Politics, Kingship, and Poetry in Medieval South India

In this compelling new study, Whitney Cox presents a fundamental reimagining of the politics of premodern India through the reinterpretation of the contested accession of Kulottuṅga I (r. 1070–1120) as the ruler of the imperial Chola dynasty. By focusing on this complex event and its ramifications over time, Cox traces far-reaching transformations throughout the kingdom and beyond. Through a methodologically innovative combination of history, theory, and the close reading of a rich series of Sanskrit and Tamil textual sources, Cox reconstructs the nature of political society in medieval India. A major intervention in the fields of South Asian social, political, and cultural history; religion; and comparative political thought, this book poses fresh comparative and conceptual questions about politics, history, agency and representation in the premodern world.

Whitney Cox is an associate professor in the Department of South Asian Languages and Civilizations at the University of Chicago. His principal interest lies in Sanskrit language and literature, premodern Tamil, and in the cultural, political, and social history of far southern India. He has been a member of the Collegium of the Berlin-based Zukunftsphilologie project since 2011 and has received awards from Fulbright-Hays, the British Academy, and the UK Arts and Humanities Research Council.

Politics, Kingship, and Poetry in Medieval South India

Moonset on Sunrise Mountain

Whitney Cox
University of Chicago

CAMBRIDGE
UNIVERSITY PRESS

CAMBRIDGE
UNIVERSITY PRESS

University Printing House, Cambridge CB2 8BS, United Kingdom

Cambridge University Press is part of the University of Cambridge.

It furthers the University's mission by disseminating knowledge in the pursuit of education, learning and research at the highest international levels of excellence.

www.cambridge.org
Information on this title: www.cambridge.org/ 9781107172371

First published 2016

Printed in the United States of America by Sheridan Books, Inc.

A catalog record for this publication is available from the British Library

ISBN 978-1-107-17237-1 Hardback

For Ken and Peter,

father and son

Contents

Figures

Tables

Acknowledgments

I imagine that most books have more than one moment of inception. This one had at least three. The first, and formative, moment occurred in Tanjavur in the waning months of 1996, when I visited the Rājarājeśvaram temple for the first time. I spent the afternoon in the complex's central courtyard, marvel-struck, as most visitors are to the place. There were eagles circling its central *vimāna*. I knew then that some day I would write a book about the Co̱las. The second moment came years later, during graduate school in Chicago, when I had asked Blake Wentworth, dear friend and fellow student, to read what would end up as the first chapter of my doctoral dissertation. Its subject was the Śaiva Tantric virtuoso Maheśvarānanda, who wrote in the early fourteenth century, but in the early rumblings of my thesis I tried to incorporate Kulottuṅga and his times. "I can't see what this has to do with anything," Blake wrote (or something like it) to me. He was right: this book was trying to fight its way onto the page, no matter how awkwardly.

A few years passed; I took a job teaching Sanskrit in London. I was sitting in a South Indian restaurant with Francesca Orsini, another dear friend and my then-colleague in SOAS. Francesca had kindly offered to discuss my research plans, including a behemoth of a book I was then considering. Describing the argument that was (yet again) incongruously tucked into the imagined study's early chapter, I warmed to the topic: I found myself talking at greater length about the preliminaries of the book-to-be, without ever coming to the main argument. Francesca suggested that maybe there was enough there for a book of its own.

Much has happened in the intervening years: I moved back to America and took another job teaching Sanskrit, but I have never stopped thinking of this as my "London book." The initial research trip to Chennai, Mysore, and Kolar in early 2010 was funded by a British Academy Small Research Grant, while the bulk of the writing was generously supported by the Arts and Humanities Research Council's award of an Early Career Fellowship in 2012–2013. Equally essential was the intellectual sustenance I received from my colleagues and conversation partners in London, especially Orsini, Rachel Dwyer, and Michael Willis. I am particularly grateful to my fellow Col̲a obsessive Daud Ali, for his constant encouragement and good advice. The SOAS library holds the personal collection of the brilliant South Indian epigraphist J. F. Fleet (d. 1917): his beautifully written marginalia supplied a treasure trove of corrections and cross-references. It was also there, and thanks again to Ali, that I was introduced to Hermann Kulke, who kindly shared with me his manuscripts of the *Cidambaramāhātmya*. The major archival research was carried out in the offices of the Archaeological Survey of India in Mysore: I am grateful to the Director, T.S. Ravishankar, to S. Swaminathan, and to the exceptionally helpful staff. I happened to be there during a visit by Y. Subbarayalu, who encouraged my work and gifted me an electronic version of his invaluable *Concordance*. K. Vijayavenugopal of the École française d'Extrême-Orient, Centre de Pondicherry, first initiated me into epigraphical studies, and has warmly supported me ever since.

I am deeply indebted to a number of my remarkable cohort of fellow scholars and friends. Special thanks are due to Leslie Orr, who has read through or discussed many versions of this argument, and has always offered wise words of encouragement and criticism. Profound thanks to Manan Ahmed, E. Annamalai, Don Davis, Wendy Doniger, Sascha Ebeling, Rich Freeman, Arlo Griffiths, Rajeev Kinra, V. Narayana Rao, Christian Novetzke, Luther Obrock, Indira Peterson, Sheldon Pollock, David Shulman, Cindy Talbot, Gary Tubb, A. R. Venkatachalapathy, and Blake Wentworth. All have helped to thrash out ideas, read drafts, and provided citations and sympathetic ears. Conversations with Yigal Bronner and Larry McCrea shaped major parts of Chapter 3; I would never have written Chapter 2 without the example of Emmanuel Francis and Charlotte Schmid's work on the *mĕykkīrtti*. Since my return to Chicago, I have been surrounded by great colleagues and wonderful students. I am indebted to Muzaffar Alam, Dan Arnold, Dipesh Chakrabarty, Thibaut d'Hubert, Rochona Majumdar, James Nye, Seth Richardson, Dan Slater, Ulrike Stark, and Christian Wedemeyer. I owe a particular debt to Margherita Trento for her superb work as my research assistant and bibliographer. The maps included in Chapter 2 were created by Olaf Nelson of Chinook Design, Inc.; Katherine Ulrich prepared the index; and I am once again profoundly grateful to Blake Wentworth for the photograph on the cover. I wrote the vast majority of the manuscript working in the Regenstein Library, and I finished it in the Franke Institute for the Humanities housed there. My thanks to the members of my class of Franke fellows, who helped me to better understand my own argument.

Three men instrumental to the book's existence passed away before its appearance. Christopher Bayly encouraged my journeyman efforts as a historian, and suggested that I submit my work to Cambridge University Press. I very much wish I could have presented him with the final product. As I was finishing the book's last round of revisions, I learned of Noboru Karashima's passing. I never met Karashima, but like all scholars of the Co̱la period, I am deeply indebted to him. Finally, just a few days after this book had gone to press, I was stunned by the early death of Barney Bate. I learned so much about politics and so very much more about Tamil from my great friend. It is still hard to believe that he is gone.

I have been fortunate to have such a loving and supportive family. My mother, Meredith Sabol; my sister, Hillary Bochniak; and Alex and Mary Morrison, *māmaṉārum māmiyārum*, have been sustaining presences throughout. And this, as with everything else, would be impossible but for Suzanne and Alice, my beautiful wife and daughter.

While writing this book, I've spent a great deal of time thinking about genealogies. My father, Kenneth Cox, taught me by example to love history. A self-taught intellectual, military officer, and practical man, he always warmly encouraged my choice of career, while being, I suspect, quietly bemused by it. I think he would have recognized what I set out to do here, and would have taken pleasure in my efforts. His grandson Peter loves history, too, among many other competing interests: he has a way of inhabiting a discovered, imagined, or invented world, of exploring it all the way to its edges. Watching him do this, I can sometimes for a moment catch a glimpse of the best version of myself.

Note on the Transliteration and Presentation of Texts

In transliterating Sanskrit, I have used the system that is universally adopted in Indological scholarship. For Tamil, I depart from the system used in the University of Madras *Tamil Lexicon* in several ways: I distinguish the short vowels *ĕ* and *ŏ* instead of their long counterparts; I give metrical Tamil texts with divisions corresponding to their word boundaries, not their prosodic units; and I mark the hyper-short *u* vowels that are dropped due to *sandhi* by a single inverted comma. This scheme of transliteration I consider to be more satisfying from a scientific as well as a historical point of view: It is consistent with that used for Sanskrit and other Indic languages, and, although the written Tamil of the medieval period did not usually distinguish the long and short *e*/*o* pairs, when necessary, its users did so through the addition of a diacritical mark (the *puḷḷi*) added to the *short* vowels. The word division here adopted is congruent with that used for Sanskrit; as there is no standard yet commonly accepted among Tamilists for the marking of significant boundaries in a line of verse – and since the habit of marking metrical boundaries appears to have only been introduced as a pedagogical aid in editions of the nineteenth century – it seems better to me to be consistent.

For the citation of personal and geographic names, I have taken a hybrid approach. In the case of Tamil proper names that contain Sanskrit elements, I have transliterated these following the latter's orthography: I thus write Rājendra, Kulottuṅga, and *brahmamārāyar* instead of Irācentira, Kulottuṅka, and *piramamārāyar*. I avoid diacritics for frequently occurring place names, but use them otherwise: thus, I write Colamandalam, Tanjavur, and Tondaimandalam, but Coḻa as a dynastic name and *tŏṇṭaiyar* as a collective noun.

Generally speaking, I have confined the citation and close discussion of primary source materials to the Notes, in order to avoid trying the patience or the endurance of the nonspecialist reader. When, however, the verbal texture of a particular passage is germane to my discussion of it,

I have opted to include the original in the main text. When citing epigraphic or manuscript sources, I retain their idiosyncrasies of spelling, except when I am reproducing the regularized text of an earlier editor; when citing the consensus of several such sources, I have regularized the orthography. Any alterations to a Sanskrit or Tamil text are preceded by an asterisk, and followed by a parenthetical reference to the source's reading; I mark such alterations – in descending order of certitude – as *corr.* (for "correction"), *em.* ("emendation"), or *conj.* ("conjecture"). Using these same signs, I have on occasion provided a more detailed apparatus of readings in the Notes; I do so when there are multiple source texts, especially multiple manuscripts, or multiple accounts of the same source.

Introduction

Once, we are told, the awesome goddess Kāḷi addressed her assembled courtiers. She was speaking, among other things, in praise of a king, who was in fact Viṣṇu come to earth to rule over the greatest kingdom of the south. The goddess detailed the story of his birth among men, his rise to eminence, and the great justice of his rule. Then she turned to describe the magnificent sight of him as he embarked upon a royal progress across his kingdom:

ma<u>rr</u>a vĕṅkaṭakaḷi<u>rr</u>i<u>n</u> utayakkiriyi<u>n</u> mel
mati kavitt'iṭav utitt'iṭum arukka<u>n</u> ĕ<u>n</u>ave
kŏ<u>rr</u>a vĕṇkuṭai kavippa micai kŏṇṭu kavarik
kulamatipputai kavitta nilav' ŏttu varave.

And so,
atop a fierce bull-elephant he comes,
like the Sun arising over Sunrise Mountain.
And just as the Moon hangs over it,
he is covered over by a warrior's white parasol,
its long yak-tail fans like bright moonlight
hovering round its orb.[1]

Elephant, king, royal emblem: mountain, sun, moon. Kāḷi's verse marries celestial harmony to the realization of a similar perfection in the physical person of the king. Royal display becomes hierophany, a momentary alignment of heaven and earth.

This syzygy and its mirroring among men contain subtle allusions to a set of further earthly conjunctions. Kāḷi never says as much – the goddess is not a genealogist – but this king, whom she calls Apaya<u>n</u>, began his life in the east, in the land where the sun's rays first touch the earth every morning. The royal family into which he was born traced its descent back to the moon, who in ages past had sired a far-reaching line of kings, among them Kṛṣṇa, another of Viṣṇu's earthly apparitions. Apaya<u>n</u>, however, rules as the rightful heir of the Co<u>l</u>as, the greatest of the dynasties of the southern Tamil country, whose distant ancestors include not only Manu the lawgiver and Rāma the perfect king (yet another of Viṣṇu's *avatāras*), but the Sun-god himself. Kāḷi's words thus enact a tableau both natural and dynastic: the all-powerful sun atop its mountain seat at once adopting as ornament and outshining the cool-rayed moon, as the ascendant imperial Co<u>l</u>a subordinates to himself the satellite dynasty of his birth. In the goddess's version of events, Apaya<u>n</u>'s accession was an act of salvation, his enthronement removing the anarchic chaos of the Kali *yuga.* Yet the fact that it is she who narrates this is unsettling: Kāḷi, the blood-drinking war-goddess at home in the cremation ground and on the battlefield, is an unlikely figure from whom to expect such an irenic vision.

It is a fiction that we can overhear the goddess's words: her speech to her ghoulish retinue was the invention of a poet, Cayaṅkŏṇṭār, in a work meant to entertain the court of this very king, whose own royal pronouncements style him as Kulottuṅga, "Lofty in his Family." The tableau is just a single moment in Cayaṅkŏṇṭār's poem, and one that cannot be understood without a great deal of tacit knowledge that the poet presumes. First of all, there is the king's ancestry: though Cayaṅkŏṇṭār's poem – it is called the *Kaliṅkattupparaṇi* – contains a detailed king-list of the Co<u>l</u>as, its version of recent dynastic history is notably and deliberately opaque. There is also the elaborate set of mythic commonplaces that assign the ruling houses in India to one of the two lines descending from the sky's most prominent luminaries. These lines had ramified down through the centuries, taking in the families at the center of each of the great epics, along with the greater and lesser kings of recent times. And there is Sunrise Mountain: this was a mobile feature of the imagined landscape of classical India, always off somewhere to the east. For the Tamil-speaking subjects of the Co<u>l</u>a, this meant the northeast, at the seaward edge of the Telugu country. This in turn summoned up the long and fraught relations between the Co<u>l</u>as and the lunar Cālukya kings who held sway in the Telugu country. But for the earliest Tamil listeners to this poem, the silence surrounding the recent past was especially deafening, as Kulottuṅga's accession was a crucial moment in the life of the kingdom, a transformation whose effects had extended far beyond the affairs of one royal family.

All fictions rely on the presumption of such tacit knowledge: it is the unsaid spaces that listeners and readers attempt to fill that make meaning possible. The martial goddess, as she relates this implied dynastic conjunction, stands in for the many makers and shapers of language, those connoisseurs of gaps and silences, for whom Kulottuṅga's public life provided an occasion for description, for poetic creation, and for individual and collective self-imagining. Cayaṅkŏṇṭār's staged ventriloquy through Kāḻi was distinct in genre, in form, and in intention from what we might call a historical narrative, but it was nevertheless a meaningful rendition of the events of the past, something that remains unobscured by the poem's many evasions and transformations. Historiography of the sort practiced elsewhere in Eurasia was vanishingly rare in medieval South India, but it produced in great abundance works of language that married poetic fiction with reference to and reflection upon the past. Cayaṅkŏṇṭār's text was one among many that so engaged with the events surrounding Kulottuṅga's accession.

So to call Cayaṅkŏṇṭār's poem a fiction is not to dismiss it. Many and varied were the fictions of Kulottuṅga's time, ranging from works that were meant to entertain, like the poet's, to the legal fictions that sustained public documents and to the elaborate confections of courtly and temple ritual. One could go so far as to claim that the greatest fiction was the Coḻa state itself, and to see it as an elaborate performance, buttressed by court ceremonies and punctuated by the spectacular acts of largesse, meant to convert the leading members of its audience into its performers and supernumeraries. Consider the following:

In the fourth year of his majesty the king Rājakesarivarman Kulottuṅgacoḻa, the emperor of the three worlds. As he was sitting in state in the Cetirāja hall in his palace in Pĕrumpaṟṟapuliyūr, the king was entreated by Pavaḻakkuṉṟanāṭ-uṭaiyāṉ, the lord of Pūṇṭi, and he graciously declared that the village of Putuppākkam should be set down in the rolls as a tax-exempt temple holding, and should be given over to the lord Śiva, master of Tirukkaccālai and master of the city of Kāñcipuram. This order was taken down by the royal secretary Muṭikŏṇṭacoḻaṉ, village elder of Pālaiyūr, and it was verified by the senior royal secretary Rājarājabrahmarājaṉ, the leading citizen of the *brahmadeya* village Keralāntakacaturvedimaṅgalam in Veṇāṭu. These were the overseers of the revenue office: Ampalavaṉ Uttamacoḻapallavarayaṉ, the master of Aracūr; Vikramacoḻa Coḻiyarayaṉ, master of Cāttumaṅgalam; Muṭikŏṇṭacoḻaviḻupparayaṉ; the revenue officer . . . Rājarājaṉ, village elder of Oṭṭaiyūr; and the revenue officer Kāñcanakŏṇṭāṉ, master of Kantamaṅgalam. From the three hundred and twenty-ninth day of his fourth year onward, the king was pleased to ordain Putuppākkam to be a temple holding.[2]

The king is presented to us in this royal communication as he held court in a certain place on a certain day, in the temple city of Cidambaram, on or around May 8, 1074, the day from which this order went into effect. He is surrounded by officials and courtiers, each meticulously located in the social space of the kingdom, most of them titled landholders from its central provinces in the Kāveri river delta. We know that this session of court took place because a copy of the order rescripted by Muṭikŏṇṭacoḻaṉ was transmitted to the temple and was inscribed on its walls, to serve as a permanent record of a part of its landed property.

This testimony would appear to be poles apart from the stylized hierophany in Cayaṅkŏṇṭār's poem. In contrast to the cosmic stillness of the image uniting sun and moon within himself, the king as captured in this record is hard at work performing the banal business of tax remission to a Śiva temple in the kingdom's northern metropolis of Kāñcī. The royal order is set firmly in time and space, lacks any sort of mythological embroidery, and is expressed in a workmanlike Tamil prose. Rather than celebrating the king's glory, the inscription captures a transaction in which he was an authorizing agent: we see here a single instance, out of many thousands, of the transfer of revenue to a religious institution, usually a temple or a conclave of learned Brahmans. One might say that where Cayaṅkŏṇṭār gives us a representation, this is a trace of a real past act. The one is perfectly good poetry; the other, the stuff of history.

It is not at all a new idea to find this distinction unsatisfactory. For one, texts like the *Kaliṅkattupparaṇi* possess a relationship to the past that itself deserves to be made an object of analysis, and declaring them out of evidentiary bounds simply ignores the problem. But more significantly, a supposedly pristine documentary source like this royal order turns out under even a cursory inspection to be just as founded upon silential gaps and tacit presumption as an imaginative work like Cayaṅkŏṇṭār's. The order is structured as a transfer of rights over land not between the impersonal institution of the state and the corporate body of the temple, but between two different lords: Kulottuṅga, the wheel-turning emperor of earth, heaven, and the underworld, and the god Śiva as he is housed in a particular site in Kāñcī. In this arresting asymmetry, the king lays claim to the entire universe as his property, to be disposed of as he wishes, while the cosmic deity is bound up within the four *prākāra* walls of a single temple, one of many such earthly addresses. All seven men mentioned along with the king appear clothed in the elaborate costume of Coḻa titulature, elevated from their place as local big men in their individual villages into the ranks of the kingdom's ruling elite. Almost all bear lordly titles issuing from the Coḻa court, rather than personal names and patronymics, and in the Tamil original, each is meticulously located in terms of his place of residence's location in the bureaucratic and customary spaces of the imperial system of land control. Each man, from local grandee to scribe, to accountant, can only be glimpsed here through the guise of an adopted and scrupulously maintained public self.

Moreover, this piece of revenue business conceals a momentous act of political transformation. This is the earliest surviving instance of the king's claiming for himself the name Kulottuṅga and the title *tiripuvaṉaccakkiravarttikaḷ*, Wheel-turning Emperor of the Three Worlds. Prior to this time, the king – then called Rājendracoḷa – had issued orders, marshaled soldiers, and made donations: he had, in short, acted like a king. But he did so in the midst of serious political uncertainty, when the Coḻa dynasty had ceased to effectively exert hegemony in its domains. Before this, the king was styled in a way that sought to connect him with his Cālukya ancestors to the northeast, while arguing for his Coḻa inheritance. But by May 1074, something had shifted: the king had assumed unimpeded control of the kingdom's central lands, and had emblematized his success by the adoption of this new regnal name. The public enunciation of this order marks the earliest extant trace of this new royal identity: that it was issued from the Śaiva temple-town of Cidambaram and that it is connected with the ancient city of Kāñcīpuram doubly mark this out as an important piece of political theater. Years of work were needed to bring this little piece of royal generosity to pass, and Kulottuṅga's graceful words are just as much the product of a ventriloquistic voicing as Cayaṅkōṇṭār's speaking through Kāḷi, decades later, in his *paraṇi*.

* * *

This book is an essay in Coḻa history, taking the emergence of the emperor Kulottuṅga I (r. 1070–1120) as its central point of focus. It seeks to answer two questions: What actually happened? And why should anyone care? The first of these questions is much the easier of the two. Many of the following pages are devoted to what happened between June 1070, when Rājendracoḷa, the Coḻa–Cālukya prince, was consecrated into kingship and his assumption four years later of his new, imperial identity. This did not take place in a vacuum, nor can it simply be confined to the domain of familial machination or court intrigue. Rājendracoḷa began to rule in the midst of polity-wide transformations catalyzed by the forging of the Coḻa imperial state-system, a process begun two generations earlier. The second half of the eleventh century saw the emergence of newly empowered elite groups, modes of property relations, and the reforging of existing caste-communities into amalgams of regional solidarity and collective action. Yet the transformation of Rājendracoḷa into the emperor Kulottuṅga was not simply the surface expression of these underlying causes, so much foam churned up from the depths of the social. Instead, in the process of this royal self-renovation, we can capture how the king's court actively sought to position itself through the calibration of public rhetoric and the assiduous fostering of a political network. The king's claim to authority was taken up in the maneuverings of often quite ordinary men and women as well as powerful grandees; royal ambition joined with local ritual observance to enact imperial kingship in novel ways. Kulottuṅga would go on to rule for nearly a half-century, and this period saw the emergence of a new settlement among the kingdom's ruling elite, the rudiments of which were put in place in the period 1070–1074. The conjuncture that brought about Kulottuṅga's accession contained within it, as the seed contains the sprout, the earliest intimations of the social forces that would trigger the slow collapse of Co̲la authority, generations later. Less an episode of the one-damn-thing-after-another of dynastic history, these events occasioned real and durable change in the medieval Tamil country.

This book is also concerned with what happens in the wake of this new imperial settlement, when this king's ascendency became an occasion for narration by others. The narratives that this provoked, crafted in Tamil and Sanskrit and in a range of genres and formats, present the events, their significance, and their practical and moral consequences in ways that are often mutually discordant. Though ranging widely in their investment in narrative facticity (the stuff of names, dates, and putative causes), none are readily assimilable to a historical – much less a historiographical – mode of explanation. But this is not to say that they did not seek to produce a coherent account of the past. These texts were written for their particular present, the time and place of their initial dissemination; and this was a present that in every case was part of the world transformed by Kulottuṅga's accession. These narrative renditions, whether court poem, inscriptional eulogy, or local myth-cycle, were not isolable, more-or-less successful accounts of what happened: they were themselves very much a part of what happened.

In each case, the rendition of the Co̲la king's coming to power enjoyed a central place in texts produced in or after his reign, and each of these texts embodied a particular complex project directed toward a specifiable social constituency. Unpacking this requires a certain practical flexibility: for all that the evidence contained within these works can suggest interpretations that are the preserve of the social historian, it is only through the tools and modes of attention peculiar to textual scholarship that these can be accessed and assessed. Understanding the individual projects constituted by these works and the ends to which they were directed can only be accomplished through attention to their linguistic fabric, with reference to the conventions within which they were structured and against which they were meant to strain. As it happens, two of these texts – Cayaṅkŏṇṭār's *Kaliṅkattupparaṇi* and Bilhaṇa's *Vikramāṅkadevacarita* – are among the major literary monuments of the period. Here philology shades over into hermeneutics, and into the work of the literary historian and critic, as attention to the place occupied by the narrative of Kulottuṅga enables a new, and better, understanding of these masterpieces.

Reading these texts in this way might be in itself interesting for some. But as much as this is necessary for the first of my questions (what happened?), it is insufficient for the second (who cares?). One might readily agree that, by carefully reading its surviving documentary and expressive traces, the murky accession of this king and its consequences can be made clear, and yet still ask why, ten centuries later, this is of any interest whatsoever. There are two answers to this question. The first of these relates to the peculiar achievements of Coḻa studies: the body of historical research on this time and place is the empirically richest and conceptually most sophisticated work of its kind for what may be called (with an audible sigh) "early medieval" South Asia. As such, it deserves to be much better known. My own training is as a philologist of Sanskrit and Tamil, not as a historian, but my esteem for these historians' work has led me to return to it repeatedly, and prompted my own attempt to add to it. I have often felt like this book was at once an extended piece of fan mail to these scholars and a love letter to the period itself, with all the potential for self-exposure and embarrassment peculiar to those two epistolary genres. To admire the work of others, however, is not to be willfully blind to its limitations, and the present state of Coḻa historical studies, for all its accomplishments, is not immune to criticism.

The second of my two answers to the question "who cares?" emerges directly from this critique of the current state of Coḻa historiography. It is my contention that the complex of events surrounding the accession of Kulottuṅga I and its subsequent interpretation should be understood as primarily *political* in character. This might appear to be a self-evident claim; it is not. I do not mean that this royal succession should be classed as what is conventionally called "political history," usually understood as the study of just this sort of thing, along with diplomatic transactions and military campaigns. Nor do I mean this in the sense that any and all human activity is shot through with and finally reducible to the self-interesting jockeying for mastery, that "it's all just politics": this may in fact be true, but it is unhelpful. I mean instead that the society over which the Coḻa kings held sway possessed an array of customary and constitutional institutions and practices that meaningfully maintained and reproduced the asymmetrical distribution of power and access to resources. This array was not exhausted by the extended household that constituted the royal court; nor, contrariwise, was the court simply a theatrical appurtenance to the actual workings of politics at the local level of patriarchy and rural domination. The polity over which the Co<u>l</u>a kings claimed control was a complexly distributed, kinetic one: its far-flung, disconnected elements could and did effectively interact with its supposed courtly center. This can be explicitly seen in the skein of events leading up to Kulottuṅga's emergence, and again in the texts that sought to repurpose this to particular collective and individual ends. In this overwhelmingly agrarian world, power ultimately depended on land and on the social relations bound up in the extension and maintenance of agriculture. But the politics of the Co<u>l</u>a state played out in poetry and legal pronouncement as well as in revenue survey and the distribution of the village grain-heap; it could be found at work in the rights claimed by caste assemblies, in the rituals of military conquest, and in acts of pious donation to gods and Brahmans.

For all that we can recognize and categorize the maintenance of the structured inequalities of this society as political, there is a distinctiveness to the institutions, imaginal modes, and practices overseen by the Co<u>l</u>as. The composition of the society and the very possibility of its dominance by the organized political enterprise of a state have been questioned and debated for decades; this has provided much of the conceptual raw material that has driven its historiography. But it would elide something of importance if the politics of the Co<u>l</u>a kingdom were to be reduced to the dry typologization of state formation. One of my chief tasks is to capture the strangeness of the politics of the period, when seen from our received notion of "the political," whether in its restricted, formal sense or in its power-is-everywhere variant, and to thus suggest that this notion can be widened and enriched by these medieval Indian materials. As a single example: among the political agents at work in the Co<u>l</u>a domains in the 1070s and after, I would not hesitate to include the goddess Kālī herself, as she appears in Cayaṅkŏṇṭār's poem and as the mistress of a temple in the kingdom's northwestern marches. To take the politics of the Co<u>l</u>as seriously, then, is to defamiliarize our ready-to-hand concept of it, and thus to critically reframe our sense of this part of collective experience.

These institutions and practices of Co<u>l</u>a politics were *legible* (that is, we can know significant things about them from the surviving evidence), they were *consequential* (the action of different agents within the array could produce outcomes that effected the workings of the whole) and – this is significant in light of the what-actually-happened question – they *changed*, both more broadly over time and as a particular outcome of the new order inaugurated under Kulottuṅga. The point of looking at the making of this particular king is that it allows us to capture the perduring structures of the meaning of politics along with the conjunctural instances in which these structures were invoked, used, and, in the process, transformed. *History* and *politics* thus shape much of the argument of this book. These are among the foundational categories of humanistic and social–scientific study; to them I would seek to add a third term, *philology*. Philology – though certainly it once rivaled its fellows here in ubiquity and significance – is now often derided, though more frequently misunderstood or simply ignored. My understanding of all three, and my use of them in this book, lays no claim to universality: on the contrary, my approach is confessedly parochial, based as it is on the medieval South Indian case, and so potentially idiosyncratic. The larger problems addressed by this extended case study and an attempt to frame it in a more general theoretical conversation provide the materials for the book's conclusions. For now, the balance of this introduction is devoted to glossing each of these three rubrics, to describing the particular senses that inform their usage, and to providing an initial précis of my own interpretative stakes in them. These glosses take the form of bibliographical critiques, and readers more interested in the stuff of the Co̱la past than in prior scholarship may wish to forge ahead to the final section of this introduction.

History

The medieval Co̱las have been subject to systematic investigation for more than 130 years. This is not the place for an extended review of this scholarly literature;[3] instead, I will concentrate on the major lines of argument subtending the field as it is currently constituted. The monument to the early phase of Co̱la studies is K. A. Nilakanta Sastri's *The Cōḻas*, first published in Madras in 1934. The style and organization of Sastri's book was conventional, its subject matter predominantly politico-military, and its outlook broadly nationalist and focused on the assessment of the Great Men of the dynasty. But none of this detracts from the lasting value of the book, at once a massive synthesis of prior scholarship and a thoroughgoing engagement with the surviving archive. *The Cōḻas* adopts a celebratory, at times almost hagiographical, tone in its characterization of the period's achievements: for Nilakanta Sastri, the Co̱la kings oversaw a profound period of civic peace and cultural efflorescence, their means of government (in an incessantly reproduced phrase) an "almost Byzantine royalty."[4] With the major narrative details of the dynasty set in place by the great historian, his students concentrated on broadly synchronic surveys on polity and economy and on extending Sastri's model to other dynastic formations. Competent and thorough, if often uninspiring, this work supplemented ongoing efforts at archaeological field survey and the collection and edition of the epigraphical corpus that still provides the mainstay of research.

The Copernican moment in the study of the Coḻas can be traced to the publication in 1973 of Y. Subbarayalu's *Political Geography of the Chola Country*. It is impossible to overestimate Subbarayalu's significance to the field; he remains at the time of writing its most important active scholar. From his earliest work, the two distinctive features of his scholarship were already in evidence: an overwhelmingly thorough empiricism and a commitment to reconstructing the areas of explicit concern in his inscriptional sources. In *Political Geography*, Subbarayalu's painstaking attention to the territorial designations that are a ubiquitous feature of the epigraphs yielded a richly textured history of the relationship between the classificatory power of the emergent Coḻa state and the customary order of the agrarian countryside. It also produced, in a precursor of much of his later work, scholarly tools possessed of utility beyond their immediate application to his argument. It includes a dozen maps (the first of any detail to be rendered of the Coḻa kingdom) and more than a hundred pages of appendices tabulating the historical names, locations, and contents of the major territorial types.

This commitment to a rigorously data-driven social history has continued throughout Subbarayalu's scholarly career; much of his later work has been produced either in partnership or in close dialogue with the Tokyo-based historian Noboru Karashima. Collectively and individually, these scholars' methods have evolved over the decades; this is especially evident in their prodigiously early adoption of the resources of information technology. Produced by Subbarayalu, Karashima, and Toro Matsui, the invaluable *Concordance of the Names in Cōḻa Inscriptions* was published in three volumes in 1978; much of the analytical work on its huge corpus of personal designations was accomplished through the analogue method of hole-sort cards. Karashima was also responsible for introducing a drive toward periodization, in order to track patterns of change over time. His division into four roughly century-long periods, tied conventionally to the reign of particular kings of the dynasty, has become a standard feature of contemporary Coḻa studies. Within this imposed structure – in which the reign of Kulottuṅga supplies the watershed for the onset of "period 3" – Karashima maintained a broad (if untheorized) commitment to a Marxist model of changing modes of production. The key transformation tracked over these centuries by Karashima is the rise of a mode of private landholding and the corresponding growth of landlordism among non-Brahmans. This massive secular change, the key point of which Karashima initially dated in the thirteenth century, saw the abandoning of the communal, village-level ownership thought to obtain earlier, and set the stage for the increasing immiseration and eventual agrarian crisis in post-Co̱la times.[5]

The shift in concern from the evaluative Great Man historiography of Nilakanta Sastri's time to the close tracking of land management and property relations in Subbarayalu and Karashima's is characteristic of the global social–historical turn in the latter part of the last century. In the Co̱la case, it played out in a markedly different mode of attention to the primary evidence furnished by epigraphy. The general shape of the inscriptional archive of the Co̱la period – the majority of which is housed on the walls of stone temples – is extraordinary, even when set against the corpora of other Indic societies. The numbers speak for themselves: of the approximately 60,000 inscriptions thought to survive in the subcontinent from premodern times, a little less than half (around 28,000) are in Tamil, the great majority of which, some 19,000, date from the Co̱la period.[6] Not all of these have been published, and doubtless many more have not even been noticed despite more than a century's concerted efforts, but the sheer number of the surviving records is astonishing. Nilakanta Sastri sought to reconstruct the period's political history, often through a cryptological level of attention to trace evidence of events. His wide-ranging knowledge of the intricacies of the records allowed him to alight upon telling details, representative cases, and interesting anomalies. Though fundamentally grounded in published and unpublished epigraphs, Sastri also cast his net more widely in his effort at producing a comprehensive study of the period: his admirable survey of literary history, for instance, remains the best English-language introduction to the subject.[7]

By contrast, the hallmark of Subbarayalu and Karashima's approach has been the exclusive attention at the level of the epigraphic corpus, rigorously controlled for in space and time. Such a demarcated data set provides the parameters to investigate the changing semantics of certain isolable nominal items – for instance, forms of land classification, revenue terms, or social categories – as projected across the scheme of their periodization. The difference in the research programs that result is striking, as can be seen in a telling example. When attempting to describe the workings of the Co̱la revenue system, Nilakanta Sastri, after a lifetime of study, is left with the sobering judgment: "To estimate the incidence of so complex a system of taxes and dues . . . would always be a difficult task and, in the actual state of our evidence, utterly impossible." Already in his early essays (some written in collaboration with B. Sitaraman), Karashima produced an exhaustive register of revenue terms and their geographical and temporal distribution, and offered some general characteristics of rates of assessment and land grading. Subbarayalu in turn extended these results. Working from the negative evidence of tax remission (the content of an enormous number, perhaps an absolute majority, of records), he imputed the staggering fact that, at the height of its imperial success, the Co̠la state laid at least a notional claim to some 87,000 metric tons of paddy per annum through its major land tax.[8]

This characteristic engagement with the evidence of epigraphy at both the finest and broadest level presents an instructive contrast to the scholarship of Burton Stein, explicitly framed as a response to Subbarayalu's earliest work. Stein's is the most ambitious, and certainly the most widely discussed, recent interpretation of the Co̠la state and society. Philological scruple and archival range were not Stein's strong suits; instead, his scholarly oeuvre, culminating in his *Peasant State and Society in Medieval South India* (published 1980), was committed to a comprehensive theorization of the Co̠la kingdom along ecological, social, and politico-moral axes. Stein's most significant contribution lies in his insistence that such a theorization was necessary: for the first time, the Co̠la kingdom as a phenomenon of time and space was seen to represent a totality of institutions, dispositions, and long-term trends that could be grasped by a historian. The first and most significant impetus for this totalization was precisely the results of Subbarayalu's early research into political geography. It is from here that Stein derived his characteristic focus on the *nāṭu*, the individual "micro-region" that supplied the atomic building block of the agrarian society. Stein wedded to this a variation on the conflict-allergic, integrationist social science that permeated the American area studies of his era, especially a particular model of social and political power dubbed "the segmentary state." This is the interpretative catchphrase most closely associated with Stein's argument; it was taken over from Aidan Southall's ethnography of the Alur, a monarchical polity in the modern nation of Uganda. In Stein's variation, the crucial fact determinative of the Co̠la polity is that sovereignty was shared within a layered, overlapping, "pyramidal" structure. This is to be sharply distinguished with the equally pyramidal forms seen in contemporary federalist democracies: in the latter case, each hierarchically ranked unit (for instance, the jurisdictions bounded by ward, city, county, state, and federal levels in the United States) possesses different responsibilities and modes of authority and domination. These multiply as you proceed up the hierarchy, with each superordinate unit subsuming some of the functions of those beneath it. By contrast, in the segmentary order, the "lower" units – those of the individual *nāṭu*s – reproduced the functioning of the "higher," with "diminishing constituencies" further down the way, coupled with "complementary opposition" between the different segments, as well as within each. The equipotent *nāṭu* segments were thus not necessarily bound together into a perduring supersegmental state: a segment could hive off, and new segments be incorporated, without creating wider turbulence.

The success of the Co̱la state thus depended, for Stein, on its inherent flexibility: the kings of the dynasty, no more and no less than the leading men of their own micro-regions, served as the impresarios of a remarkable, centuries-long orchestration of an expanding network of *nāṭu*s, which for a time encompassed practically the entire macro-region of South India. While power was parcellated and segmentary, "authority" and "legitimacy" were not: these were a property of the center or apex of the system, the royal court. The king exercised direct domination over a circumscribed region, while the ability to compel loyalty and to direct resources outside this area depends on his privileged access to a purely "ritual" sovereignty. The mode of this sovereignty was primarily distributive: the king enjoyed the ability to disburse his largesse in the form of land given to temples (*devadāna*, "gift to the gods") and to Brahmanical estates (called variously *agrahāra*s or *brahmadeya*s), women exchanged in marriage with "chiefly" lineages, and war booty given to martial groups. In Stein's view, then, the structure of Co̱la political culture rested on a profound dualism: the ritual sovereignty exercised by the center versus the actual power vested in the leadership of the individual *nāṭu*s. This view possesses classical Indological precedents in the distinction articulated in works written in Sanskrit between *kṣatra* (power as force) and *rājadharma* (righteous rule).[9] In the Co̱la case, however, Stein proposed that actual power did not itself depend on a naked appeal to violent coercion, or to the elaborate ascriptive hierarchy of the caste system as it was realized in the north. Instead, power in the *nāṭu* derived from a transhistorical attunement of interests – an "alliance" – between Brahmans domiciled in their scattered estates and the leading "peasants" of each micro-region.[10]

It was this adventitious calibration of local interest and royal grandeur that allowed for the centuries of Co̱la rule, not anything resembling a state in the conventional sense of the term. This arrangement was in turn to be superseded by another social formation, which emerged from within the Co̱la peasant state's virtuous matrix. New collectivities – *pĕriya* ("great") *nāṭu*s, agricultural combines, trading guilds, and self-styled "right-" and "left-hand" caste clusters – came to overshoot the boundaries of the individual micro-regions, a process Stein labeled "the transition to supra-local integration." This metastatic process of late twelfth and thirteenth centuries interrupted the delicate balance adumbrated by the Coḻas, who returned to their old role as just locality leaders, eventually paving the way for the very different mechanisms of the Vijayanagara war-state to be imposed from without on the Tamil country.

There is much to admire in such a notably bold attempt at synthesis as Stein's, and it is easy to be skeptical of some of the lines of criticism that it has engendered.[11] Some of these appear like persnickety efforts at positivist faultfinding; still others are limited by their unwillingness to admit the desirability or even the possibility of such a theorization. Others have been perfumed by more than a whiff of nativism, as in the persistent critical claim that a model derived from anthropology was not in principle suited to interpret such a major civilizational complex as Coḻa-period Tamilnadu. Still others have plumped for rival theories, notably the variation on Marx's model of European feudalism pioneered in the history of medieval North India. Certainly, Stein's linguistic and archival competence was limited: nothing in his work evinces the easy familiarity with the sources so apparent in Nilakanta Sastri or Subbarayalu. And while the segmentary state model is beset with considerable difficulties, this ultimately has little to do with its African anthropological origins.[12] In the wake of subsequent research, Stein's central claim about the lack of efficacy and formal structure in the Coḻa state apparatus now looks embarrassingly underinformed. Internal to the argument, the exclusively "ritual" status he ascribes to the royal center is, if anything, even more problematic. Stein's identification of the "ritual" dimension of sovereignty with a peculiarly royal propensity for public generosity, besides being falsified by the thousands of private donative inscriptions that crowd the walls of the region's temples, stands in unresolved tension with his equally significant positive evaluation of the Brahman-dominant peasant axis. If this possessed a distinctive moral character, did it express itself in an idiom that was remote from redistributive ritual? If so, how? And, given the overwhelming positive character that Stein ascribed to the upper echelons of his peasant society, what do we make of the Coḻa state's capacity for organized violence, as attested in its own bellicose rhetoric and in the accounts of its rival kingdoms? Still more, there is the endemic violence of agrarian life itself. Did the "ritual" character of Coḻa kingship render it ipso facto immune from this?

The adaptation of Marx's model of feudalism to the evidentiary and ideological peculiarities of medieval northern India has proven a hugely successful research program, producing reams of doctoral dissertations, monographs, and scholarly articles, of uneven quality.[13] Its application to the linguistically, environmentally, and socially distinct terrain of the far south has been the work of two Kerala-based scholars, Rajan Gurukkal and Kesavan Veluthat. Veluthat's *Political Structure of Early Medieval South India* remains the single strongest, and most scathing, critique of the conceptual and evidentiary inadequacies of Stein's argument; in this, it is very effective. But the entailments of the feudalism model – agrarian involution, deurbanization and demonetization, political immobility, the instrumental use of religion to reinforce a stolidly casteist social order – are largely epiphenomenal to Veluthat's supple engagement with the epigraphical and textual archives of Co̠las and his adduction of the parallel evidence of the Pāṇḍya and Cera kingdoms. A more sustained effort at theorization employing broadly Marxian methods is James Heitzman's *Gifts of Power*. Eschewing the feudalism framework, Heitzman's approach is eclectic: grounded in a historical materialist commitment to tracing the means and relations of production and their coherence into a social formation, Heitzman focuses on the differential realization of modes of "lordship" within particular local societies. Cognizant of Stein's skepticism of earlier claims of an overweening centralized imperial apparatus, and adopting the periodization and source-critical exhaustiveness of Karashima and Subbarayalu, Heitzman's short book represents the most significant large-scale conceptualization of the Co̠la state to have emerged in their wake.

Over the past forty years, the historical study of the Co̠la polity has been thus transformed. For all its many internal differences, this body of scholarship has been united in the privileging of the documentary details of its epigraphical sources, its attention to phenomena of the long-term, and its typological character. These foci have led to some notable areas of underemphasis. One of these is gender: other than Stein's superficial interest in elite marriage alliance (where royal women are characteristically reduced to tokens of exchange), there has been little attention to the lives of roughly half of the humans who resided in the territory claimed by the Co̠las. Leslie Orr's *Donors, Devotees, and Daughters of God* (2001), a work firmly in the Karashima–Heitzman trajectory, marks a notable corrective to this. This absence is symptomatic of a wider problem, which might be glossed as a persistent underdetermination of historical agency. While this can be seen in the inattention to the evidence of the actions performed by women – often only furtively available in the records, as Orr has demonstrated – it extends into the levels of the literate male elite that are the principal focus and audience of the epigraphs and other texts. In tracing the changes to social power and the state over the *longue durée*, the description and explanation of the individual and collective projects of real historical agents tend to be bracketed out, as does any account of what these agents may have represented themselves as doing. But it is only in the wake of the remarkable successes of recent social history that attention to these projects became not only possible but also potentially elucidating. In the informing context of long-term change, it is possible to discern what was structurally constrained and what was genuinely creative in particular conjuctural instances, as in the case of Kulottuṅga's coming to power. In turn, the possibilities of future action were opened up or constrained, in a relation of path dependency, precisely by the outcome of such instances. It is in this tension between structure and conjuncture – a dichotomy possessed of a long ancestry in historical studies – that the acts, whether physical, verbal, or ideational, of individuals and groups take on their significance in human societies. That is to say, it is here that we can locate the second of the three guiding rubrics for this study.

Politics

In trying to provide a definition of the category of the "political," one could do worse than to begin with Max Weber. Politics for Weber was "the striving to share power or striving to influence the distribution of power, either among states or among groups within a state." It was here that his well-known taxonomy of the modes of legitimate domination (traditional, charismatic, legal) could play itself out. The major corollary to this – the celebrated definition of the state as a community that sought to maintain a "monopoly on the exercise of legitimate force within a given territory" – seems a poor fit to the ramshackle plurality of the Coḻa case, or to many other medieval states across Eurasia. Indeed, though never directly engaging with Weber's argument, Stein's characterization of the segmentary character of the polity seems directly opposed to such a model. Weber's core distinction within the political "vocation" or "calling" (*Beruf*) between those individuals living "for politics" and "by politics" might seem equally inappropriate in this case. In fact, these are not inappropriate at all: the emergent Coḻa state apparatus from the mid-eleventh century included figures productively assimiliable to these ideal-typical models. But these corollaries, as the essay from which they are derived explicitly discusses, are bound up with Weber's efforts at a sociology of his own revolutionary present ("Politik als Beruf" was first delivered as a lecture to radical students in Munich in 1919); typically, they were advanced in the context of a much wider historical view, one at once cognizant and inclusive of the Indian past. In Weber's insistence that premodern India possessed a politics that could be captured, analyzed, and compared, his work already compares favorably with Marx's reliance on high-colonial officialdom's vision of the rigid dualism between the ephemeral swarm of endlessly skirmishing royal dynasties and the utterly static, inwardly turned village communities of premodern India.

In this same essay, Weber briefly alights on the *Arthaśāstra* attributed to Kauṭalya. Weber's en passant reference merely repeats the major cliché of its interpretation (it represents "a really radical 'Machiavellianism,' in the popular sense of this word"); but it is remarkable that the German sociologist was aware of the work only a decade after the appearance of its Indian *editio princeps.*[14] The Kauṭalyan text has structured almost all modern scholarly discussions of early Indian politics; while it is a work of genuine and abiding interest, this has had significant unforeseen consequences. Two of these, closely related but distinct, can be characterized as a "lexicalist" concentration on the formal vocabulary of politics, and a strong focus on the doctrines of normative and prescriptive texts, to the expense of other kinds of potential sources.

Lexicography and the study of historical semantics, of course, are perfectly legitimate ways to produce knowledge, and their use is hardly restricted to this particular field. The lexical orientation of the study of classical Indic politics arguably emerges organically from the interpretation of the *Arthaśāstra* itself: as any reader of the Sanskrit text can attest, its vocabulary is strikingly unusual, though whether this is an artifact of age or of disciplinary or authorial idiosyncrasy remains an open question.[15] But in this case, these methods have possessed an outsized influence – almost a monopoly – and have tended to be used as the privileged means of articulating a fundamental *difference* to Indic politics as set against a presumed (European) standard. Semantic investigation maps out the boundaries for a notably stable class of terms, often structured around a dichotomy between the this-worldly model of the Kauṭalya tradition and the transcendent standards of, say, the *Gītā* (this commonplace is already seen in Weber). This is not to discount the scholarly legitimacy of such lexical investigation, nor its utility in mediating between a modern audience and the very distant world of the premodern Indian past. This method does, however, leave unanswered the lingering problem of whether a complexly articulated theory, complete with rhetorical nuances, explicit and tacit interlocutors, and significant presuppositions, could ever be productively reduced to a discrete list of nouns, whose unpacking forms the sole task of analysis.[16]

Similarly, it is no condemnation to say that the pursuit of early Indic politics has been largely confined to the abstractions of prescriptive texts. "Political theory" is of course just that, and it can and should be studied in terms of its propositional and argumentative content. Normative works are all too often the only evidence we possess, which touch upon the political life and ideas of enormous swathes of Indian space-time. But the intellectual history of classical political theory is oddly truncated: the *Arthaśāstra* is one of those interventions, common in the literary history of Sanskrit, that served to eradicate all traces of its predecessors, save what it incorporated. There is no major later treatise that approached its complexity: the most valuable later texts were explicitly epitomes of it. Singh's recent study of the *Nītisāra* of Kāmandaka, commendable in many ways, is illustrative of the evidentiary limits of these descendant texts.[17] Careful to mark the differences in doctrine between Kauṭalya and Kāmandaka, Singh's effort to situate the latter within a changed world of "medieval" politics runs afoul of difficulty in historicizing it, as it lacks any geographical reference and can at best be assigned to a several-century-long spread of the first millennium of the Common Era.

Turning to a place and a time like that of the Co̱ḻas, the limitations of the sole reliance upon the exegesis of classical works of theory is readily apparent. There appear to be no points of contact between Kauṭalyan theory and the political practice of the Co̱ḻas and their subjects. In fact, the one work studied here that has recourse to the *Arthaśāstra*'s typologies – Bilhaṇa's long poem – did so at a rival court hundreds of miles away, and with an intent that was conspicuously subversive.[18] Politics – the striving for power and influence within the elite actors of the kingdom – was conducted in a sophisticated, palpably self-conscious manner without reference to this classical or postclassical corpus of theory. It is instead from a wide skein of other discourses, many of them narrative rather than systematic and derived equally from Sanskrit and Tamil antecedents, that the language of Co̱ḻa politics was knitted together.

Perhaps the most eloquently symptomatic attempt to provide a theoretical model exhaustive of ("Hindu") Indian politics is that attempted by the anthropologist Louis Dumont. The establishment of civilizational difference through lexical investigation and the subordination of historical practice to transhistorically valid theory are both on prominent display in Dumont's writings; but so too is a powerful synthetic intellect. In Dumont's view, politics exists in the classical Indic ideological universe as a remnant of what troublingly could not be subordinated to the caste system's overriding logic of status: "Being negation of *dharma* in a society which continues to be ruled by *dharma*, the political sphere is severed from the realm of values."[19] Where "status," which for Dumont is equivalent to ritual and thus social purity, is the exclusive source of value, "dominance" is left as its shadowy complement: the brute fact of control over the land is assimilated to the Indological trope of *kṣatra* and the ethnographic stereotype of the "dominant caste" within a particular local social system. Caste being the ideological centerpiece of the entire society, the medium whereby all material and symbolic goods were distributed and all legitimacy channeled, politics becomes consigned to the domain of the purely adventitious, and thus to the unthought. To make this work, and to account for the actual stuff that appears to have happened in the Indian past (for which Dumont gamely asserts the need to study "the inscriptions"[20]), Dumont produces the mediating third – "authority" – with which raw power is charged in order to render morally coherent judgment over dominated inferiors, and which remains ineradicably "plural rather than singular."[21] The ability to reflect on this organization of social life from within – and here Dumont is explicitly thinking of Kauṭalya – depended upon a prior transformation of consciousness into a radically isolated individual: the political thinker resembles the religious renouncer in his self-imposed exile for normal society.

Dumont's was an expressly idealist effort to think through the consequences of a mode of collective life fundamentally different from that found in the modern West. Rigorously familiar with the details of the ethnographic record of his day, Dumont cannot simply be dismissed on account of his level of abstraction. A vigorous attempt to counter Dumont's structuring caste-politics dichotomy can be found in Dirks's *The Hollow Crown*, which inverts *Homo Hierarchicus*'s subordination of the political and relativization of the historical in its account of the caste society centered on the ruling lineage of the little kingdom of Pudukkottai. Situated in a detailed précis of the medieval history of the Tamil country, Dirks's ethnohistory ultimately derives much of its rhetorical and argumentative power from the intersection of the ancien régime of the Tondaiman little kings and the priorities of the colonial state. By contrast, it is the long premodern history of the practices of power that supplies the central theme of Ronald Inden's *Imagining India*. Though more broadly a critique of the Indological variant of a wider Orientalism, Inden's work includes a commitment to advancing politics as the central term to both India's past and the study of that past. This is embedded in a crucial terminological distinction: eschewing as both amorphous and essentialist the customary appeal to "society" as a descriptive and explanatory term, Inden reserves its use for delimited, purposive associations – for example, his usage of "court society," adopted here. Following Collingwood, Inden opts for the general covering term "polity" as it "focuses attention on the relationship of ruler and ruled and on the agreement and conflict that are integral to the ongoing making of a 'society' as an empirical entity."[22]

This salutary focusing on the ongoing work of the political undergirds the constructive operation with which Inden's book ends, a sketch of the Rāṣṭrakūṭa kingdom, the dominant polity of the Deccan from the mid-eighth to the late tenth centuries. Of necessity, the sketch is compressed: only a few epigraphical sources are translated and interpreted, and these are taken as exemplary instances of perduring patterns of discourse, rather than as traces of conjunctural instances in the kingdom's history. The burden of the brief account is dedicated to a polemical variation on the lexicalist theme, with Inden proposing a series of altered translations for much-used terms, while arguing for the centrality of others (for instance, *jānapada* and *paura* as rural and urban collectives of "subject-citizens"; *tejas* as "luminous will") in order to exfoliate a tacit premodern Indic understanding of political power.

Despite the incommensurabilties of this large and contentious body of scholarship, it is unified in view of some of its presuppositions. First of all, there is such a thing as a premodern (or perhaps better, a classical and medieval) Indian politics: its existence and significance are not optical illusions of retrospection. And while it is subscribable to the generic categories of a historical sociology, there is a specificity of time, space, and cultural situation that makes the study of a premodern Indian politics a coherent enterprise in its own right. As said earlier of the particular Co̱la case, politics in early India was legible; that is, it is available for our reconstruction. It was also consequential; that is, productive of outcomes that were not already determined by other factors, though for some theorists (above all, Dumont), political consequences were the result of sheer accidence within an otherwise totalizing social order. Whether premodern politics was subject to change remains a controversial matter in the existing scholarship: this is something that its conjoint methods of the elucidation of key terms and the unpacking of clasic authoritative texts can only capture with difficulty.

Recent work, while operating within these presuppositions, has done much to explore their limits. This is usefully typified by the scholarship of Daud Ali and Cynthia Talbot. Ali's *Courtly Culture and Political Life in Early Medieval India* can be considered a panoramic expansion of Inden's concluding exercise. Focusing especially on the historical semantics of the court over a vast geographical and temporal spread, Ali usefully brings together the testimony of prescriptive treatises with epigraphical attestation and literary representation. It is the latter focus, on works of Sanskrit *kāvya*, that is especially valuable, as it prompts an innovative investigation mapping the outlines of the affective dimensions of the political. This is a notable lacuna elsewhere in the scholarship: already in Weber, and especially in the studies of Indic theory and practice, there is precious little acknowledgment of the degree to which politics is invested in the harnessing and channeling of emotional energy and the controlled direction of collective passions. Ali's recovery of the courtly content of aesthetic theory supplies a powerful corrective lens to this myopia. So many of the classics of Sanskrit literature, like the theoretical treatises in which they were in dialogue, trafficked in carefully nuanced stereotypes, resistant to more local and particular mediation. Taking these sources on their own terms, Ali's interpretation is thus one of the long-term, of the timeless and placeless standard that authors writing in Sanskrit labored to evoke for their audiences. Talbot's *Precolonial India in Practice* is set in a very different argumentative register, its singular focus provided by the Kākatīya kingdom that emerged from the cultures of upland Andhra from the late twelfth century. Talbot meticulously pursues the protean social character of the parvenu warriors who made up the Kākatīya kings' "political network" (another phrase that I adopt here) as well as the Brahman temple officiants, *agrahāra* denizens, and mercantile groups who were their co-participants in it; the work also devotes notable attention to the donations of certain cadres of elite women. Almost a photographic negative of Dumont's picture of the caste system, Talbot's Telangana is a social landscape of new men defined by their martial and donative deeds, not their position in a hierarchy of status, and on the crucially shifting loyalties through which hegemony was maintained.

It is broadly in the center of the lines of force plotted by Ali's and Talbot's works that the present account can be situated. The two projects operate at very different levels of scale, and it is through an effort at synthesis between these – between the level of culturally situated stereotypy and practical instantiation – that the category of politics becomes as it were actualized. How this can be captured depends on the analysis, evaluation, and interpretation of the surviving traces of the Coḻa polity. Among these traces are material remains, plastic representations, and volumes of quantitative and geographical data: these are all certainly significant. But it is those traces cast in perduring linguistic form, that is texts, that are privileged here, as they are the most complex evidence of this time and place to which we will ever have access. And it is the means of this access that provides the third and final of the rubrics addressed here.

Philology

If history supplies the field in which the argument of this book operates, and politics a lens through which to observe it, the eye that does the observing is a philological one. This is confessedly as much a matter of personal inclination as it is a methodological program; in the context of Coḻa studies, it has a recidivist air. The first modern studies of the dynasty and its kingdom were undertaken by epigraphists, notably Eugen Hultzsch, Franz Kielhorn, V. Venkayya, and H. Krishna Sastri, themselves a part of a larger levy of brilliant scholars with similar interests.[23] The entirety of the earliest systematic knowledge of the dynasty, including the sum of its dynastic history, depended on these men's skills in paleographic decipherment, formal chronology, critical edition, and textual interpretation: that is to say, on their philological skills. As the massive project of corpus production got under way in the last century, subsequent scholarship came to depend largely, though by no means entirely, on the published volumes of *Epigraphia Indica* and *South Indian Inscriptions*, and on the thousands of transcripts housed in the offices of the Archaeological Survey of India, themselves philological interventions of no mean sort. Over the ensuing decades, this textually centered side of Coḻa historical studies gave way to the colligation of volumes of evidence and increasingly to cliometric analyses of the sort typified by Karashima's scholarship.

I do not intend here to reject the massive gains in our knowledge that this sort of research has produced in favor of a reactionary return to an earlier set of scholarly methods. Instead, it is in wake of the transformed field of social history that a renewed attention to the formal and linguistic composition of the sources seems potentially of value. There is nothing especially radical to this impulse: it is perhaps little more than yet another call for a "cultural" or "linguistic" turn in the study of Coḻa history, and a belated one at that. In preferring the label of "philology" for the kind of scholarship practiced here, I am in good company.[24] But of what do I speak when I speak of philology?

By it, I do not refer exclusively to textual editing, though parts of what follows depend upon my own editorial reconstructions of certain Sanskrit and Tamil sources. Nor, contrariwise, do I wish to subordinate this sort of editorial work, along with lexicography, metrical study, or grammatical analysis to the status of disciplinary second-class citizens and to propose, say, a division into "primary" and "secondary" philologies, that is to say between textual criticism and hermeneutics.[25] Perhaps the best general way to frame this is Pollock's minimalist characterization of philology as "the discipline of making sense of texts," one freely drawing upon such widely differing skill-sets as that of cultural historian and the grammarian in its efforts.[26]

A project like this one, concerned with philology as a means for the reconstruction of a distant politics, could thus be founded on an appeal to a virtuosically "close" reading paired with an effort at "contextualization," or to a Geertzian "depth" of interpretation or explication. But I find that a better account can be had in adapting some of the ideas of Mīmāṃsā, the classical doctrine of Vedic textual exegesis. This might come as a surprise: as a philosophical enterprise, Mīmāṃsā was marked by an evacuation of historical referentiality and a naturalization of the inequities and asymmetries that are the stock in trade of political power.[27] But there are few thinkers in world intellectual history who have thought more carefully and relentlessly about how texts, in fact, make sense. Such an appeal has the further use of clarifying my insistence on the limits of what I call the "lexicalist" dimension of the study of India's premodern politics.

Words refer, the Mīmāṃsaka teaches, confident in the unique perfection of Sanskrit: words in that language always and invariably capture their meaning. Every individual correctly formed vocable is thus imbued with *abhidhā*, the capacity for denotation, and each securely delivers its payload of meaning with every token usage. Language, however, is more than just a matter of words; and in any case, the token can only ever point to a type, to an utterly abstract, if entirely real, generality. To account for how a collection of these reliable meaning-vehicles can ever cohere, or refer to a concrete particular, the Mīmāṃsaka posits a second capacity innate to language, *lakṣaṇā* or "the indicatory." It is this function that accounts for sentential meaning; how (to use the stock example) we can hear the sentence "Bring the cow" not as an aggregate of simples referring to cowhood as such, the verbal meaning "to bring," and the insinuating undertow of the imperative mood, but as a particular command to do a particular thing to a particular animal. It is this second operation that is the necessary condition for there to be sentences, and thus communication, at all. But it is also this exact same mechanism that opens up a space for figuration, for metaphor, and for the other, nonliteral resources of language. The Mīmāṃsaka philologists describe these as phenomena of words that have become *skhaladgati*, which have gone askew or tripped themselves up. It is only in this eccentric swerve of the otherwise-reliable act of reference that these further possibilities are disclosed, through a mechanism closely allied to that which makes words hang together as sentences in the first place.

To suit my purposes, there is some considerable violence that needs to be done to many of the commitments driving the Mīmāṃsā theory. It must be dragged from its exclusive attachment to an inerrant and fixed Sanskrit, from the impersonality of the Veda, and from the impulsions of its sacrificial cult. Still, this can be reformulated in a reconstructive shorthand with a historical purpose: words do certainly refer, and they pick out past ideas and states of affairs. We may, under certain circumstances, take these words' meanings as objects of our study, whether be it to a long-dead man's name, a technical term, or an item in a mythic ancestry. Lexical reference is thus certainly an important part of the story; it is just not the whole story. It is instead to the subsequent, *lākṣaṇika* dimension of language to which the philology of this book is generally addressed, to the emergent totalities of sentences, and so of texts, whether they be in Tamil or Sanskrit, prose or verse, documentary report or work of the imagination or (as it sometimes happens) a mixture of all of these languages, forms, and registers. It is only the attention to the way these texts are put together and how they work, and to their stumblings, whether intended or inadvertent, that we can disclose something of this distant world in a way that other methods simply cannot.

There is a further basic commitment to this book's philology, one which the Mīmāṃsaka, alas, did not share: it aspires to transparency. The poems, court pronouncements, genealogies, political communications, notarial records, and Tantric scriptures with which I reckon in the following pages were written long ago, in languages that are distant from my own, and it is very likely that I have misunderstood them. As such, I try throughout to make the raw materials of my understanding available to my reader, so that she may decide how close to the mark I may have come, or how far from it I have fallen. Though this amounts to little more than the primary-school injunction to "show your work," it will on occasion make greater demands on my reader than might seem fair. At the same time, some of this accessory detail formed the most intellectually interesting work that went into the book's writing; certainly I derived the most enjoyment in parts of its writing. It is often forgotten that there is no philology without *philia*.

But there is more at stake than just the pleasure that this book has furnished its author. The whole of the book amounts to a polemic for and an enactment of the need for a renewed attention to the text in the studies of premodern South Asian history. It is surely an unintended consequence of the work of historians like Subbarayalu and Karashima that their methods have drawn attention away from the verbal workings of the sources of the Co̱la past at precisely the moment when competence in the historic languages of India has entered a steep (some would say terminal) decline. It is not enough to disaggregate the corpus of Co<u>l</u>a inscriptions into a data set of nouns, ready to be tallied up.[28] Even the seemingly straightforward Tamil prose of the epigraphs embed within them significant semantic depths and rhetorical complexities, which only philological attention can bring out. This commitment is built into the structure of this book: the notes that accompany the main text are meant not merely to provide the necessary apparatus of reference, but also to provide the explanatory philological scaffolding to the arguments set out in the main text. In a similar way, the notes also strive toward transparency in their assessment of prior scholarship, and in accounting for the book's methods more generally. As such, they tend at times to be extensive; while their linguistic, interpretative, text-critical, methodological, and argumentative details are not necessarily of interest to every reader, for some – this reader included – they are central to the enterprise of the sort of a philological history of politics that this book attempts.[29]

I adopt as a model for this sort of scholarly project the so-called Cambridge school of historians of European political thought, notably Quentin Skinner and J. G. A. Pocock. The published scholarship of these two scholars alone is complex and dauntingly large, to say nothing of their students, contemporaries, and critics. But to venture a very unnuanced gloss on their shared project, both Pocock and Skinner are preeminently concerned with looking at the shifting languages of politics over time, from the central texts of classical antiquity through their recovery in the Renaissance, to the early modern and modern canon of political philosophy.[30] Rather than understanding this as the working out of a single telos and an exploration of certain perennial themes, they insist that the Western discourse on the political was invariantly plural ("the *languages* of politics") and that the articulations of these languages in particular texts were meaningful interventions into their particular historical (and so social, political, religious, etc.) contexts. Further, both men are emphatic as to the diversity of the genres in which the languages of politics can be studied. By argument and example, Skinner's and Pocock's practical exercises in scholarship, as well as their writings on method, urge the connection between a thoroughgoing historicism and a philological scruple in the recovery of the past's discourses on the political; in Skinner, a variety of philology is productively conceived through a conversation with Austin's philosophy of language. Beyond their value as exemplars and theorists, Pocock's and Skinner's works supply a provocative contrast with the current study: as already described, the formal theory of classical and medieval India has practically no role to play in the interpretation of Co<u>l</u>a-period politics, while historiography of a recognizable sort is nonexistent. Instead, it is to the domain of literary trope and the shifting idioms of administrative classification, or to the architectonics of ritual performance, that we must turn in order to interpret the dynamics of the Co̱la polity. The period presents its student with a seeming paradox: the problem of political thinking without political thought. Working through this paradox forms this book's principal challenge; its attempt at resolution is its most significant result.

Plan of the Book

Each of the four major chapters that comprise the book takes its title from one of the names assumed by the man eventually called Kulottuṅga, and in the body of Chapters 1, 2, and 3, the king is referred to by that name. So it is that, in the period before the issuing of his first records, the prince is referred to as Rājiga, following the probably derogatory usage of Bilhaṇa, itself suggestive of the prince's Andhra origins. For the crucial period 1070–1074, the subject of Chapter 2, I employ the name given in the new king's own records, Rājendracoḷa, to be distinguished from his grandfather Rājendra and his various maternal uncles and cousins using variations of the same title. The watershed of mid-1074 marked the proclamation of the now-emperor's new title Kulottuṅga, a regnal name that marked a sharp departure from previous royal naming conventions. From this point onward, in Chapters 3 and 4 I use this name exclusively, though the king continued to possess a wide spectrum of official names. Cayaṅkŏṇṭār almost never refers to him by this most common name, preferring instead Apayaṉ (Skt. *abhaya,* "fearless") and Cayataraṉ (*jayadhara,* "the victorious"); in his natal region of Veṅgī, the king is celebrated under a welter of conventional heroic epithets and by the local regnal name Viṣṇuvardhana VII. Names mattered in medieval South India, especially for rulers or those who wished to rule, and drawing the reader's attention to this serves to buttress one of the central claims made here, that the creation of the public identity of Kulottuṅga Co̱la was something accomplished over time and through the efforts of multiple actors and institutions.

Chapter 1 ("Rājiga") begins with the standard explanation for Kulottuṅga's imperial accession, in which politics is symptomatically reduced to its most primordial form of kinship relations. In the reinterpretation presented here, the established facts of the king's descent – that he was a matrilateral cross-cousin of the main line of the family and the product of several preceding generations of marital alliances – are located within a wider network of interdynastic relationships, paradigms of action anchored in myth, public narratives, and conjunctural events of the 1060s. All of these suggest the wider complexities that inflected the Co<u>l</u>a dynastic situation. This chapter also includes a compressed account of the nature of the mature state-system that emerged under the Co<u>l</u>a family's stewardship in the decades leading up to 1070. This is meant to be synthetic rather than historiographical: elements from several of the positions outlined earlier reoccur there, in newly configured form. Besides introducing the major institutions and forces at play within the mature imperial state, this sketch occasions a turn to the contingent details of the period 1063–1070, the reign of the eventual king's uncle Vīrarājendra, and the structural causes of the burgeoning crisis that preceded Kulottuṅga's emperorship.

Chapter 2 ("Rājendracoḷa") takes up the critical years 1070–1074. At the beginning of this period, the new king was one member of an unstable triarchy with his uncle and cousin; by its end, he had weathered the death of both of his corulers and the apparent near-collapse of Co<u>l</u>a authority to emerge as sole ruler. It was the efforts of his court society in this period, even more than Rājendracoḷa's dynastic bona fides, that made possible the emergence of the emperor Kulottuṅga. For Rājendracoḷa's court, as well as that of his ill-fated cousin Adhirājendra (whose brief reign fell in the period 1069–1072), the crucial arena for political action was Tondaimandalam, the northern part of the Co<u>l</u>a territory and the erstwhile home of the earlier Pallava dynasty. The ruling societies of both kings' courts sought to recruit the Tŏṇṭaiyar elite to their cause, in a time when royal authority appears to have ceased to function in the central lands of the Kāveri delta, through such diverse means as the calibration of inscriptional rhetoric, intervention into relations in land on behalf of elite clients and, in Rājendracoḷa's case, the conspicuous forging of alliances with upland warrior colonists and the martial goddess Kālī.

Chapter 3 ("Kulottuṅga") turns from the reconstruction of these events to the very different literary narratives of the king's coming to the throne. Differing in genre, medium, language, and emphasis, these three renditions are united in the centrality they accord to Kulottuṅga. In each, the narrative is deployed with a particular and historically identifiable audience in mind, and in the service of a particular and stipulable socio-textual project. In detailing these, I reconstruct the ways that the representation of Kulottunga's rise became unmoored from its original circumstances, to be repurposed by his rivals, his feuding would-be heirs, and even by the complex factions of his own court society.

Chapter 4 examines the long aftermath of Kulottuṅga's rise in a single place, the local world centered upon Cidambaram, the home of the celebrated temple to Śiva as Naṭarāja. Set in the zone intermediate between Colamandalam and Tondaimandalam, Cidambaram had for centuries been a significant, though not an especially prominent, part of Tamil Śaiva sacred geography. But with the rise of Kulottuṅga and the establishment of his new political settlement, this area was rapidly transformed, with the Cidambaram temple set on its way to becoming the quintessential center of southern Śaivism. This transformation can be seen in the patterns of donation by members of the royal court and by the emergence and consolidation of its local Brahmanical culture; the textual transactions that emerged from these intertwined to produce the distinctive local society centered on the temple-town, which was to endure for centuries after the final Coḻa decline.

The book then concludes by engaging with some contemporary theoretical reflections on the theory of the historical event and the transformations that these can catalyze, in order to situate the making of this long-dead South Indian king within a wider conversation about the possibilities of a theoretically interested study of the past.

1 Rājiga, before 1070

The *Marumakan̲*

The origins of kings and rivers are obscure, the *Mahābhārata* tells us. But we all know how the Veṅgī princeling Rājiga became the Co̲la emperor Kulottuṅga: for more than a century, this has been the subject of scholarly consensus, providing the theme for a polyglot chorus of opinion remarkable in its consistency. Briefly, as the result of three generations of marital alliances between the Co̲las and the Veṅgī Cālukyas, Rājiga and his immediate family were "plainly Chôḷas at heart, far more than Chalukyas." Owing to the Dravidian way of reckoning kinship, Rājiga was both agnate and affine of the Co̲la family, and thus a man "who was tightly bound" (*gāḍhaṃ sambaddho 'bhūt*) to it; having "spent his childhood in the palace of his maternal grandfather," he "[spoke] Tamil as his mother-tongue" (*tan̲ tāyppāṭṭan̲ araṇmanaiyir̲ ... vaḷarntu ... tamil̲ mŏl̲iyaiye tāymŏl̲iyāka kŏṇṭu payin̲r̲u*). In the course of a mysterious "time of troubles" in the latter part of 1070, Rājiga was able to assume the throne of his matriline; whether he "acquired the Chôḷa crown by hostile invasion and conquest" or otherwise "unlawfully gained power" (*unrechtmäßig zur Macht gelangten*), the circumstances "could not have been bloodless."[1]

Seen from the perspective of the Co̲la patriline, the story is a pathetic one: the family's generational alliance with the dynasty to their northeast proved a misalliance, one that ended in the cashiering of the main line of the Tamil kings. Contrariwise – if one wished to adopt Rājiga as the hero of the piece – the vagaries of these political and familial ties allowed this singularly able and ambitious man to vault over the limited options his regional kingdom would have allowed him and seize the main chance that ended with him ruling over the greatest kingdom of the south. Whatever their partisan coloring, in all of these explanations, the emergence into history of the man who would rule for a half-century as Kulottuṅga Co̲la relied on merely the execution of the logic of the kinship system itself, coupled with the law of unforeseen consequences.

The version of the Cālukya–Coḻa's accession given in Nilakanta Sastri's monumental *The Cōḷas* provides the classic account. Unique among the kings in the book's political history, the doyen of medieval South Indian history allots to Kulottuṅga two chapters, the first of which is devoted entirely to his career before 1070. Admitting that many of the events surrounding the accession will never be known – and carefully discounting some of the many proposed reconstructions as implausible – Nilakanta Sastri's version of events has the young Rājiga ejected from the succession in Veṅgī as a result of the maneuverings of his paternal uncle Vijayāditya and the collusion of Vīrarājendra, the then-ruling Coḻa king; this was followed by a lost period encompassing 1063–1070, during which time the prince may have "carved out a small principality for himself" near modern Chhattisgarh. When, just a few weeks after his coronation, Adhirājendra, the direct heir to the Coḻa throne, "lost his life in a fresh rebellion," the Coḻa–Cālukya prince was well positioned, both genetically and politically, to take full advantage. His status as a cross-cousin, however, remained enough of a potential source of embarrassment that later eulogists (among them the poet Cayaṅkŏṇṭār) had to concoct different narratives of Kulottuṅga's settled place in the lineage.[2]

There is much to recommend in this version of events and its focus on genealogical detail. First of all, it has the advantage of being true (see Figure 1.1): the Veṅgī prince whom we may, for now, call Rājiga was in

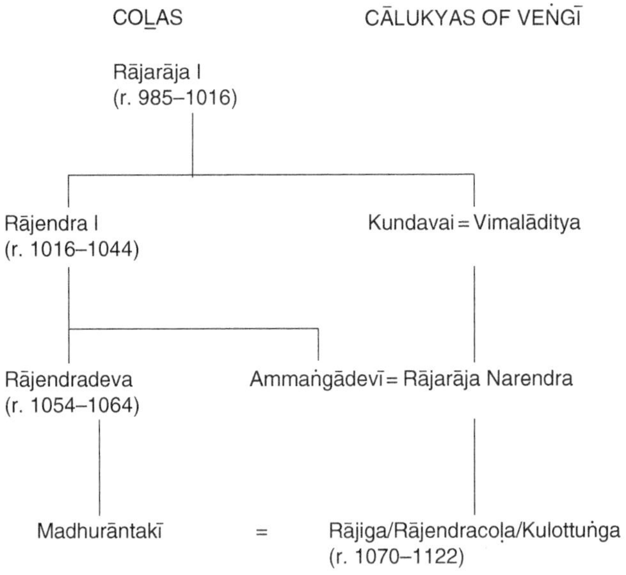

Figure 1.1 Coḻa–Cālukya marriage alliances

fact the son-in-law, nephew, and great-nephew of the Co<u>l</u>a kings; over the preceding two generations, the ruling Co<u>l</u>a family had indeed given out some of its cohort of daughters in marital alliance with the eastern Cālukya line. The underlying condition of possibility here seems to have been a temporary political disaster in Veṅgī, in which the Cālukya king Dānārṇava (r. 970–973) was unseated by one Jaṭācoḍa Bhīma, who went on to reign until 1000. During this period – which later Cālukya records imagined as a period of acephalous anarchy in Veṅgī – Dānārṇava's heirs settled in the Co<u>l</u>a court of the emperor Rājarāja. Cālukya royal donors would continue to appear in Colamandalam temple inscriptions for decades to come, suggesting that at least part of the family remained in – or simply remained connected to – the Co<u>l</u>a heartland after the dynasty's restoration as Co<u>l</u>a clients.[3] It was thus during this period of interregnum that the alliance was struck between the two families. While the temporarily dispossessed Cālukyas evidently stood to gain, the proposal may have come from the Co<u>l</u>a side: a similar marital strategy had, in the immediately preceding generations, successfully welded the Irukkuveḷ family of Koṭumpāḷūr, a lineage of influential kingmakers based to the southwest of the delta, into the Co<u>l</u>a line. The extension of this strategy of alliance to the Cālukyas speaks to the inflated ambitions of Rājarāja's time, when the Co<u>l</u>as began to expand prodigiously beyond their core in the Kāveri delta.[4]

Seen through the explanatory lens of the Dravidian rule of cross-cousin marriage, the relationship of alliance could have continued indefinitely: daughters of the Co<u>l</u>a patriline could marry their father's sister's sons, and thus produce Cālukya heirs ever more fused to the Co<u>l</u>a family, while males of the Co<u>l</u>a patriline could have wed their father's sister's as well as their mother's brother's daughters, or indeed the daughters of their elder sisters who had been sent to Veṅgī. Rājiga, as the *marumakan̲* (at once "sister's son" and "son-in-law") to the main line, was duly wedded to his mother's brother's daughter, Madhurāntakī, who shared with him a common grandfather in the great Co<u>l</u>a emperor, his namesake Rājendra. The alliances could easily have perpetuated themselves – the hallmark of the Dravidian system being, after all, "perpetual affinity" – had not fate and ambition intervened, and Rājiga somehow proven able to interpose himself into the succession of his *māman̲ār*, his maternal uncles and their analogues.

All of this is an elegant demonstration of the ways that kinship has functioned for millennia in South India, as it is of the salience of the methods and evidence of ethnography to the study of the distant past. It is also a tribute to the industry and skill of the heroic generation of Indologists and historians who first pieced the story together from disparate, scattered sources in a diversity of languages and media. And it makes a very good story. The strategy, intermittently but steadily pursued for decades, was meant to win for the Tamil kings one of the great prizes of the peninsula, the rich and cultured tracts at the mouth of the Godāvari, and thus to end the cycle of usurpation and seasonal warfare there. But it was not to be: the *marumakaṉ* Rājiga proved ruthless enough at courtly politicking or the practice of violence, and so the centuries-old line of the Co̱las came to an end, the unwitting loser in the unraveling of a scheme of its own design.

Yet, despite all of this, to see the transformation of Rājiga into Kulottuṅga and all of its attendant consequences solely through the lens of royal kinship is deeply misleading. The burden of this chapter will be to provide a more adequate context in which to understand this transformation. This is not to say that the argument from descent must be entirely abandoned. Certainly it is the case that in a hereditary kingship, the system of kinship and the system of political rule must necessarily overlap.[5] But the incorrigible fact of these cross-cousin marriages cannot in itself exhaust a historical explanation of the events of Kulottuṅga Co̱la's imperial emergence, nor can it account for the wider consequences that ramified from it. It is the case, first of all, that the ways in which royal figures were represented in their relation to their genetic ancestors and successors were not limited in medieval India to the facts of kinship and descent in the strict sense. Instead, the sources attest to the importance of modes of family-centered narrative emplotment and other, nongenetic, ways of reckoning succession and affiliation. In the majority of our sources, these alternate genealogical modes are given much greater attention; it is in fact only in a few closely interrelated texts, composed in Sanskrit and far away from the Co̱la center, that the details of Rājiga's parentage are given with any clarity.[6] These documents, further, were only issued in the following generation, by the rival court societies of the then-emperor's sons: it was only then that Kulottuṅga's conjoint parentage took on any public significance, that it supplied the elements of an "actionable" past.

There is a wider lesson to be learned from all of this. One way to approach this resembles the critique of the notion of supposedly primordial kinship relations launched decades ago by Pierre Bourdieu. In what he, in a typically sibylline phrase, styled as "the objective limits of objectivism," Bourdieu insisted that we understand the facts of descent and relation to be themselves subject to the skewed, self-interested rendition by local witnesses, and to magnification or distortion by subsequent analysis.[7] David Henige's methodological criticism of the "modern dynasticising" habits of Indian historians may be read as an intramural application of this idea: Henige suggests that "historians have tended to ignore, mask, absorb and perpetuate" the biases and weakness of epigraphical data, especially their characteristic suppression of collateral lines and anything other than the supposedly normative patrilineal pattern of succession.[8] What both of these critiques of genealogical reason suggest is the need to allow as broad a definition as is practicable of what underlay the representations of descent and kinship in Rājiga's time and place; and that this needs be done with an eye to the suppressions and obfuscations that – as a cynic might say – are the genealogist's stock in trade. In a great many sources, the narrative framing of Rājiga's two families as descendants of the Sun and Moon, and so members of the *sūrya-* and *somavaṃśa*s, supplied a major mode of dynastic self-understanding. This framing was both retrospective and proleptic: it provided not only ways to understand the past but lenses through which to envision the future. Further, the customary adoption by the paramount member of the family of serially alternating titles, which I will call "cognomen," provided a means to organize the dynastic history of the Coḻa family in a way that had nothing to do with descent or martial alliance. This was simply a logic of access to political power, and by tracking it, it becomes possible to infer tensions and conflicts in the dynasty that are left otherwise unmentioned in the extant documents.

For all that these dynasty-internal positionings were significant, looking at them in isolation tells us very little about the politics of the medieval South. To venture an interpretation of this politics, it is necessary to set these dynastic wrangles within the skein of institutional and cultural networks that constituted the Coḻa polity. From the perspective of the vast majority of the surviving evidence, the Coḻa royal family was only a single, albeit central, node within a heterogeneous world of actors, institutions, and practices. The burgeoning dynastic crisis into which Rājiga interposed himself did not occur in a superstructural vacuum; instead, it was conditioned by the massive changes that the polity had undergone in the preceding two generations. These decades witnessed incessant and escalating seasonal warfare, unprecedented territorial consolidation, attempts at dynastically driven social engineering, and the proliferation of both state apparatus and novel forms of elite comportment. The details of these transformations are the stuff of the certain achievements of the social historical scholarship of recent decades. These can be set alongside the evidence of the eulogistic or rhetorical output of the court societies of the Coḻa kings of the mid-eleventh century, which was centrally concerned with the crafting of an evolving set of intertextually connected statements about royal authority and succession. Both of these – the nature of polity and the nature of the Coḻas' aestheticized claims about their authority within that polity – changed dramatically in the period prior to Rājiga's emergence.

The complex strategies of elite kinship and royal self-understanding; the changing fabric of the basic variables of Co<u>l</u>a polity; the claims made in the poetic and ideological statements issuing from the royal center: all of these come together in the conjuncture of the later 1060s, especially what can be reconstructed of the frenetic activity associated with the court of Rājiga's *māma<u>n</u>* Vīrarājendra (r. 1063–1070). Much of what we can say about this king's brief but consequential reign relates to his military and diplomatic transactions: above all, his attempt to decisively outflank the Kalyāṇa Cālukyas of the western Deccan and so solve the problem of Veṅgī's endemic dynastic instability. This furnished Rājiga with major features of the political terrain he traversed; just as significantly, Vīrarājendra's own rise to power fomented an internal crisis of dynastic legitimacy that effected the situation of his Cālukya *marumaka<u>n</u>*. In restoring, however tentatively, the possibilities, tensions, and incipient problems of these few years, we gain a valuable perspective of the still greater transformations that would follow.

Epic and Cognomen

In Figure 1.2, the three-generation series of Co<u>l</u>a–Cālukya marital alliances is situated within a wider genealogical frame of reference. This expands outward to show the lines of descent and of access to rule that were articulated in a diachronic parallel to the articulation of Rājiga's immediate ancestry. The table is not exhaustive: it is restricted to members of the Co<u>l</u>a family who underwent the ritual of royal consecration, and largely suppresses those female members of both houses who were not involved in major inter-dynastic marriages. Rājiga, for instance, had two sisters whom we will not encounter until late in his reign as Kulottuṅga.[9] But within these limitations, this representation of the relationships in the two families reveals much that is left opaque in the genealogical argument exclusively concerned with the particular inter-dynastic marriages whose final product was Rājiga. Once again, to adopt this perspective does not simply deny the significance of the cross-cousin explanatory model. Genealogy is of self-evident importance in the reproduction of a dynastic monarchy, but the reckoning of a significant genealogy can only be assessed within the wider order in which it occurs. Certainly there were wider cultural factors that supplied resources for the public version of events for contemporaneous agents, and these need to be accounted for in any adequate historical explanation of those events.[10]

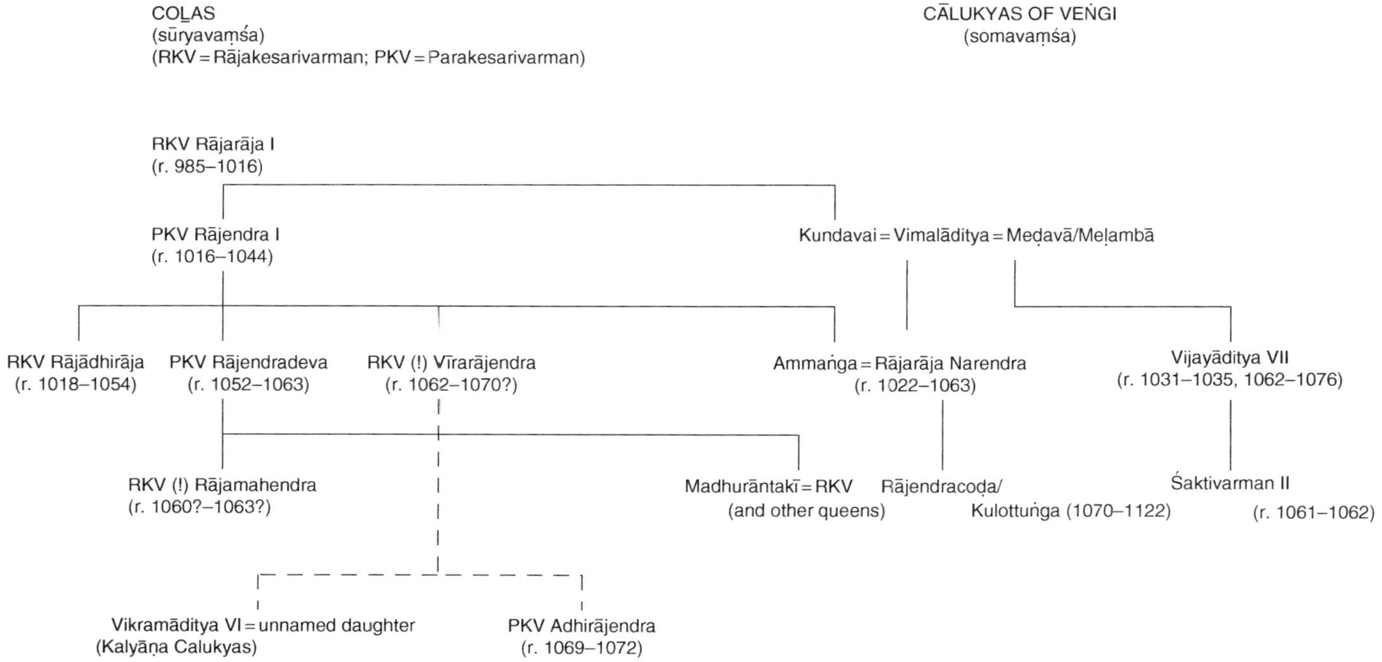

Figure 1.2 The Coḻa and Cālukya dynasties, 985–1072: an expanded view

As mentioned already, the same scholarly consensus on the cross-cousin explanation for Kulottuṅga's rise to power is unanimous regarding the rationale behind the prior marital alliances: from the Co̲ḻa side, these were meant to secure a claim over the eastern peninsula's other major riverine–agrarian heartland, as part of its rivalry with the western Cālukyan family ruling from Kalyāṇa in what is now northwestern Karnataka.[11] From the perspective of the two generations of Veṅgī Cālukyas who allied themselves with the powerful kings of the south, this alliance emerged *faute de mieux* during the family's temporary exile from 973. Adversity seems to have brought close together the brothers who ruled after the Cālukya restoration in Veṅgī around the year 1000, as the succession of Śaktivarman I (r. 1000–1011) and Vimalāditya I (r. 1011–1018) occurred without incident. This was an exceptionally pacific interlude in the otherwise fractious and opaque history of internecine conflict among the Veṅgī family.[12] This had been especially acute in the previous century: since the reign of Bhīma I – who succeeded his paternal uncle Guṇaga Vijayāditya in 892 and who ruled until 922 – the dynastic history of the Andhra region was a tangle of multiple rulers, month-long reigns, and repeated conflicts over whether the right of succession belonged to the brothers of a king or to his sons.

The briefly ruling Dānārṇava, whose death in battle against Jaṭācoḍa Bhīma had led to the family's Tamil exile, had himself come to the throne as an old man, after a rebellion against his younger brother Amma II, whose reign was marked by a scrum of rebellion and invasion. The familial harmony that attended the Cālukya restoration at the outset of the eleventh century was not perpetuated in the generation that followed. Vimalāditya conducted two prominent marriage alliances, in an apparent effort at political triangulation: one was to Rājarāja Co̲ḻa's sister Kuntavai, the other to a Meḍamā (*var.* Meḷambā), apparently the granddaughter of Jaṭācoḍa Bhīma. Both women gave birth to sons who went on to claim the Cālukya throne. Rājarāja Narendra, Kuntavai's son and *marumakan̲* to the Co̲ḻa emperor, allied himself with his mother's powerful family, marrying his cousin Ammaṅgādevī, daughter of Rājarāja's successor Rājendra. Lacking such connections, the son who would eventually rule as Vijayāditya VII had to pursue his own policy of triangulation. Proof of an incisive political mind on his or his courtiers' part, Vijayāditya's public life was marked by constant shifts, with different records declaring him the ally of the Kalyāṇa Cālukyas – he appears to have been essentially adopted by his cousin-dynast Someśvara I – and then of the Gaṅgas and eventually the Co̲ḻas under Vīrarājendra. Much remains unclear in the several accounts of Rājarāja Narendra and Vijayāditya's alternately serial and simultaneous reigns, but the most likely narrative has them running each other out of the Veṅgī's capital Jananāthanagarī (modern Rajahmundry) as their political and martial fortunes seesawed, intensified by their alliances with their powerful, self-interested neighbors to the west and south. At the beginning of the 1060s, Vijayāditya had placed his son Śaktivarman on the throne in Veṅgī, only to have him die, evidently through violence, after only a year of rule. The period of Rājiga's youth and adolescence was thus a time of unceasing internecine conflict.

If all of this seems eerily reminiscent of the explosive family politics of the *Mahābhārata*, this should come as no surprise, as so it seemed to those contemporary to the events. In the hands of the eulogists attached to both Rājarāja Narendra's and Vijayāditya's court societies, the account of the Bhārata war supplied a dramatis personae, a lexicon, and a series of fixed narrative tableaux to which the family's conflicts could be readily compared. A clear example of this can be seen in Vijayāditya's Ryāli plates, where Śaktivarman's early death is equated to that of Abhimanyu, Arjuna's young and gallant son cruelly cut down on the Kurukṣetra field by an army of his kinsmen. Here, of course, the epic comparison come freighted with additional consequences: overwhelmed by grief, Vijayāditya is still an equal to Arjuna, and like his epic counterpart, is impelled to act and to seek revenge. The crucial fact underlying and empowering these identifications was the Veṅgī Cālukyas' self-understanding as *somavaṃśin*s, kings who looked to the Bhārata clan as their own distant ancestors. Once again, this is not limited to the case of these Andhra kings: as Sylvain Brocquet has argued, the corpus of Sanskrit panegyrics for each South Indian dynasty may be conceived of as fragments of an expanded, implicit epic, in which the historical present interpenetrates with the ancient past, in both tropic comparison and genealogical continuity.[13]

In the Veṅgī Cālukya case, the effect of epic narrative models extended beyond the retrospective and annalistic, and supplied a framework through which royal actions were imagined and evaluated. The two Sanskrit epics presented two very different modalities of power: to adopt Pollock's concise formula, if violence and evil in the narrative world of the *Rāmāyaṇa* is "othered" – displaced onto a deranged and monstrous enemy – then the *Mahābhārata*'s violence is "brothered," "brought home" within the family itself.[14]

This is not to suggest that the royal actors and their attendant agents in medieval India lived their public lives in a state of perpetual hallucination, unable to distinguish epic prototype from contemporary fact. Rather, the model of the kings' putative ancestors in the solar and lunar houses provided a rhetoric for the conception and evaluation of action: these were not set in stone, nor did narrative models necessarily overwhelm political exigency. These models were a set of flexible cognitive and political instruments, subject to revision, partial adaptation, and, of course, alternative interpretation. A clear instance of this, returned to below, can be seen in the repurposing of the Co̱ḻas' quintessential *sūryavaṃśa* exemplar of Rāma Dāśarathi in the hands of the court eulogists of Vīrarājendra.

The pressure upon the possible actions exerted by epic exemplars seems to have achieved an unprecedented, self-conscious articulation during Rājiga's father's reign. Harried by wars with his brother and with the western Cālukyas, with years lived in exile far from the settled heart of coastal Andhra, Rājarāja Narendra's court was nevertheless the site of the invention of Telugu literature, or at least of that work of poetic art that the subsequent Telugu tradition looked back upon as its founding moment.[15] Nannaya Bhaṭṭa, himself a Brahman émigré from the Tamil country (and who thus plausibly entered the family's service during its Coḻa exile), tells his readers in the metapoetic preamble to his *Mahābhāratamu* that it was Rājarāja Narendra's personal request to his poet–guru that set in motion the composition of the Bhārata war in the form of a Telugu *campū*:

> The illustrious Chālukya king, supremely knowledgeable in *dharma*, gently said:
> I've listened to many ancient books with a stainless heart.
> I've learned the ways kings must rule, and people live.
> I've watched many surpassing plays, read eloquent poems vibrant with meaning.
> I've set my heart on temple texts that speak of God.
> Nonetheless, ceaselessly I desire to hear what the *Mahābhārata* seeks to say . . .
> my lineage begins with the moon, and then proceeds
> through Puru, Bharata, Kuru, and King Pāṇḍu.
> The stories of Pāṇḍu's famous sons, virtuous and beyond blame
> are ever close to my heart. . . .
> With all your learning, please compose in Tenugu
> a book that makes clear
> what the celebrated Kṛṣṇa Dvaipāyana spoke,
> the proven meaning bound to the *Mahābhārata* text.[16]

It seems entirely appropriate that this was the case. The fractious familial politics that ran through the whole of Rājarāja Narendra's public life resonated with the story of his ancient ancestors in the lunar dynasty: cast into a new, local idiom, the *Mahābhārata* succinctly captured the courtly world of eleventh-century Andhra. Just as the "honey and coconut" of Telugu represents at the phonaesthetic and lexical levels the interpenetration of Sanskrit and the Dravidian language, so Nannaya's *Mahābhāratamu* was at once witness to and instrument of a wider convergence of the epic narrative and local idioms of martial poetry, and the enduring cultural structures that these give expression. And at the heart of this convergence, we are again confronted by the reckoning of kin: here, however, it is the intersection between two different cultural schemes that defined the fault lines between affiliation and schism, love and bitter antipathy, within a single family. Mythical paradigms and the immediate generational position of the males of the Cālukya line are here not antimonies but conjoint elements of a more comprehensive genealogical imagination.

The driving conflict of the *Mahābhārata* depended on the ineradicable rivalry between paternal cousins, *bhrātṛvya*, exemplified by the epic's Pāṇḍavas and Dhārtarāṣṭras. But this rivalry, articulated in the epic and rearticulated in *praśasti* and in Nannaya's courtly *campū*, existed in a tense dialectic with the alternately patrilineal and patrilateral dynastic succession seen in the Cālukya genealogy: either sons or younger brothers provided the usual candidates for royal succession. The axis between paternal uncle and nephew – between *pitṛvya* and *bhrātrīya*, exactly the genealogical chiasmus of Rājiga and Vijayāditya versus Rājarāja Narendra and Śaktivarman – becomes the preeminent point of tension and potential conflict. This is in plain contrast to the epic framework, where the relationship of paternal uncle and nephew is not one of potential violence but of solicitude and deference. The epic prototypes here are Dhṛtarāṣṭra and Yudhiṣṭhira, whose respectful bond never wavers even in the face of family holocaust. All the while, each passing generation produces another crop of notional *bhrātṛvya*s; this was a role available to Rājarāja Narendra and Vijayāditya who, as non-uterine brothers, were assimilable to parallel cousins. In a world suffused with the Epic narrative, this supplied a standing, genealogically hardwired pretext for intra-dynastic conflict. This might explain something of the obscure early history of the Veṅgī line. The narratives of explosive conflicts of the *somavaṃśa* provided a self-fulfilling – and self-perpetuating – story that the internally cleaved courts of Veṅgī repeatedly told themselves.

Coupled with these fractiously multiple worlds of his patriline, and ultimately of far greater importance to Rājiga's public career, were his links with the imperial Coḻas. As with so much of Rājiga's early life, there is much that is unknown here: did the young prince, his family, and his retinue speak Tamil among themselves? During his early years in Veṅgī, was he brought up to think of the distant world of the Tamil plains as "home"? There is no way to know this, yet certainly for the prince and the world that surrounded him, the pull of the southern court could only have been a powerful one. The Veṅgī dynasts' contending alliances with the Co̱ḻas and the Kalyāṇa Cālukyas were no accident: Rājiga's father and uncle were linked to the two most powerful political formations of the time, whose endemic warfare saw territories alternating between their control. Even granting the highly stylized martial language of eulogy and court poetry, this points toward a rising tide of violence in these years, attributable in large part to the remarkable consolidation overseen in the first half of the century by Rājarāja and Rājendra Co̱ḻa. Such unprecedented success seems to have led to a cascade of unforeseen consequences for the Co̱ḻa polity, returned to below. But one such consequence is of immediate import: the internal politics of the dynasty transformed in the wake of Rājendra's long reign. The history of his successors stands as a testimony to this: although the order and chronology of the Co̱ḻa rulers in the middle decades of the eleventh century has been securely reconstructed,[17] this period still presents many unanswered questions and tantalizing anomalies. This can be clearly seen through the most basic fact of kingly public presentation, the regular pattern of regnal names.

As can be seen from Table 1.1, the mid-eleventh century witnessed a dramatic expansion in the number of potential claimants to the title of Co̱ḻa king and a contrapuntal diminution in the variety of royal names. With the partial exception of Rājādhirāja (who bore the alternate title Vijayarājendra[18]), most of whose long reign was spent as junior partner to his father, all of the Co̱ḻas possessed names that were simply variations on or expansions of Rājendra's, who seems to have been transformed during his sons' lifetimes from a father–predecessor into a totem ancestor, whose sons and grandsons calibrated their public selves to capture his charisma. The successions of the 1050s and 1060s are made theoretically intelligible by the distinguishing titles Parakesarivarman and Rājakesarivarman, the alternating cognomina used by the Co̱ḻas. This practice is consistent with that of other southern dynasties; in the Co̱ḻas' Sanskrit *praśasti*s, this convention is traced back to fictitious early members of the lineage,

Table 1.1 *Co̱ḻa regnal names, 1018–1072*

Rājakesarivarman Rājādhirāja	Son of PKV Rājendra	r. 1018–1054
Parakesarivarman Rājendradeva	Son of PKV Rājendra	r. 1052–1063
Rājakesarivarman Rājamahendra	Son of PKV Rājendradeva	r. 1058/9–1063?
Rājakesarivarman Vīrarājendra	Son of PKV Rājendra	r. 1063–1070?
Parakesarivarman Adhirājendra	Son of RKV Vīrarājendra	r. 1069–1072

whose names were adopted by the subsequent kings in the order of their consecration into kingship.[19] The order of these cognomina is a matter neither of generational succession nor of a claim about independent rule: when a member of the lineage exercised authority, he did so under the sign of Rājakesari or Parakesari, in the alternating serial order of his ritual establishment. More than one Co̱ḻa king could exercise authority at a time, as when Rājakesarivarman Rājarāja I and Parakesarivarman Rājendra I ruled jointly from 1012 to 1014, or the latter's corule with his son Rājakesarivarman Rājādhirāja from 1018 to 1044.

The Coḻa *-varman* titles were thus, formally speaking, not a part of the reckoning of kinship, but served as indices of the sequential access to the ritual of consecration. The use of the alternating titles formed a part of a skein of publicly displayed markers of Coḻas' collective identity. But this skein had begun to unravel in the decade before Rājendracoḷa's own consecration in 1070. For the two preceding generations, the reigning Coḻa king had ensured the succession by associating himself with his heir, duly bearing the alternate *varman* title. The transition from Rājarāja to Rājendra to Rājādhirāja, further, had followed the order of primogeniture. This was a narrative commonplace of the solar dynasty: the scandal of the *Rāmāyaṇa*'s *Ayodhyākāṇḍa* is that Daśaratha violates this tradition when he passes over Rāma in favor of his brother Bharata. But after this three-generation patrilineal succession, where the Coḻa rule moved from father to eldest son, the transition from Rājādhirāja to Rājendradeva was patrilateral, that is, brother to brother.

This anomaly appears to have been less a shift in the customs of the Coḻa family than a contingent response to potential catastrophe. Court eulogies from the 1050s onward attribute this to the Rājādhirāja's death in the battle of Koppam and Rājendradeva's ritual consecration on the field the following day. Rājendradeva attempted to resume the patrilineal succession by consecrating his own son as Rājamahendra. This strikingly failed, as can be seen by the disruption of the regular pattern of the cognomina, both Rājamahendra and his paternal uncle Vīrarājendra being Rājakesarivarmans. Some have seen in this the evidence of Rājamahendra dying while still *yuvarāja*, but this fails to accord with the fact that all later Coḻa genealogies place Rājamahendra in the succession of Coḻa kings, an otherwise inexplicable lapse in court protocol. It seems likely that uncle and nephew – notice that this is the fraught relation of *pitṛvya* and *bhrātrīya* – each claimed the succession for himself. This time, the uncle proved successful: Rājamahendra's few records were seemingly issued while his father was still alive, and so Vīrarājendra's adoption of the Rājakesarivarman cognomen may have been as a deliberate act of *damnatio memoriae*, an effort to excise his nephew from the dynasty's genealogical reckoning.

If this is correct, the outcome of the disputed succession may have borne consequences for Rājiga's early life. Rājamahendra's sister, Madhurāntakī, was the eventual Kulottuṅga's chief queen, and it is likely that they were already married in the early 1060s.[20] Rājiga may have been a part of the aggrieved party of Rājendradeva's family, who saw the kingship as theirs by right of direct inheritance. It is thus only when Rājiga's relationship as *marumakaṉ* to the Coḻa main line is set within this intersection of mythic stereotype and the adventitious contention for primacy with both his Coḻa and Cālukya kin that we can begin to plot the lines of force that not merely made him eligible to assume power in the southern kingdom but produced the conjunctural opening that made such an outcome possible.

The Coḻa State, 985–1069: An Interpretive Sketch

Ruling families, whatever their pretensions, are not the sole makers of their own destiny. It is only (to borrow a phrase) within the setting of a wider structure of politics that the projects, ambitions, successes, and failures of kings and their courtiers were of any significance, and so it is only with some sense of this wider context of relevance that a history such as this one can proceed. This, however, necessitates a change of focus: from the intersection of mythic model and familial machination in the 1060s, we must turn to the longer history of the Coḻa polity, and to the reasons for its transformation into the great imperial state-system it had become by the second half of the 1000s. What were the reasons for the spectacular successes of this one South Indian kingdom, and what were the dynamics that governed it?

At the beginning of the tenth century, the Coḻa dynasty had been no different from any of a number of other ruling lineages scattered across the southern peninsula. The Pāṇḍyas, the Ceras, the Āys, the Cālukya houses of Veṅgī and Vemulavāda, the Pallavas in their postimperial desuetude: all these shared with the family ruling from Tanjavur a circumscribed territorial footprint and a similar pattern of seasonal warfare and public gifting to Brahmans and religious institutions, recorded in stone and copperplate inscriptions. The Coḻas, along with the Pāṇḍyas and the Ceras, possessed a family name connecting them with the enormous regional prestige of Tamil classical poetry. There is, however, no reason to take this self-identification as anything but an empowering fiction. Under the first dynast with anything more than local ambitions, Parakesarivarman Parāntaka (r. 907–955), the Coḻas began to seriously extend their control beyond the upper stretches of the Kāveri delta. Parāntaka's armies won significant victories to the south and north, entering into Pāṇḍya territory (he bore the epithet "who took Madurai") and reducing smaller lineages to the north of erstwhile Pallava territory, while successfully conducting a marital and martial alliance with the Ceras to the west. But these ambitions were sharply checked by a campaign of the Rāṣṭrakūṭa overlord Kṛṣṇa III, at the time the south's dominant ruler. The Coḻa army was catastrophically outmatched at Takkoḷam in 949, where Parāntaka's heir apparent was left dead on the battlefield. The subsequent Rāṣṭrakūṭa occupation of Tondaimandalam, an earlier arena of Coḻa territorial extension, threw the final years of the king's reign into chaos.[21]

Rājakesarivarman Aruṇmŏḻideva Rājarāja emerged in 985 from a post-Parāntaka dynastic tangle whose ambiguities were as great as those that surrounded his great-grandson Rājendracoḷa eighty-five years later. Rājarāja's reign marked the beginning of a process of state-building unparalleled in medieval India. Initially working outward from the reduced dynastic patrimony in the Kāveri delta, this took as its raw material the basic fabric of agrarian society in the Tamil-speaking lands. This consisted of a discontinuous landscape of small, independent regions, determined in the last instance by the access to water sources adequate to support riziculture. The country centered on the dynasty's homeland resembled an archipelago, dotted by autarkic, inwardly turned clusters of habitation, irrigation, and cultivation called *nāṭu*s ("country" is perhaps the best equivalent). Each of these constituted a "discrete social universe," possessing a conventional, stable name, usually coined after a single *ūr* or settlement, or a feature of local topography.[22] Extending above the level of several individual cultivating habitation-clusters, these *nāṭu*s were alternately compact (when nearer to perennial sources of water such as the Kāveri) or widespread (when in drier parts of the region). Within these, the Dravidian patterns of kinship identification and matrimonial alliance reinforced at a social level the confines of topography and hydrology.[23] Ranging between and alongside the region's many *nāṭu*s – some 550 of which can be identified in Colamandalam and its adjoining territory between the years 1000 and 1200 – were the open spaces of pastoralism and tribal societies, the terrain of swidden agriculture and the collection of forest produce, and the tracks traversed by peddlers, tradesmen, and bards. But it was the *nāṭu*s that supplied the building blocks for the project of the Coḻa state begun under Rājarāja. Within the evolving network of the *nāṭu*s, there were three distinct social groups from whose ranks were drawn the ruling societies of the Coḻa kings: magnates, gentry, and Brahmans. There were other types of persons whose actions can be traced in the surviving sources, especially members of merchant enclaves (*nagarams*), but also forest peoples, mobile traders, artisans, and warrior groups from outside the delta. Yet these three groups were by far the dominant sources of the kingdom's political elite.

The Co<u>l</u>a kingdom, first of all, was not the only local polity whose ambitions extended over a multitude of individual *nāṭus*. Spread over a broad arc relative to the Co<u>l</u>a deltaic center, extending from the western uplands to the boundary zone between Colamandalam and the former Pallava heartland of Tondaimandalam, was a constellation of smaller polities, each encompassing a number of constituent *nāṭus*, among them Ma<u>l</u>anāṭu, Iruṅkoḷappāṭi, Milāṭu, Vāṇakoppāṭi, and Tirumu<u>n</u>aipāṭi.[24] These were dominated by martial dynasts analogous in their culture and royal comportment to the Co<u>l</u>as themselves: indeed, Rājarāja's ancestors had only emerged from obscurity by displacing one such lineage, the Muttaraiyars, as the lords of Tanjavur; the Co<u>l</u>as continued to intermarry with them into imperial times. Well within the era of Co<u>l</u>a success, these older magnate rulers ("chiefs" or "feudatories" in earlier scholarship) continued to arrogate to themselves a measure of kingly public dignity. A key example is furnished by the lords of Milāṭu, a polity centered on the ancient temple site of Tirukkovalūr, who maintained regalian pretensions even within the mature Co<u>l</u>a state-system, claiming such kṣatriya appurtenances as a *gotra*-identity and the *-varman* name element distinctive of that *varṇa*, going so far as patronizing the creation of a long epigraphic eulogy on themselves and their country, written in passably classicizing Tamil verse, and dated in Rājarāja's regnal years.[25] These magnate families would continue to be powerful throughout the centuries of Co<u>l</u>a dominance; though small in numbers, magnates gave gifts, led bands of armed men, and acted as local rulers and as state officials.

Within the customary boundaries of each *nāṭu*, the work of agrarian domination – control over patriarchy, the administration of local justice, maintenance of irrigation networks, and the periodic marshaling of cultivators and agrestic workers for corvée labor and armed force – was the preserve of a condominium of landholding gentry and local Brahmans.[26] The gentry – whom earlier scholars have classed as "peasants" – formed the membership of the governing society of each individual *nāṭu*, itself (confusingly) sometimes simply referred to as "the *nāṭu*." In what follows, this group is sometimes referred to by the collective caste name "Veḷḷāḷa." It is uncertain what local ascriptive category the gentry might have used as a form of collective self-reference, if any such term existed; the use of Veḷḷāḷa should accordingly be considered as a sort of historical-sociological shorthand for what was likely a far more granular social reality.[27] These are the men encountered throughout the epigraphical record as the *nāṭṭār* ("the men of the *nāṭu*") or – in the juridical voice of the records themselves – as *nāṭṭom* ("we of the *nāṭu*"). It is in this first-person plural voice that the gentry rendered decisions and granted assent to the acts of agents from outside the *nāṭu*, preeminently those of the Co<u>l</u>a state itself.

When named as an actor in or a witness to a piece of local business, a man of the gentry generally appears with the title x-*uṭaiyā<u>n</u>*, where "x" refers to some habitation (i.e. an *ūr*) within the given *nāṭu*. The widely shared -*uṭaiya* ("possessor") title was diagnostic of the greater and lesser lordships of the region, up to and including members of the magnate families and the Co<u>l</u>a kings themselves; it was also borne by the deities of local temples in their juristic aspect as owners of property. The relationship between leading gentry, magnates, and the incumbents of the Co<u>l</u>a dynasty was a scalar one, with only continued martial and political success and putative *kṣatriya* status producing a perceived qualitative difference between the royal figures and the less powerful rural dominants. Below the level of the royal court – or in certain cases even within it, given the history of royal–magnate marital alliances – lay a shifting terrain marking the difference between magnate and gentry: all of the -*uṭaiya* titleholders, human and divine, thus shared in the fact of their "lordship," however limited or aggrandized.[28] Thus, "magnate" and "gentry" mark points along a continuum, and social mobility between the two groups, broadly considered, was certainly possible. It is not always entirely clear whether an individual falls into one category or the other. In the first instance, a figure may be identified as a magnate when his name connects him with one of the lineages of sub-imperial families (whose patrimonies I call "magnate polities"). Contrariwise, men described as the "possessors" of a certain village may be understood to be a member of the gentry. But the distinction is by no means definitive. In particular, the ranks of the magnates were not closed. Seemingly, the most direct means of entry into the magnate class was the practice of violence: joining the members of older lineages were the martial leaders on whom the Co<u>l</u>a kings' warmaking increasingly came to depend. These newer magnates were of ascriptively diverse backgrounds: some were certainly members of the gentry, but some evidently hailed from martial communities from beyond the pale of the delta. The emergence of these martial new men was among the most recognizable and consequential social transformations of the Co<u>l</u>a period, as we shall see.

From the time of the Pallavas onward, the *nāṭṭār* gentry had appeared in records lending their assent to the creation of new land grant Brahmanical estates, *brahmadeya*s, within the territory of their *nāṭu*. While Brahman families were certainly domiciled in villages throughout the region, it is these large, royally sponsored foundations that were the most spectacular evidence of their leading place in the rural social order. The presence of one or more *brahmadeya*s within a *nāṭu* serves as an index of its agrarian wealth, particularly its ready access to perennial water sources, especially the Kāveri and its major tributaries. For the historian, the *brahmadeya* villages thus provide crucial evidence of intra-*nāṭu* development: where an inscription establishes the existence of one, the presence of circumambient settlements classed as *veḷḷāṉvakai* ("cultivator type") can be reliably inferred, even when they themselves go unmentioned. This evidentiary status, however, points to a larger epistemological conundrum: the testimony of copperplate foundation charters and the lithic records found on temple walls are skewed disproportionately toward recording the details of Brahmanical life and landed privilege. Thus the epigraphic documentation of the arrangements for local administration – the classic example being that found in the lengthy tenth-century records of the *brahmadeya* of Uttaramerūr in modern Kanchipuram district – has been uncritically taken as the presumptive standard for all of the settlements of the medieval Tamil country.[29] While this is an illegitimate overextension of the value of these particular records, to overcorrect in the opposite direction and to devalue the Brahmanical settlement in the rich lands of the Tamil country – to see it either as epiphenomenal or as a parasitic incursion – is equally misguided. The Brahmanical presence in the riverine parts of far Southern India was many centuries old by Rājarāja's time, and, despite some efforts to imagine it as an intrusive mass colonization from elsewhere in the subcontinent, its agents were linguistically and ethnically a part of the fabric of their local societies.

In a region of strikingly little urbanization, aside from the ceremonial capitals of Tanjavur and Gaṅgaikŏṇṭacoḻapuram (those twin Brasilias of the medieval Tamils) and the ancient metropolis of Kāñci at the northern edge of the core Coḻa territory, many of the central-place functions elsewhere associated with cities were scattered across the landscape in the *brahmadeya*s. Education, adjudication, and archival storage were all, if not monopolized in Brahman-dominated villages, strongly associated with them. And, of course, the *brahmadeya* villages housed temples, often as the geographical heart or "nerve-center" of the settlement, and it was these that supplied the physical and social space for many of these central-place functions: the long-term trend of the twelfth and thirteenth centuries was to see these sacred sites consistently expand themselves at the expense of the individual Brahman freeholders.[30] The degree to which *brahmadeya*s offered mediated access to divine grace and power should not be treated lightly, but neither should their denizens be entirely reduced to purveyors of the sacred, that is, to "priests."[31] The assemblies that governed individual *brahmadeya*s, noncultivating elites set throughout the rural landscape, served as principal loci of investment and capital accumulation and, in turn, of such development initiatives as the extension of irrigation networks and land reclamation.[32] Outside of such evidently this-worldly activities, the culturally sanctioned Brahmanical command over knowledge is not reducible to the strictly "religious." Calendrical calculation, medicine, basic engineering, customary law and juridical procedure, theories of policy, martial arts, and the control over language and thus public eloquence: all of these modes of formal learning were part of the Brahmanical syllabus, alongside the Veda and the domains of śāstric scholarship. *Brahmadeya* residents did not by any means monopolize either formal or tacit learning, the evidence for which can be seen in the specialized literacy and numeracy that were the preserve of the *ūrkkaṇṇaku*s or village accountants, or in the subsequent appearance of highly trained professional literati among the gentry. Nevertheless, the intersection of a secure place atop the rural social hierarchy and the cultural sanction for the pursuit of scholarly and practical knowledge allowed at least a segment of the Brahman communities to pursue careers beyond their natal villages, as a mobile professional elite who proved amenable to recruitment into state service.[33]

Over the course of Rājarāja's long independent reign (985–1012), during the brief dyarchy with his son Parakesarivarman Rājendra (1012–1014) and – with ever-increasing pace – in Rājendra's own reign (1014–1044, from 1018 associated with Rājādhirāja), the discontinuous patchwork of parcellated *nāṭu*s, subregional magnate polities, and Brahmanical estates was stitched together into a new, imperial whole. Throughout the vastly increased area where the Coḻas issued inscriptions, but especially in the core territories of Colamandalam and what would come to be called Naṭuvilnāṭu ("the land in the middle," to the south of Tondaimandalam), we can perceive the workings of a linked policy of martial mobilization and the forging of a transregional state cadre out of the condominate gentry and Brahman elite. The six decades of these kings' combined rule seem marked by an unprecedented expansion of the number and social standing of the armed men in service to the Coḻas: if it did not number the 900,000 soldiers attributed to it by a contemporary Cālukya inscription, nevertheless the marshaling of the Coḻa army was the catalyst for a pronounced militarization of the kingdom.[34] Recruitment appears to have been drawn from the upland regions on the fringes of the cultivated Colamandalam heartland, but there is evidence that suggests the importance of peasant levies, the most significant of which can be seen in the earliest appearance of the "Right Hand" (*valaṅkai*) designation in the names of martial groups. This label would subsequently come to be adopted as emblematic of cultivator communities across Southern India. It is possible that in its early, expressly martial incarnation, the *valaṅkai* consisted of upland peoples only in the process of entering into settled agrarian life; but whatever their social constitution or regional origin, these armed men and their entourages would have been an omnipresent fact of life in the Kāveri delta, serving as the conduit through which the mobile wealth seized on these campaigns was introduced into the core territories of Colamandalam.[35]

Taking advantage of the regional power vacuum in the wake of the Rāṣṭrakūṭa imperial collapse after 973, the armies of Rājarāja and Rājendra's time were hugely successful: during Rājarāja's reign, they subjugated the Pāṇḍya and Cera domains to the south and west, waged destructive campaigns hundreds of miles into the Deccan, and unseated the kings of Sri Lanka from their traditional capital at Anurādhapura. Under Rājendra, these territorial gains culminated in the putative "conquest" of the Gaṅgā and the campaign against the Srivijaya thalassocracy in the Indonesian archipelago.[36] Alongside the largely gestural gains involved in these dramatic undertakings, Rājendra's rule saw the establishment of Co<u>l</u>a imperium as a political and administrative reality, with outright Co<u>l</u>a control of the Pāṇḍya country and Kerala, intervention (as we have seen) into the dynastic scuffles in Veṅgī, and continuous military pressure on the Kalyāṇa Cālukyas.

All of this depended, as already suggested, on the enormous marshaling of military labor. However, the reigns of Rājarāja and Rājendra oversaw another, even more consequential, mobilization: the recruitment of the regional rural elite into the emergent structure of the imperial kingdom. Military leaders appear to have been drawn overwhelmingly from the magnate class and, interestingly, from Brahmans, who are well represented among those possessing the high martial title of *senāpati*.[37] In this same period, magnates totally disappeared as independent rulers of their own patrimonial little kingdoms, which were encompassed within the newly minted Co<u>l</u>a imperial nomenclature, especially that of the *vaḷanāṭus* ("prosperity *nāṭus*"). These territorial divisions were an innovation of Rājarāja's time, the end product of a kingdom-wide revenue survey. Each of these new divisions was initially named after epithets of Rājarāja himself: so the erstwhile Ma<u>l</u>anāṭu tract, for instance, was swallowed up into the newly designated Rājāśrayavaḷanāṭu ("The Refuge of Kings"), while the central royal preserve around Tanjavur was renamed Pāṇḍikulāśanivaḷanāṭu ("Thunderbolt to the Pāṇḍya family"). This internal reorganization is perhaps the most eloquent testimony to the gathering ambition of the state-making project in the first three decades of the eleventh century.[38]

Something similar to the royalist project of the *vaḷanāṭu*s can be seen in the names of the elite actors of the epigraphic record. Central to the Coḻa imperial success in this period is the wide-ranging incorporation of magnate, gentry, and Brahman figures into a shared system of honors and distinction, traceable through the awarding of titles associated with the charisma of the royal family. Though present in a rudimentary form since Parāntaka's time, the wide dissemination of such honors was an innovation of the reigns of Rājarāja and Rājendra. The title *mūventaveḷaṉ*, to take the most significant example, was broadly adopted by gentry figures throughout the Coḻa territories, especially those distinguished by the "possessor" (*-uṭaiya*) name segment that set them out as local landholders. This title was almost invariably preceded by a name or epithet of the Coḻa king (or a *nāṭu* name, in a much smaller set of instances); the Brahmanical equivalent *brahmarāyaṉ*/*brahmamārāyaṉ* is equally associable with Coḻa regnal titles.[39]

Due to this remarkable grafting of royal onomasty, the kingdom's dominant figures could, over the course of just a generation's time, look out across the region and find men assimilable to themselves, part of a hierarchy of honor that descended from the Coḻa family. Many of these acquired their place in this hierarchy through state service: distinct from these titles of honor, but relatable to them, are the names of various offices into which the elite were recruited. The distinctive office of the early eleventh century, present in record after record throughout the kingdom, is that of *atikāri* (Skt. *adhikārin*, met often in the honorific form *atikārikaḷ*), "official" as such. These men – more than half of whom are identified as *mūventaveḷar* – were the primary instruments of the royal center's will. A great many further officeholders were associated with chancellery duties, with the recording and verifying of the king's oral commands and their transformation into written orders to be transmitted and later inscribed in stone and copper. Here *mūventaveḷar* dominated in the performance of secretarial duties (*tirumantiravolai*, the office "of the palm-leaves of royal counsel"), while *brahmarāyar*s were predominately responsible for oversight and rescripts (*tirumantiravolaināyakam*).[40] Most conspicuous in its development – as stands to reason, given the growth of the state apparatus – was the revenue office, the *puravuvaritiṇaikkaḷam*. Institutions going under a similar name had existed since Parāntaka's time, and some of the magnate domains had earlier maintained their own inchoate *tiṇaikkaḷam*s. Over the course of the eleventh century, the office came to possess an increasingly complex internal hierarchy, as the royal center evidently succeeded in its efforts to quantify, capture, and redistribute an enormous quantity of agrarian wealth, as well as interpose itself into the region's monetized economy, which was strongly associated with the mercantile enclaves or *nagarams*, which dotted the agrarian landscape.[41]

In a very literal sense, the rapid development of the imperial polity was iconized in monumental form by the Rājarājeśvara temple complex in Tanjavur.[42] Not only is this rightly the most celebrated example of medieval South Indian monumental architecture, its enormous inscriptional archive records the summoning into being of a far-flung network of revenue, goods, and human capital centered on the temple and its environs.[43] The Tanjavur temple complex was an argument in stone about royal power, from the stunning donations of ornaments and precious metals by Rājarāja and his elder sister, to the clusters of villages, set in terrain only newly opened by the expansion of Co̱la agriculture, meant to forward their annual revenue contribution to the temple's upkeep in perpetuity. Other villages, located far outside the kingdom's core, were also included in the temple's revenue network: these included settlements in the old Pāṇḍya country, in northern Sri Lanka, and, most spectacularly, deep in the northwestern Deccan. With these, the argument shades over into one about the projection of Co̱la armed might beyond the Kāveri.[44] Something similar can be said for the named martial groups ("regiments") prominently included among the temple's donors, a testament to the militarization of the kingdom's public life. The command economy centered on the temple thus served as an enormous engine for actualizing the dynasty's imperial ambition, as it "brought Rājarāja I and numerous local leaders of the *nāṭu*s into a single administrative system headed by the king."[45]

The success of this new imperial order – which again was articulated remarkably quickly, in only about a generation's time – brought with it a host of unforeseen problems. The enabling factor here lay in the sheer scale of the agrarian and human resources that the Co̱la kings were able to mobilize from within their home region. The products of the region's agriculture literally fueled the dynasty's building projects and armies, and its conjoint Brahman and gentry elites were linguistically, ethnically, and culturally integrated long before the turn of the eleventh century and the dawn of Co̱la imperial ambitions. The contiguous regions that were the bases of other Tamil- and Kannada-speaking polities, along the Sinhala-speaking kingdom centered on Anurādhapura in Sri Lanka, simply possessed no comparable resources, and were massively outmatched by the marshaled forces of this regionally unique social and material amalgam.[46] By the period of shared rule between Rājendra and Rājādhirāja (1018–1044), even excluding the distant and highly ritualized power projection into the northeast and across the Bay of Bengal, the Coḻas laid claim to a wider swath of territory than any earlier southern polity, and they attempted in a desultory way to reproduce their nascent state-system throughout.

Yet from the middle of the eleventh century, two intertwined contradictions underpinning the Coḻa polity become increasingly apparent. The dynasty's state-making project depended in the first instance upon the integration of the elite sector of Colamandalam's rural societies, upon whose hegemony the region's exceptional productivity and internal development had depended. Yet this regional ascendancy, though guaranteeing exceptional agrarian and material wealth and with it state revenue, was balanced by the counterforce of the logic of endemic martial competition that dominated the relationships between the peninsula's multiple kingdoms, upon which Coḻa expansion at the expense of their neighbors depended. This led to an unprecedented militarization of the society that was disruptive of the Brahmans' and Veḷḷāḷas' settled civilian regime. Much of this potential for armed violence was directed outward, and successfully so; but the conquests of the Coḻa armies brought under the dynasty's control new territories that lacked the social matrix from which the Colamandalam ruling society was drawn. The very success of the dynasty's elaborating network of entitled officials thus led to efforts toward its reproduction among societies with very different local forms of domination. The outer fringes of the Coḻa imperial territory – far drier and wilder than the settled spaces of rice cultivation in the kingdom's core – retained the character of jagged frontiers, despite the efforts to accommodate them within the Coḻa system of nomenclature and land tenure. Military recruitment in the kingdom's drier uplands catalyzed demographic and economic transformations in its deltaic heartland: warrior groups distinct from, and ascriptively inferior to, the Brahman–Veḷḷāḷa condominates emerged increasingly as landholders in the central regions of the kingdom, accelerating the emergence of private property, which had begun in the context of class differentiation internal to the rural elite.[47] Along with the physical domiciling of these fighting men and their families in the midst of Colamandalam's cultivator locales, the inevitable effects of a permanent seasonal war footing on the kingdom's adult males could only have had palpable consequences. In a period when at least two members of the dynasty were killed in battle, there can be no doubt that families at every point in the social order were directly touched by war. This series of asymmetries between the kingdom's settled agrarian center and its expanding frontiers, especially the limits of the Cola state's need to identify and recruit its martial cadres outside the kingdom's core, formed its first structuring contradiction.

If this first contradiction lay in the extension of the Cola state into new territory, the second contradiction developed internally. The intensification of the political and revenue apparatus built up by the Cola kings – the ability of the nascent state to intervene in local customary life and to extract surplus from the cultivators – was, throughout the kingdom's core, marked by its withdrawal or abeyance in precisely the locales marked by the greatest concentration of wealth and local power, the Brahmanical estates and flourishing temple sites scattered throughout the region. The entirety of our knowledge of the Cola state's operation depends upon the recorded instances of its controlled surrender of rights, most often of the state's claim to some stipulated amount of landed revenue, to the benefit of a religious institution or the governing *sabhā* of a *brahmadeya.* Even assertive royalist political power, through the workings of a remarkably successful discourse of false necessity, remained permanently inclined toward spectacular acts of generosity to Brahmans and to the gods domiciled in constructed temples. The creation of new estates, the ceding of the proceeds of agrarian land to temple upkeep, and the outright surrender of regalian control over justice and right of access produced an overlay of particularist, autonomous zones throughout the space of the state. This appears to have also touched – though in a far less systematic fashion than the liberties of the *brahmadeya* – on the public lives of magnates and gentry, whose own attested interactions with individual temples frequently amount to pious tax evasion. Settled within or inextricably bound up with these areas marked by the occultation of state power was much of the elite Brahman-gentry strata, even (perhaps especially) those directly in state service.

The limits of the control that a medieval polity could exert over a wide territory, which the military machinery of the Cola had overshot in the course of its rapid expansion, began to assert themselves on the dynasty's statecraft by mid-century. Those newly subjugated regions with long independent dynastic traditions of their own – northern Sri Lanka, Pāṇḍimaṇḍalam, and Kerala – were hived off from the Cola patrimony, and were for a time taken over as appanages by junior members of the dynasty. These rulers (earlier scholarship's "viceroys" and "governors") adopted local styles of entitlement, and seemingly imported Colamandalam elites as their officials.[48] This system of appanage proved to be short-lived: though Rājiga's own early public life as an independent Cola ruler derives from this logic of royal devolution, the system was abandoned over the course of his subsequent reign. Despite this shedding of central administrative control over newly conquered territory, the machinery of entitled officeholders and revenue bureaucrats continued to proliferate, reaching the apogee of its top-heavy complexity during the reign of Rājendradeva.[49] Within the southern peninsula's kinetic system of interdynastic martial competition, the success of Co<u>l</u>a state-building had another consequence in the ever-escalating violence of the seasonal warfare between the Co<u>l</u>as and the Kalyāṇa Cālukyas. We have already encountered the consequences of this escalation: above all, the battlefield death of Rājādhirāja– himself more generalissimo than king – and the subsequent turbulence within the Co<u>l</u>a succession, culminating in the hyperactivity of Vīrarājendra's seven years on the throne.

For all of its extraordinary success, the Co<u>l</u>a state inaugurated under Rājarāja and continued by his son and grandsons should not be seen as more stable than it actually was. For all the granite of its practical apparatus and the glittering ornament of its new aristocratic order, the system was remarkably precarious, its mortar of customary observance and institutional inertia unset. It was an act of deliberate royal initiative that made Rājarāja's great monument at Tanjavur into a metonym for the imperial state of which it was the apex. Yet the massive network centered on the Rājarājeśvara was severed less than twenty years after its founder's death, when his son and successor redirected the revenue of at least eight of the providing villages to fund the upkeep of his own massive monument, the Gaṅgaikŏṇṭaco<u>l</u>īśvaram at the heart of the new capital of Gaṅgaikŏṇṭaco<u>l</u>apuram. Tanjavur would no longer continue as a major residential or ritual center for the Co<u>l</u>a kings.[50] The marvelously cut letters of the Rājarājeśvara's epigraphs, easily the finest extant achievement of Co<u>l</u>a-period orthography, in the end described an order that only briefly outlived its royal initiator.

The *Mĕykkīrtti* as Political Text

The *mĕykkīrtti* had been an innovation of the inscriptions issued in Rājarāja's reign, a stereotyped preamble in Tamil verse, which serially described the king's major martial accomplishments while depicting his possession of a range of royal virtues, chiefly his association with the goddesses of prosperity and victory.[51] Rājarāja's *mĕykkīrtti* text – essentially just a brief catalog of his major conquests – seems to have been adapted from Pallava and Rāṣṭrakūṭa antecedents;[52] from Rājendra's reign onward, the preamble grew precipitously in length and internal complexity. That this form of poetic royal self-presentation took shape under these two successive kings is a matter of record; that their reigns oversaw the emergence of a regionally unprecedented imperial state is another. The emergence of this style of public poetry and the emergence of the Coḻa imperial order were thus processes that unfolded simultaneously over the first half of the eleventh century. Simultaneity suggests concomitance: the *mĕykkīrtti* as a textual genre was so bound up with Coḻa state-making to only be intelligible within the logic of the dynasty's emergent political settlement.

There are a few initial clarifications to be made about the *mĕykkīrtti* form. It needs first of all to be kept distinct from other epigraphical and literary genres: for all of its surface similarities, it must especially be distinguished from the cosmopolitan Sanskrit *praśasti* or praise-poem. *Praśasti* is less a genre than an overarching pragmatic category – it can be prose or verse; mythical, historical, or both in content; in honor of a single figure (royal or otherwise), or the account of a dynasty, revised with every ruler. By contrast, the Coḻa *mĕykkīrtti* is tightly regimented in its form and in its descriptive *topoi*, and it is invariably and unwaveringly focused on a single figure, the Coḻa king in whose name it is issued.[53] The form's peculiarity relative to the stylistic norms of other modes of Tamil public poetry needs also be recognized: while there were earlier (as well as later) forms of eulogy composed in Tamil – what are in fact vernacular *praśasti*s, such as those encountered in the Pāṇḍya charters of the eighth and ninth centuries – the *mĕykkīrtti* was at least initially a Coḻa-specific phenomenon, as can be gathered from the close match between the Coḻa texts and the generic checklists found in such later poetic grammars as the *Paṉṉiruppāṭṭiyal*.[54]

In its austere, self-consciously "classical" diction, the *mĕykkīrtti* can equally be distinguished from the wider world of contemporaneous Tamil poetry. While the extant corpus of integral Coḻa-period Tamil literary works dates from the end of Kulottuṅga's reign in the early 1100s, there is ample surviving evidence in works on metrics and literary theory that demonstrates the preferred forms of courtly literary expression prior to this time. This evidence powerfully underscores the *mĕykkīrtti*s' status as stylistic outliers. Though composed in verse, they were without exception cast in a simplified version of the old *akaval* or *āciriyappā*, the dominant meter of the Caṅkam anthologies, as opposed to the exuberant spectrum of other metrical forms then available. Further distinguishing them, and again suggestive of a deliberate filiation with classical norms, the *mĕykkīrtti*s show only a limited interest in the use of figures of sound – for instance *ĕtukai* or front-rhyme – that were otherwise requisite in Tamil verse of the time. To this conservatism was wedded a certain anonymity. None of the extant eulogies of any Coḻa king is ascribed to a particular author: they seem to have been the product of official culture at its least individual, a poetry by and for elites possessed of a modest literary education.[55]

This is not to dismiss the peculiar poetic virtues of the *mĕykkīrtti* form: individual eulogies were certainly composed with careful eye to their expressive and rhetorical effect. To take a single, influential example: in the list, much discussed by modern scholarship, detailing the king's conquests across the sea, the composers of Rājendra's *mĕykkīrtti* produced a catalog of exotic place names, tamed through their reproduction in Tamil orthography and a series of etymological wordplays, and set out in an artfully patterned, chiming parataxis.[56] Individual eulogies can include impressive set-pieces of verbal art; yet it is only when read as a corpus that the peculiar power of the *mĕykkīrtti* becomes clear. Above all, there is its remarkably rapid internal evolution. Departing from the model of Rājarāja's brief versified preamble, Rājendra's eulogy grew to prodigious size over the course of multiple expansions and redactions, coming in time to dwarf most of the temple records to which it was appended. During the decades of the mid-eleventh century, over the course of the several successive reigns of Rājendra's sons, the form's complexity increased yet more pronouncedly. The courts of Rājādhirāja, Rājendradeva, and Vīrarājendra produced multiple texts of varying length and ambition: Rājendradeva's reign alone saw the promulgation of five independent *mĕykkīrtti*s (only Kulottuṅga would issue more). At the same time, the eulogies of Rājādhirāja and the kings who followed him were marked by an expanding dramatis personae, with multiple-named figures – family members especially, but also other Coḻa notables, members of the rival Kālyāṇa Cālukya dynasty, and their own underlords. This new personalization remains tied to the figure of the Coḻa sovereign, but the specificity with which the king interacts with named individuals heightens the *mĕykkīrtti*'s characteristic fusion of epideictic elaboration and annalistic rapportage.

Coḻa imperial expansion and consolidation were marked, as we have seen, by a number of structuring contradictions, and the rhetorical form of the *mĕykkīrtti* can be understood as an attempt to confront these contradictions through expressive means. Insofar as the process of Coḻa state-making met with success, and as more of its ongoing work was performed by newly established, quasi-bureaucratic institutions, and as the kingdom's armies swelled with forces from outside the pale of the deltaic social world, the public argument for the authority of the Coḻa incumbent becomes radically personalized. The king himself, and conspicuously *not* his ancestors, whether mythic or more recent, was vested in his *mĕykkīrtti* with charismatic and martial power. Yet for all that the right to rule remained cast in this predominantly personal idiom of valor, more and more figures begin to crowd into scene: the field of kingly action is made into a stage for a small cast of aristocratic heroes and villains, the martial celebrities of the time. A heroic king cannot claim credit for the defeat of the nameless masses of his enemies' armies, and so the eulogies came to include litanies of names of notables from the other side. So too the parcels of territory distributed to members of the Co̱la family that feature in the eulogies from Rājādhirāja's time onward: these are not admissions of the failure of direct Co̱la rule, but rather accounts of the dissemination of royal charisma down from its pinnacle at the Co̱la king's parasol-shadowed lion throne. The marked instability of those members of the family who participated in this signals a shifting landscape of potential heirs-presumptive, answering to the dynastic turbulence seen around the accession of Vīrarājendra and, a decade later, of Rājendracoḷa.

All of these figures, allies and enemies both, a supernumerary *corps de théâtre* carved on the walls of temples throughout the Co̱la domains, are in the end always subordinate to the king. The Co̱la sovereign was the sole actor on the stage of his *mĕykkīrtti*, to whom the other personalities were, like the jingling foreign place names of Rājendra's eulogy, so much stylish ornament. The cult of royal particularity ramified beyond the eulogies themselves. The Vaiṣṇava theologian Yāmunācārya, casting around in the mid-1000s for a ready-to-hand analogy for his god's relationship to the cosmos, pointedly alighted on the figure of the Co̱la king: unassailably dominant, one without a second, yet always accompanied by his sons, his retainers, and his wives.[57]

It is thus simple enough to correlate the expansion and elaboration of the *mĕykkīrtti* form with the processes of the imperial elaboration of the Co̱la state, as the parcelization of authority throughout the newly expanded imperial territory, the rising intensity of warfare, and the burgeoning problems of succession all seem to find their place there. But how can these representations connect in a constitutive way with the ongoing task of Co̱la state-making in this time? How – to revert to the strong argument – can we understand the poetry to only be intelligible in terms of polity? The reply to this sort of question by historians has typically been a simple one: the *mĕykkīrtti* played a part in rendering legitimate Co̱la rule, in overawing the dynasty's subject peoples through its themes of regalian dominance and the maintenance of *dharma*. This was the stuff of kingly public display throughout India's medieval period, either "a dark noise to impress the impressionable and to induce in them a trembling awe" or "the spiritualizing of material interests and the fogging over of material conflicts."[58] The effect of such a representation, so the argument goes, was to render natural the unstable apparatus of Co̱la rule, to make the contingent seem necessary. This idea is presumed to be self-evident throughout Co̱la historical studies: even the most outstanding recent scholarship falls back on just this sort of explanatory mechanism, when the role of the *měykkīrtti* has been thought worthy of explanation at all.[59]

We should be cautious of the possibility of, or even the necessity for, such a manufactured consensus in medieval South India. The question of the applicability of this notion of legitimation, born of the social–scientific explanation of capitalist modernity, to the premodern, precapitalist non-West has been critically explored elsewhere, as has the notion that the cultivators who made up the vast majority of the subjects of the Coḻa kings were in any way motivated or coerced by an appeal to their ruler's putative right to extract surplus from them.[60] More to the point, this sort of broadly applicable covering explanation removes the need to actually come to terms with the content of a supposedly legitimationist text, the work of which is already done by the fact of its mere existence.

A useful starting point was furnished some years ago by Richard Davis, when he suggested that the Coḻa *měykkīrttis* "are best viewed . . . as a type of rhetoric . . . [as] poems meant for a large audience, intended to persuade them that the Cōḻa king was the rightful king by virtue of his great achievements." This is a deceptively simple formulation, and Davis himself does not pursue it further. Nevertheless, he struck upon the crucial idea of seeing them not as overwhelming ideological displays but as genuinely political texts, that is, as making more or less successful arguments for the sake of persuasion.[61] Characterizing the *měykkīrtti* form as an instance of political discourse rather than a vehicle of legitimation might seem to some to be a distinction without a difference; it could be thought to rest on an anachronism no less vitiating than that of legitimation theory. In what way can we even meaningfully speak of the politics of the medieval dynastic state in India?

Some interpretations, among them those burdened with the outmoded European phantasia of Oriental despotism, would deny the very possibility that the kingdoms of premodern times could possess a politics at all; others would subordinate any ostensibly political actions to an extrinsic religio-cultural ideal. As was already argued in the Introduction, I presume that medieval India possessed a politics that is at least potentially reconstructible. The Coḻa dynasty was faced with a situation analogous to all other middle-period polities, major and minor; the fact that they were so peculiarly successful suggests the need to look for some specific cause or set of causes. Certainly, some causal efficacy may be assigned to the ecological and social terrain of Colamandalam, the network of the *nāṭus* and their ruling elites: these preceded the Coḻa expansion and served as conditions of its possibility. But the particular success of the Coḻa state lay in its transformation-through-co-option of these ruling elites in part into officials and generals, but more broadly and more significantly into those casually accepting of its suzerainty. This was accomplished neither through overwhelming force nor through smoke-and-mirrors trickery. It was accomplished through politics, which may be broadly defined as the ability to control and allocate material and symbolic resources through collective action, and so to influence outcomes within a particular social order. In regard to the apportionment of tangible, material resources – above all the agrarian surplus – the scholarship of recent decades has given us a remarkable purchase on the politics of the Co<u>l</u>a period. But an understanding of the politics of the intangible remains fugitive. So too does an understanding of the ways in which locally meaningful action can be connected to intended and unintended consequences, of how the history of the Co<u>l</u>a period was the amalgam of contingent undertakings by historical agents, and not just the more or less mechanical outcome of impersonal processes.

Generally speaking, political action and political actors may be characterized in terms of their connection with the efficacious use of language. This, in another jargon, is referred to as language's performative capacity, the ability to create new states of affairs and to open or foreclose modes of action through verbal or textual acts. The Co<u>l</u>a-period act of the comprehensive renaming of the landscape of the central Tamil plains and the grafting of the onomastic conventions of the ruling family onto the personal names of elites throughout the region may both be understood as political acts in this sense. The Co<u>l</u>a court and chancellery did not force the adoption of its new toponymy upon its subjects at spearpoint, any more than some landowner was coerced into publicly styling himself as Rājarājamūventaveḷā<u>n</u>. This was a circulatory process: new ways of conceiving the Co<u>l</u>a land and new styles of public honor radiated outward from the royal court, but it was only in the taking up of these by local dominants that the elusive fact of Co<u>l</u>a imperial hegemony can be traced.

So too with the *mĕykkīrtti*. As a mode of political communication, the Tamil eulogistic form was at its outset the result of royal initiative, and it was in light of advantageous circumstances of terrain, both physical (in its network of temples, the preeminent sites of permanent record) and social (among the Brahman and gentry condominates), that the innovative Co<u>l</u>a genre was calibrated. The *mĕykkīrttis* of Rājarāja, Rājendra, and their successors' reigns were publicly articulated arguments about the individual royal incumbent, keyed in a conservative, classicizing register evidently meant to appeal not to a group of avant-garde connoisseurs but to a wide Tamil-speaking social elite, those for whom the rhythmic litany of the *akaval* served as an immediately familiar marker of literariness.[62] These agrarian elites on whom the work of domination rested, only the minority of whom would have possessed a formal literary education, formed the franchise of epigraphical actors throughout the period, and served as the target audience for the royal charisma broadcast from the Co̱la court. Some of these would adopt Co̱la royal titles as part of their personal name, and would act as direct agents of the dynasty's will; many more were only passive in their incorporation into the political society of the kingdom's expanding core.[63] Like the kingdom-wide system of titles and honors, and increasingly like the agents of the state itself, these inscriptional preambles were indices of the common political culture operative throughout the territories to which the Co̱las laid claim.

However, considering the *mĕykkīrtti* solely from the perspective of the royal center broadcasting the king's idealized poetic image gives a falsely totalitarian impression of Co̱la hegemony, and fails to account for the efforts at calibration that can be detected in some of its instances. The links between the royal court and the wider elite society were continually being made and remade: Co̱la imperial sovereignty was itself a work in progress, if not dependent on the consent of the governed then on the ongoing material and rhetorical suasion of different sectors of the elite. But the deployment of the *mĕykkīrttis* was equally indicative of certain elites' own, locally circumscribed political projects, in which the refracted imperial glamor of the *mĕykkīrtti* was a resource employed to their own advantage. The distribution of the *mĕykkīrtti* texts thus delineated the boundaries of a circulatory system of political charisma, the medium through which the Co̱la polity was constituted.

Evidence for this process, and suggestions toward a periodization of it, can be seen in Francis and Schmid's latitudinal study of the occurrence of *mĕykkīrttis* within the corpus of inscriptions in the modern Union Territory of Pondicherry.[64] They conclude that the habit of opening Tamil temple inscriptions with a king's *mĕykkīrtti* was introduced under direct royal impetus during the reigns of Rājarāja and Rājendra and continued under Rājādhirāja. The relative fixity of these texts, which were periodically expanded under the latter two kings, is suggestive of a coherent central initiative, in parallel with the development of the wider state apparatus. This led to the establishment of certain temples as loci of eulogistic significance – "*meykkīrtti* sites" – which continued to serve as the locale of such display during subsequent reigns. From Rājendradeva's time, royal initiative ceases to be the central motive for the recording of the *mĕykkīrtti*; instead, the occurrence of a eulogy came to signal independent action on the part of local elites, either in soliciting the imprimatur of the royal center or in simply linking their actions with it as a distant source of authority.[65]

Vīrarājendra: Crisis and Revolution

The end result of this process of formal elaboration can be seen in the inscriptions of Vīrarājendra. The third of Rājendra's sons to take the throne did so under uncertain and perhaps contested circumstances sometime in mid-1063. As already mentioned, his adoption of the cognomen *rājakesarivarman* was an anomalous violation of Co<u>l</u>a dynastic custom, and may suggest an effort at the public dememorialization of his brother's (and so analytically, "his") son Rājamahendra. Political–aesthetic display assumed a newly prominent place in this king's court; this was especially so in the closing years of his reign, which saw the dissemination of an innovative mytho-historical *praśasti* in Sanskrit and the assumption of a revised short *mĕykkīrtti* text. The longer of his two standard *mĕykkīrtti*s, which appears throughout his reign, beginning in records of his second year, is notable for both its frenetic narrative energy and its mutability.[66] Its opening remains stable (and highly conventional) throughout its issue: "Taking up the circle of the earth – like a jewelled ornament – in his mighty arms, in which Śrī flourishes; caring even more than a mother for the world's creatures that have come to the shade of his jewel-decked warrior's parasol." This preamble concludes with a reference to the omnipresent crowd of other kings gathered at Vīrarājendra's feet, and the serpent-like Kali, banished to a bolt-hole in the earth. In the first four years of his reign (*ca.* 1063–1067), this is followed by a list of territorial appointments made to members of the royal family, in a manner consistent with the records of Rājādhirāja and Rājendradeva. The contents of this list fluctuates from record to record – in its earliest published version from Tiruveṅkāṭu (dated to his year two, day 233, sometime between November 1064 and February 1065),[67] it claims that Vīrarājendra "according to established order" (*mu<u>r</u>aimaiyil*) crowned with bright jewels his celebrated elder brother Āḷavantā<u>n</u>, calling him "Rājādhirāja, famed throughout the wide world," and "granted Tondaimandalam to his dear son Maturāntaka<u>n</u>, whom he crowned with a beautiful crown, fit to brighten the eight directions, and with the name 'Coḷentira<u>n</u>, with his army of swordsman.'"[68] Coḷentira<u>n</u> disappears from later versions, while the mysterious Āḷavantā<u>n</u>, which might refer to Rājādhirāja, who had died a decade earlier, is referred to as "Rājarāja" in subsequent versions. The apportionment of rights and honors to the king's family then gives way to a depiction of the victories won against the Kalyāṇa Cālukyas. The first of these, significantly recounting a victory in Veṅgī, centers on a horrific image:

he slew the *mahādaṇḍanāyaka* Cāmuṇḍarājan̲, cut off his head, and – what's more – he disfigured the nose and face of his only daughter, Nākalai, the wife of Irukayan̲, who was lovely as a peacock.

The eulogy goes on to account Vīrarājendra's defeat "for the third time" of Āhavamalla Someśvara, and to describe the enemy war-leaders killed in battle and the booty seized from their army, before rounding out with the king sitting in state, accompanied by his queen.

In a series of records issued in his fifth and sixth years, this text, itself already wavering in its individual realizations, appeared in a heavily revised format. Gone are the references to family members: while the Veṅgī campaign remains, the account of Vīrarājendra's wars with the Cālukyas is massively expanded. The eulogy takes on a hallucinatory quality in its description of an event that never took place, a martial rematch against the Cālukyas at Kūṭalsaṅgamam, the site of an earlier victory of Vīrarājendra, referred to throughout the public pronouncements of his reign. The eulogy's account of the event (which occurred sometime in 1067) describes how Āhavamalla, thinking "death is surely better than a life filled with shame," dispatched a letter to Vīrarājendra demanding another battle, "so that everyone might know it," with the taunt "whoever fails to appear out of fear is no king at all, but only a man ruined by this great shame come from war."[69] In fact, it is Āhavamalla who fails to appear, and after Vīrarājendra waits for him for a month at Kūṭalsaṅgamam, he erects a pillar of victory and – parodically inverting the parceling out of appanages to members of the Cola house – calls out "the ruined one, who had come before" (seemingly an effigy of Āhavamalla), anoints him as the Cālukya king, and conducts in absentia an elaborate ritual humiliation of him and his sons.[70]

In this long *mĕykkīrtti*'s early recording of royal prerogatives awarded to his family, its remarkably detailed accounting of the deaths and mutilations of named figures among Vīrarājendra's enemies, and in the elaborate theater of power staged at Kūṭalsaṅgamam, we are met with details of the king's central involvement in managed public spectacle. The greatest and most abundant surviving evidence of this is the promulgation of the multiple *mĕykkīrtti* texts themselves. All of this is consistent with the fact that Vīrarājendra's court was the setting for an attempt at transforming Tamil as a language of literature: the king is honored as the patron and namesake of Puttamittiran̲'s grammatical and literary-theoretical treatise, the *Vīracol̲iyam*, an innovative, if largely unsuccessful, attempt to coordinate the linguistic and poetic facts of Tamil with the cosmopolitan Sanskritic standard.[71] In a way that sets out Vīrarājendra from his brothers, or indeed from any of his Coḻa predecessors, his court evinced a strong commitment to the aestheticization of politics. As can be seen elsewhere in the surviving documents of Vīrarājendra's brief reign, there is a palpable energy evident here, a concerted and yet constantly shifting effort to calibrate the king's public persona in the representations emanating from his court, plainly intensifying the habits of his father's and his brothers' courts.

The style of Vīrarājendra's public presentation suddenly changed in his seventh regnal year (1069–1070). Most spectacularly, these changes can be registered in the appearance of a Sanskrit *praśasti* in his honor, two copies of which appear almost simultaneously in far-flung parts of the Coḻa dominions, one carved over a series of pillars found in a temple *maṇḍapam* in Kanyakumari and the other inscribed on copperplates found in Cārāla in modern Nellore district. This wide dissemination of the text served in itself as an index of imperial grandeur and control, and provides yet another intimation of the seriousness with which Vīrarājendra's court attended to poetic and rhetorical presentation. Vīrarājendra's *praśasti* draws explicitly on the *Rāmāyaṇa*, extending the long-standing Coḻa claim to membership in the solar dynasty. Though earlier Coḻa eulogists had drawn upon the solar mythos in their accounts,[72] Vīrarājendra's court poet Candrabhūṣaṇabhaṭṭa composes in a new key. In the course of his brief account of Rāma, in fact, he writes in a way that is quite independent of the usual *praśasti* style:

> He didn't kill the lord of the *rākṣasa*s out of anger, nor out of desire did he bring back his beloved: he fulfilled the duties of a king, completely and fully.
>
> If you think that he did not, then why did he strike down the Śūdra [i.e. Śambūka] who was practising *tapas* on Mount Malaya with his sword? And why did he abandon Sītā again, when she possessed such matchless beauty and virtue?[73]

Departing from the standard celebratory register of the *praśasti*, and addressing the events that have long troubled the *Rāmāyaṇa*'s readers, this suggests a recognition of the difficult things that kings must necessarily do. Following closely upon the text's reflections on Rāma, it turns to the Coḻas' founder–ancestor, meant as a clear analog to the *Rāmāyaṇa* hero[74]:

> Into that [solar] lineage was born a king called Coḷa who, laying waste to hordes of rulers with his great power, was like the Death-god himself to kings; as he ruled the whole earth as if it were his capital city, tracts of wilderness everywhere made themselves into his pleasure-gardens.

He was the equal to Śiva in his glory. Once, that treasure-house of courtesy passed some days, which afforded him some chance for relaxation, wandering in forests frequented by groups of holy men.

Another time, as that patient man was intent upon the bold act of hunting down herds of deer, he wandered in still other forests, with only a few of his troops accompanying him. It was then that all of the sudden a *rākṣasa* in the form of a deer seized him, and the innately well-mannered man [*prakṛtidakṣiṇaḥ*] went to the Southern quarter.[75]

As he was silently following that deer with his swift horse, he came to another forest, filled with great trees. The leaders of his hastily-marshalled forces, always ready for distant campaigns without end, followed him.

The king slew the night-stalker, and along with his many secret agents, he wandered [*vicacāra bhūricāraḥ*] there along the Kāveri river, which bore the nectar that the gods gained through churning the milk-ocean, right there on earth, in the guise of its waters.

He bathed, and wished to give wealth to Brahmans; the calm-minded man found none there. So then he brought eminent savants – the best of their kind – from the Āryan lands, and he settled them there on its banks.[76]

The eponymous ancestor had appeared in earlier Co̱la genealogies, but the description of him here is unique. That Rāma is Coḷa's prototype is transparent: this replicates the central motivating event of Vālmīki's *Araṇyakāṇḍa*, the ruse by the shape-shifting *rākṣasa* Mārīca that leads to Sītā's abduction. But the departure from the epic prototype is equally evident. Most obviously, there is the telling absence of any loss suffered by Coḷa as a result: the traumatic separation that is the emotional core of the *Rāmāyaṇa* is replaced by the king's serendipitous discovery of the unspoilt Kāveri country. Still other anomalies are difficult to explain from this distance: why do Coḷa's generals follow hard at his heels, a violation of the narrative topos of the solitary wandering king? The transformation of forest into garden is more readily explicable: Coḷa goes on to clear-cut the woods along the Kāveri and plant areca palm and betel-vine, essential ingredients for Brahmanical hospitality; along with the foundational act of Brahman settlement, this rhymes with the eulogy's subsequent focus on Vīrarājendra as a founder of new *brahmadeya* estates. The five verses on the ruling king conclude with an evocation of the solar-dynastic context of the whole *praśasti*:

A ruby called the Essence of the Triple World was set [by Vīrarājendra] in the crown of the great Śiva, Pārvatī's husband, who dances in the glorious small assembly hall. So it seems to me as if the blessed Sun, the founder of his own lineage, had been mounted there to spell the ruin of the Moon, the first member of the family of his foes, who serves as Śiva's crest-jewel.[77]

From his seventh regnal year, contemporaneously with the issue of Candrabhūṣaṇabhaṭṭa's *praśasti*, only the shorter of Vīrarājendra's two *měykkīrttis* is used, in a heavily revised format, with an altogether different set of rhetorical valences.[78] Where the short *měykkīrtti*, like the longer text, had been fixated on the struggle with the Cālukyas of Kalyāṇa and their repeated humiliations at the Co<u>l</u>a's hands, its new revision moved away from the spectacular martial grandiloquence of the earlier records, replacing it with a new note of consolidation. The text is even shorter than its earlier recensions; in its entirety it reads:

> With heroism as his sole aid, and generosity his sole ornament,
> driving off black Kali with his upraised straight sceptre,
> he took the head of the southern king, took tribute from the Cera,
> and subjected the Sinhala lands to his will;
> five times he saw the back of Āhavamalla;
> in recovering the Veṅkai country,
> he made good on the vow made by his elder brothers;
> he conquered Kaṭāram and gave it to the king
> who had taken refuge at his ankleted feet;
> he gave a country to Vijayāditya, who came and paid worship to his feet, and
> tying the necklace of heirship upon Vikramāditya – fit to make the eight
> directions sparkle – he conquered the entirety of the 750,000 country of Raṭṭapāḍi,
> and gave it to him, who had been pleased to take refuge at his feet.
> Seated in state, along with his queen, mistress of the entire world, the emperor,
> Rājakesarivarman Śrī Vīrarājendraco<u>l</u>a, in his seventh year.[79]

Some of the material here is remounted from the earlier versions of the text: besides the opening phrases and the paradigmatic claim that the king forced the retreat of the Cālukya king (and so "saw his back") five times, the description of Vīrarājendra as redeeming his brothers' oaths by recovering Veṅkai (=Veṅgī) had been included since at least two years earlier. It is difficult to say what the underdetermined assertions of the defeat of the Pāṇḍya, the successes in Kerala and Sri Lanka, and the alliance in the Malaya country really amounted to, as this *měykkīrtti* contains the only references to them. But it is the notably specific claims about Vīrarājendra's new allies Vijayāditya and Vikramāditya, respectively Rājiga's paternal uncle and Āhavamalla's second son, that are of signal importance here. The interpretative key to this lies in a series of rapid changes in the structure of interpolity alliances, what Nilakanta Sastri justly deemed revolutionary.[80] The circumstances for Vīrarājendra's political coup begin with the death by religious suicide of the ailing Āhavamalla Someśvara in late March 1068.[81] In an unprecedented move, Vīrarājendra intervened in the Cālukya succession at Kalyāṇa, backing his own candidate for the throne of his family's perennial enemies, then helping him to carve out a breakaway principality in the southern part of the Cālukya domains. Where Vikramāditya had been the object of the earlier version of the *mĕykkīrtti*'s contempt, which travestied him through the insulting deformation of his name as *vikkalaṉ* (perhaps "the cripple"), he was now referred to in his proper fashion, and even granted the appurtenance of royalty, being described as *aṭi aṭaintu aruḷu-kiṉṟa vikkiramātittaṉ*, acting with the *aruḷ* of a king at the moment of his submission to the Coḻa. This dramatic rhetorical reversal would have been readily apparent to the Coḻa subjects who were the *mĕykkīrtti*'s audience: copies of the revised text can be found close by the older version, as was the case for instance in Kīḻūr in central Miḷāṭu.[82] The testimony of the eventual Vikramāditya VI's court poet Bilhaṇa, for all its obfuscations and complexities, supplies the further detail that this political alliance was cemented through the marriage of one of Vīrarājendra's daughters to Vikramāditya.

While references to successes in Veṅgī had been a staple of the king's earlier *mĕykkīrtti*s, the announcement that Vīrarājendra had installed Vijayāditya there marks a stunning surprise: in some versions of the revised text, this is underlined with the explicit declaration that "*cāḷukki*" Vijayāditya was receiving Veṅgī. Rājiga's *pitṛvya* was unrelated to the Coḻa house through blood or marriage, and had served as an underlord of Āhavamalla, honorifically referred to in his own records as his "son" (*maga, nandana*).[83] Having successfully sowed dissension among Āhavamalla's actual heirs, the fact that Vīrarājendra turned over the much-contested Veṅgī to such an unlikely king seems astonishing; certainly to Rājiga and his followers, it must have been a completely unanticipated disaster. From Vīrarājendra's view from the lion throne, things doubtless looked different: perhaps he recognized in Vijayāditya's crafty maneuvering between the peninsula's different powers the workings of a political intellect similar to his own. For it is difficult not to credit this diplomatic revolution to the ability, energy, and ambition of the king himself. For more than a generation, the Coḻas had been locked in a series of increasingly costly conflicts with their neighboring kingdoms. In what must have been a furiously active reign by a man who came to the throne already in middle age, Vīrarājendra and his court society overcame this impasse. By 1069, only a year or so after Āhavamalla Someśvara's death, the Coḻa hegemony over the western and eastern Deccan would seem to have been a fait accompli, an event that was memorialized by the Tamil and Sanskrit eulogies issuing from the Coḻa chancellery. Rhetorical ambitions and actual accomplishments did not exist in a vacuum from each other. The move away from the vivid *mĕykkīrtti* of the early years of the reign can be read as a part of this new politics of consolidation: the war-poetry that marked the years of harsh campaigning in the mid-1060s might no longer have had a place in a world where seemingly the Cola had no real enemies left to fight.

But in contrast to the diplomatic and literary-aesthetic éclat of Vīrarājendra's court, the king's orchestration of Colamandalam's internal politics was sclerotic. This can be seen from the account of a grand darbar convened by the king in Kāñcīpuram sometime between mid-December 1068 and mid-February 1069. The record of this session of court is contained in perhaps the most significant document from Vīrarājendra's reign, a huge, rambling, and now mutilated inscription on the central shrine of his father's great temple at Gaṅgaikōṇṭacoḻapuram.[84] It is the earliest surviving record found on the site of Rājendra's monument, and provides the most extensive reckoning of the Gaṅgaikōṇṭacoḻīśvara's network of supporting villages, many of which had earlier directed their revenue to the Tanjavur complex. Vīrarājendra's royal order details the arrangements made in otherwise unknown royal orders issued by Rājendra (referred to as "my father, who was pleased to conquer the eastern country, the Gaṅgā, and Kaṭāram") in 1035–1036 and by Rājādhirāja ("my elder brother, who conquered Kalyāṇa and Kolhapur, and died on the back of an elephant") in 1044 and 1048; these are confirmed and expanded upon in numbing actuarial detail, in a field-by-field survey of the produce of the granting villages. This evidently made good the lack of two decades' worth of public records on the maintenance and upkeep of Rājendra's signature building program. The most detailed document of Vīrarājendra's seven years of reign, a time marked by fervid military and diplomatic activity, was a literal settling of old family accounts.

The retrospective character of this royal initiative is mirrored in the composition of the courtiers and officials whom the inscription describes in great detail. While damage to the record obscures some of its testimony, the names, titles, and oikonyms of some fifty men responsible for the acclamation (*evutal*) of the order can be made out, as can another seventeen officials, either chancellery men responsible for its drafting and rescripting or bureaucrats of the *puruvaritiṇaikkaḷam*. The composition of these two groups is very telling: unsurprisingly, members of the gentry and Brahman elite form a supermajority: of the fifty courtiers, twenty-two are *mūventaveḷar* or are described as the *uṭaiyar*-possessor of a specified village, while thirteen are Brahmans. The two groups thus comprised 70 percent of those figures whose identities can be ascertained. Given pride of place among the Brahmans is none other than Candrabhūṣaṇabhaṭṭa, the composer of Vīrarājendra's Sanskrit *praśasti*, here bearing the loyalist title Vīrarājendrabrahmādhirājar. The two men responsible for the initial transcription of the king's oral order are a Brahman and a man bearing the title *pallavarājan̲*; among the thirteen scribes and members of the revenue office, there are four *mūventaveḷar*, and four other likely Veḷḷāḷas (identified as *-uṭaiyān̲*, or *veḷān̲*) and one Brahman; the social identities of the other figures are not ascertainable, whether due to damage to the record or otherwise.[85]

All of this is unsurprising. What is surprising are the absences among these leading figures of Vīrarājendra's court. There are, first of all, hardly any figures that hail from the magnate families that had been recently folded into the Co̲la apparatus of honor: though a few figures in the list bear semi-royal titles, only a single member of a major magnate lineage is represented.[86] Also surprising is the court's overwhelmingly civilian character: despite the kingdom's militarization throughout the 1050s and 1060s, and despite Vīrarājendra's own constant campaigning, there are no men bearing a martial title like *senāpati* or some other marker of military service. But the pronounced regional bias of the composition of this elite forms its most striking irregularity: despite the darbar's location in Kāñcī, only two of the fifty courtiers were from Tondaimandalam, while only a single junior official was from the region.

These are isolated data, but they speak to wider patterns. Though only partly overlapping in its members, the composition of this list is similar to another record of court held by Vīrarājendra concerning the foundation of a hospital at Tirumukkūṭal (the only record of Vīrarājendra's longer than the Gaṅgaikōṇṭaco̲lapuram order, also of the fifth year but lacking a day) and another record from 1081–1082 revoking an earlier, undated decision taken in Vīrarājendra's time.[87] Significantly, all three of these records, the most significant documents of Vīrarājendra's court society, concern arrangements first made in Vīrarājendra's brothers' time, which the king was endorsing or carrying out. As the Co̲la king was enacting the brilliant diplomatic coup of his final years, his local actions within the kingdom seem premised on an ideal of internal political stasis.

That Vīrarājendra surrounded himself with the gentry and Brahman elite of Colamandalam makes perfectly good sense. It was these men that his grandfather, father, and brothers had relied upon to build up the mechanisms of court and state that had created a political enterprise of unprecedented magnitude. But while this political transformation had spread the Co̲la claim to rule into territories well beyond its former deltaic core, it had introduced new figures and collectivities into its matrix of ruling power, and had perceptibly sped up the process of the condominate elite's self-aggrandizement, to the expense of the state's own ambitions. These processes, the contradictions of Co̲la success outlined earlier, had by the late 1060s already created new martial caste groups, and had accelerated the consolidation of landed property, which was the decisive social–historical change of the *longue durée* in the Co̲la period. Among those who benefited most from this were evidently the old magnate lineages: the men of these families were already controllers of substantial resources in land. Geography abetted this process, as the old magnate territories abutted Jayaṅkŏṇṭaco̲lamaṇḍalam, the erstwhile Tondaimandalam, which was to prove an incubator of the social forces emerging in this period, as we shall see in the next chapter. Vīrarājendra and his ministers appear curiously aloof from these changes. There is, of course, nothing to suggest that the Co̲la state had either the interest or the ability to conduct any sort of census of its subject people, and the last cadastral survey of which we have any evidence dates from Rājarāja's era, nearly a half-century earlier. But the degree to which the changed political realities were to obtrude themselves into elite life even in the polity's deltaic core became clear almost immediately upon Vīrarājendra's death, less than a year after the diplomatic revolution he successfully stage-managed.

Certainly among those who were attentive to Vīrarājendra's brittle new order were his Veṅgī nephew and members of his own burgeoning court society. If in fact some sort of Co̲la campaign had taken place in the east Godavari deltaic zone – if the message in Vīrarājendra's short *mĕykkīrtti* was not just the announcement of Vijayāditya VII's backing by his powerful imperial neighbor – there is no evidence that Rājiga had taken any part in it. Yet Vīrarājendra had since his fifth year (*ca.* 1067–1068) claimed victories in Cakrakoṭṭam (in modern Chhattisgarh), the same area that Rājiga is himself placed by his own early records, and where Bilhaṇa records a campaign by the young Vikramāditya. Whether Rājiga fought for or against his paternal uncle, or for the distant family of his matriline alone, is unclear, as is the relationship between this and Vijayāditya's subsequent backing by the Co̲la king. One likely scenario would have Vīrarājendra affirming the situation on the ground, and so supporting Vijayāditya despite the closer ties of relation with Rājiga, his sister's son and his late brother's daughter's husband. As a sort of consolation prize, then, Rājiga may have been allowed to exercise a certain authority close to the core regions of Colamandalam, in the area linking his two dynastic heartlands, in Tondaimandalam and Nolambavāḍi, as it was in this area that his first inscriptions are concentrated from his second regnal year onward. Placing a seemingly loyal and indebted near-relation in a position of authority close by, rather than as an independent ruler along the distant Godavari, might have been an extension of Vīrarājendra's wider project of consolidation. If this were so, seemingly such careful students and practitioners of the art of power as Vīrarājendra and his ministers stunningly mistook or failed to comprehend the early maneuverings and proliferating ambiguities that surrounded Rājiga, the might-have-been lord of Veṅgī.

Summary

The existing explanation for the Veṅgī Cālukya prince Rājiga's sudden emergence as an heir presumptive to the Coḻa throne is that he was eligible as the result of several generations of marital alliances. This is not so much incorrect as it is insufficient. The grafting of the Cālukya prince into his Coḻa matriline instead provides a unique opportunity to see the multiple ways in which different modes of power – royal, political, institutional, and rhetorical – were operative in maintaining the political society at whose apex the Coḻa kings ruled. Kingship was dependent on metaphor as much as it was on the harnessing of violent force: royal public presentation and possibly self-conception were invested in the pan-Indic tropes of the solar and lunar lineages, and these mythic stereotypes shaped the available possibilities of action, especially within dynasties.

The centuries-long endurance of the Coḻa order was the work of more than the imagination, however. Over the course of the first decades of the eleventh century, the local elites of Colamandalam and its surrounding regions increasingly came to act within a supralocal system of domination, overseen by an apparatus of rule that ranged over the adoption of personal names linked to Coḻa royal charisma, the growing presence of elite court officials within locality decision-making, and the rise of a revenue bureaucracy and a formalized chancellery. We can thus speak of a perduring Coḻa state, the reach and efficacy of which far exceeded that of any other contemporary polity in the peninsula. This unprecedented success saw the expansion of the zone of Coḻa political control far beyond the dynasty's core territory in the Kāveri delta. This new, imperial phase of Coḻa history is iconized by Tanjavur's Rājarājeśvara temple, whose network of revenue assignments extended deep into the Deccan and Sri Lanka.

The classicizing eulogy form called the *mĕykkīrtti* became the distinctive form of Coḻa public rhetoric at precisely the same time as the emergence of the imperial state-system. In their extreme personalization of royal rule, the *mĕykkīrtti*s articulated a series of rhetorical arguments, in striking counterpoint to the multiplex nature of the kingdom's political reality. The strongest evidence of the expressive nature of Coḻa kingship can be seen in the remarkable products of the court chancellery of Vīrarājendra (r. 1063–1070). In this reign, the repeated attention to the calibration of the court's public presentation worked alongside a brilliant series of martial and diplomatic successes, which briefly saw an apparent solution to the peninsula's endemic interpolity warfare. This may be contrasted with the court's evident misapprehension of the kingdom's internal politics. It was in the wake of seven years of frenetic rhetorical argument and brittle high politics that Rājiga the Cālukya prince first entered into the public life of the far south.

2 Rājendracoḷa, June 1070–May 1074

Introduction

When, in June of 1070, the Cālukya prince Rājiga was initiated into the Co<u>l</u>a kingship as Rājakesarivarman Rājendracoḷa, he assumed a place at the pinnacle of the kingdom that had been ruled over by his grandmother's, mother's, and wife's male relations. The imperial polity over which the Co<u>l</u>a kings reigned was arguably the most prosperous and militarily the most powerful in India; it was certainly the most conspicuous in its rapid development into a regional superpower over the previous three generations of its kings. This prominence had, however, come at a cost within the Co<u>l</u>a family: two kings – Rājādhirāja, Rājendracoḷa's *māma<u>n</u>* or maternal uncle, and Rājamahendra, his parallel cousin (and wife's brother) – had both died in battle, and the reign of Vīrarājendra, the paramount ruler in 1070, had been marked by ambiguities in the succession and thereafter by a brilliant, frenetic effort at royal self-presentation and diplomatic machination, issuing forth in a welter of Tamil and Sanskrit political-poetic texts, and a newfound focus on courtly aesthetics.

Rājendracoḷa, evidently outmaneuvered in his natal Veṅgī by his father's brother Vijayāditya VII, entered into the upper reaches of Co<u>l</u>a dynastic politics as the third member of an unprecedented triarchy, Vīrarājendra's son having been consecrated as Parakesarivarman Adhirājendra two years earlier. But these three kings were only single players in a much wider elite political society: extending outward from each of their courts, this was inclusive of the gentry and Brahman leadership of the kingdom, along with the new men of the upland fighting castes who had made Co<u>l</u>a martial expansion possible.

It was, evidently, a complicated time to be a Co<u>l</u>a king: the massive successes of the first half of the eleventh century had given way to a prosperous but fragile imperial order. New players were crowding the center of the kingdom, while its outlying marches were a shifting landscape of seasonal fighting marked by the enduring presence of martial and agrarian peoples as yet unassimilated to the Co_la style of titlature, comportment, and land control. Public arguments emanating from the several court societies were addressed to the kingdom-wide elite constituencies upon whom continued hegemony depended; as in Vīrarājendra's court, the primary medium of these arguments was the royal eulogy, the *mĕykkīrtti* or "true fame" of the king, which survives as the opening to many inscriptional texts.

"His Sword and His Two Shoulders"

Of central significance here is the earliest of Rājendracoḷa's public texts, the first public notice of his transformation from Co_la–Cālukya prince to the emperor Kulottuṅga. When Rājendracoḷa began to issue orders in his second regnal year – and when those elites declaring their allegiance to him begin to publicly proclaim as much in their own, local decisions – these are prefaced by a *mĕykkīrtti*, in proper imperial fashion and in a notable departure from earlier subimperial rulers. Rājendracoḷa's principal eulogy is brief, compared both to the grandiloquence of his predecessors and to the texts he would later issue as Kulottuṅga. While the interpretation of its patent text is relatively straightforward, the *mĕykkīrtti* repays close scrutiny, harboring ambiguities and significant departures from the standard set by earlier instances of the form. Prior scholarship has managed, with considerable success, to elucidate the details of geography and chronology scattered throughout, and to establish its overall sense.[1] Many of these same historical data are returned to in Kulottuṅga's subsequent *mĕykkīrtti*s, often in a way that presumes familiarity with this earliest statement. Concentrating on this single text, however, it can be read not just as a work of verbal art, but as a complex position-taking within the wider domain of Co_la political rhetoric. This is especially so in light of the two other *mĕykkīrtti* texts that were in circulation at the same time.

Like other examples of the form, the *mĕykkīrtti* takes Rājendracoḷa as its sole grammatical as well as eulogistic subject. Structured by the pauses afforded by verbal forms, which in turn map onto its major narrative and thematic elements, the text can be parsed into four segments of roughly equal length:

tirumaṉṉi viḷaṅkum iru kuvaṭ' aṉaiya
taṉ toḷum vāḷum tuṇaiy ĕṉak keḷalar
vañcaṉai kaṭantu vayirākarattuk
kuñcarakkuḻām pala vāri ĕñcalil
cakkarakoṭṭattut tārāvaracaṉait
tikku nikaḻat tiṟai kŏṇṭ'aruḷi

As if his only aid was his sword and his two shoulders,
like great mountains shining with the goddess of fortune,
overcoming the trickery of his foes,
he seized great troops of elephants in Vayirākaram,
and in faultless Cakkirakoṭṭam,
he was pleased to levy tribute from Tārāvaracaṉ,
enough to make bright all the directions

The *mĕykkīrtti*'s very first word, *tirumaṉṉi*, not only calls to mind the opening to the *mĕykkīrtti* of his grandfather and namesake (Rājendra's often-revised text consistently begins *tirumaṉṉi vaḷara*, "To make the goddess of fortune prosper"), but also possesses propitious magical force as an auspicious opening.[2] *Tiru* is the equivalent of Sanskrit *śrī*, the embodiment of royal sovereignty, and thus both a proper name and an honorific extension to a name. *Maṉṉi*, however, is less clear: it suggests a feminine version of *maṉṉaṉ*, "king," or – more rarely – an elder brother's wife.[3] The borrowing of the language of Rājendra's eulogy may rest on more than just the identity of the king's regnal names, or on the prestige of the earlier emperor. The reference to Śrī-Lakṣmī as *tirumaṉṉi* seems to imply a subtle acknowledgement of another, senior claimant to the Coḻa kingship, just as Rājendra's eulogies were first issued during his brief corule with his father Rājarāja. The goddess is then linked to the king, or rather to his body. She is set upon his shoulders, the quintessential masculine repository of strength, virility, and erotic attraction, which are "like two mountains" *iru kuvaṭ' aṉaiya*, where she "shines," *viḷaṅkum*, like sunlight playing on a distant slope.

The king's physical strength, thus charged with the divine, and his warrior's sword are "like aids," *tuṇaiy ĕṉa*, to him. This subtly gestures yet again toward a specific precursor, the opening to Vīrarājendra's programmatic short *mĕykkīrtti, vīrame tuṇaiy ākavum tiyākame aṇiy ākavum* ("With heroism as his sole aid, and with generosity his sole ornament"), the revised text of which, we have seen, heralded the promulgation of Vīrarājendra's last years of rule. This is the first intertextual acknowledgment of Vīrarājendra's *mĕykkīrtti*, to which much of Rājendracoḷa's own eulogy can be read as a response.[4]

The text then shifts into its main matter. The initial claim that "he overcame the treachery of his foes" has little to draw it into higher focus, beyond the conceptual rhyme with the king's autonomous heroism ("as if his only aid . . ."; the two phrases are linked through grammar) and the phonetic rhyme that it introduces (*vañcaṉai . . . kuñcara- . . . ĕñcalil*). With the reference to the elephants of Vayirākaram (identified as modern Wairagarh, now in eastern Maharashtra), the text makes its first, tentative foray into the realm of historical-denotational style. The *mĕykkīrtti*'s most pronounced gesture to this style immediately follows: in Cakrakoṭṭam, Rājendracoḷa levied tribute on Tārāvaracaṉ. This has been convincingly established as part of modern Chhattisgarh; presuming it to be the modern Chitrakoot, this is about a fortnight's march, a little more than 200 miles away, from Vayirākaram/Wairagarh. The ruler in question, moreover, has been identified as one Dhārāvarṣa, a minor ruler of a line of Nāga kings.[5] Cakrakoṭṭam had been claimed as conquered territory by the Coḻas as early as Rājendra; but it was contested territory around 1067, to which period the events alluded to here must refer. In one of the final redactions of Vīrarājendra's long eulogy, it is claimed that the king "sent his army on campaign against all throughout the domain of Cakrakoṭṭam" (significantly, this comes right before the account of Veṅgī); the same region also witnessed an early campaign by the future Vikramāditya VI.[6] The presence of both future kings suggests that this was more than just a series of shatter-zone skirmishes, but a major front in the seasonal warfare between the Coḻas and Cālukyas. The subjugated king's name – "Rain in Torrents" – summons up the dry, martial uplands of Rājendracoḷa's preregnal life: claiming a victory over such a figure thus serves to establish the prince's warrior bona fides. The final, telling detail of the verbal supplement *aruḷi* ("was pleased") places the whole tableau in higher relief: to act with *aruḷ* is to behave with the kind of grace-in-resolution characteristic of a king, not just a soldiering princeling.

arukkaṉ utaiyatt'ācaiyil irukkum
kamalam aṉaiya nilamakaḷ taṉṉai
munnīrk kuḷittav annāḷ tirumāl
ātikkeḻalāki ĕṭutt' aṉṉa
yātuñ caliyā vakaiy iṉit' ĕṭuttut
taṉkuṭai niḻal kīḻ iṉp'uṟa iruttit

Gently, so as to leave her completely unruffled,
he took up the earth-goddess, like a lotus
resting in the direction of the Sun's rising
just as on that day long ago when Tirumāl, as the primal Boar, took her
when she had plunged into the sea's ancient waters
and set her at peace beneath the shade of his parasol

Though grounded in tropic stereotype, that of the king placing the earth beneath his royal parasol, this segment marks a dramatic shift in poetic intensity. It is the most syntactically elaborate phrase of the entire text – thirty syllables, almost three entire metrical lines, separate grammatical object and verbal argument (*tirumakaḷ taṉṉai* . . . *ĕṭuttu*), with an extended mythic simile and an adverbial parenthesis interposed between them. The embedded simile, gesturing toward similar constructions in classical poetry, marks a departure from the received norms of the *mĕykkīrtti* style: earlier Co<u>l</u>a *mĕykkīrtti*s had not turned to the fund of purāṇic mythology (this is yet another contrast between the Co<u>l</u>a eulogies and wider world of Sanskrit and vernacular royal *praśasti*). This shift into the distant past is stitched into the steady flow of *akaval* lines by the temporal marker *a<u>n</u><u>n</u>āḷ* ("that day"), a central point of poetic attention signaled by the double grammar of the phrase it culminates: *nilamakaḷ* is at once the agent of the adjectival participle *kuḷitta* and the object of the participial doublet *ĕṭuttu* ... *ĕṭuttu*, one bounded by the simile, the other modifying Rājendracoḷa. The myth here is that of the boar *avatāra* of Viṣṇu, who rescued the earth from beneath the waters of the ocean. In the gentleness with which Rājendracoḷa, for all his martial might, "rescues" the earth, he is like Tirumāl (=Viṣṇu), who "becoming the primal Boar," *ātike<u>l</u>al āki*, is equally delicate in his restoration of the land atop the chaos of the waters.

However, this straightforward poetician's reading of the simile fails to capture what is really at work here. The Vaiṣṇava boar was the emblem of the Cālukya family into which Rājendracoḷa was born, and this trope notably marks the sole acknowledgment of his birth and early life in Veṅgī. This goes unmentioned in any of Kulottuṅga's *mĕykkīrtti*s, while his later court poet Cayaṅkŏṇṭār's passing admission remains wrapped in multiple deferrals and ambiguities (see Chapter 3). This is thus a consequential claim: along with its declination from the conventions of earlier Co<u>l</u>a eulogies, this appeal to the mythic repertoire obliquely introduces its subject's unusual place in the dynasty. Seen in the particular light afforded by this recourse to dynastic myth, the simile *kamalam a<u>n</u>aiya nilamakaḷ*, "the earth-goddess, like a lotus," which otherwise seems poorly matched to the *avatāra* comparison that follows it, takes on its contextual significance. The phrase *arukka<u>n</u> utaiyatt'ācaiyil irukkum kamalam* is grounded in a double meaning: at once (as translated above) "resting in the direction of the Sun's rising" – referring elliptically but unambiguously to the east, home to Sunrise Mountain and to Rājendracoḷa's paternal homeland[7] – and "abiding in the desire for the Sun's rising." The crucial word here is *ācai*: like its Sanskrit etymon *āśā*, this means either "direction" or "desire." The import of this punning comparison is clear: a lotus only opens at the touch of the sun's rays, so too the country of the east – governed by the Cālukyas, of the lunar dynasty – only attains its fullness at the arising of the sun, the mythic founding ancestor of the Co<u>l</u>a kings. Rājendracoḷa was not in control of his patrimonial homeland, and subjects of the Co<u>l</u>a king no doubt knew this to be the case: it had been announced in Vīrarājendra's late records that he had given Veṅgī over to Vijayāditya, Rājendracoḷa's uncle and potential rival. Rājendracoḷa, veteran of the Deccani campaigns of his youth, at once Cālukya boar and Coḻa sun, is figured as the genuine king of the east in this subtly conjoint appeal to dynastic symbology.

tikiriyum puliyum ticaitoṟum naṭāttip
pukaḻun tarumamum puvitoṟum niṟutti
vīramum tiyākamum māṉamum karuṇaiyum
taṉ urimaic cuṟṟamākap piriyāt tarātalam
nikaḻac cayamum tāṉum vīṟṟ'iruntu
kulamaṇimakuṭam muṟaimaiyil cūṭit

He has sent the wheel and the tiger in every direction,
and in every land he has established fame and *dharma*;
heroism, generosity, honor, and compassion are his companions
by right,
and, as a result, the surface of the earth shines forth in its entirety;
He and Victory sit in state together,
with a crown upon his head set with fine jewels,
that has come to him through lawful succession;

With this, both the direct and oblique claims to prior kingly deeds conclude. The remainder of the eulogy contains nothing in the annalistic-referential style – the young king may not have accomplished any other deeds worth recording – and instead shifts to a virtuosic rendition of commonplaces taken over from earlier *mĕykkīrtti*s. *Tikiri* and *puli*, wheel and tiger, are regal accoutrements that long predate the Coḻas' imperial heyday. The former, as dependable an emblem of sovereignty as any in classical India, invokes the ideal of the *cakravartin*, the wheel-turning king; it also possesses strong Vaiṣṇava connotations. The latter, the Coḻa totem, offers a parallel and complement to the reference to the Cālukya boar a few lines before.

The wheel and tiger are followed by an identically matched pair of abstracts, *pukaḻ* or fame and *dharma*, given in an exactly parallel construction.[8] The symmetry of this set of matched pairs is interrupted – deliberately so – by the four-term series that follows upon them. The opening pair here – *vīram* and *tiyākam*, heroism and generous renunciation – once again directly invokes the opening to Vīrarājendra's short eulogy, *vīrame tuṇaiy ākavum tiyākame aṇiy ākavum*; these royal attributes are complemented, in a clear case of competitive extension, by the addition of *māṉam* and *karuṇai*, honor and compassion. This augmented set of four are said to be *taṉ urimaic cuṟṟam āka*, Rājendracoḷa's "rightful companions." The metaphor – it is in fact closer to the *utprekṣā* or fanciful conceit of the Sanskrit poeticians – is unattested in the earlier eulogies, although there are similar examples in the Tamil classics.[9] The pregnant use of *urimai*, "right, property, intimacy," here is significant: a word found in the earlier *mĕykkīrttis* of Rājarāja, Rājendra, Rājādhirāja, and Vīrarājendra, this supplies one of the foundational terms in the appeal to each king's particular right to rule. It is remounted here as the enabling condition for Rājendracoḷa's demonstration of this spectrum of royal virtues, exceeding the claims of earlier kings' eulogists.[10]

Given the martial contents of the *mĕykkīrttis* as a whole, occurrences of *cayam* ("victory"; variant spellings include *jayam* and *cĕyam*) are omnipresent, and thus hardly probative. But the phrase *kulamaṇima-kuṭam muṟaimaiyil cūṭi* ("with a crown upon his head set with fine jewels, that has come to him through lawful succession") pointedly gestures to the model of earlier Coḻa eulogies. Much as with the sense of *ācai* earlier, *kulamaṇi* ("fine jewels") embeds a double meaning: *kula* can, in Sanskrit and Tamil both, refer to the superiority of a gem, a mountain, or a woman; but it may, in its simplest sense, just mean "family." To refer, however obliquely, to Rājendracoḷa's ancestry in the course of a text whose rhetoric draws on both his Coḻa and his Cālukya heritage stages a deliberate ambiguity, one that would later become central to this king's public self as the emperor Kulottuṅga, "lofty in his family [/families]." *Kula* (generally meaning "family") can be found in the *mĕykkīrttis* of Rājendra, Rājādhirāja, and Rājendradeva; so too *muṟaimai* "order, succession" is attested in the texts of the first two of these kings, and in the long eulogy of Vīrarājendra.[11] In this passage of the *mĕykkīrtti*, the subject matter really becomes the constitutive intertextuality with the accounts of the Coḻa kings of earlier generations; the differences in Rājendracoḷa's text distinguish him from the earlier examples by either addition or the subtle drawing of attention to his place in another dynastic order.

> *tan kaḻal tarātipar cūṭac cĕṅkol*
> *nāvalam puvitoṟum naṭāttiya*
> *kov irācakesarivaṉmarāṉa*
> *uṭaiyār śrī irājentiracoḷatevarkku yāṇṭu iruntāvatu*

> With kings gathered around his warrior's anklets,
> he has sent forth the straight sceptre of his rule
> to every corner of the Rose Apple continent:
> the king, Rājakesarivarman, lord and master, Śrī Rājendra Coḻa,
> in the second year of his reign

The closing lines really add nothing to the cunning game of adoption and differentiation of the eulogy's earlier sections. Instead, in their stereotyped invocation of subservient kings and the king's emblematic sceptre, they round out the text of the eulogy, culminating in the final, standard array of royal titles and regnal year. Even this, however, needs be seen against the model it faithfully reproduces, that of the consensually admitted phrases by which a Coḻa king exercises his authority. For all the absence of a concluding flourish, the reproduction of the standard template demonstrates the anonymous author's final argument: this is a king whose authority follows from the formal apparatus of his chancellery's language as much as from his martial accomplishments.

In addition to the *mĕykkīrtti*s of earlier generations of Coḻa kings, there is another, decisive text against which Rājendracoḷa's *mĕykkīrtti* needs to be read. As we have already seen, by adopting the official cognomen Rājakesarivarman, Rājendracoḷa tacitly acknowledged two immediate predecessors, his maternal uncle Vīrarājendra (himself styled Rājakesarivarman) and his cross-cousin, publicly known as Parakesarivarman Adhirājendra. The relative paucity of Adhirājendra's surviving records and the influence of the highly perspectival account of Bilhaṇa *Vikramāṅkadevacarita* have skewed this king's brief reign in the eyes of modern scholarship: for Nilakanta Sastri, he "ruled for a few weeks" before "[losing] his life in a fresh rebellion."[12] When Nilakanta Sastri's wrote, Adhirājendra's accession date was as yet unsettled; it is only due to an epigraphical discovery decades after the publication of his magnum opus that this is now set as June 1, 1068.[13]

Of the nineteen records issued in Adhirājendra's name that are now available, only three are dated in his second regnal year, the remainder of the records in his name are assigned to his third year; that is, between June 1070 and May 1071, most of which lack an exact date. This is significantly the period immediately following Rājendracoḷa's own coronation, but before the appearance of any of his own records. The *mĕykkīrtti* that begins most of these records, then, was an immediate predecessor to Rājendracoḷa's own eulogists' efforts; a close comparison demonstrates their distinct intertextuality, shading over into subtle argument:

tiṅgaḷ er malarntu vĕṇkuṭai maṇṭilam
maṉṉuyir toṟum iṉṉaruḷ curantu
niṟainiḻal parappi niṟpa muṟaimaiyiṟ
cĕṅkol ticai toṟum cĕlva taṅkaḷ
kulamutal paritiyiṉ valan oḻi nīvaṟku
oṟṟaiy āḻi ulāva naṟṟavat
tirumalarccĕlviyum irunilappāvaiyum
kīrttiyaṅ kiḷḷaiyum porttaṉipūvaiyum
matuvaiyiṟ puṇarntu pŏtumai tuṟantu taṉ
urimait teviyar ākki marapiṉil

cuṭarmaṇimakuṭam cūṭṭi nĕṭunilam
maṉṉavar muṟaimuṟai taṉṉaṭi vaṇaṅka
vīramum tiyākamum āram eṉap puṇaintu
māppukaḻ maṉuvuṭaṉ vaḷartta
kopparakecarivaṉmarāṉa
uṭaiyār śrī adhirājendradevarukku yāṇṭu 3āvatu[14]

As the circle of his white parasol, blossoming like the full moon,
stands, extending his kind affection for all living creatures
and spreading dense shade;
as his straight sceptre, come down in good succession,
goes forth to all corners of the earth;
as his matchless wheel processes in order to wipe away
the decline of the might of the Sun, his family's progenitor;[15]
joining, in his strength,[16] with the lovely flower-goddess of noble austerities,
the lady of the wide earth, with the parrot-like beauty that is his fame,
and with the matchless goddess of battle,
rejecting all commonality, taking them as his deserved queens,
and decking them out in shining jewelled crowns, as is only customary;
with row after row of kings worshipping his feet,
ornamented with a garland of heroism and generosity,[17]
increasing, along with Manu, his great fame,
Kopparakesarivarma, Lord Adhirājendra, in the third year of his reign...

The text is a bit shorter than Rājendracoḻa's; it also conspicuously lacks any historico-referential information. Potentially, Adhirājendra did not have any martial accomplishments to celebrate: following Sethuraman's plausible suggestion, he may have earlier served as the Coḻapāṇḍya ruler in the far south, and likely did not participate in any martial campaigns in that then-pacified portion of the Coḻa territories. That difference of curriculum vitae aside, the two cousins' eulogies evince deep parallels in their relationship to their textual precursors and in their implied arguments about their subjects. Rājendracoḻa's text, as we have seen, borrows its opening from both men's grandfather, the empire-builder Rājendra; it introduces an ambiguous innovation into the *mĕykkīrtti* matrix with its mythopoetic reference to his Cālukya origins; and delivers a series of controlled variations on the lexical and thematic stock of earlier eulogies, especially that of Vīrarājendra, its subject's maternal uncle and Adhirājendra's father. The opening words to Adhirājendra's *mĕykkīrtti, tiṅgaḷ er*, reproduce the opening of Rājādhirāja's, as does the text's direct invocations of the Coḻa family's solar origins (*kulamutaṟpariti* in Adhirājendra's eulogy approximates *aṅkatirkaṭavuḷtŏlkulam*, "the ancient family of the hot-rayed god," in Rājādhirāja's) and rightful succession (as coded in the shared *muṟaimai*). The choice appears deliberate: Rājādhirāja was the dynasty's quintessential warrior-king who, as co-regent for many years with Rājendra, provides an argument for dynastic continuity not seen in the decades intervening since his death in battle. For a king without martial deeds to recommend him, navigating the transition to independent rule with his father still on the throne, Rājādhirāja's example was a potent one; Adhirājendra's regnal name, of course, also recalls that of his uncle. And again, like Rājendracoḷa's eulogy, Adhirājendra's text tries to refract some of the regal glamor of the closing public argument of Vīrarājendra's time: there is once again the invocation of the Coḻa sun (paralleling his father's Sanskrit *praśasti*) and, even more prominently, the adoption of the *vīramum tiyākamum* formula: here, these twinned kingly virtues are metaphorically woven together into a garland, just the sort of token of honor passed from bridegroom to bride, continuing the *mĕykkīrtti*'s central marital trope.

The overriding theme here is *muṟaimai* or succession, obliquely introduced here by the adverbial description of the subordinate kings bowing *muṟaimuṟai*, "in row after row," as it is joined with *marapu* or "custom." Significantly, the latter term does not occur in any earlier Coḻa *mĕykkīrtti*s. The importance of this appeal to orderly patrilineal succession is starkly put: it is this, and only this, which preserves the sun's descendants' workings in the world. The contrast with Rājendracoḷa's eulogy is palpable: the scion of the direct succession of the Coḻas is presented as the heir to an unbroken royal line, and his joining to the feminine hypostases of rule as a fait accompli, something that can be referred to immemorial custom. Rājendracoḷa's text, likely drawn up in direct response to Adhirājendra's, is premised by contrast on its subject's only partial reliance on his imperial ancestry: he is instead figured as a veteran of the northern marches in the Deccan, tied to another great royal tradition and intent, like Viṣṇu's Boar *avatāra*, upon sweeping in to secure what is rightfully his.

Scenes from Coḻa Tondaimandalam

In looking so closely at the linguistic, intertextual, and rhetorical fabric of these brief eulogistic texts, there is the danger of losing the forest in the trees. Certainly, both Rājendracoḷa's and Adhirājendra's *mĕykkīrtti*s drew on the language of earlier models, but it is hard to overemphasize just how repetitive and formulaic the *mĕykkīrtti* genre in fact was.[18] And even if the complexities and nuances that I find in their texts may be attributed to the intentions of the work's courtly authors, was there really an audience receptive enough to catch these ambiguities, borrowings, and subtle recastings? When either of these texts was declaimed before a contemporary gathering or when it was later incised on the wall of a local temple, who would have cared about the finely etched details of the celebration of these kings?

It has been argued a priori that all texts, and the sort of texts of interest to historians and literary critics especially, are necessarily to be seen in light of some preexisting conversation or argument, which they are meant to reframe or into which they are meant to intervene.[19] Given the public dissemination of these particular texts and the evident care with which they respond to the verbal texture of earlier examples, simple hermeneutic charity insists that we presume that at least some of their audience was alive to the repetitions, reinventions, and subtle polemics encoded in the Co<u>l</u>a *mĕykkīrttis*. Less abstractly, however, it is possible to specify within the world of the late eleventh-century Co<u>l</u>a country to whom exactly the argument staged between these royal cousins was meant to make a difference.

The entirety of the surviving epigraphs dated in Adhirājendra's regnal years and those dated in the years of Rājakesarivarman Rājendracoḷa are plotted on Figure 2.1. The nineteen records of Adhirājendra range all the way to the southern limits of Co<u>l</u>a territory, with two inscriptions found in Polonnuruwa in Sri Lanka and one near Tirunelveli in the far south of the peninsula. Almost all of the records are concentrated in riverine areas, mostly along the Pennar and Palar rivers, as well as a scattering of five records from the Kāveri delta. Among the records from the Kāveri region – in the heartland of Colamandalam – are the three records dated to the king's second year, and the index record by which the absolute limits of his reign can be calculated. The majority of these traces are located in the northern part of the Co<u>l</u>a domains, either in Tondaimandalam (Jayaṅkŏṇṭaco<u>l</u>amaṇḍalam in the Co<u>l</u>a territorial imagination), the northerly region centered on the ancient city of Kāñcīpuram, or in old magnate domains on its southern borderlands.[20] A complementary pattern of distribution obtains in the records dated in Rājendracoḷa's years. There are seven records in his name from the delta, half of which are among the latest inscriptions issued; the great majority of his records (thirty-one altogether) is concentrated in the region of Jayaṅkŏṇṭaco<u>l</u>amaṇḍalam or its adjoining territories, just as in Adhirājendra's case. And just as there is a scattering of records in Adhirājendra's name in the far south, Rājendracoḷa possesses a set of northwestern outliers in Nikarilico<u>l</u>amaṇḍalam, near the source of the Palar in what is now Karnataka's Kolar district; several of these are among the earliest of his issues.

Figures 2.2–2.4 illustrate the ways in which the contents of both corpora of inscriptions reinforce the impression lent by their geographic distribution. More clearly than simple objective cartography, this reveals

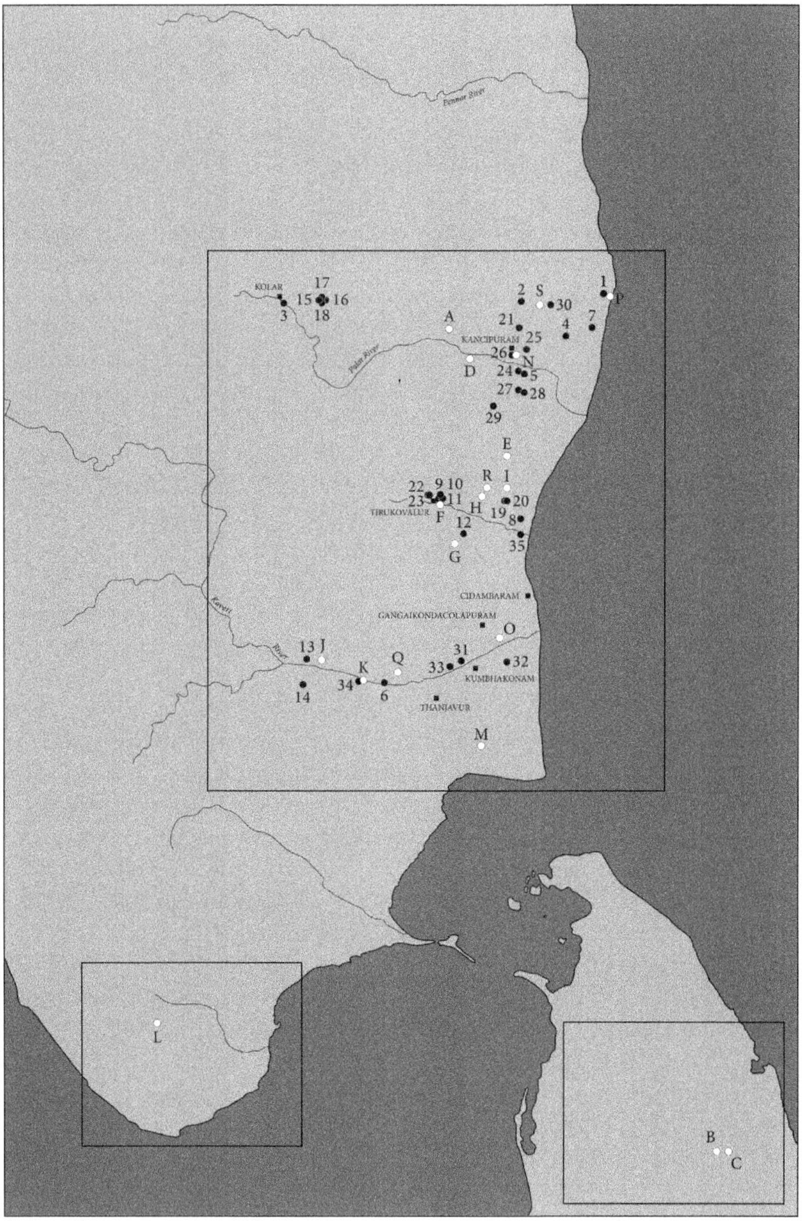

Figure 2.1 Rājendracoḷa (black circles) and Adhirājendra (white circles) inscriptions, 1069–1074. Legend on p. 84

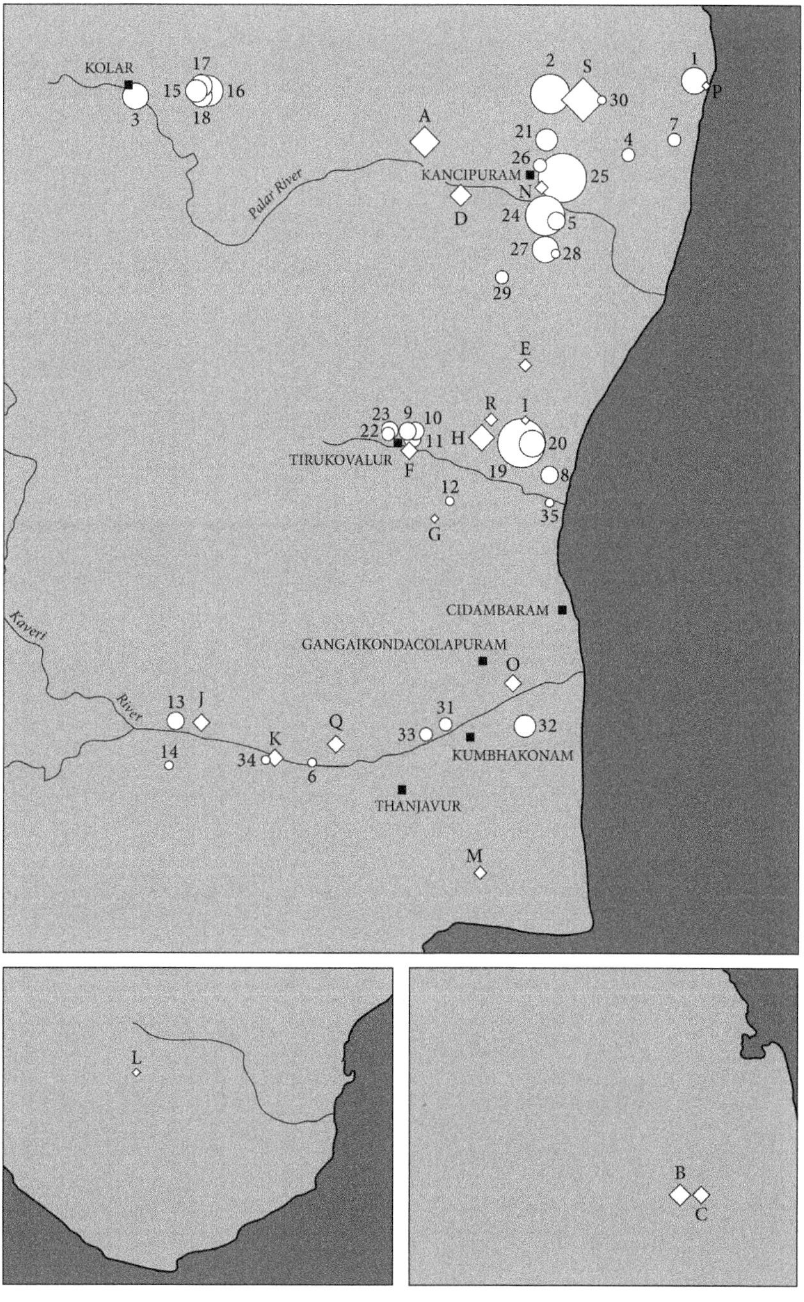

Figures 2.2–2.4 Rājendracoḷa (circles, numbers) and Adhirājendra (diamonds, letters) inscriptions, weighted by contents. Legend on p. 84

Rājendracoḷa Inscriptions

1. Tiruvoṟṟiyūr SII 3:64 (ARE 106 of 1892), year 2 (1071/2)
2. Tiruvaḷaṅkāṭu SII 3:65 (ARE 14 of 1896), year 2 (1071/2)
3. Kolār EC 10 Kolar 108/106d (SII 3:66; ARE 131 of 1892), year 2 (1071/2)
4. Comaṅkalam SII 3:67 (ARE 182 of 1902), year 3 (1072/3)
5. Kavantaṇṭalam SII 3:77 (ARE 206 of 1901), year 4(1073/4)
6. Kovilāṭi SII 7:498 (ARE 278 of 1901), year 3 (1072/3)
7. Tirucūlam SII 7:541 (ARE 315 of 1901), year 3 (1072/3)
8. Vākūr PI 28 (SII 7:807; ARE 180 of 1902), year 4 (1073/4)
9. Kīḻūr/Tirukovalūr SII 7:875 (ARE 247 of 1902), year 4 (1073/4)
10. Tirukovalūr SII 7:876 (ARE 248 of 1902), year 4 (1073/4)
11. Tirukovalūr SII 7:877 (ARE 249 of 1902), year 2 (1071/2)
12. Tirunāmanallūr SII 7:979 (ARE 349 of 1902), year 3 (1072/3)
13. Mahādānapuram SII 8:701 (ARE 386 of 1902), year 4 (1073/4)
14. Vayalūr SITI 743, year 3 (1072/3)
15. Mulbagal EC 10 Mulbagal 49a, year 3 (1072/3)
16. Mulbagal EC 10 Mulbagal 105ab, year 4 (1073/4)
17. Mulbagal EC 10 Mulbagal 106b, year 4 (1073/4)
18. Mulbagal EC 10 Mulbagal 119, year 3 (1072/3)
19. Tirupuvaṉai PI 113 (ARE 185 of 1919), year 3 (1072/3)
20. Tirupuvaṉai PI 114, year 3 (1072/3)
21. Tākkoḷam ARE 243 of 1921, year 3 (1072/3)
22. Grāmam ARE 193 of 1906, year 4 (1073/4)
23. Iṭaiyāṟu ARE 279 of 1928/9, year 3 (1072/3)
24. Ārppākkam, ARE 138 of 1923, year 2 (1071/2)
25. Kāñcipuram ARE 68 of 1920/1, year 4 (1074)
26. Kāñcipuram ARE 522 of 1919, year 3 (1072/3)
27. Tirupulivaṉam ARE 395 of 1912/3, year 3 (1072/3)
28. Tirupulivaṉam ARE 398 of 1912/3, year 3 (1073)
29. Karaṉai ARE 232 of 1958/9, year 4 (1073/4)
30. Tirupaccūr ARE 133 of 1930, year 2 (May 1072)
31. Tirupurampiyam ARE 334 of 1927, year 4 (1073/4)
32. Iñcikkuṭi ARE 431 of 1954/5, year 4 (1073/4)
33. Ālaṅkuṭi ARE 497 of 1920/1, year 3 (1072/3)
34. Tiruvaiyāṟu ARE 157 of 1918, year 3 (1072/3)
35. Tirupāpuliyūr SII 7:748

Adhirājendra Inscriptions

A. Tiruvallam SII 3:57, year 3 (1070/1)
B. Polonnaruwa SII 4:1388 (ARE 594 of 1912), year 3 (1070/1)
C. Polonnaruwa SII 4:1392 (ARE 596 of 1912)
D. Kalavai SII 7:442 (ARE 228 of 1901), year 3 (1070/1)
E. Kiṭaṅkil SII 7:854 (ARE 227 of 1902), year 2 (1069/70)
F. Kīḻūr, Tirukovalūr SII 7:884 (ARE 256 of 1902), year 3 (1070/1)
G. Tirunāmanallūr SII 7:985 (ARE 355 of 1902), year 3 (1070/1)
H. Viḻuppuram SII 8:754 (ARE 438 of 1903), year 3 (1070/1)
I. Tiruvākkarai SII 17: 227 (ARE 205 of 1904), year 2 (1069/70)
J. Śrīnivāsanallūr SII 17: 653 (ARE 603 of 1904), year 3 (1070/1)
K. Śrīraṅgam SII 24: 25 (ARE 181 of 1951/2)
L. Maṉṉārkoyil SITI 821, year 3 (1070/1)
M. Siddhamalli ARE 5 of 1945/6, year 3 (May, 1071)
N. Kāñcipuram ARE 273 of 1955/6
O. Tiruviḷākkuṭi ARE 123 of 1926, year 2 (1069/70)
P. Tiruvoṟṟiyūr ARE 219 of 1912, year 3 (1070/1)
Q. Kukūr ARE 280 of 1917, year 3 (1070/1)
R. Paṉaiyapuram ARE 322 of 1917
S. Tirupaccūr ARE 113 of 1929/30, year 3 (1070/71)

Legend for Figures 2.1 – 2.4

the extent to which elite, courtly, and royal initiative was unevenly apportions in different parts of the kingdom. Each of the records seen in Figure 2.1 is here weighted according to a set of qualitative criteria, depending upon the record's rhetorical valence (especially the inclusion of a *mĕykkīrtti*),[21] the presence of different sorts of named individuals, and the nature of the donative act it records.[22] Seen in this way, the distribution becomes even more pronouncedly oriented toward the northern edges of the Coḻa imperium, while both kings' scattering of inscriptions in the Kāveri region shrink into relative insignificance: in many cases in the delta, the reference to either king amounts to little more than the notarial reference to a regnal year. The five-year period depicted in these maps can, further, yield a skeletal diachronic narrative, in which Adhirājendra's court society begins from its base in the south and undertakes a brief burst of activity in the kingdom's north in the king's final year, while Rājendracoḷa's court, from a base in the north and west, extends itself into the core.

More than a century ago, Eugen Hultzsch suggested that "the southern limit of the dominions of [Rājendracoḷa] in the second year of his reign is perhaps roughly indicated by a line connecting Tiruvoṟṟiyūr, Tiruvālaṅgāḍu and Kōlār,"[23] roughly the meridian defined by the modern cities of Chennai and Bangalore. Hultzsch further argued that it was only from his fifth year, and the beginning of records by the renamed Kulottuṅga I, that the king came to be in possession of the whole of the Coḻa imperial patrimony. The pattern of distribution presented in these figures broadly supports Hultzsch's conjecture. But his claim prompted a strong refutation by Nilakanta Sastri: in his efforts to falsify the earlier epigraphist's contention, Sastri produced a number of inscriptions dated in Rājendracoḷa's early years from points further to the south than Hultzsch's imagined boundary line. A number of the records listed by Sastri have been included in these figures; others were misattributed.[24] But to partly concede the point in Sastri's favor, there are enough records from the Kāveri delta to falsify the strong version of Hultzsch's claim; that is, that the future Kulottuṅga was confined in his authority to the far northern fringes of the kingdom. Medieval territorial boundaries were porous and socially fluid: there was no hard border demarcating the area of possible action of this king, his contemporaries, or their proxies. In any event, the degree of territorial control evinced by inscriptional location is highly relative: individual records range on a scale from the direct interventions of royal agents through to local notables declaring their support of a king, through to the use of a king's name and regnal date out of purely conventional norms. As political documents, inscriptions – whether prefaced by a royal eulogy or not – existed at the intersection of multiple modes of social power.

It is in this light that the shared concentration of Adhirājendra's and Rājendracoḷa's records in the northern end of the kingdom takes on particular significance. Jayaṅkōṇṭacoḻamaṇḍalam, the location of the balance of both sets of records and overwhelmingly the site of the most significant of these, was the Coḻa recasting of the ancient Tondaimandalam, the former heartland of the Pallava dynasty. That the two kings' inscriptions center on this region is reminiscent in the first instance of the earlier system of regional appanages that had been instituted under Rājendra and continued by his sons. Adhirājendra had likely been an incumbent in this system, if he had earlier reigned in the far south as Jaṭāvarman Uṭaiyār Coḻapāṇḍyadeva.[25] And while Rājendracoḷa's early actions were atypical in many ways of these lesser Coḻa lordships – above all, in the issuing of orders in the Coḻa courtly style – these appear to be an extension of the same logic. The Tondai country had long been integrated into the Coḻa imperial order, with Kāñcīpuram serving as one of the dynasty's several capitals. And yet the court societies and elite partisans of Adhirājendra and Rājendracoḷa undertook evident efforts to establish themselves in the region. This can be seen most tellingly in the public dissemination of their eulogies, and also in the substantive acts recorded in the business of the surviving records. What does their concentration in the Tondai country and its environs tell us?

In terms of its ecological and social matrix, Tondaimandalam was similar to the rest of the Coḻa territory: the ruling elite of the region was formed by Brahmans and Veḷḷāḷas ruling over agrarian societies similar to, if generally drier than, those further south. But despite its integration into the Coḻa kingdom for more than a century, in 1070 the erstwhile Pallava country remained distinct in its economy, its social constitution, and, above all, in its politics. The open, scrub-filled plains of modern Kanchipuram and Chengalpattu districts were where the green, watered country of the Kāveri opened up onto the broad expanses of the Deccan; lacking the hydraulic resources of the Coḻa heartland, Tondai country was poorer in its agriculture, though its long experience of urban life around Kāñcīpuram saw a relatively higher penetration of commercial development. This can be seen in the presence of the ancient merchant's guild of the Aiññūṟṟuvar, the Five Hundred Masters of Aihole, and in the high concentration of *nagaram* sites, the enclaves that supplied the nodes of the transregional network of trading and marketing.[26] Though integrated into the Coḻa system of nomenclature since the final years of Rājarāja I's reign,[27] the region's assimilation to the kingdom-wide landed order was only partial. Some of the evidence of this rests on matters of convention, as for instance in the survival of the term *koṭṭam* for a territorial unit existing above the level of the individual *nāṭu* (a list of twenty-four such *koṭṭam*s can be found in later literary accounts).[28] More substantively, the region had yet to be integrated into the characteristic Co<u>l</u>a system of *vaḷanāṭu*s. As these were the chief units of record for the Co<u>l</u>a fisc, the Tondai country was evidently a separate entity unto itself in the all-important matter of its revenue settlement. In place of the centrally instituted system of *vaḷanāṭu*s, the region possessed its own characteristic institution in the form of the *ta<u>n</u>kū<u>r</u>u* ("independent zone"), which later came to be called the *ta<u>n</u>iyūr* ("independent settlement").[29] The nucleus of these territorial clusters was generally a *brahmadeya* village, the foundation of which often dated from Pallava times. These spatially distributed clusters, each "a supreme example of rural-urban continuum" served as the principal nodes for the actions of the Co<u>l</u>a state in the region; their character as extended central places may have inspired the Co<u>l</u>a efforts at territorial integration within the kingdom's Kāveri heartland. The network of *ta<u>n</u>iyūr*s lent the region its distinctive character; equally important was the long metropolitan memory of Kāñcīpuram itself, as well as the durable royal traditions of the Pallava court.[30]

It is from the Tondai region that the major accounts of Brahmanical self-governance derive, including the celebrated early tenth-century records of Uttaramerūr. The managing institutions of this and other *brahmadeya* villages cannot be overgeneralized to the Tamil country as a whole: their peculiar concentration in the Tondai country, if anything, points to the degree they are nonrepresentative cases. Yet the region's distinctive political culture extended beyond these exclusively Brahman institutions. There is, for example, the widespread occurrence throughout Co<u>l</u>a records of the title *pallavaraiya<u>n</u>* ("lord of the Pallavas"), usually preceded by a royal epithet. The title's exact semantics are unclear: in its form, it resembles the naming conventions of magnate lineages, but its frequent occurrence and strong association with royal service plausibly associates it with the ranks of Tŏṇṭaiyar warrior-gentry recruited into the proliferating state apparatus.[31]

The most remarkable evidence of the political constitution of Tondaimandalam lies in the precocious development there of collective institutions extending across the customary boundaries of individual *nāṭu*s and endogamous caste communities. The appearance in the surviving records of these collective institutions, especially the agriculturalist group styling itself as the assembly of the *cittirame<u>l</u>i* ("Shining Plow"), has long been noted. While understood by their earliest interpreters as evidence of complex systems of provincial governance instituted by the benevolent and omnicompetent Co<u>l</u>a state, these records were alighted on in Stein's revisionist understanding as testimony for the centrifugal tendencies (the "transition to supralocal integration") that heralded the terminal decline of the kingdom's precarious hegemony. Such interpretations, for all their differences, were in perfect concord about these institutions' periodization: they could be dated to the late twelfth and thirteenth centuries, during the unwinding of Coḻa imperial sovereignty.[32]

It was thus a major revision of the accepted understanding when the epigraphic remains of the Tiruvagnīśvara temple in Tāmaraippākkam (modern Tiruvannamalai district) were published at the end of the last century.[33] Three of the inscriptions housed in this temple feature decrees by a *cittirameḻi* assembly; two of these can be reliably dated to Rājendradeva's fifth and tenth years, 1057 and 1062, some five or six generations prior to their previously established attestation. Nor do the Tāmaraippākkam accounts reveal the institution in its inchoate infancy. In the three judgments issued by the assembly, we can see most of its later features on full, precocious display.[34] By far the most detailed of these records is the earliest, which gives the results of a criminal trial: the death sentence of one Pĕriyāṉ, guilty of murdering his brother, is commuted into a temple donation in perpetuity and the requirement that he care for his aged, indigent parents. In this record, the *cittirameḻi* accorded itself the full share of nearly regal dignity evident in its much later pronouncements. The Coḻa king's truncated *mĕykkīrtti* is followed by a Sanskrit verse and a brief Tamil eulogy imitative of the royal style, both in reference to the assembly itself, and no further reference is made to an external authority to the assembly's ability to issue decisions with the force of *dharma*.[35]

Although perhaps not as immediately exciting to the historical imagination, the other two Tāmaraippākkam *cittirameḻi* records are more eloquent in their social content. The first is speciously dated in the fifth regnal year of Rājendra,[36] and pointedly pertains to the land tenure of a named portion of Jayaṅkŏṇṭacoḻamaṇḍalam. Those territories enrolled as *devadāna* lands (tax-free temple holdings) in Paṅkaḷanāṭu, part of Palkuṉṟakkoṭṭam, had been infringed upon by unidentified figures holding rights to the collection of certain levies, as well as certain other rights to the land, all of them prerogatives issued by the royal center. Summoning one Rājarājapiṭārar (possibly an official, though the title is anomalous, as is his pleonastic description as "performing the *piṭāram* for this country"), the assembly – here identified as the *pĕriyanāṭu* "gathered in the Rājendracoḻa [hall]" – seemingly registers his disposition of formal opposition to these royal imposts before itself ceremoniously refusing to accept them.[37] The third and latest record (TK 26), dated to Rājendradeva's year ten or 1062–1063, sets the revenue rates for several different grades of agricultural land. These otherwise typical contents are remarkable for the agents responsible for their issue: a named collective of the ruling elites of ten different *nāṭu*s (three of them old magnate territories), explicitly located in Jayaṅkŏṇṭacoḻamaṇḍalam, arrogated itself the control of *nāṭṭāṇmai* ("governance"), and so the authority to set the terms of land tax without any reference to the royal center beyond the token reference of the record's truncated opening eulogy.[38]

Although these are isolated records from an out-of-the-way part of the kingdom, their significance cannot be underestimated. They attest to an emergent process of social differentiation, the first visible fissure in what would later become a yawning gap in the cobbled-together edifice of the unitary Coḻa polity. Combined with the other, more perduring features of Tondaimandalam regional difference (in landed nomenclature, in urban and quasi-urban development, and especially in the collective self-understanding of dominant groups in its society), this suggests a friction over the integration of Tondaimandalam and of the Tŏṇṭaiyar elite into the kingdom-wide order. That this emerges into the historical record during the mid-century reign of Rājendradeva is especially eloquent: it was in this period, as we have seen, that the Coḻa state apparatus bulked the largest, and when it encountered the limits of its own internal elaboration.

Without reducing deeply contingent social processes to a too-simple play of force and counterforce, a structural explanation suggests itself. Despite Tondaimandalam's long-term political integration into the Coḻa kingdom, it was the mid-century subsumption of the old magnate territories into the Coḻa imperial core that appears to have catalyzed these changes. The magnate polities had for centuries acted as a buffer zone between Colamandalam and Tondaimandalam, and their dissolution in this period produced an incongruity within the system of Coḻa imperial control. In the short run of the post-Rājendra era, the most obvious effect of this was an aggrandization of Jayaṅkŏṇṭacoḻamaṇḍalam, which swiftly became the notional location of old magnate lands as far to the south as Tirukkovalūr, the chief temple-town of the old Milāṭu realm on the south bank of the Pennai. These newly integrated lands ranged over an area mapping closely onto that demarcated by the joint agreement of the *nāṭṭār* seen in Tāmaraippākkam.[39] This territorial expansion served as the proximate cause for the first major assertions of local particularism, catalyzing a collective recognition by the magnate and Brahman–gentry elites of the precariousness of their local customary rights in the face of the proliferating Coḻa state. This particularist recognition cannot be characterized as rebellion or "state resistance," however conceived. In ascriptive, linguistic, and broadly speaking ethnic terms, the magnates,

Brahmans, and gentry of Tondaimandalam were assimilable to their deltaic counterparts. If anything – especially if the *pallavaraiyaṉ* title did in fact possess a regional basis – these figures were somewhat more likely to be drawn into the network of state affiliation, accepting official roles such as *atikāri* or entering into the revenue bureaucracy of the *puravuvaritiṇaikkaḷam*. We might perhaps best see the Tāmaraippākkam charters as an effort to secure a collectively advantageous place in the transregional political hierarchy, at the very moment when Tondai particularism was becoming an endangered species.

Adhirājendra's Tondaimandalam Mobilizations, 1070–1071

It is in this context that the epigraphic traces associated with Adhirājendra and Rājendracoḷa need to be situated. Given that the distribution of both corpora evinces a strong bias toward Tondaimandalam, it was clearly there that these princes' court societies and political networks labored to assert and reproduce themselves. In the case of Adhirājendra, presuming an initial base in the Pāṇḍya country to the far south, his first year after his coronation centered upon shifting his attention (and likely his physical presence) to the north; Rājendracoḷa, on the other hand, was based in the interstitial zone between the northern marches of the Coḻa lands and his erstwhile home country in Veṅgī.

Seen from this vantage, the rhetorical choices made in either princes' *mĕykkīrtti* assume a clearer outline. Adhirājendra's eulogy – with its studied invocations of family origins and orderly succession – presents an open bid to the authority of continuity: Coḻa rule had after all been good for the Tŏṇṭaiyar elite. This argument, embedded in the verbal texture of the eulogy, can be correlated with the distribution of Adhirājendra's surviving records. There is much that is dark here: as we have already seen, it is often impossible to reconstruct the social agencies that led to the production of a given inscriptional text, just as the collective calculus – the play of affiliation between figures of the court, local elite societies and particular individuals – remains obscure. In many cases, the reference to the king may be purely conventional, a means of recording a date without further significance beyond a vague and inconsequential recognition of royal authority.[40]

Adhirājendra's few surviving records do, however, supply a number of occasions in which the work of practical politics can be clearly discerned. In two of the three records dated to his second regnal year (from June 1069 to May 1070), we can see something of these efforts. One, from Tiruvākkarai, fails to mention Adhirājendra, save in its opening date formula, and is cast in a style that sets it from the ordinary run of Coḻa epigraphs. Comprising a single Sanskrit verse and a short passage of Tamil prose, it documents the reconstruction in stone of a brick temple's central tower. The honoree is named as Kumāri Centaṉ (erratically Sanskritized as Śendana), who is described as the *kuṭippaḷḷi* of the village of Poypākkam, and bears the quasi-magnate title Cayaṅkŏṇṭacoḻaviḻupparaiyanāṭāḻvāṉ.[41] This would seem as if it were an act of private pious philanthropy in which the mention of Adhirājendra was purely notional, were it not for the other record of the second year, from Kiṭaṅkil, some thirty miles away. Once again, there is no *mĕykkīrtti* and seemingly no strong presence of Adhirājendra or his court; yet the transaction recorded is more detailed and more significant. The leading citizens of Kiṭaṅkil (referred to by its conventional name as well as Mummuṭicoḻanallūr, a prototypical example of royalist rechristening) announce their sale of a considerable parcel of cultivable land to one Cĕṅkaṇicāttaṉ nālāyiravan, alias Kalikālacoḻaccĕṅkaṇināṭāḻvaṉ, the *kuṭippaḷḷi* of Paṇḍitacoḻacaturvedimaṅgalam in Oymānāṭu.[42] The record shifts into its inevitable report of tax remission, in this case to support a ritual endowment for "the dancing Śiva of the Shining Plow," for whom – the record has Cĕṅkaṇicāttan nālāyiravan report in his own voice – "I had erected in the Gaurīśvara temple in this village."[43]

The two central figures in these documents are united in their social and political identities: given their closeness in space and time, they were certainly known to each other and likely related, whether directly or through the far-branching subtleties of Dravidian kinship. Both are identified as the *kuṭippaḷḷi* ("cultivator" or "settlement" *paḷḷi*) of two villages, one of which was certainly a *brahmadeya*. The title is an interesting one, combining the name of an upland warrior caste community with an adjective suggestive of a landed, indeed landholding, style of life. Onomasty here recapitulates social history: the middle decades of the 1000s had witnessed the emergence of warrior groups who had previously been outside the pale of delta society as landed property holders in the core territories of the kingdom. That one of the two named *kuṭippaḷḷi*s was domiciled in a *brahmadeya*, previously the exclusive preserve of Brahmans, is especially significant, as it was from the matrix of the Brahmanical estates that the practice of private landholdings first emerged.[44] Equally suggestive is the coincidence in these two men's social identity of the lordly title *nāṭāḻvāṉ* ("lord of the country"), of rising importance throughout the second half of the eleventh century and the hallmark of the warlord families that would emerge in the 1100s.[45] These men were members of warrior groups hailing from outside of the Kāveri core, newly assertive in the wake of the wars of mid-century, as they entered into the social space of the old magnate lineages; their donations attest an attempt to forge a connection between these figures and the public charisma of the Coḻa prince.

It is unclear whether this connection was actively solicited by Adhirājendra's court. Possibly these two local strongmen were simply arrogating to themselves the imprimatur of the newly ruling king. But the fact that the second of these two public pronouncements was blazoned with the presence of the *cittirameḻi* suggests a process of triangulation at work in this one local lord's public self-presentation. In invoking his new king as well as the emerging forms of collective belonging in his home country (representatives from Oymānāṭu were among those issuing the *nāṭṭāṉmai* pronouncement in Tāmaraippākkam), Cĕṅkaṇicāttan is emblematic of the complexities of Coḻa elite politics in 1070.

This self-assertion by *arriviste* warriors recently entered into the magnate ranks can be juxtaposed with the surviving evidence of what were certainly deliberate actions undertaken by members of Adhirājendra's court society. These emerge from the accounts of a public assembly held in the precincts of the Smaśāneśvara temple in Kāñcīpuram, which are recorded in two inscriptions, one dated to November 9, 1070 (the 161st day of Adhirājendra's third year) from Kāñci's Tirukalīśvara temple, and the other, dated to December 18 of the same year (or Adhirājendra year 3, day 200) from the Bilvanātheśvara temple in Tiruvallam, some twenty-five miles away. While the full text of the earlier of the two is no longer available, they obviously both derive from an identical formulary.[46] They report the issuance of a public order from the Smaśāneśvara's eastern *maṇḍapa* by two officers, the *atikārikaḷ* Pūraṉ Ātittadevaṉ, bearing the title Rājarājentiramuventaveḷān and hailing from Pulāṅku in Puṟakkiḷiyūrnāṭu in Pāṇṭikulāśanivaḷanāṭu, and the *senāpati* Rājarājaṉ Paraniruparākkataṉ, alias Vīracoḻa Iḷaṅkoveḷan, the *kiḻaṉ* of Naṭār in Tiraimūrnāṭu in Uyyakŏṇṭavaḷanāṭu. The announcement is executive in character: after conducting an inquiry among the accountants for the villages attached to either temple, these officials refer to revenue assessments put in force "from the year following upon the seventh year of the emperor Vīrarājendra" for a host of levies and customary duties, significantly paid in cash rather than in kind.[47] The earlier record then breaks off; the account from Tiruvallam goes on to declare that revenue deriving from two villages in the old magnate territory of Perumpāṇappāṭi had been previously unaccounted for, and should henceforth be given over for previously unfunded expenses.

A group of nine notables, most of them *mūventaveḷar*, took the decision to disburse these funds for a series of temple food offerings for named deities and their consorts, in an amount slightly in excess of the previously unallocated revenues.

The social identities of the two officials delegated to make these arrangements are clear, and very telling. The *atikāri* Pūraṉ Ātittadevaṉ's home was on the southern bank of the Kāveri, deep within the core Coḻa patrimony, and he had earlier served as a courtier of Adhirājendra's father, having appeared at Vīrarājendra's Kāñcī darbar two years before.[48] The *senāpati* Rājarājaṉ Paraniruparākkataṉ, also from the Kāveri heartland, was a scion of one of the most eminent of magnate lineages, intermarried over generations with the Coḻa royal family; his *biruda*-like personal name (a Tamil transcription of Sanskrit *paranṛparākṣasa*, "a rakshasa to enemy kings") bespeaks the family warrior credentials that went along with his martial office.[49] These were thus men from the uppermost echelons of the state elite, and loyalists to the ruling line. But they were distinctly outsiders in the environs of Kāncī, at the furthest northern edge of any of the records issued in Adhirājendra's name.

The men upon whom they devolve the task of distributing the newly discovered (perhaps "discovered") revenue present a distinct contrast to these notables. These included a ranking official from the revenue office, and also a Colamandalam man, Vidiyaṉ Tirumāliruñcolai, bearing the title Kuvalayadivākaramūventaveḷaṉ, and a revenue bureaucrat from Tondaimandalam, Kaṇṭanīṟaṇintāṉ, a *pallavaraiyaṉ*. All of the rest of the men bear similar honorifics (five are *mūventaveḷar*, one *pallavaraiyaṉ*, and one *tamiḻataraiyaṉ*); all but one are from the Tōṇṭai country, hailing from different named *koṭṭam*s.[50] These were all local men, though none were from Kāñcī. In lending their imprimatur to these several new observances, they gained more than merit accrued for the afterlife: seeing to the distribution of food to devotees, they both gained honor for their charity and recognition that their worldly success was a mark of divine favor, invoking the benefit of Śiva as Lord of the Burning Ground in the metropolis and the more localized benefits of the god as Bilvanātheśvara. They may well have gained more than that: it is easy enough to see in the public recording of this charity an emolument offered to these men, rendering over to their responsibility not just revenues in paddy, but easily converted (and readily pocketable) income in coin.[51]

These are admittedly sparse data, but from them we can impute something of the wider political intentions of Adhirājendra and his supporters around 1070. It is clear that Jayaṅkōṇṭacoḻamaṇḍalam was the focus in this: the landed warriors identified as *kuṭippaḷḷi* from points to the immediate south of the old Pallava domains were among the first to lend their support to the new king, recently arrived from Pāṇḍya country. The references to him in their records, lacking a *mĕykkīrtti* – perhaps his court had yet to compose one in his honor? – show a modicum of public deference, but were meant to register deeds performed in their own name. The situation was especially complex in the case of Cĕṅkaṇicāttaṉ, both in the dedication of his offerings to a deity of the *cittirameḻi* and in his pious landgrab in the vicinity of Kiṭaṅkil: the engrossment of his own estates may have necessitated covering his bets, as it were, with both the royal center and the assertive agrarian society of his home country. Adhirājendra and his agents may well have welcomed the support. As a new ruler who himself conspicuously lacked any martial credentials, Adhirājendra was thereby linked with representatives of the new men who had emerged from the endemic warfare of mid-century.

While the *kuṭippaḷḷi* records detail the independent actions of two men declaring their connection with Adhirājendra, the proceedings from the Smaśāneśvara temple evince an open bid for the loyalty of members of the northern gentry, via the redistributive mechanisms of the region's temples.[52] The two officials from Colamandalam were evidently dispatched to the north in order to secure the support of local gentry elites, using a combination of public honor and private enrichment complementary to that seen in the record from Kiṭaṅkil. There may have been an urgency to this: Vīrarājendra, who was certainly alive in June of 1070, was likely succumbing at this point to the illness that would eventually kill him.[53] With his father's courtiers and the resources of the Kāveri delta nominally at his command, Adhirājendra could have advanced his rhetorical program of orderly succession and Coḷa dynastic continuity to secure the loyalty of the magnates, gentry, and Brahmans of the Tondai country.

It was, however, not to be. From across the Coḷa kingdom, there are at least three inscriptions dated in Adhirājendra's third year, recording donations to support observances in the hopes of restoring him to health. Whatever effect these might have had, he died at some undetermined point after the second half of 1071.[54]

The story of the sickness unto death of a Coḷa king may have been refracted, generations later, in the Vaiṣṇava hagiographic fable of Kṛmikaṇṭha, the "worm-throated" Coḷa king. The closing *sarga* of Garuḍavāhanapaṇḍita's *Divyasūricarita* (thirteenth century?) contains a lurid account of the otherwise saintly Rāmānuja's black magic assassination of the Coḷa king, a fanatical Śaiva who had killed and tortured members of his order. The poem's grotesque description of how after a dream-visitation by Viṣṇu, "masses of worms ceaselessly emerged from the hole in his throat, where it had been struck by [the god's] weapon," might contain a reflex of the real illness (cancer? gangrene?) that was the death of Adhirājendra. The devout poet, himself supposedly a *vaidya* or medical practitioner at Śrīraṅgam, has Tyāgarāja, the Śiva of Tiruvārūr and "foremost of Viṣṇu's devotees" declare that this marked "the final seal on the imperium of the Coḷa line of kings," in what is perhaps a distant memory of the cessation of the family's main branch. While it would be folly to see in this mélange of historical detail and narrative invention a straightforward account of the events of the early 1070s – especially so given the lack of any other evidence of the religious persecutions at the story's heart – there may be some glimmer of the Adhirājendra's grim misfortune, as recast by a pious poet centuries later.[55]

Forging Rājendracoḷa's Political Network, 1071–1073

We have already seen the degree to which the evidence furnished by inscriptions is partial, underdetermined, and recalcitrant to historians' reconstructions. For all their remarkable abundance, the surviving records of Coḻa times allow a glimpse of their surrounding society and its politics only through a very restrictive, indeed myopic, set of lenses. Presenting the settled outcome of complex social actions otherwise lost, inscriptions give only the heavily redacted public transcript of collective dealings. A virtue can be made of the necessity imposed by these sources: inscriptions supply us with nearly real-time evidence of the ongoing work of the creation and maintenance of hegemony across the many local societies that existed beneath the Coḻa imperial parasol. Karashima suggested that they might be considered as the libretti of the ongoing dramas of social power in this world.[56] For all its attractions, this notion overstates the dynamism of the patent text of the Coḻa records: they are less like little dramas than a series of carefully composed *tableaux vivants*, within which one can only occasionally glimpse the slight movement of their players.

There is also question of the records' cast of characters. The franchise of epigraphically attested persons was a small and socially restricted one, the rare named laborer or low-caste litigant notwithstanding. The individuals who adopted the roles of the speakers, witnesses, and authorities in the records were often the single representatives of wider collectivities, who were themselves at best supernumeraries on the epigraphic stage. In the case of a successful martial leader or rural big man, we can cautiously infer the wider society in which they operated, but only in negative awareness of the fact that the vast silent majority of that society – the female, the agrestic laborer, the subaltern – fell outside of epigraphical representation altogether. In focusing here especially on the interactions between the Co<u>l</u>a kings' courts in local societies throughout the region, there is a danger of provoking an optical illusion, in which the local worlds only seem to change due to the stimulus of the royal center. This is, of course, patently untrue, as much of the brilliant historiography of the last several decades has shown. But it is in these records of courtly interventions into local worlds – with their cross-cutting projects of state officials, local dominants, assemblies, and collectives, all of them overhung by the images of authority, righteousness and controlled violence constellating around the figure of the king – that the density of interaction is most pronounced. In these tableaux of power, it is often difficult to detect where agency in fact lies, whether with the members of an assembly issuing the inscribed order, with the royal officer acting as a guarantor, or with the figure of the deity in whose juridical personality a donation is made. This makes the value of these documents difficult to capture; it is also what makes them interesting.

Even the social elites who do find mention in the records answer to no clearly demarcated conventions of identification. Sometimes records can be extremely liberal in the information they transmit about a given individual: when (as in a donation from Mahadanapuram near Tiruchirappalli, dated in Rājendracoḷa's fourth year, 1073–1074) we are met with a figure referred to as Cempaṅkuṭi Kauśikan Maturāntaka Vīrapāṇṭiyanāna Co<u>l</u>abrahmamahārājan, we learn a great deal indeed. At a glance we learn this one man's natal village (Cempaṅkuṭi), his Brahmanical clan or *gotra* (Kauśika), and his father's name (Maturāntaka, a prototypically Co<u>l</u>a royal name), as well as his personal name and high title of honor.[57] Elsewhere, the historian is not met with such precision, as in the records composed in the collective voice of the *ūr* or *sabhā* of a given locale. Even when individuals are named, they are often only given in the anonymous lineaments of their titles: the many overlapping local worlds of Co<u>l</u>a times possessed no notarial protocols governing when an individual must be assigned an oikonym and patronym, for instance, or when he or she might only be recorded under the sign of one of the interchangeable honors connected to the Co<u>l</u>a royal establishment.

So it is that in seeking to interpret the politics of the years that Rājendracoḷa issued inscriptions, there is much that cannot be reliably known. The social and personal identities of the agents who appear in these records are often difficult to reconstruct; there is, further, the question of the degree to which the agency of the court can be attributed to the recorded transactions. However, there is much that can be recovered. Compared to the records of Adhirājendra, first of all, there are simply more data to work with: the records in Rājendracoḷa's cousin's name appeared over the course of what was likely little more than a year, while Rājendracoḷa's records bear dates in his second, third, and fourth years: all told, Adhirājendra's nineteen records against thirty-five for Rājendracoḷa. These may be plotted along a spectrum: from the anonymous accounts paying only conventional lip service to his dating formulae through those recording the actions of social elites connecting themselves with Rājendracoḷa and his court, to the occasional public enunciations that can be credibly linked to acts of policy, and to the deliberations and decisions of the king and his court.

Those records detailing temple donations in the voice of the local *sabhā*, which lack any proper names and are usually without a *mĕykkīrtti*, may be placed at one end of this spectrum: at the most, these serve as control evidence, and as diffident attestations that some salient of Rājendracoḷa's political network was at work in their region.[58] Even when records convey personal names, and even when these names are suggestive of courtly provenance or connection, this is often the limit of what we can say about these agents or their actions. So it is that an inscription from the *brahmadeya* of Vākūr records the names and pious donations of two "maid servants" (*veḷḷāṭṭi*) Māṟi and Ceṭṭi, without any other details of their social identity; two earlier records from the neighboring Tirupuvanaṉi complex even mention that prototypical figure of Coḻa central authority, the *atikārikaḷ* or officer, but the figure – likely a member of the magnate lineage that formerly ruled over the territory of Vāṇakoppāṭi, some distance away – remains masked behind his title Uttamacoḻavāṇavarājar.[59]

Elsewhere, a deep sedimentization of local practices is evident in the inscriptional records, linked tenuously with the royal center. Thus, in a significant cluster of donations in the Vīraṭṭāṉeśvara temple near Tirukkovalūr, magnates bearing titles associated with the old Muṉaipāṭi and Milāṭu lordships ostentatiously gave livestock to endow lamps in the names of their relations. These are punctiliously prefaced by Rājendracoḷa's short *mĕykkīrtti*, but in their formulary, they are identical to donations made almost 130 years earlier, in the reigns of Parāntaka and Kṛṣṇa III Rāṣṭrakūṭa; a similarly formulaic donation, dated in Adhirājendra's third year, was made in the same temple shortly before the earliest of these records. These erstwhile little kings, while evidently eager to appear politically correct, seem equally eager to retain the contours of their own local habits of public life.[60]

In one partial and problematically dated record,[61] named members of the *sabhā* of Tiruppātirippuliyūr (Paranṛpaparākramacaturvedimaṅgalam in Co<u>l</u>a nomenclature) sell a parcel of land to Cāttan Pirattāli, the consort (*ākamuṭaiyāḷ*) of Iraṇṭāyiravaṉ, alias *senāpati* Rājendracoḻavesālipperayan, the *kuṭipaḷḷipperumāṉ* of a *brahmadeya*. Here – though the inscription breaks off before the description of the disposition of the land and its revenues – we can see the operation of a social nexus identical to that of the *kuṭippaḷḷi* donations associated with Adhirājendra. The same logic – the appeal to particular powerful individuals, and their public linkage to the authority of the king – is apparent in Rājendracoḷa's earliest definitively dateable record. This record, from Kāñcīpuram and including the *tirumaṉṉi mĕykkīrtti*, mentions a royal order in the 142nd day of Rājendracoḷa's second year – approximately November 2, 1071, likely while Adhirājendra was still alive – that exceptionally transfers the entire village of Pūtamaṇinelvāyil (save some revenues for temple support) to the possession of a single man, Netināyaṉ Cuntaracoḻamūventaveḷāṉ, previously just a landholder in the same village. The co-occurrence of a royal order – in the earliest historical trace of Rājendracoḷa, no less – and the unusual attestation of a prebendal individual village grant in Tondaimandalam point to a public gesture by this new king, perhaps rewarding a loyalist or lending his authorization to the fait accompli of a local big man, a man of the gentry plausibly in the process of emerging as a new magnate.

Another very early royal order shows a similarly interventionist court at work: a second-year record from Tiruvālaṅkāṭu,[62] lacking an exact day, documents the settlement of a group of twenty-five families of oilmongers (members of the *caṅkarappāṭi* caste), to provide oil for temple lamps, in the process renaming them as "Rājendracoḻappāṭi," in what seems to be an extension of the Coḻa habit of rechristening to the level of the caste-community. Several different officials – including a *tirumantiravolai* and an *atikārikaḷ* – were involved in this piece of local social engineering, which involved provisions for the *caṅkarappāṭi*s' access to grazing land, water, and cremation grounds. Another second year record, opening with Rājendracoḷa's long *mĕykkīrtti*, from the ancient and prestigious temple of Tiruvoṟṟiyūr, documents a purchase of land by the temple from numerous local *ūrār*, funded by a cash donation from a magnate *senāpati* from the Kāveri delta.[63] This figure is none other than Paranṛparākṣasanār, alias Vīracoḻa iḷaṅkoveḷār, the same man who had earlier overseen Adhirājendra's distributivist program in Kāñcīpuram. While the lack of exact dates make it impossible to narrow down a precise window of time, this suggests an effort by this courtier to publicly transfer his loyalty to Rājendracoḷa, possibly after the death of his former royal patron.

Finally, in another second year record, again prefaced by the *tirumaṉṉi* eulogy, from the Ādikeśava temple in Ārppākkam, near Kāñcīpuram in the heart of the Tondai country, a cluster of lamp donations is headed off by that of a queen of Rājendracoḷa's, referred to as Trailokkiyamāteviyār, acting in concert with her mother Umainaṅkai and dedicated to one Vikramakesarippallavaraiyar.[64] In another of the donations in this fragmentary document, one of a pair of pastoralists bears the title *cittir-ameḻikoṉ*, "king [or perhaps 'shepherd'] of the Shining Plow."[65] This tantalizing detail, coupled with the presence of the royal women, again suggests the complex political negotiations of these years.

Taken together, these records suggest a pattern of intentional public acts, directed at multiple constituencies throughout the Tondai region and centered on ancient and prestigious temple sites. It was here that the deeds of Rājendracoḷa's court, as well as the polished eloquence of his *mĕykkīrtti*, were concentrated, in a series of early enunciations of his lordship. All of this presents a notable contrast with the early records from the vicinity of the Kāveri delta. Though some inscriptions there do bear the *tirumaṉṉi* eulogy, the records of Rājendracoḷa's regnal years (only one of which dated to his second year) present a staid, anonymous picture of *sabhā*s notarizing local donations and land transactions in the Coḻa king's name.

The major exception to this suggests a crisis of royal power in the kingdom's central territory. This is furnished by a highly anomalous (and apparently no longer extant) record from the village of Vayalūr, in modern Karur district. Dated in Rājendracoḷa's third year, it purports to record the order (*kaṭṭalai*) of three lordly figures, setting certain taxes in cash on agrarian produce in order to provide for the upkeep of the local Tiruvagnīśvara temple and setting fines to be exacted by its governing body. The order ends with civil sanctions and imprecatory formulae, none of which are in the Coḻa chancellery style.[66] Despite the inclusion of Rājendracoḷa's regnal years, this order's issuers appear to act very much under their own authority. By this point – June 1072 to June 1073 – Adhirājendra was certainly no more, but Rājendracoḷa's authority in the heart of the Coḻa country was little more than nominal. There is some evidence to suggest that the Kāveri core was subject to intermittent public chaos in this period: a later document dates a disturbance in the *brahmadeya* of Rājamahendracaturvedimaṅgalam (near Papanasam) to June–July of 1071, at the very beginning of the king's second year. Allegedly, communal conflict between left-handed and right-handed caste groups resulted in the sacking and destruction of the Brahman village's main temple, a loss only rectified nine years later.[67]

It would thus seem to be a mistake to project backward from the king's fully secured reign as Kulottuṅga, and to see the consolidation of his imperial authority as inevitable. It was nothing of the sort: the Co̲la family was large and likely stocked with heirs, and there is no reason to suppose that the mechanisms of royal succession should have worked at all. For elites like the magnate donors of Tirukkovalūr or the ruling troika in Vayalūr, the obedience paid to the royal house was purely a formality. In the period of 1071–1073, the Co̲la state apparatus seems to have ceased to function in its core territories. This returns us to the genuinely political work done by the *mĕykkīrtti*, in all of its rhetorical and intertextual complexity. Tondaimandalam, aggrandized by the old magnate polities, was the scene of the concerted efforts by the courts of Adhirājendra and Rājendracoḷa to secure a loyal elite clientele and a territorial base. Yet both kings' agents in their inscriptions appear to have been drawn from throughout the Co̲la kingdom: like Adhirājendra, a number of Rājendracoḷa's officers hailed from the Kāveri delta, and in at least one case – the magnate Paranṛparākṣasa – it proved possible for a delta aristocrat to navigate from one king's retinue to the other. The evidence for the territorial composition of the official elite for both kings is meager, though this kingdom-wide spread of officials' origins appears typical of earlier kings as well.

It is only in retrospect, then, that we may see that Rājendracoḷa's recruitment of the Tondaimandalam elite was decisively successful, and that this success would prove significant for the later history of Co̲la politics. The martial leaders who would prove to be the two most prominent lords of Kulottuṅga's later court – Karuṇākara Tŏṇṭaimā̲n and Maturāntakateva̲n Po̲n̲nampalakkūtta̲n, alias Naralokavīra – notably linked themselves to their natal region in their courtly self-presentation.[68] Yet more evidence is furnished by the court poetry of the next Co̲la emperor, Vikramaco̲la (r. 1118–1135), in whose court the significance of men from the Tondai country and the erstwhile magnate lordships bulked ever larger. Of those courtiers who can be localized from among the list of court notables contained in Oṭṭakkūttar's *Vikkiramaco̲lavulā*, over half hailed from Jayaṅkŏṇṭaco̲lamaṇḍalam.[69] The evidence of this Toṇṭaiyar junta surrounding Kulottuṅga's son and successor is illuminating in retrospect and prospect both: it casts light both on the crucial transition in the early 1070s and on the warlordism that would mark the closing decades of Co̲la rule, drawn from this same social stock.

Poetic or rhetorical strategies cannot be univocally translated into historical causes: there is nothing that allows the assumption of the efficacy of Rājendracoḷa's anonymous eulogists' text upon the subsequent actions of the Tondaimandalam elite. Nevertheless, in placing the doings of the king's agents at the intersection of the rhetorical and the practical – emblematized in the seamless transition between the verse of the *mĕykkīrtti* and the legalese of the surviving records – some cautious inferences can be ventured. To repeat: Rājendracoḷa, like his ill-fated cousin Adhirājendra, made a project of ruling over the distinctive local societies of Jayaṅkŏṇṭacoḻamaṇḍalam; it is there that the balance of his early records can be found, and the preponderance of those attesting to direct courtly interventions. The work of the *mĕykkīrtti* needs to be situated within this give-and-take of emolument and clientage, as the controlled exercise of a species of public argument. A great many of the Coḻa kings' subjects may have heard the sonorous phrases of their preambles as just so much verbiage. But some listeners at least must have heard in these an appeal to the imagination, one that resonated with what they knew of the king and what they saw realized by the men and women of his court in their own local worlds.

Kolar: In the Court of the Vermillion Queen

One must look just beyond the frontiers of Tondaimandalam for the clearest case of the intersection between local interests and courtly designs. Traveling upstream along the Palar river – the most important watercourse of the northern Tamil plains – leads to the ancient country of Kuvalāḷanāḍu, what is now Karnataka's Kolar district. Distinct from the surrounding countryside of the southern Mysore plateau, with its rich red soil and heavy forest, it is a terrain of boulder-studded mountains jutting out of scrubby ground: even today it has the feel of a borderland. This region, which had once been the home-land of the Gaṅga kings of Tālakāḍu, had been the scene of a series of epigraphical interventions by Rājarāja and Rājendra. But the Kuvalāḷa country was in 1072 fallow lands for Coḻa court influence – with the exception of a single short record dated in Vīrarājendra's years (in Tamil but of purely local style, commemorating a *satī*), there had not been a single Coḻa inscription in the region for fifteen years.[70] Rājendracoḷa crucially had the region all to himself. The diverse nature of his early inscriptions in this confined territory lays bare the complex process by which Rājendracoḷa's court and local actors came into relation. More to the point, the king's early actions here make clear the decisive part played by the ideational in the creation of his emergent hegemony. In its most dramatic form, this serves as a provocation to rethink the limits and even the nature of what we conceive as the politics of the medieval Co<u>l</u>a world.

Located directly to the west-northwest of the Tondai country, Kolar was even more arid and less hospitable to agriculture.[71] But it lay in the direct path of expanding Co<u>l</u>a power, especially in the context of the intensifying military competition with the Cālukyas, and the early decades of the 1000s saw the old Gaṅga and Noḷamba lines extirpated, and the region incorporated into the imperial territorial imagination as Nikarilico<u>l</u>amaṇḍalam.[72] Kolar supplied a marchland and possibly a secure staging area for the Co<u>l</u>a campaigns to the north and west: it is not a coincidence that it was during the reign of Rājendra, whose *mĕykkīrtti* gave pride of place to his Deccani victories in Raichur, Banavase, and Kulpak, all to the northwest, that the Co<u>l</u>a involvement in Kolar really took off. This involvement seems to have extended beyond the pattern, typical of the delta and the Tamil-speaking southern plains, of the support of local elites and carefully calibrated acts of religious generosity. In a region that differed in its spoken language, its social complexion and – most significantly – in its structures of rural domination, the Co<u>l</u>a kings appear to have introduced settlers from their own lands in order to shore up their local power.[73] Certainly the Co<u>l</u>as and their agents sought to reproduce the imperial system there, issuing inscriptions in Tamil and integrating the region into the system of titles and nomenclature.

This is the background against which one can read a much-discussed pair of inscriptions dated to Rājendracoḷa's third year, from the villages of Avani and Uttanur.[74] Beginning with the *tirumaṉṉi* eulogy, these two almost-identical documents record the judgment (*matam*) of the *pĕriya-viṣayam* of "Śrī Rājendracoḷa's eighteen countries" and the *mahāseṉai* or "Great Army," said in one text to belong to the *valaṅkai*, the right-hand caste sodality. While the bulk of the records is given over to the details of rates of assessment, exemptions from tax, and standards of land mensuration, the records begin with a sweeping gesture:

> By the favor of the king, Śrī Rājendraco<u>l</u>a, the sacred plow of all the lands has come together[75] and made up the seventy-eight *nāṭu*s of Colamandalam and the 48,000 territory of Tondaimandalam . . . the *pĕriyaviṣayam* of Śrī Rājendracoḷa's eighteen countries which is made up of . . . and the heavily-armed Great Army [of the Right Hand] have agreed to [*kaṇṭa*, lit. "seen"] the following judgment: Ever since the appearance of the illustrious family of the Co<u>l</u>as, there has not been a tax on either cows or buffalos. In these eighteen countries, this spurious [?] tax has been imposed . . . The *atikārikaḷ* A<u>l</u>akiyaco<u>l</u>amūventaveḷār, since this spurious tax on cattle and buffalos has now been imposed [?[76]], declared, "This tax should not be paid."[77]

After setting a schedule of revenue standards and the rods for field measurement, the records conclude:

Thus have we made inscribed and issued this order [*cācaṉam*], inclusive [?] of the judgment agreed to by the *pĕriyaviṣayam* of the eighteen countries and the heavily-armed Great Army [of the Right Hand]. Whatever tax that has been cancelled by the *pĕriyaviṣayam* of the eighteen countries and the heavily-armed Great Army ... anyone who pays the tax, he destroys brahmans cow, tawny cows, and *nirai* kine on the banks of the Ganges, and [brahminicide is the result / they destroy Vārāṇasī, becoming great sinners]

The text from Avani breaks off here; that of Uttanur continues:

they become enemies of the *pĕriyaviṣayam* of the eighteen countries and the heavily-armed Great Army. Those who maintain ... this stone inscription ... they gain the power of this judgment in perpetuity [?]. Thus we of the *viṣaya* of the eighteen countries and the heavily armed Great Army have made this stone inscription.[78]

The record then ends with conventional imprecations in Tamil and Sanskrit.

In their language, in their areas of explicit concern, and in the social dynamic that can be seen at work within them, these two records from Kolar bear obvious comparison with the *cittirameḻi* records from Tāmaraippākkam discussed earlier. For all that they set themselves out as drawing from the whole of the Tamil-speaking Coḻa dominions, this connection, along with considerations of geography, suggests that the collective groups mentioned here were likely settlers from Tondaimandalam; they might well be classed as "military colonists" hailing from the region's "conquering peasantry."[79] The *mahāseṉai*, with its evident connections to the "right-hand" warrior sodalities attested since the early 1000s, links these documents yet again to the militarization of Coḻa society,[80] but it is the name of the other collective, the *pĕriyaviṣayam* "of Śrī Rājendracoḷa's eighteen countries," that is especially telling. This name forges the strongest link with the Tāmaraippākkam declarations of two decades earlier, reproducing the formula seen there of the *pĕriyanāṭu* "gathered in the Rājendracoḻa hall" as the collective agent rejecting a claim to exaction. The change from *nāṭu* to *viṣayam* likely reflects the transition to the different system of land-tenurial practice observed in Kannada country, where the *nāḍu* pertained to a different level of the landed order than it did in the Tamil plains, while the totemic reference to the eighteen countries suggests the links provided by such translocal social conglomerates as the Ayyāvoḷe 500 merchant syndicate, who may have provided the circulatory medium by which these collectivities extended and reproduced themselves.[81]

The domestication to local norms visible in the shift from *pĕriyanāṭu* to *pĕriyaviṣayam* captures the social strain productive of this collective judgment. The gentry and armed cultivators who made up these two collectives pointedly rejected the imposition of a poll tax on livestock precisely because it was uncustomary in their Tamil-speaking natal region in the Coḻa domains, invoking a sort of *ius Damilicum* in their right to exemption. The language of these records – whose textual constitution leaves much to be desired – is ambiguous, but these men's awareness of this perceived injustice and their decision to reject it and to impose their own terms in the revenue settlement took their bearings from precedent extending back to the Coḻa expansion of Rājendra's time and figured around an appeal to his royal favor or *aruḷ*, as well as the support garnered from that king's grandson and namesake, as mediated by his official Aḻakiyacoḻa mūventaveḷār.[82] This understanding of the record would mean abandoning the interpretation advanced by Nilakanta Sastri that these inscriptions documented Aḻakiyacoḻaṉ's depredations as the acts of "a self-willed or autocratic ruler or chieftain," whose illegitimate exactions were resisted through appeal to the higher justice of the king.[83] The language of the records and the parallel furnished by the analogous records from Tāmaraippākkam suggest, on the contrary, that the presence of this man of the gentry was meant to lend imprimatur to the decision of the collective, and to provide a channel for the king's authority.[84]

These records furnish a test case for observing the rhetorical work of Rājendracoḷa's *mĕykkīrtti* up close. The image of the king that his eulogy constructed – veteran of Deccani campaigns, heir at once to the legacy of the lunar line of the Cālukyas and the brilliance of the Coḻa sun, a soldier-king whose success was a consequence of his fighting spirit, generosity, and charisma – seems calibrated to attract precisely the sort of men who made up the *pĕriyaviṣayam* and the *mahāseṉai.* Self-consciously a part of the Coḻa order yet physically, socially, and culturally distinct from it, eager to place themselves in a pedigree linked to the Tamil plains while remaining attentive to their particularist localism, proudly assertive of themselves and their martial bona fides, these men might have seen in the carefully maintained image of the young Coḻa–Cālukya king a man very much like themselves. Inasmuch as these collectivities were in communication with similar groups further down the Palar in Jayaṅkŏṇṭacoḻamaṇḍalam – for which the accord between these two records and those of Tāmaraippākkam supplies evidence – we can hypothesize the wider reception that the *mĕykkīrtti* may have garnered. It was on the shoulders of men like these that Rājendracoḷa ultimately rode to his imperial accession around 1074: here we can see the emerging accord between these men and his court in vivo.

Figure 2.5 Kolaramma temple, exterior (showing Rājendracoḷa's inscription)
From *Epigraphia Carnatica*. Edited by B. Lewis Rice and R. Narasimhacarya. Volume 10: Kolar District. Bangalore: Mysore Government Central Press, 1905, frontispiece. Reproduced by kind permission of the Syndics of Cambridge University Library.

But before the issue of this proclamation, men of Rājendracoḷa's court had already been active in Kolar. Among the eight surviving records dated in his second regnal year, by far the longest is the remarkable inscription housed on the outer walls of what is now called the Kolaramma temple in the chief town of the modern district. The temple is strikingly unlike the Coḻa temple architecture of the plains, its compact fortress-like bulk forcibly resistant to the influence of the surrounding hills; while only moderately decorated with exterior sculpture, its squat shape prefigures the later Vorticist masterpieces of the Hoysala temples of Belur, Somnathpur, and Halebid (see Figure 2.5). Its current form dates to the reign of Rājendra, whose court devoted particular interest to the site; one record from his time details a panoply of donations in land to the temple's resident goddess (*piṭāriyār*) in the king's seventh, eleventh, and sixteenth years; another, dated to his twenty-second year, describes the reconstruction in stone of the brick structures in the complex, overseen by an official from a prominent Colamandalam Brahman family.[85]

The investment in the goddesses of this region in Rājendra's time is not limited to this temple site. Two inscriptions from about seven miles to the northwest, one of them dated in Rājendra's sixth year (*ca.* 1018), announce the joint actions by local Tamil settlers and seemingly a member of the king's household to maintain the ritual sacrifice of a goat on every Tuesday of the year, dedicated to Cāmuṇḍeśvarī, the goddess of Jayaṅkōṇṭacoḻacaturvedimaṅgalam and the *kuṟaṭṭiyar* of the *nāṭu*. This was apparently a newly instituted practice, rather than a local customary observance, as they record fines in gold to be levied against the (Kannadiga?) local headman should the animals not be provided.[86]

These sparse fragments cast significant light on the huge document of Rājendracoḷa's second year incised along the walls of the Kolar temple. The record begins with two men, the *atikārikaḷ* Ampalavan Tiruppontaiyār, bearing the title Vīracikāmaṇimūventaveḷār, and Nirupacikāmaṇi Viḻupparaiyaṉ, a *mukaveṭṭi* or mid-level bureaucrat of the *puravuvaritiṇaikkaḷam* revenue office, both from Tondaimandalam, opening a hearing in the outer enclosure of the temple. Questioning an unnamed *kannāṭapaṇḍitar* in control of a local monastic establishment and a group of temple priests, the *atikārikaḷ* is said to ask whether sufficient revenue in gold (*māṭai*) had been converted into paddy from temple lands to provide for the deity and her servants. Receiving the answer that such endowments were not in place up until the present, the officer launches into an enormous account of incoming revenue and a calendar of ritual observances for an entire pantheon of deities headed by the goddess Cāmuṇḍeśvarī, some daily, some monthly, some solsticially, and some annually, all calculated in the exact amounts of food, cloth, and coin to be received.[87]

Even more remarkably – in fact, uniquely – this meticulously detailed document accords precisely with an extant textual authority, a work calling itself the *Brahmayāmala*, cast in the register of Sanskrit typical of Tantric texts. This discovery was made by the doyen of scholars of Śaivism, Alexis Sanderson, who demonstrated the relationship between the temple's observances and the liturgical details of this work, which differs from the Śākta scripture of the same name, the so-called *Brahmayāmala-Picumata*. The southern work has some evident ties with the earlier text, taking on the names of its core pantheon of goddesses and the all-important hardware of its central *mantra*-system.[88] But whereas the *Picumata* is above all focused on the acquisition of magical powers and visionary encounters with wild female spirits, the temple-*tantra* presents a detailed liturgy meant to secure royal victory and success.[89] The many observances provided for in the temple inscriptions are of a wider amplitude than the prescriptions of the *tantra*, but there are distinct continuities. So, for instance, the Vedic recitation provided for in the epigraphs finds no correspondence in the *Brahmayāmala* text, while the offering of alcoholic drink (*matiyapāṉam*) for the worship of both male and female Tantrics does. Even more arresting, temple epigraph and tantric injunctions both enjoin the offering of a goat every Tuesday of the year, just as in the nearby inscriptions dated in Rājendra's years.[90]

The inscription's opening scene of the hearing between the two Tŏṇṭaiyar men and the temple's officiants is brazenly fictive. The records dated in Rājendra's regnal years belie the central claim that the temple had been operating without endowments. Something had evidently changed in the temple's administrative and liturgical order: this alerts us to the composition of the dramatis personae represented in the bulk of the record, especially those awarded incomes in its new arrangement. The greatest beneficiary of the new order, at 180 *kalam* of paddy per annum, was the same *kannāṭapaṇḍitar* who was given pride of place in the record's opening. This figure, whose title perhaps connects him with the regionally prominent Kālamukha Śaiva order, was a *parvenu* in the temple's epigraphical culture, appearing in no earlier records. The next two most highly compensated figures, at sixty *kalam* a year – note the steep difference! – were a Brahman priest called Māraciṅkabhaṭṭaṉ, seemingly an incumbent from the temple's earlier regime, and a tantric Śaiva virtuoso (*bhayiravamutali*, "chief of the *bhairava* ascetics"), one Irājentirak Kaliyugabhairava.[91] Ranged beneath these eminences was an *équipe* of non-Brahman temple priests, Vedic reciters, *tāntrika*s, and assorted service personnel (watchmen, potters, sweepers, etc), each allotted a share of the temple's income. But it is in the relationship between the three major figures of abbot, Brahman officiant, and tantric renouncer that the temple's institutional dynamic can be inferred. Earlier records refer to a highly conventional liturgical order, with Brahmans performing the same observances seen throughout the Coḻa domains. The order to which Tiruppontaiyār and Nirupacikāmaṇi lent their imprimatur, by contrast, was an unusual amalgam of local practices such as the Tuesday goat-offering, the mantric and iconological underpinnings of the *Brahmayāmala*, and the emerging forms of the pan-regional southern temple cult. The liturgical and practical arrangements instituted in this long record thus marked a de novo resetting of the temple's calendar as well as its internal hierarchy, with the *paṇḍita* and his officiants in charge, the representative of the old Brahman priesthood incorporated yet subordinate, and the institutionalization of an entirely new mixed regime of worship, both orthoprax and esoteric.

Among the service personnel given allotments is a figure tasked with "teaching grammar and *Yāmaḷam*": it was this figure who may himself have produced the surviving scriptural guide for this very specific temple culture. *Tantra* and inscriptional corpus likely emerged conjointly, through a process of mutually reinforcing composition. While it might be objected that the poor Sanskrit of the *tantra* seems unlikely to be from the hand of an instructor in *vyākaraṇa*, one notes that this lecturer's salary was the same as the temple clerk and carpenter: a craftsman meant to yield workmanlike results, rather than a product of an elite literary training and sensibility.[92]

For all the interest that this evidence affords – and it is among the rarest pictures we have of the real mechanics of medieval South Indian temple practice – the question of motivation remains. Why did the workings-out of the organization of a regional temple elicit the interest of Rājendracoḷa's court, still more the massive intervention to which the inscription attests, by far the longest of the king's early records? Given the court's involvement in the declaration of the Tamil settlers in the region less than a year later, one could argue that support for the temple may have helped to render legitimate the rule of the arriviste king, that it lent some of its glamor to him in the wake of his support for the new regime of the *kannāṭapaṇḍitar* and his Tantric co-religionists. The abbot, the antinomian ascetic, and the Brahman priest from the temple's old dispensation were all political actors in their own right, and their recruitment to Rājendracoḷa's cause was as consequential as that of the gentry, lordly, and Brahman figures who declared for him in the Tamil plains.

Certainly these men and their followers merit consideration in this way. But these were really only figures of significance in Kuvalāḷanāṭu itself; their reputation and authority do not appear to have extended farther than the town in which they lived. There is nothing to suggest that the temple's officiants participated in any wider network that ramified into the Coḻa country; in this, they present a notable contrast to the collectives of the *pĕriyaviṣayam* and the *mahāseṉai* of the Avani and Uttanur records. If Rājendracoḷa's agents were actively engaged in winning over a local agent, that agent was of an altogether different sort than these temple functionaries. I refer to the goddess herself.

This goddess was, just like the ritual of her temple, a confection of several parts. She combined within herself the figure who had been worshipped in the stony landscape of Kolar for at least two generations prior to 1072, the demon-slaying warrior-maiden long considered to be native to the Deccan, and the wild Tantric power-goddess of the Yāmala cult. In her mythic and ritual profile, she thus embodied a cosmopolitan ideal distinct from that of the network of royal courts from which Rājendracoḷa emerged. This fusion of roles was already under way in Rājendra's era: the great empire-builder, for whom Kolar served as a martial staging-area – a spearhead pointed at the heart of the Cālukya country – paid evident homage to this war-goddess, to the point where his servants coercively extracted local livestock for her propitiation. With the integration of the ritual and mantric technology of the *yāmala* cult, the goddess was augmented yet more. In the new order, her temple became an engine for converting material goods – cloth, paddy, and the flesh and blood of goats, among other things – into martial and thus political power. When I visited the Kolāramma temple in early February 2010, a *pūjā* conducted by a group of women worshippers obliquely captured something of this sanguinary heritage. In place of animals, they had prepared a massive lamp offering, each single light made from a hollow half of a lime, filled with oil and smeared with vermillion. With their soft flesh, ultimately consumed in the act of worship, and their thick daubs of brilliant crimson, these were evident surrogates for the blood offerings once given to the goddess.

Like his mother's father, Rājendracoḷa retained designs over southern Karnataka; but his service to Kolar's presiding goddess was likely motivated as much by the powers she lent him in his maneuvers within the Coḻa country. The Kannada-speaking uplands were connected to the Tondai plains, and beyond them to the heart of the delta itself, and this blood-drinking feminine power would be a commanding ally to have at the young king's back as he embarked on the path to the throne.[93] There is, in fact, a hint in Rājendracoḷa's early life, before the issue of his first inscriptions, of his awareness of the powers to which such transgressive deities could give access. Among the spare inscriptional remains of the kings of Cakrakoṭṭam – the scene of the young Rājiga's early soldiering, awarded such a prominent place in Rājendracoḷa's *mĕykkīrtti*s – is a copperplate charter detailing provisions for the royal sponsorship and maintenance of a regime of periodic human sacrifice. This cult, remnants of which endured into Bastar's colonial modernity, was certainly active during Rājiga's sojourns there, as the charter is punctiliously dated to October 1065.[94] It is possible to imagine that Rājendracoḷa or members of his circle were aware of this practice. In any event, as Rājendracoḷa advanced in the world to the point where he began to issue his own public orders, one of the first recorded acts bearing his imprimatur was a massive investment in the ritual power of this Tantric warrior goddess, one whose cult, while not demanding the ultimate transgression of human offerings (the *mahāpaśu* or "great beast" of the Tantric ritual imagination), nonetheless depended on offerings of blood and liquor, revolting to Brahmanical orthodoxy.

But what does it mean to speak of Cāmuṇḍeśvarī or Bhadrakālī as a political actor? An easy answer would default into an explanatory logic of representation: the goddess was a figment of collective imagination, a screen onto which the local people of the Kolar country and the Tamil émigrés could project their own culturally specific ambitions, anxieties, and desires. There once was a man who wished to be king: he convinced himself and others that the goddess could help him and, as luck would have it, he succeeded. With its reductively Bergerian (or Kauṭalyan!) social psychology, this representationalist understanding is unsatisfying, in that it drives a wedge between the putatively real and the putatively imaginal politics of Rājendracoḷa's time, or tends toward a chilly relativism ("that's what they thought"). This relativist argument, further, can only be made to work through an astigmatic foreclosure of further interpretation and analysis: we run up against the limits of intelligibility the moment historical actors cease to behave in ways that we ourselves might do. But it is the first of these two options – premised on the historian's ability to divide out the real and the imaginary – that points toward a way out of this impasse. By introducing a divide between historical action that is potentially coherent and that which is spurious, and so interposing categories of genuine and false consciousness into the account of the past, a space opens into which these very dualisms may be collapsed. If a fictive person like Cāmuṇḍeśvarī consists only as a play of representations differentially available first to the people in this time and place and then – processed through the aleatory filter of the passing of centuries – to us, can we speak any differently of a substantive person like Rājendracoḷa? To be certain, one was a confection of language, inert material, and imaginative energy; the other was a self-aware biological creature subject to physiological processes, and capable of autonomous action: someone who ate, slept, spoke, fathered children, got sick, and died. But it is not casuistry, much less a surrender of secular historical reason, to insist that as prior entities who provoked and incited the actions of others, and who supplied occasions for description, invention, and contestation through language, goddess and Coḻa king were crucially alike.

However paradoxical it is to admit it, our reliable sense of the physical existence of the goddess actually far outstrips that of the once-living man. No images of Rājendracoḷa survive, no personal paraphernalia, and – a few stylized lines of poetry or royal proclamation notwithstanding – not a single word that can be dependably assigned to his mouth or pen. By contrast, we can summon up a very clear image of the goddess's worldly existence. Both inscription and *tantra* agree that to make Cāmuṇḍeśvarī fit to receive offerings in her place in Kolar, her central *mantra* – her ontologically prior, acoustic form – needed to be installed in a pot, either alone or as accompanied by the mother-goddesses of her retinue, similarly fixed. The *tantra* provides a template for the temple's ritual prescriptions; read together, the idealities of the Sanskrit scripture and the accountancy of the Tamil records snap into alignment. A square of nine pots should be set up in the temple's *maṇḍapa*, with the goddess's pot in the center and two sets of four ancillary goddesses each installed in the cardinal and intermediate directions. The *tantra* explains that the pots should be made of gold, silver, or copper; only in the absence of these can they be earthenware. Both *tantra* and temple record agree that the goddess's pot is to be wrapped in a cloth, for which the inscription records an allowance of one-eighth of a *kācu* for the replacement at the time of solstices and eclipses. It is only in the presence of this more primary form that the goddess could then be translated to an anthropomorphic image, through the successive imposition of yet more *mantra*s.[95]

All of this is meant to take place under the supervision of a head officiant, an *ācārya*, conversant in the *Brahmayāmala*, who in the eyes of *tantra* is the orchestrator of the whole performance. Beyond this figure, however, the summoning of the goddess involved a whole complex division of labor and a complex entanglement of the material, the linguistic, and the imaginal. The pot that served as the material locus of the goddess's realization, with its irreducible thingyness, rested at the center of this network of persons, objects, phonemes, and mental events, but was not simply reducible to any of these. This material locus is strangely fitting, recalling as it does the Sanskrit logician's stock example of the potter and his handiwork: What is the interplay between the potter, his wheel, and the materials on which he works? Does the pot exist within the lump of clay, or does it somehow endure after shattering into pieces? When, after all, does a pot begin (or cease) to be "a pot"? So too with the bloodthirsty goddess whom *tantra* and official document insist is uniquely instantiated in just such a pot: she emerges from a set of intersecting continua – the clay or metal worked by human hands, the livestock offerings, the Sanskrit *mantra*s uttered by human vocal apparatus, the swirl of associations and preexisting cultural stereotypes that inform the mental image of a wild, virginal divine warrioress, the local projects of the Śaiva religieuses of the temple, and those of the Tŏṇṭaiyar men dispatched to negotiate with them – without being reducible to any of these.

This sort of an approach has an uncanny undertone to it, to be certain, and it opens up further questions (Was the goddess worshipped in state at Kolar "the same" as the *kuṟaṭṭiyar* worshipped nearby a few years earlier? Was she "the same" goddess whom Cayaṅkŏṇṭār made the center of his *Kaliṅkattupparaṇi* a generation later?) But it supplies a point of oblique comparison for the varied skeins of individual effort and contingent chance, of material resources, action, belief, intention, and suasion, that made it possible for one publicly imagined person – the prince

Rājendracoḷa, with just his sword and his two shoulders – to be translated into another, the emperor Kulottuṅga.[96]

Conclusion: "Lofty in His Families"

The earliest surviving pronouncement of the Co<u>l</u>a king Rājakesarivarman Kulottuṅga is dated May 1074.[97] It records a royal order, issued from the Cetirāja hall in the royal residence in Pĕrumpaṟṟapuliyūr, the modern Cidambaram, and took the form of a communiqué sent to Śiva as master of the temple of Tirukkaccālai in Kāñcīpuram. We have seen this order already, in the Introduction: at the request of one Pava<u>l</u>akuṉṟanāṭuṭaiyāṉ, a member of the gentry of Pūṇṭi, a village in the nearby *koṭṭam* of Kāliyūr was converted into tax-free *devadāna* land in the temple's favor. Rescripted by two officials of the *puravuvaritiṇaikalam* and witnessed by a cluster of officials (all of them from the delta), the royal exemption was passed on to the temple and subsequently incised on its walls.

The significance of this small piece of court business is easy to miss. It is, to begin with, notable that the order was issued from Cidambaram. This is the first such documented connection between the king and that temple, which was long a site of Tŏṇṭaiyār religious interest and which would prove to be of enormous significance for the king's family and his courtiers. The temple's Dancing God would come to far overshadow the goddess of Kolar as an important actor in the kingdom and beyond. It also marks, possibly for the first time, the use of a new *mĕykkīrtti* formula, and the abandonment of the *tirumaṉṉi* eulogy. The new preamble, beginning *puka<u>l</u>mātu viḷaṅka jayamātu virumpa* [/] *nilamakaḷ vaḷara kamalāmakaḷ puṇarka* ("as the Lady Fame shines, as the Lady Victory grows desirous, as the Earth-goddess flourishes, as the Lotus-goddess joins with him"), would go on to be used for another four decades, alternating with a much longer text with which it shares its first word (*puka<u>l</u> cū<u>l</u>nta puṇari*, "Surrounded by his fame," introduced some months later);[98] except for the desultory mention of victories over the Cera and Paṇṭiya kings, the *puka<u>l</u>mātu* eulogy makes no effort at historical reference, much less the complex rhetorical gambits of the earlier text. A no less important shift can be seen in the royal style of Kulottuṅga's title: along with his new regnal name, he is referred to as *tiripuvaṉaccakkiravarttikaḷ*, the Wheel-Turning Emperor of the Three Worlds. It is the first time that a Co<u>l</u>a king claimed such an honor.

Though no records attest to a second coronation or any other commemoration, the Co<u>l</u>a court sought in its changed formulary habits and in its public ceremonies to demarcate a clear dividing line with the past. The emperor would only ever be subsequently referred to as Rājendracoḷa by members of his own family; henceforth to his subjects he was Kulottuṅga. The name was an inspired choice: breaking with the onomastic conventions of the preceding six incumbents on the Co<u>l</u>a throne, it was evidently meant to convey a royal dignity above the fray of what had been the chaotic internal machinations of the Co<u>l</u>a dynasty. It also contained a subtle hindward glance at its bearer's early life, leaving tantalizingly indeterminant just how many *kula*s it referred to: for at least one later promoter of Kulottuṅga's fame, the poet Cayaṅkŏṇṭār, the king was explicitly "supreme in *both* families," the product of the successful union of the Co<u>l</u>a and Cālukya crowns.[99] The transformation from ambitious prince to the king of kings appears from this point onward to have been an accomplished fact.

Such anyway was the picture Kulottuṅga's court sought to convey. It was, however, by no means the case that this had been the only possible outcome of the events of the early 1070s. The former Rājendracoḷa had publicly emerged in the kingdom ruled by his mother's relations with a great deal already in his favor: his pedigree within the ruling line stretched back to the kingdom's imperial foundation under Rājarāja; his place within it was further buttressed by his marriage to his cross-cousin, who would come to be called Maturāntaki. Yet security of lineage was not alone sufficient to ensure his eventual succession, even had it not been the case that Adhirājendra had met an early death. While there is no need to posit a civil war or an Orientalist fantasia of palace assassination to account for Adhirājendra's death, the inscriptions issued in the two royal cousins' names clearly describe distinct if overlapping patterns of action, jockeying for power in the northern reaches of the kingdom's Tamil-speaking territories. That Tondaimandalam served as the theater of royal competition jibes with its significance in the Co<u>l</u>a landed order – as the entryway to the open country of the Deccan, as the natal region of a significant proportion of the empire's gentry and Brahmanical officialdom, and as the heart of its mercantile endeavors. It is also suggestive of the complex cocktail of social forces at play there. Greatly expanded by the cashiering of the older magnate polities, and possessed of long traditions of local particularism and civic life, Tondaimandalam was the scene of the appearance of new forms of collective organization like the *cittirame<u>l</u>i* assemblies and the site of the landed settlement of arriviste groups of warriors like the *kuṭippaḷḷi*, the quintessential new men of the second half of the eleventh century.

When exactly Vīrarājendra died, or when he ceased effectively to rule, is unclear, but it would have clearly ratcheted up the stakes of the competition between the societies centered upon Adhirājendra and

Rājendracoḷa. The ambience of conflict may have been more generalized, leading to anarchic conditions even in the core regions of Colamandalam, and efforts there to establish pockets of independent rule. While the practical elaboration of a network of political clients and dependent allies can be seen in the operative portions of both men's inscriptions, the richest and most eloquent testimony of their careful positioning is in their *mĕykkīrtti*s. Adhirājendra's eulogy, the first to appear, deftly argued for the legitimacy and priority of direct royal succession, both in its patent argument and in its subtle linkages to the eulogies of his predecessors, especially his father Vīrarājendra's spectacular short *mĕykkīrtti*. Rājendracoḷa's *mĕykkīrtti*, crafted in evident response, takes this intertextuality a step further, while setting out its subject's distinctive early history and arguing for his warrior bona fides.

Much of the work that went into marshaling the political network that would change Rājendracoḷa into Kulottuṅga likely took place after Adhirājendra's death: the crucial period seems to have been 1072–1073. As the capillary work of patronage and public acclamation went on in Tondaimandalam and increasingly in Colamandalam, the by-then solely ruling king's court invested particular effort in shoring up its basis in the vicinity of Kolar, the Nikarilicoḻamaṇṭalam of the Coḻa state imaginary. These efforts were conspicuously at work in the pronouncements of the self-styled *pĕriyaviṣayam* and Great Army of the Right Hand, whose public independence and social composition link them to the emergent collectivities of Tondaimandalam. But even greater significance inheres to the court's efforts to adapt, localize, and channel the fierce powers of Kolar's martial cult of Cāmuṇḍeśvarī. The power of this cult's tutelary goddess, formerly directed toward the Coḻa's Deccani antagonists, was turned back into the kingdom's heart, so to blazon the warrior credentials of its royal patron. It is this ambidexterity of the king's relationship to the Tantric divinity's real and worldly power that may have suggested to Cayaṅkŏṇṭār some of his theme in the *Kaliṅkattupparaṇi*.

Kulottuṅga's imperial success was not just a consequence following from the fortuitous circumstances of his birth and lineage, or from his good fortune to have been the last man standing when it came time to crown a new emperor. The accomplishments and individual efforts of this one man were in only a minor part of the complex tangle of projects and longer historical trajectories, a tangle that can only be partially picked apart at the great remove from which we now know of it. To be certain, the king supplied a focal point; but the shifting configurations of courtiers, literati, aristocrats and a certain war-goddess can be traced around him, and it is these configurations that constitute the bulk of our knowledge of the kingdom's politics.

We lack a robust indigenous lexicon with which to speak of these politics. Kings, queens, and deities all behave with *aruḷ, atikāris* make petitions (*viṇṇapañ cĕytal*) and proclaim (*evutal*), and poets known and anonymous compose (*iyaṟṟal*) and praise (*pārāṭṭutal*). But there is little in the way of an emic language for the sort of collective and individual actions that the evidence presents us, and thus no way to capture what it was the political actors understood themselves to be doing.[100] It was more generally the case that there was lack of a tacit or explicit political theory suited to the kinetic nature of the medieval Indian state.[101] And yet, it moved: the forging of an alliance between the royal line and the lords and gentry of Tondaimandalam would prove to be of enormous consequence over the course of the twelfth century, supplying the enabling conditions that would give rise to the warlords typical of the kingdom's terminal decades. Less perceptibly, but plausibly, the regime inaugurated by Kulottuṅga seems to have accelerated the rise of the region's collectivities and caste sodalities (the "transition to supralocal integration") that was to supply the major dynamic of the social history of later times.

This was not simply the adventitious outcome of historical processes occurring behind the backs of its actors. On the contrary, we are presented with evidence of knowledgeable agents whose actions, whatever their unintended consequences, were coherent, legible, and at least partly amenable to our understanding. The contradictions of the mid-century Coḻa polity – the chronic overextension of its authority due to its unprecedented martial and political success, and the ongoing and irreversible surrender of its constituent institutions in the face of *brahmadeya* liberties and temple exemptions – were not resolved by Kulottuṅga's imperial accession: such contradictions do not admit of simple solution. But the alliance between Kulottuṅga (and his heirs) and the Tondaimandalam elite temporarily welded one potentially restive part of the kingdom firmly to the center. This also helped to secure temporary Coḻa access to the king's native region of Veṅgī, almost the equal of the Kāveri delta in its agrarian wealth. Though sometimes read as a symptom of Coḻa decline, Kulottuṅga's subsequent abandonment of the Coḻa foothold in Sri Lanka, his resumption of indirect rule in Pāṇṭimaṇṭalam, the streamlining of the proliferating network of officials, and the lack of further territorial aggrandizement are all suggestive of a clear-sighted *realpolitik* among the kingdom's ruling society. The periodic crises of the recent past and the seeming chaos of the first years of the 1070s gave way to a retrenchment of the Coḻa state, and the creation of a new political settlement.

Kulottuṅga was to go on to rule for almost five decades after 1074, and many of the innovations ushered in under the new settlement were to become well-worn parts of the landscape during his reign. His own court poets would include a sidelong acknowledgment of the early martial successes – the stuff of the old *tirumaṉṉi* eulogy, forever abandoned after 1074 – speaking of them as occurrences *iḷaṅkoparuvattil*, "during his days as a prince." But his translation from Rājendracoḷa to Kulottuṅga was to remain otherwise unspoken in his court's later pronouncements. That his reign marked a real break with the past is something, perhaps understandably, about which the authors of his later *mĕykkīrtti*s remain silent. But in the hands of others, Kulottuṅga's coming to power was to provide the subject matter for a kaleidoscopic diversity of interpretations, each of which laboring one way or another to capture something of the caesura that it represented. It is in the work of poets, then, rather than in any theory of politics, where we can find evidence of the spectrum of understanding about the nature of political agency and the logic of historical change that was available to Kulottuṅga and his contemporaries.

Summary

In June of 1070, there were three Coḻa kings; by 1074, there was only one. There is no direct indication of political violence or civil war, but a considerable amount to evidence allows us to track the different court societies' maneuverings. Vīrarājendra, the senior-most member of the triad, died within months of its formation; the dauphin Adhirājendra didn't last much longer, dying probably in the closing months of 1071. Adhirājendra's court and clients nevertheless left enough textual traces of their actions that a complementary pattern can be observed between them and the actions undertaken by the court society surrounding Rājendracoḷa. Both courts concentrated their efforts on political control of Tondaimandalam, a region that for all of its connections to the Kāveri heartland possessed particular features in its social complexion and its political culture. Both courts issued complex rhetorical appeals in their *mĕykkīrtti*s, which were full of intertextual echoes of earlier eulogies. The strategies each pursued in the northern parts of the imperial kingdom were straightforward: martial magnates were publicly associated with the particular kings, and local groups materially benefited from the disbursement of courtly largesse.

Adhirājendra's death, however it transpired, did not simply leave the path to the imperial throne open to Rājendracoḷa, as the Coḻa hegemony underwent an evident crisis in its core territory for at least another year.

The precise events that underlay its stabilization remain obscure, as do those events leading up to Rājendracoḷa's public transformation into Kulottuṅga. But what can be reconstructed of the actions of the eventual emperor's court tells us a great deal about the politics of the Coḻa state, and raises larger conceptual questions about medieval Indian politics in general. Above all else, Rājendracoḷa's conspicuous attempt to renovate the materials and social and liturgical frameworks of Kolar's temple to Cāmuṇḍeśvarī suggests that our interpretation of what makes up an efficacious political agent in this world can be expanded, in a direction that is counterintuitive to normal social science. The temple's Tantric goddess can herself be intelligibly placed within the explanatory account of the imperial accession of Kulottuṅga, and our ready-to-hand political vocabularies of power, agency, authority, and efficacy can thus be seen in a new and more capacious manner.

3 Kulottuṅga

The King and the Poets, ca. 1087–1115

Introduction

The first several years of Rājakesarivarman Rājendracoḷa's reign saw the king remade as emperor through the successful creation and extension of a political network centered upon the old Pallava heartland of Tondaimandalam. The Co̱la–Cālukya prince's court society gradually came into being through the work of the rhetorical arguments contained in his *mĕykkīrtti*s, the successful elaboration of local alliances with landed magnates and gentry, and the public propitiation of a martial goddess. The emperor Kulottuṅga did not suddenly emerge out of nowhere to claim the right to the throne of his mother's family; instead, his court's maneuverings evince an assiduous negotiation of the changing political landscape of the Co̱la state.

This version of events contrasts with the inherited scholarly consensus, which has treated Kulottuṅga's accession as depending in the first and last instance upon the logic the intersecting genealogies of the Co̱la and Cāḷukya families, and on his sudden seizure of the Co̱la throne in a coup d'état. This consensus, reviewed in Chapter 1, is grounded in a series of arguments adumbrated in the closing years of the nineteenth century by Eugen Hultzsch, Georg Bühler, Kanakasabhai Pillai, and John Fleet. Working from scattered and internally heterogeneous literary documents, these scholars managed to recover the tissue of connections uniting the two South Indian dynasties, and to locate the shifting public image of Kulottuṅga within them. This was a remarkable feat of historical reconstruction, especially given the recalcitrance of these sources, none of which readily accord with conventional historiographical standards of evidence. These men were certainly right in their discoveries, and are eminently deserving of the credit for them. Yet it is remarkable how little the interests and the priorities of these sources connect with the evidence that survives from the crucial period 1070–1074. With the exception of a single oblique invocation of Sunrise Mountain in Rājendracoḷa's *mĕykkīrtti*, there is no mention in any of the earliest sources of the Co̱la king's twinned lineages, their geographical location, or their connection with the pan-Indic kingly trope of the solar and lunar dynasties, all mainstays of the later poetic accounts. Nor is there any suggestion of a court intrigue that resulted in the elimination of Adhirājendra, something tentatively advanced by Fleet and repeated so often since to have become the default interpretation of these events.[1]

The sources for this earlier consensus, all of them composed in the decades following the onset of Kulottuṅga's reign and differing widely in language, genre, medium, and presumed audience, are: Bilhaṇa's great eulogistic *mahākāvya*, the *Vikramāṅkadevacarita*, completed around 1087 in honor of Vikramāditya VI in the Cālukya capital of Kalyāṇa; a set of three Sanskrit copperplate charters containing the royal orders of two of Kulottuṅga's sons in his natal region of Veṅgī (issued respectively in 1086–1087, 1090–1091, and 1092–1093, and attributed to a eulogist called Viddayabhaṭṭa); and the *Kaliṅkattupparaṇi* of Cayaṅkŏṇṭār, a poet of Kulottuṅga's own court, whose Tamil poem commemorating a Co̱ḻa campaign in the Kalinga kingdom was composed at some point after 1115.[2]

One line of approach to these texts might suggest that, given their literary character and their distance from the early events of Kulottuṅga's reign, their testimony should be accorded a very limited value, especially when compared to the "hard" prosopographical and material evidence already surveyed. This sort of simple positivism, however, is entirely inadequate to these materials. Works of literature – texts constructed in accord with canons of structure and taste, the creation and the understanding of which represented acts of considerable cultural virtuosity – possess a different, not an inferior, evidentiary significance. Simply put, Kulottuṅga's accession provided an occasion for narration, as an event in recent history that merited addressing. Each of these three texts attempted to integrate and domesticate the Co̱ḻa emperor's coming to power within its own particular rhetorical, symbolic, and generic priorities, but all were united in seeing the king's career as a provocation for narrative. The very fact that this event was considered important, and that it required explanation within the different formal mechanisms embodied in these texts, is itself historically significant, and relevant for the event's interpretation. It necessitates close attention to the linguistic, aesthetic, and pragmatic particulars of each of these literary realizations.

This is not a small task. First of all, in none of these three cases was Kulottuṅga's accession the sole focus of the narrative. Instead, each of these three complex texts contains an account of the accession that is in some way relevant to its larger project. Each may be regarded as a perspectival articulation of the event of the accession as subordinated to its wider literary and political priorities, what I will refer to as a "rendition." In approaching these three renditions, these differing priorities need to be constantly kept in mind, as does their location – in all three cases self-consciously marked – within the particular set of social boundaries that inflected their creation and their initial sphere of circulation and reception.

It is an unhelpful truism to claim that literary works are meant to be consumed by their audiences; the task of localizing a text, especially a work of literary art, cannot rest content with relying on external notices of it or relating it to some underdetermined social collective. Instead, the fundamental *worldliness* of these works provides a precondition for their intelligibility, and for the place enjoyed by Kulottuṅga within their narrative and poetic order. "Worldliness," a term coined by the late Edward Said, is a useful angle of approach to historical works of literature precisely because it leaves the question of their address to the world an open one. Literary texts possess "ways of engaging with the world that are both numerous and complicated," and it is the job of the critic or the historian of literature to remain alert to how these ways can differ, sometimes radically so, even among works that are contemporaneous.[3] The shared worldliness of these three renditions suggests that they be seen as differentially related to each other; despite their formal and linguistic diversity, there are nevertheless significant areas of overlap between them, beyond their shared narrative focus on Kulottuṅga.

To begin with, all three are works of "courtly culture"; that is, all were produced within the distributed societies centered on particular royal households. This in itself does not tell us all that much: these individual court societies were heterogeneous, as were the larger polities of which they were each the supposed apex. So too, the relationship between king and poet differs radically in the three cases. At the level of their linguistic codes, the renditions divide out into two works in Sanskrit and one in Tamil. This demarcates an important limit to their accessibility: those in Sanskrit could circulate anywhere in the wider cultural universe of Indic high culture, but only there. Access to Sanskrit was an elite preserve, though that elite may well have been considerably broader than the Brahman intelligentsia to which it is often presumed to have been limited. But language choice was not in any simple way a selection between a local and a translocal audience. The most conventionally historical, or better annalistic, account among the renditions is that furnished by the charters from Veṅgī: here, the use of Sanskrit obeyed an analogous logic to their incision on metal plates, meant to ensure stability and legibility within their circumscribed local world. Conversely, the Tamil of the

Kaliṅkattupparaṇi is certainly cast in a high poetic register and its author's cultural horizons extended well beyond the confines of the far south. It is only Bilhaṇa's *mahākāvya* that sought, and in fact achieved, a cosmopolitan readership outside the context of its creation; it is here that the idiosyncrasy of the émigré poet's work really takes root.

Two of the renditions – the Veṅgī copperplates and the *Kaliṅkattupparaṇi* – we may describe as "Co̱la" works. That is, they were the products of court societies that had Co̱la kings at their center, either Kulottuṅga himself or his sons. These shared an idiom of royal self-presentation, and an inclination toward celebrating the king's accession as a major event in the history of the world, something Bilhaṇa's biography of Kulottuṅga's Cālukya nemesis most definitely did not. It is in the Co̱la renditions that the structuring metonymies of the solar and lunar dynasties and their instantiation in the Co̱la and Cālukya family lines provide significant parts of a shared language of kingly authority. Yet these were not the product of a unified program of royal propaganda, and this figural lexicon is expressed in markedly different ways, and to different ends. Though ostensibly celebratory of Kulottuṅga, in both cases there are other figures of honor who are interposed between the Co̱la king and the poet, and it is these figures that are central to any worldly reading of them. Correlatively, Bilhaṇa's Sanskrit work shares with Cayaṅkoṇṭār's *Paraṇi* an appeal to courtly poetic entertainment, as opposed to the charters' yoking of eulogistic and annalistic verse to legally efficacious prose. Further, Bilhaṇa and Cayaṅkoṇṭār were literary celebrities, composing works meant to appeal to a particular audience, but these audiences differed in ways that are significant to the poems' interpretation.

The events of Kulottuṅga's accession are not the central narrative matter of any of these works, but their renditions of them can be read as symptomatic of the larger preoccupations of these works. As such, they reveal more of interest than just whatever positivist data that they can be made to yield. In all three renditions, the figure of Kulottuṅga emerges not as a blank slate suited for poetic embroidery but as a crucial element in each text's wider symbolic structure. But each realizes this in markedly different ways, and so the narrativization of Kulottuṅga's career enables us to better understand the diversity of medieval literary form, of the ways and means of poetic language within the polyglot world of courtly South India.

Bilhaṇa's Double Game

Of the three renditions, Bilhaṇa's *Vikramāṅkadevacarita* (*The Deeds of King Vikramāṅka*, hereafter *Carita*) is at once most studied and least understood by modern scholarship. For a work remarkable for its suave form and acerbic wit, Indological discussion of the *Carita* has, until very recently, remained preoccupied with its assessment as a positive historical source, and with the question of Bilhaṇa's supposed mendacity as a Cālukya propagandist. This is perhaps all too predictable: in trying to wring every last detail of dynastic chronology from the poem and in prejudging its author as a flattering courtier, even the *Carita*'s most attentive modern readers have labored precisely to occlude its wider significance.[4]

Amidst all of its many accomplishments – the sustained flow of verbal dexterity, extended passages of consummately realized poetry of praise, and the reimagining of older tropes and subtly elaborated intertextual linkages with earlier works of *kāvya* – the *Carita* intermittently incorporates some of the most strident denunciations of kingship ever seen in courtly Sanskrit, and it is precisely here that the figure of Kulottuṅga becomes vitally important. Further, in the poet's explicit account of his own life, we possess perhaps the single most valuable testimony of the inner world of a medieval Sanskrit literary figure. Understanding Bilhaṇa as just a talented hack writing a one-sided narrative of his patron Vikramāditya's rise to power elides both this dissident undercurrent and the conspicuous work of the author's self-fashioning. Bilhaṇa figures himself as a consummate outsider, a misanthropic Kashmirian living in seeming semi-exile in Karnataka, and in this virtuosically realized verse portrait of his patron, the poet's own impression is that of a successful man who longed above all else to escape from the scene of his greatest success, to bite the hand that feeds him, and to recoil from the institution of kingship itself.

"Though the working of my speech be dry and tasteless, it will be honored on account of the king's great deeds": with an utterly conventionalized mock-humility, strikingly discordant with its surroundings, Bilhaṇa claims in the *Carita*'s prologue (1.28ab) that the special virtues of his patron are what make his poem worth reading. The early years of Vikramāditya's princely life supplied much in the way of narrative raw material, though little of it may have seemed promising as the stuff of eulogy. The Cālukya prince, whom contemporary sources variously style Vikrama, Vikramāṅka, Vikramāditya, Vikramārka, and (by the Coḻa *mĕykkīrtti* authors, with deliberate misprision) Vikkalaṉ, was the second of the three sons of Āhavamalla Someśvara I (r. 1044–1068). Like Kulottuṅga, Vikrama's early public life was bound up in the dynastic tangles of the late 1060s, and especially in Vīrarājendra Coḻa's short-lived diplomatic solution to the peninsula's endemic warfare. The resemblances between Vikrama and Kulottuṅga, in fact, are many and uncanny: as princes, both led likely simultaneous martial campaigns in the vicinity of Cakrakoṭṭam; both were Cālukyas who married into the Coḻa line, and so were bound together in multiple degrees of kinship; and both would go on to eventually rule for a half-century. And neither was the first in line for his family's succession, though here the record of Vikrama's actions presents a starker example of royal power-politics than Rājendracoḷa's pre-imperial political maneuverings. Āhavamalla died at the peak of the hot season of 1068, and was succeeded by his eldest son, who adopted the regnal name Bhuvanaikamalla Someśvara (in the conventions of modern scholarship, Someśvara II).[5] Based in the Banavāsi 12,000 territory, Vikrama at first acknowledged his brother's suzerainty for a number of years. Though the sequence of events is not clear, he then apparently rebelled against Someśvara, overthrew him, and was by 1076 secure enough to issue royal orders of his own and to adopt the year of his accession as the start of a new epoch, the Cālukyavikrama era, timed to roughly coincide with the end of the Śaka millennium. Jayasiṃha, the youngest of Āhavamalla's sons, was for a time given Vikrama's former appanage in the southwest of the kingdom, but eventually launched his own unsuccessful rebellion, perhaps in 1081–1082. Nothing is known of Vikramāditya's brothers after their defeats: they were most likely killed.

Our sense of Cālukya elite politics is far less defined than that of the Coḻas, and it is not possible to get any clear idea of the composition and workings of Vikramāditya's court society, either before or after his accession.[6] While it is apparent that the dynastic turbulence present in the Coḻa line was, if anything, even greater among their northern rivals, how far this can be correlated with wider social transformations remains unclear. It was this series of intradynastic skirmishes, however, that provided Bilhaṇa with the rudiments of his theme: the Kashmiri poet's task was to transform a king whose most notable victories had been won against his own brothers into a subject fit for conventional eulogy. Bilhaṇa was more than capable of this, and on the surface the *Carita* is placidly unconcerned with the contradiction between amoral realpolitik and the celebration of its subject's dharmic virtues.

The gap between events and their representation in the poem, far from undermining the poem's value, raises the question of the place of historical referentiality within it. When, for instance, in a verse-montage in the *Carita*'s fifth chapter, Bilhaṇa describes a period of Vikramāditya's life in *vanavāsamaṇḍala* (i.e. the Banavāsi region, encompassing parts of the modern Shimoga and Uttara Kannada districts) as an erotic interlude taking up "just a few days' time" (*dināni katicit*, 5.23), it takes no great effort to show this to be a poetic distortion of events. Vikramāditya had long been connected with this important region, which was assigned the high reckoning of a 12,000 territory in the Cālukya land tenurial system.[7] Whatever assignations he enjoyed must have been eked out during the leisure-time of a busy regional lord. This is after all the point: Bilhaṇa transfigures the events of the real world into the stuff of literature, in a way surely as recognizable for his initial audience as for the modern reader in search of reliable historical evidence. In a complementary manner, however, what verifiable historical details Bilhaṇa includes in the *Carita* are deliberately there, and meant to serve a purpose within the poem's narrative and moral logic. Specifying what this logic might be, and especially what it might be in the case of his schematic presentation of Kulottuṅga's rise to power, depends upon both a sense of the whole poem, and of its author.

The *Carita* is a long work, in keeping with both the conventions of the *mahākāvya* and the ambitions of its author. It begins with the mythic origins and heroic past of the Cālukya dynasty (*sarga* 1), before moving on to the deeds of Vikramāditya's father Someśvara I, including the founding – actually the renovation – of the capital city of Kalyāṇa (*sarga* 2).[8] Vikramāditya's early life and the events surrounding his contested assumption of Cālukya kingship provide a major portion of the poem (*sarga*s 3–6), as do the details of his wooing and winning of his chief queen Candralekhā (*sarga*s 7–9), and the royal couple's lovemaking and amusements (*sarga*s 10–13). The king subsequently puts down a revolt by his younger brother Jayasiṃha (*sarga*s 14–15) and returns to his capital just in time for the hunting season (*sarga* 16). Following a further desultory skirmish with the Coḷas (*sarga* 17), the *Carita* closes with the poet's final description of his homeland and the events that lead him far from home and to the southern emperor's court (*sarga* 18).

Given the dynastic tumult surrounding Vikramāditya – with two internecine wars fought in the early years of his reign – it is easy enough to imagine that joining the circle surrounding him was a potentially dangerous decision. It was, however, a good fit for Bilhaṇa, in whose hands the art of poetic expression took on a notably eristic, even aggressive, tone. This much is clear in the *Carita*'s introductory verses, a critical broadside preemptively delivered to Bilhaṇa's fellow poets and would-be critics. Though he was following in the tracks of models both classical and contemporaneous, Bilhaṇa's opening gambit is notably bold:[9]

Fellow poets: You must guard that ambrosia for the ear that you have churned up from the sea of eloquence. Just like the anti-gods, verse-thieves are ever at the ready to snatch it away. (1.11)

> Some frauds think themselves clever in the company of dull wits, but who are these poor bastards, when faced with the words of good poets? Water may be proud to put out a fire, but what can it do the luster of even a tiny gem? (1.18)

To the conventional topos of *kukavinindā*, the condemnation of bad poets, Bilhaṇa adds the new wrinkle of his pointed dismissal of an ungrateful and uncultured audience: the finely honed jeweler's chisel of a poet's art is unsuited to do the hatchet-work of appealing to such low tastes, and the unkind reader is likened to a camel on the hunt for thorns in a pleasure-garden.[10] Through his prologue, in which Bilhaṇa returns repeatedly to the same figures of jewels, thieves, master poets, and hayseed audiences, the master image is that of a goldsmith's touchstone or *kaṣapaṭṭikā*: it is only when assayed by a truly knowledgeable audience that the value of his poetry is really apparent.[11] The tone throughout is one of constant jockeying for dominance between poets, and between poet and audience, with the ever-present risk of theft, fraud, and counterfeit hanging over the whole enterprise. This antagonistic, even paranoid theme, however, is played across Bilhaṇa's self-conscious adaptation of the gently musical, decidedly unaggressive *vaidarbhī* style of Sanskrit poetry, that "downpour of ear-nectar from a cloudless sky, down-payment for the attainment of the felicity of poems' language."[12] Poetry is a risky business, Bilhaṇa sweetly says: above all when you work for a king. It is in the course of this opening that he includes the patently insincere disavowal of his own ability and celebration of the virtues of his patron. All of this is sketched in just a few opening verses: Bilhaṇa's arch insouciance is without real precedent in Sanskrit poetry.

This opening salvo is counterbalanced by the *Carita*'s lengthy coda, on the wonders of Kashmir and Bilhaṇa's own early life. This was an essentially independent autobiography in verse, a form that, while departing from elements found in Bāṇa, is original to him.[13] In it, Bilhaṇa supplies a litany of courts in which he won fame and humiliated his rivals, while hinting at his own past failures and disappointments. While he ends on the upbeat note of his spectacular success at the Kalyāṇa court, the dark undertones added throughout remain. Bilhaṇa thus bookends his long poem on the regnal, martial, and erotic excellences of his patron with the condemnation of small-minded critics and untalented fellow-poets, and with his own verse self-portrait, in which he not-so-subtly bemoans his dependence on a royal patron of any kind. From the poet's perspective, kings are unctuous philistines, the stain of whose attentions he had to wash away in the purifying waters of the Ganges.[14] The poem's final verses underline its author's hardly concealed contempt by returning to a theme of the prologue, issuing a stern injunction to potential patrons to support poets of his caliber or risk being forgotten forever.[15]

Bilhaṇa's authorial personality is thus marked by a tensely maintained autonomy, which can be seen as a carefully projected artifice of the poet's self-image, as evidence of alienation, or as the effect of a physical and subjective mobility. But there is something more at work here than just self-promotion at the expense of others. Underlying this virtuoso hauteur lies a deeper, almost subliminal idea, a potentially radical critique of kingly power and legitimacy itself. Seen from this angle, a central theme (perhaps *the* central theme) of Bilhaṇa's poem is not the celebration of Vikramāditya but a repudiation of kingship as a whole, using his patron's own fratricidal rise to power as a surreptitious proof-text. It is here that the poet's reliance on the man whom he disdainfully calls "Rājiga" becomes critical to the larger design of the *Carita.*

Kulottuṅga only figures in the narrative in a few scattered verses, but crucially it is in these that the poem's dissident subtext is allowed to rise to the surface. When Bilhaṇa turns the full brunt of his scorn onto a king, it is not on his patron, or even his patron's evil brothers, but onto Vikramāditya's greatest rival, whom the poet paints as a usurper filled with murderous yet ultimately impotent rage toward the Cālukya king. But displacing the worst things that the poem has to say about kings and kingship onto the Co<u>l</u>a does not blunt Bilhaṇa's subversive edge. In the poem, as in real life, Kulottuṅga and Vikramāditya are eerily twinned. The two kings are really shadows of each other, a fact of which Bilhaṇa takes full advantage. Bilhaṇa debuted his poem at some point between 1085 and 1088,[16] when much of the striking parallelism between the two men's reigns had yet to emerge. The poet could not have known that the two kings would continue to war against each other for the next four decades, or that their reigns would both mark moments of disruption of the patterns of statecraft that came before them. Bilhaṇa's poem thus takes on a salience that extends beyond his value as a historical source: in the poet's subtle linking of these two kings' lives, his work is oddly prophetic.

It is an extended sequence early in the poem, comprising the fourth through the sixth *sarga*s, which narrates Vikramāditya's early victories and his conflict with his elder brother, that forms Bilhaṇa's core statement on the nature of power and politics. It is here that he included his oblique and easily misunderstood account of Rājendracoḷa's seizure of the Co<u>l</u>a throne. The sequence begins with Vikramāditya embarking on a campaign – a *digvijaya* or world conquest – to the south of the Cālukya territories. The destruction that he visits on the recalcitrant southern kingdoms, especially those of the west coast, is all described in the conventionally extreme terms of martial poetry: so, in an act of ecocide, the Malaya mountains are denuded of their famed sandal trees, and the ocean is "befouled with the blood of the kings of Kerala."[17] After encountering ill omens on the road back from an incursion into Coḻa territory, Vikramāditya is met by a messenger from the court, carrying awful news: Vikramāditya's beloved father Someśvara had fallen ill and opted "to draw this horrid charade of embodied life to a close in the embrace of the Tuṅgabhadrā." (4.59). Carrying out this wish, the old king and his court marched to the river, where (4.68):

> He entered the river's water neck-deep
> and so it was then that, to the crashing accompaniment
> of the river's surging wave,
> he went to the city of moon-crested Śiva.

Upon hearing the messenger's news, Vikramāditya's emotional collapse is total: as his throat fills with howling cries and he collapses into apoplexy, his attendants take away his dagger to prevent him from self-harm. That this occurs to the poem's hero and patron who a few verses earlier was figured as an unstoppable warrior is totally in keeping with Bilhaṇa's tightly wound, emotionally demonstrative style. Recovering, the young prince performs his funeral obsequies and returns to Kalyāṇa in mourning. There he has a tearful reunion with his elder brother, whom he shortly sees installed as Someśvara II (4.92–93). Immediately, however, the new king turns to evil, as Śrī, the goddess of royal power, proves as intoxicating and as addictive to him as strong liquor (4.98). Bilhaṇa goes on to depict a world that warps around the new king's dementia, as he is deafened to the good council of his advisors by the din of his royal musicians, and as his elephants – sensing his inner corruption – begin to sluice off their backs after he has ridden them (4.99, 102). Someśvara's increasing lunacy provides the first opportunity for Bilhaṇa to question the institution of kingship itself:

> It was as if Fortune were a she-ghoul:
> As he had come to know its taste from kissing her,
> he craved blood from the opened necks of all those around him.[18]

Faced with this deteriorating situation, Vikramāditya worries that in his warped state, his elder brother would be unable to fend off an attack from his Coḻa enemies, and so decides once again to begin a campaign to the south (4.117–18). He flees the capital with his younger brother Jayasiṃha (5.1), suggesting to his readers that great model of fraternal love, Lakṣmaṇa accompanying Rāma into exile.

After a series of skirmishes with troops dispatched by Someśvara II – in which Vikramāditya proves himself "a god of death to rival kings" who "swallows whole the armies pulverised by his elephants" (5.7) – the prince stops in the Vanavāsa country (5.19–23). He meets with Jayakeśin, the king of Koṅkaṇa, who donates treasure to this cause, and he wins over the wavering Āḷupa king (5.25–26). In the description of the forging of these alliances, Bilhaṇa reaches out into the domain of politico–historical reference: these were actual kings whose support of Vikrama no doubt was an accomplished fact when he wrote. This shift to the poetic embroidering of Deccani realpolitik, moreover, supplies a transition to the major political and affective link forged by Vikrama in his pre-imperial phase with the Co̱la king. Often simply called "the Tamil" (*drāviḍa*), the king is unnamed, but it is Vīrarājendra who is meant. The sea-change in the relationship between the Co̱la king and the Cālukya prince is heralded by the arrival of a Co̱la ambassador to Vikramāditya's camp, whose long and beautifully ornate speech is a masterpiece of the Sanskrit poetry of ingratiating persuasion (5.31–46). The king wants Vikramāditya for an ally, not an enemy, and – the envoy eventually comes to his main point – would happily offer up his daughter in marriage to seal their friendship.

The two men finally meet on the south bank of the Tuṅgabhadrā, companionably share a single seat, and negotiate Vikramāditya's marriage to the Co̱la's daughter (5.85–88). After his marriage, Vikramāditya is reticent to let his father-in-law leave him, and with good reason it turns out: he soon hears of the old king's unexpected death (6.7). Grieving yet again, Vikramāditya marches on Kāñcīpuram, where he is admired by the local women, in one of Bilhaṇa's wonderfully suave erotic asides (6.10–20). He then moves on to Gāṅgakuṇḍa (that is, Gaṅgaikŏṇṭaco̱lapuram) in order to ensure the succession of his brother-in-law (only called "the Cola's son," *colasūnu*, this is Adhirājendra, 6:24). Bilhaṇa transparently manipulates chronology in the interest of narrative coherence here: Vīrarājendra was likely dead by the middle of 1071, with Adhirājendra dying some months later, while Vikramāditya still acknowledged his brother's authority until at least 1074.

Vikramāditya's pre-regnal career is thus structured around his movement further and further into the Co̱la orbit: from a despoiling conqueror, he is transformed into a loyal son- and brother-in-law, and the protector of the Tamil dynasty's integrity. Here, in characterizing the most momentous happenings of Vikramāditya's early life, Bilhaṇa relies on the description of masculine intimacy, of the intense and often tempestuous relationships between male kin or would-be kin.[19] With his father dead, and his elder brother in the grip of a demonic madness, Vikramāditya must look elsewhere for the support and sustenance that should rightly be found among his male relations; and in making Vikramāditya's brief but intense friendship with Vīrarājendra into one of the emotional crescendos of the poem, Bilhaṇa figures the Coḻa king as a surrogate guru-elder in place of Vikrama's departed father and deranged brother-king.

Within this affective logic, the role of the man whom Bilhaṇa calls Rājiga is that of a piece of moral and affective antimatter. His appearance in the narrative is sudden: after the brief month that Vikramāditya spends in the Coḻa capital with his brother-in-law (*māsamātram*, 6.24 in a rare exact reference to time), and a quick expedition against refractory "tribal bowmen" somewhere in the wild country to the north of the Coḻa country (6.25), the prince returns to the banks of the Tuṅgabhadrā, the southern border of the Cālukya lands. Rājiga then abruptly enters onto the scene, in a pair of tightly interwoven verses narrating the last of the great reverses of Vikrama's early career:

> *atha katiṣucid eva daivayogāt parigaliteṣu dineṣu colasūnoḥ* |
> *śriyam aharata rājigābhidhānaḥ prakṛtivirodhahatasya veṅgināthaḥ* || 6.26
> *kuṭilamatir asau viśaṅkamānaḥ punar amum eva parābhavapragalbham* |
> *praguṇam akṛta pṛṣṭhakopahetoḥ prakṛtivirodhinam asya somadevam* || 6.27

> But then, when only a few days had drifted by, through the workings of fate, the Cola prince was struck down by *prakṛtivirodha*, and the lord of Veṅgi, called Rājiga, snatched away his sovereign power.
>
> He had a twisted mind, that one, and fearing that [Vikrama] alone could oppose him once more, he made Somadeva, the *prakṛtivirodhin*, ready, in order to harass him from the rear.

Bilhaṇa was a poet of subtleties, and this is especially evident in this compressed account of the Coḻa succession.[20] The chief ambiguity here rests on the doublet *prakṛtivirodha*/*prakṛtivirodhin*, linked significantly to Vikramāditya's unlucky brother-in-law (the unnamed Adhirājendra) and his mad brother, here called Somadeva. *Prakṛtivirodha*, a hostility or opposition (*virodhaḥ*) that either comes naturally (*prakṛtyā*) or which is found among a kingdom's populace (*prakṛtīnām*), is a term of art that resonates with the formal language of classical political theory, especially that of the *Arthaśāstra*. While the compound terms *prakṛtivirodha* and -*virodhin* do not occur explicitly there, it provides all of the linguistic and ideological raw material needed to coin them. The ambiguities that result from this, however, begin in Kauṭalya's text itself, where the two senses of *prakṛti* ("subjects" and "nature") are already difficult to disentangle; an identical or closely similar set of terms is also part of the shared stock of the language of politics in Deccani epigraphy throughout the medieval period. Something similar is at work in Bilhaṇa's term *pṛṣṭhakopahetoḥ* ("in order to harrass him from the rear"); this alludes to *paścātkopa* or "disorder in the hinterland," an element of Kauṭalyan strategic calculus.[21] The poet is not simply beholden to the *Arthaśāstra*'s technical language; rather, this vocabulary was part of a larger suggestive framework to Bilhaṇa, allowing him to play upon his source text's own ambiguities, turned to his own ends and resonating with his own poetic idiom.

Judging from Bilhaṇa's idiom elsewhere in the poem, in calling Someśvara *prakṛtivirodhin*, he slyly depicts his patron's brother as adverse *to* nature, a freakishly unnatural near-monster. By comparison, Rājiga becomes perhaps the greater villain, an exemplar of the cruelly self-advancing ideal of the Kauṭalyan *vijigīṣu* or expansionist king. Bilhaṇa archly indexes this when he describes him as *kuṭilamati*, "crooked-minded," subtly evoking the sinister connotations of the common (mis)construal of the *Arthaśāstra*'s author's name. Here we have a sort of interpretative key to this terse version of the Coḻa imbroglio: the events, Bilhaṇa insinuates, are to be read under the sign of Kauṭalya, as Bilhaṇa joins fratricidal psychosis and Machiavellian will-to-power together in uncanny alliance.

There is, however, a further set of connotations toward which the term *prakṛtivirodha* gestures. Once again, the reference is not exact, but both elements of the compound word resonate with classical Ayurveda's descriptive taxonomy of disease, where *prakṛti* denotes the set of a patient's genetic predispositions, and *virodha* and its related forms are prominent among Ayurveda's vocabulary of the causes of illness.[22] This play of resonance between the political and the medical – a crisis in the constitution of the Coḻa and Cālukya families, coupling madness, degenerative illness, and moral depravity – appears to be a deliberately staged ambiguity of Bilhaṇa's. He directs his readers toward one interpretation of the ambiguous phrases, in which the ambition of Kulottuṅga and the madness of Someśvara are seen as pathologically allied. Describing Adhirājendra as *prakṛtivirodhahata*, "struck down by an opposition with (in?) his constituents," thus retains the nuance of morbidity. As we have seen, it is quite possible that the briefly ruling king's early death is attributable to disease, rather than violence. Whether reports of this were available at the Cālukya court in faraway Kalyāṇa is impossible to say, and is perhaps beside the point.[23] In Bilhaṇa's hands, these distant events of almost two decades earlier are integrated into his vision of high-stakes dynastic politics: his patron's enemy is cast as an unscrupulous villain, whose presence taints by association his by-then disappeared brother. While containing a surface acknowledgment of actual events – Adhirājendra's sickness, Rājendracoḷa's accession, Vikrama's outmaneuvering by his brother and the Coḻa – it reassembles the stuff of the past into materials amenable to his own intentions.[24]

This remarkably dense and compact set-piece supplies the pretext for a further, and much more subversive, gambit by the poet. The alliance between Rājiga and Someśvara, bearing all the marks of the amoral politics of the *Arthaśāstra* as well as the taint of criminal insanity, supplies the occasion for the move to kingly denunciation *en clair*. Over a series of eleven remarkable verses (6.28–38), Bilhaṇa shifts completely from his narrative mode and speaks in a tone of open contempt for and condemnation of kings and kingship as such.[25] Such poetry of dissent is not lacking elsewhere in Sanskrit *kāvya*, but it is rare enough, and its occurrence here starkly disturbs the eulogistic fabric of the poem. The denunciation begins with a sudden shift in narrative register, from the particular and historical to the mythic and gnomic:

> Does Śrī entrust herself to prudent men? No. Rather she
> gives herself over to madmen, as if her tender feet were sorely
> wounded in her wanderings on the whetted sword-blades of so many
> warriors. (6.28)

The goddess of royal power dwelling on the tips of warrior's swords is a standard trope. In Bilhaṇa's reinvention, Śrī is no longer a prize to be won through martial valor, but an object of pity, a once-desirable woman crippled by ill-use, willing to give herself over to any man who desires her, instead of waiting for a suitable lover. Here, the sixth *sarga*'s stumbling, asymmetrical *puṣpitāgrā* meter comes into its own: in classical *kāvya*, uneven meters often iconize a moral or narrative disequilibrium. This sense of formally bounded unease, lurking in the background of Vikrama's lament for Vīrarājendra and the sudden death of Adhirājendra, now snaps into prominence.[26] This subtly produces a sense of vertigo, of the world out of joint, which hovers over the entire passage. The flaws of kings in the Kali age are not limited to their unworthiness and madness; they are at once impious and locked away in a pathological solipsism:

> Their servants keep them so sheltered from the outside world that
> kings see the whole damn thing as if it were nothing.
> Foolish by nature, they don't give a second's thought to the world to
> come. (6.32)[27]

> "Only fools think these balled-up contraptions of stone and
> gemstones to be God." Secretly, wicked kings think just this, and
> so they falsely reverence even Lord Śiva's liṅga. (6.33)

The condemnation then takes on a more general and more radical tone:

> It is as if all their manhood has melted away from spending all their time in the company of thousands of nubile girls: fearful at every step, kings suspect danger all around them. (6.34)

> The miserable harlot is always ready to run off to another man across the broad road of a battlefield, thick with bloody mud. That's why as soon as this royal Śrī's set foot in kings' hearts, she leaves a stain. (6.35)

The first of these two verses – playing with a theme that dates back to Kālidāsa – begins with a wonderfully plastic evocation of the swirl of available women said to surround kings (*aviratataruṇīsahasramadhya-sthitivigalatpuruṣavratā ivaite*), and the vertiginous sexual exhaustion that inevitably results from this, coupling this to a notion of paranoia as a sort of venereal disease. The second is the crescendo of this sequence, itself arguably the dark center of the whole *Carita*. The trope of staining or marking is a favorite of Bilhaṇa's; where in the opening of the denunciation Śrī was absolved of any guilt – worn down by her suitors' violence, she had merely followed the path of least resistance and settled for a poor choice of mate – here, the goddess is transformed into a faithless harlot, a figure of scorn as well as bathetic pity.[28] While the commonness, even the prostitution, of the royal goddesses Śrī and Lakṣmī is regularly met with in political poetry, there is always the possibility that they might be reformed and turned back to the patriarchal ideal of settled and subordinate monogamy. Here, there seems no hope of such a recovery. Śrī is irremediably corrupt and corrupting, just as Bilhaṇa had earlier transformed her doublet Lakṣmī into a bloodthirsty demoness. With his last, general comment, Bilhaṇa's picture is complete:

> Kings fail to consider what has been decreed by Fate, that in their family *someone* must go on to be king. So it is that, in their lust for power, they'll even destroy their own house. (6.37)

This verse, the last of the denunciation, is jarring: Bilhaṇa's abrupt conclusion (*bhūpāḥ kulam api nirdalayanti rājyalubdhāḥ*) reads practically like prose: there is no effort to prettify this, or to embed it in intertextual poet's games. "Rājiga" may have supplied the pretext to launch into this tirade, but there is nothing in what the poet has told his audience that would lead them to consider his patron's Coḻa enemy to be a sexually dissolute atheist; even the claim of usurpation rests only on the poet's ambivalent insinuations. Yet, in the passage's eleventh and final verse, as Bilhaṇa pulls away and sets the denunciation back into his narrative, this is exactly the intimation:[29]

What wrong had that noble-minded man ever done to his brother,
such that he joined with their family's enemy, Rājiga the Cola,
in the hope of doing him harm? (6.38)

Despite this conspicuous effort to direct the onus here at the Coḻa king, it is impossible not to notice that the blast which Bilhaṇa delivers against Kulottuṅga applies much more to Vikramāditya, an ambitious prince (and, as we already know, a promiscuous sexual athlete) on the verge of unseating his own elder brother – of in fact diving headlong into the destruction of his own house. Kulottuṅga's crucial role in the *Carita*'s narrative logic is to supply an excuse for showing kingship in all its malignancy, and to provide the poet with what can be called plausible deniability: of course, it is only to kings like the wicked Machiavellian Rājiga that this patently general denunciation applies. In fact, this broadside against the very fact of kingship connects what comes before with what follows: like a lamp in the doorway, it illumines both.

Bilhaṇa's rendition of the events in the Coḻa country, then, is less a piece of historical narration than the deliberate and careful subordination of the stuff of history to his own moral and aesthetic preoccupations. Kulottuṅga functions as a device within the poet's carefully crafted semiotic order, placed in an artificial and finally self-subverting opposition with the poem's real "target," Vikramāditya. The shadowy role of the Coḻa king within the wider poem seems to bear this out. He appears, very briefly, three other times in the narrative: he is present at Candralekhā's *svayaṃvara* husband-choice, as the last of the kings that she indifferently passes by before laying eyes on Vikramāditya (9.123–130, *cf.* 9.142); it is to him that Vikrama's younger brother Jayasiṃha turns for support as he prepares his unsuccessful rebellion (14.12) and he is ignominiously defeated near Kāñcī at the end of the poem (17.43–67), supplying a suitably victorious closure to the narrative. In a moralizing touch, this final defeat is meted out as punishment for the Coḻa's role in Jayasiṃha's treachery, where the derangement of the proper relation between brothers and its replacement by amoral self-aggrandizement is made the inevitable consequences of contact with the wicked southern king.[30]

It is impossible to gather anything of Kulottuṅga's real-world deeds amidst the studied ambiguity of Bilhaṇa's language. Bilhaṇa's success as a court poet, and his reputation in the later literary imagination, depended on just this tension, on his double game of polished courtly praise and carefully crafted subversion hidden in plain sight. The poet seems to court this risky business, owing to his self-professed independence from his patron's control, and his place within the world in which he moved and labored: he presents himself as a man bold enough to insult his patron-king to his face, and clever enough to get away with it. There is a wider lesson to be learned here, perhaps, about the workings of court culture in medieval India. The literary (and other) products of kingly patronage were by no means merely engaged in a straightforward celebration of royal power, or in papering over the inequities of their societies. Sometimes court poets could address their patrons as mocking critics, even as rivals.[31] Later literary memory celebrates Bilhaṇa as a practitioner of this sort of brinksmanship, and of its consequences: whether as a poet fallen out of favor railing against his former patron or as the seducer of royal princesses caught in flagrante delicto and saved from execution by extempore verse-craft.[32]

This wider literary reputation won by Bilhaṇa in the centuries after his great work's debut signals something important about the protocols of reading that it presumed, and about the sort of reception that it was meant to gain. To read the *Carita* as a historical source for the medieval Deccan, or even to understand Bilhaṇa as a figure strongly located in the Kalyāṇa Cālukya court, is to do violence to the work and to the intentions of its author. The acerbic Kashmiri is unambiguous, about this at least: for all that he had found literary fame and fortune in a southern kingdom, this was for him a tolerable, but by no means ideal situation. His real audience, as he emphasizes over and again in the poems' opening and final cantos, was that of the far-flung world of still-cosmopolitan Sanskrit, above all those connoisseurs living far away in Kashmir. His local materials are only that, the stuff to be transformed by the poet's craft into something meant to last on the tongues and in the minds of those people who really mattered to the poet: the *habitués* of *sabhā*s throughout India. The events of Vikramāditya's reign could be denuded of their specificity in the course of their transformation into stylish Sanskrit verse: Kulottuṅga's successfully making himself a king was less a significant waypoint in the recent history of the south as it was an opportunity for Bilhaṇa to focus his attention on the repellent, fascinating world of royal power.

This was not the product, it needs to be stressed, of a deficient historical or political sensibility on Bilhaṇa's part. The Cālukya kingdom, like the Co̱la, was a complex society that produced clear-sighted accounts of both the distant and the recent past, and there is some evidence to suggest that the poet familiarized himself with the historical-annalistic *praśasti*s which, like the Co̱la *mĕykkīrtti*s, headed up royal pronouncements.[33] All the same, the events of the Co̱la succession are cast into ominous shadow, used as scenic dressing for the playing out of Bilhaṇa's elaborate acts of poetic sedition.

Moonset on Sunrise Mountain

The *Vikramāṅkadevacarita* was composed far from Kulottuṅga's court, and was meant to circulate in a world disconnected from that of the Coḻas, to travel throughout the entirety of the Sanskrit cosmopolis. It was, further, a work whose circulation was mediated through manuscript copies as well as through its citation by professional readers such as critics and anthologists. Though also composed in Sanskrit, the second of the literary renditions of Kulottuṅga's coming to the Coḻa throne emerged under very different material, social, and practical conditions. There is a further important contrast to the Kashmirian's unitary poem: though the three charters issued by two of Kulottuṅga's sons in his natal region of Veṅgī share a single named author – and hold the majority of their patent text in common – they differ profoundly in their verbal texture, in their rhetorical character, and in the ritual and juridical undertakings they were meant to subserve. It was the shared depiction of Kulottuṅga's ancestry found in all three charters that first provided the evidence to modern scholarship to reconstruct the pattern of cross-cousin marriage between the Coḻas and the Cālukyas that came to dominate the understanding of his coming to power.[34] The question, however, of why reference to Kulottuṅga's ancestry took on its particular significance in the charters' time and place went unasked by positivist historiography; so too did the question of the charters' existence as durable material objects, or their place within the world of Veṅgī politics. It is this practical, social dimension to their historical existence that marks the charters' peculiar character, and which must guide their interpretation.

Incised on sets of copperplates and bound together with seal-rings, the charters were meant for a specific locale and a specific group of readers and auditors, in contrast to Bilhaṇa's far-flung potential audience.[35] While the earliest of the three addresses itself to an audience extending over the entirety of modern coastal Andhra Pradesh,[36] their circulatory world was embedded in the deltaic micro-region of Veṅgī, in what is now East Godavari district. From the perspective of the vast, dry, and warlike Deccan plateau, Veṅgī formed a tiny enclave on its eastern edge, a well-watered and prosperous little cosmos unto itself. The region's agrarian wealth, and its long-term importance as the hub of Andhran high culture should not, however, lend a falsely pacific image to what over the centuries had been hotly contested real estate. We have already seen how the intrafamilial Cālukya conflicts of the middle decades of the eleventh century marked the life of the young Rājiga before his earliest appearance in the historical record, and how these conflicts were structured around the Veṅgī dynasty's collective self-conception as heirs to the

Mahābhārata's warring *somavaṃśa* families.[37] The kingdom of Veṅgī was far from the central lands of the Coḻa kingdom, and though Kulottuṅga's turbulent early years were at least partly spent in the region, there is no reason to believe that he ever set foot there again after establishing himself further to the south in 1070. Nevertheless, the Cālukya–Coḻa emperor remained a felt presence in his old homeland, and his royal charisma strongly inflects the charters, occasioning their obvious departures from the earlier model of the public documents of the Veṅgī Cālukya family.

The three charters are all dated in Kulottuṅga's regnal years. The earliest, the Teki plates, was issued in his seventeenth year (1086–1087) by Rājarāja Coḍagaṅga,[38] and its purpose was to legally confirm certain customary rights to members of the Teliki caste-community (*telikikulalabdhajanmānaḥ*), including an extensive list of subcastes. This group, said to have emigrated from Ayodhyā with the Cālukya founding ancestor Vijayāditya, is confirmed in its rights to ride horses through the streets on the occasion of their wedding festivals, and the newly married couples of the caste are allowed to present the king with betel on a golden platter at the conclusion of their wedding (T, ll. 93–98). The charter's poetic preamble (*praśasti*) is the longest of the three, and the most aesthetically ambitious in its narration of the intertwinned histories of the Coḻa and Cālukya families. The second set of plates, from Chellur, is dated four years later, to Kulottuṅga's twenty-first year (1090–1091) and was issued under the authority of Vīracoḍa. This charter memorializes a subordinate named Meḍamārya, the son of one Potana, and establishes a royal grant of land to a Viṣṇu temple patronized by him. The verses in praise of Meḍamārya, his father and his gotra-ancestor Mudgala form another mini-*praśasti* within the donative portion of the inscription (vv. 22–37). The third set, the Pithapuram plates, is dated to Kulottuṅga's twenty-third year (1092–1093), and was again issued by Vīracoḍa. The business of the donation here is truly extraordinary, as the plates detail an extensive land grant in order to found an *agrahāra*, Vīracoḍacaturvedimaṅgalam, given over to a massive list of 536 Coḻa Brahmans, seemingly induced to migrate to Veṅgī from the Coḻa heartland. The *gotra*-wise list of the donees, along with their names and the distribution to shares is prefaced by another mini-*praśasti* on the merits of the Brahman *varṇa*. This supplies a small creation myth drawing on significant stories from the epics and *purāṇa*s (Triśaṅku, Nahuṣa, Śiva as Tripurāntaka), illustrative of the greatness of the caste. These basic details are given in Table 3.1.

Table 3.1 *Details of the Veṅgī copperplate charters, 1086–1093*

Name and reference	Issuing king	Year (Kulottuṅga's regnal year and CE)	Extent	Nature of grant
Teki (EI 6: 35)	Rājarāja Coḍagaṅga	Year 17, 1086–1087	5 plates, 109 lines, 48 verses; includes long passage in *gadya* prose	Awarding special privileges to members of the Teliki caste-community
Chellur (SII 1: 39)	Vīracoḍa	Year 21, 1090–1091	5 plates, 114 lines, 40 verses	Granting a village to a Viṣṇu temple founded by the Brahman *senāpati* Meḍamārya
Pithapuram (EI 5:10)	Vīracoḍa	Year 23, 1092–1093	9 plates, 280 lines, 35 verses	Creates a new *brahmadeya* village, Vīracoḍa-caturvedimaṅgalam; includes a list of the names of the 536 donees

The contours of the inscriptional culture that the local world of Veṅgī sustained were markedly different from those of the Coḻa country. As we have seen, in the second half of the eleventh century, the Coḻa epigraphic order was dominated by stone inscriptions on temple walls, largely composed in Tamil and issued by a range of elite social actors. The Coḻa emperors issued occasional royal orders on copper, as in the enormous Karandai Tamil Sangam plates issued by Rājendra *ca.* 1020, weighing some 216 pounds.[39] But even the most gigantic of these are dwarfed by the sheer quantity of stone epigraphs. By contrast, copperplates remained the main technology of epigraphic dissemination by the Veṅgī Cālukyas: while stone temple inscriptions occur, their numbers do not approach what is seen in the far south. This can be correlated to a broadly different mode of rule, as the portable copperplate epigraphs, there as elsewhere, were meant to perform a different function than stone records. While the latter tended to confirm endowments or legal rights enjoyed by the institution, usually a temple, which served as the site of inscription, copperplate charters were portable documents meant to establish specific rights and prerogatives for individuals or collectivities, and were almost invariably associated with royal power.

The habit of the making of copperplate charters possesses a long history particular to the Veṅgī region: beginning in the late ninth-century reign of Guṇaga Vijayāditya III, the Cālukyas employed a standard epigraphic template, composed in an unambitious register of Sanskrit prose, notable for its assignment of relatively exact dates to the length of each king's reign.[40] This model of a compact king-list appended to the head of the Cālukyas' royal orders underwent a further elaboration in the first half of the eleventh century, with the addition of a common narrative armature uniting the Veṅgī Cālukyas' records with those of their more imperially ambitious cousins to the west in Kalyāṇa. The degree to which the new format may have been directly catalyzed by an infusion of the political rhetoric from the western family remains undetermined; there appears, however, to have been a real circulatory network operating between the two dynastic centers.[41]

While the earlier king-list begins with the historical fact of the early seventh-century division of the two Cālukya lines, with Pulakeśin II ruling in the west and his brother Kubja Viṣṇuvardhana dispatched to the east, this was downplayed in the new format, first seen in the grants of Śaktivarman I (r. 999–1011). Instead, the revised texts favor of a grander epic vision of the dynasty's past and future, grafted onto the existing template.[42] The new format introduces a doubled mythic origin for the Cālukya family, in line with the tradition being invented at the same time in Kalyāṇa. The family traces its origin through the lunar dynasty and thus through the protagonists of the *Mahābhārata* war, while the account also has the family's forebears ruling for fifty-nine unbroken generations at Ayodhyā, the capital of the *Rāmāyaṇa*'s solar dynasts.[43] To this reimagining, shared between the two branches of the family, the Veṅgī texts add a distinctive narrative element: the first named ancestor to move to the south from Ayodhyā, Vijayāditya, dies unexpectedly ("through the machinations of fate," *daivadurīhayā*), and his pregnant widow is adopted by a Brahman, called Viṣṇubhaṭṭasomayājin. Her son is named Viṣṇuvardhana, thus establishing the order of the alternating cognomina for the Veṅgī Cālukyas, parallel to the Coḻa practice. It is he who, processed through the rituals of both his Kṣatriya and Brahman families, obtains the favor of the goddess Nandā atop Mount Calukya, providing his descendants with their customary sobriquet.[44]

While this brief narrative innovation was constructed at least partly out of the formulaic materials shared with the Kalyāṇa base-text, its inflection here is the first instance of the impress of local influences upon the records' design and rhetoric. In the Brahmanical "adoption" of the founding ancestor, we can perhaps see an ethnohistorical gloss on the place of the warrior family within the heavily Brahmanized social world of the Godāvari delta, paralleling the adoption of the idiom of the Bhārata family, which provided the eastern Cālukyas with narrative resources to act out their own intramural tensions and conflicts.[45] This narrative matrix appears in all of the Veṅgī charters of the early eleventh century: it is there in the records of Vimalāditya, Rājarāja Narendra, Vijayāditya VII, and Śaktivarman II, respectively, Kulottuṅga's paternal grandfather, father, paternal uncle, and parallel cousin.[46] But the model was not fixed. Individual realizations of it could rework the description of each individual king, expanding upward from the bare fact of the king's name and the length of his reign into a more ornate description. As the king-list grew nearer to the particular issuing king's time, simple prose gives way to verse, and so into a full-fledged *praśasti* of the king and his immediate ancestors.

Within this space of possibilities we may situate Viddayabhaṭṭa, the named author – the so-called *kāvyakartṛ*, "poem-maker" – of all three of the charters issued by Kulottuṅga's sons. By this title, we should perhaps understand "the creator of the [new] poetry," the figure responsible for revising and extending the inherited matrix-text. The colophons found at the close of all three records are unanimous in attributing the works to Viddaya working in collaboration with a scribe (*lekhaka*) named Pennācāri, who actually produced the draft copy for the coppersmiths.[47] This straightforward attribution, however, glosses an altogether more complicated situation. It is difficult, first of all, to sort out what the division of labor was likely to have been between these two men: evidently one or both of them also served in some way as an editor, responsible for sorting through the existing versions and choosing the best one from which to depart.

More significantly, over the period of their issue, the three Coḻa–Cālukya plates evince a pattern of partial revision and retooling, based on the pragmatic circumstances of their particular donations, among other concerns. Within them, we can trace the ways in which other, unnamed agents contributed to the charters, introducing changes in the verbal matter of the text ranging from minor corrections of grammatical or metrical usage to wholesale revision of the text's explicit political message and its poetic framing. While Viddaya (or Viddaya-Penna) is thus the attributed author of the plates' eulogies, we are witness here to a complex process of collective authorship. All the same, and purely for convenience's sake, in what follows I will refer to the author of the shifting text as Viddaya.

The interrelationship between these three texts is an intricate one that resists a straightforward narrative of redaction. Taken together, a picture emerges of three very different works, possessing particular aesthetic and practical dimensions, which happen to largely coincide in their language. Though able to work in a range of complex meters and art-prose, and showing a command over *alaṃkāra* and a range of purāṇic references, Viddaya was not always observant of the niceties of grammar and prosody, and his verses undergo changes over time that testify to the hand of early readers and critics of his work. Within the three versions, we are thus privy to a process of textual editing and revision that is otherwise almost unprecedented in a medieval author. It is the irreducibility of these differences, however, that provides the impetus to understand how each of the charters sought to affect a doubled intervention, into the dynastic narrative of the Coḻa and Cālukya families and into the world of the Veṅgī kingdom.

Rājarāja Coḍagaṅga and Vīracoḍa, the two sons of Kulottuṅga who were the issuing authorities for the charters, each stepped into the unstable role of the semi-independent ruler of Veṅgī just as it was in the process of being integrated into the Coḻa landed order, an effort that was to prove ultimately ephemeral.[48] In hiving off the rule over the northeastern kingdom, Kulottuṅga appears to have adapted the mid-century Coḻa system of appanage, while maintaining the customary appearance of Cālukya rule. Coḍagaṅga and Vīracoḍa had not been the first of Kulottuṅga's sons who held this post, and Vīracoḍa did so twice, after a gap of some years. There are no surviving records from the first of the Coḻa princes deputed to Veṅgī, and even his name is uncertain: called Mummuḍicoḍa in Coḍagaṅga's record and Rājarāja in the two issued by Vīracoḍa,[49] he only held the office for a year before (we are told) "finding that kingship was not as pleasant as the pleasure of serving the feet of his elders" he returned to Colamandalam.[50] Vīracoḍa was dispatched next, sometime in 1077–1078; there are no inscriptions from this period, however, and after six years he was himself recalled, as his father either "called him back out of his desire to gaze upon the loveliness of his form, unequalled in its youthful beauty" or "brought him back since his sole desire was to be reunited with his parents and brothers."[51] For the next five years Coḍagaṅga ruled prior to himself being recalled (presumably so: the two later grants are silent on this point) and Vīracoḍa allowed to resume his reign.[52] Note the marked contrast to Bilhaṇa: Viddayabhaṭṭa's several accounts all made explicit reference to time, references that can be collated with the dates given in the Śaka era of the royal orders themselves.

The dissonance between this evidently turbulent decade and a half, a period which saw three different kings ruling in quick succession, and the placid, sentimental language seen in these brief quotations illustrates a core feature of the charters' narrative imagination. What were likely to have been cases of recall, familial tension and tentative or open bids for independence within a fluid, unstable political environment are cast into the register of paternal loyalty, masculine intimacy, and family melodrama, in a way that connects Viddaya's charters to Bilhaṇa's otherwise very different work. The stakes of ruling over Veṅgī were very high indeed, in both material and symbolic terms. A notably rich agrarian region, Veṅgī was the third side in the asymmetrical triad of the kingdoms of the south, and, in light of the dispositions inflecting the power politics of the medieval period, it was strikingly, even troublingly, anomalous. Ruled over by Cālukyas, but those of putatively Somavaṃśin extraction in contrast to the Sūryavaṃśins ruling in Kalyāṇa, and the brightest corner of the green and settled east set all around by dry, warlike uplands, Veṅgī had for decades been caught in a shifting field of force between the Kalyāṇa cousin-dynasty to the west and the Coḻa south.[53]

When Rājendracoḷa was first making his fortune in the northern marches of the Coḻa lands, his natal kingdom was ruled by his uncle Vijayāditya. As these plates attest, it was around 1076, two years after the king's imperial Coḻa accession, that control over the Andhra kingdom reverted to his authority. Veṅgī then became a proving ground for Kulottuṅga's sons: for this new generation of Coḻa-Cālukya kings, the need to retain favor back in Colamandalam was cross-cut by the more immediate tasks of local control and the maintenance of political alliance. Veṅgī possessed its own landscape of power, its own caste-based lordships and its own very prominent Brahmanical dispensation, and the operative portions of the plates attest to the differing strategies of rule practiced by the Coḻa incumbents, ranging from the recognition of local customary rights to the wholesale importation of Tamil Brahmans.

There are thus three intertwinned projects at work in these texts. First, there is the narration of the past, explaining how the present king came to enjoy his position: this is based upon the narrative that the Cālukya kings had been telling and extending for generations. But recent history bulks large in all three versions, attesting to an acknowledged transformation in the nature of Veṅgī kingship: it is here that the story of Kulottuṅga is told. Each of these texts further aimed to produce a consummate image of the currently ruling king, Coḍagaṅga or Vīracoḍa. Here, the material is more unstable, and more liable to shift in emphases between versions. The varying past narrated by the three texts and the present person of the issuing king are of course not dissociable: the particular man's position in the genealogy, and the narrated history of his relations with his imperial father constrained Viddayabhaṭṭa's focus to particular genealogical and expressive angles of vision. Finally, there is the declaration of the donative act itself, and of the *pātra*, the worthy vessel of its receipt. This differs completely in each text: besides providing the connection between the work of praise and the world of local agents, this donative impulse colored the eulogistic text, affecting the presentation of the kind of king who undertook such a gesture.

While the text of Viddaya's *praśasti* is given in (mostly) good Sanskrit, and composed according to aesthetic canons that would have been recognizable throughout the cosmopolis, there is a subtle undercurrent of the local and the vernacular discernable within it. This Andhra nuance can be seen in details of textual genre and in the flavor of individual verses in a way that would have registered with the charters' initial audience, and which would itself have served the projects of their issuing kings. This is exactly in keeping with the larger work of the charters, their attempt to set the kings within the local, while gesturing toward grander epic and imperial narratives. Viddaya's three texts largely coincide in their opening, reproducing the inherited king-list matrix, and bringing the account of the Cālukya kings up to Vimalāditya, the issuing kings' paternal great-grandfather.[54] All three then turn to the account of Kulottuṅga's conjoint ancestry in the Cālukya and Co<u>l</u>a families: it is this passage that first spurred the genealogical reconstruction that has dominated the earlier discussion of Kulottuṅga's accession. To emphasize: it is in texts from Veṅgī – but *only* there – that we first find any clear testimony to Kulottuṅga's doubled ancestry. While Rājendracoḷa's earliest *mĕykkīrtti* alluded to his Cālukya heritage, and (as we shall see) Cayaṅkŏṇṭār's *Kaliṅkattupparaṇi* would later include an equivocal account, these earlier and later poetic figurings of the Co<u>l</u>a king's ancestry would be uninterpretable without the evidence furnished by the data contained in his sons' orders, issued far away from the Co<u>l</u>a kingdom's core.

It was thus only in these records, and in the Veṅgī context in which they were disseminated, that the question of Kulottuṅga's doubled origins was considered important: it was only there that its narration took on the character of an "actionable" account of the past. Chief among the resources that Viddaya had at his disposal was the narrative stereotype of the solar and lunar lineages. The eulogies of earlier generations of Co<u>l</u>a and Cālukya kings certainly employed these stereotypes: Rājendracoḷa's first *mĕykkīrtti* makes passing use of the topos of dynastic sunrise, and Candrabhūṣanabhaṭṭa's innovative Sanskrit *praśasti* on Vīrarājendra sustains a lengthy narrative of the Co<u>l</u>as' *sūryavaṃśa* credentials. But the mythic resonances of the two families, especially their linkage with the events of the great epics, are all but ignored by Viddaya, and these traditional materials instead take on a changed significance. Instead of the mythic past, it is the coming together of sun and moon in Veṅgī's present time that provides a heavily overdetermined means to describe his patrons' place within their world.

It is here that the variation between the three records becomes significant, as the differences between them were clearly motivated by more than just grammatical, metrical, or literary-critical scruple. This level of consequential variation impinges upon the records' interpretation: this is not just a technical matter of interest only to a pedantic paṇḍit or a modern philologist-editor, but a core feature of the charters' textuality that repays direct attention by anyone who might wish to understand them. For instance, in referring to Kulottuṅga's parents, the texts divide into two partly overlapping versions, where Teki and Pithapuram read together against Chellur:[55]

That king [Rājarājanarendra] lawfully took as his queen the lady famed throughout the world by the name Ammaṃgā, whose power lay in her beauty, suited to [his own], and who purifies the entire earth [C: He had as his queen the lady famed throughout the world by the name Ammaṃgā, who was totally without fault on account of her righteous deeds, the sole dwelling place of every auspicious quality, who purifies the entire earth]: just as the Gaṅgā was born of Jahnu, Gauri from Himavān, and Lakṣmī from the milky ocean, she was born of the Coḍa Rājendra, the ornament of the dynasty of the Sun.

Here, in the charters' first reference to the solar lineage,[56] the variation characteristic of this section of the *praśasti* is immediately apparent. Though all three of the verses convey the same information, the reading of Chellur stands apart; strikingly so, given that it falls between the other two records in time. Chellur was the first grant to be issued by Vīracoḍa, and the two brothers were evidently rivals, and it is prima facie possible that the revisions there might have been motivated by a desire to distinguish the issuing king from his possibly disgraced half-brother. However, Pithapuram, issued two years later, reverts to the readings given in Teki, both here and elsewhere.

There is thus no decisive motivation for the changes introduced in Chellur, which change the verse's grammatical armature and substitutes a few, trivial details in the description of the kings' Coḻa grandmother.[57] The next verse, which all three charters share in common (except for a trivial error in Teki), continues the theme:[58]

> As Śiva and Parvatī had Kārttikeya, the two of them had a far-famed son, whose unimpeded power [/spear] laid waste to the hordes of his enemies, called Rājendracoḍa, a bright light among the race of kings.

The very next verse reverts to the divided readings (Chellur versus Teki/ Pithapuram) in its description of the young Cālukya Rājendracoḍa's first successes, and in its statement of the solar theme:[59]

He first set himself to rule over Veṅgī, the source of the arising of the radiance [of his fame], just as the thousand-rayed sun first sets itself on Sunrise Mountain, and then proceeded through his (and its) brilliance to the corners of the earth.

Here, the changes in the Chellur text are slight enough to be unnoticeable in translation. In a reverse of the situation seen elsewhere, its revision introduces a grammatical solecism; otherwise the Chellur text appears to have been revised with an eye to removing such errors.[60] Nevertheless, the real interest to this verse, present in all of the versions, lies in the *śleṣopamā* or punned simile. Crucially, in a concatenation of the mythic and geographical registers, Rājendracoḍa begins his glorious rise – like the sun – in the land of Sunrise Mountain, indexing Veṅgī's real location while connecting him with the radiant charisma of his maternal lineage. This provides the organizing metonymy for representing the experience of Kulottuṅga's rise to power, reminiscent of Rājendracoḷa's own early *mĕykkīrtti*'s invocation of Viṣṇu's boar *avatāra*. In the verse immediately following, the Chellur text again shows revision, this time substantial: the young king's fame (*kīrtiḥ*), simply called "matchless" (*atulā*) in the other two versions, is described via a rearrangement of the verse's final line to be "as white as the nectar-rayed moon" (*sudhāṃśudhāmadhavalā*), a beautifully alliterative phrase that supplies a lunar counterpoint to the preceding stanza's solar theme. Here again Chellur's changes register as improvements.

The crescendo of this whole set-piece, however, is found in the verse that follows (TP 10, C 11):

bhogīśābhīlabhogapratimanijabhujabhartsitātyantabibhyan-
nānābhūpālalokaprahitabahuvidhānarghyaratnābhirāmam |
dhatte mauliṃ parārdhyo mahati nṛpakule yaḥ kulottuṃgadevo
devendratvād anūne surapatimahimā coḍarājye [']*bhiṣiktaḥ* | |
bhogapratimanijabhujabhartsitātyanta-] TP; *bhogapratibhayabhujanirbhartsanātyanta-* C
-arghya-] CP; *-argha-* T

He, Kulottuṅga, supreme among the entire great race of rulers,
as powerful as the lord of the gods,
was embued with the sovereign power of the Coḷa kings,
itself not inferior to Indra's role in the heavens –
placing upon his head the crown made lovely by the great many perfect jewels
offered up by all the many kings of the world, terrorstruck by the threat of his
arms, like [C: as frightening as] the awful coils of the lord of the snakes.

The verse is composed in the long and regal art-meter *sragdharā*, and its first half verse consists of a forty-two syllable barrage of aspirate and labial sounds, suggestive of the mass and power of the serpent's coils they describe. This remarkably forms a single long compound word, an adjective to the seemingly innocuous *maulim*, "crown," set at the join between its two halves. The remainder of the verse, though less grandiloquent than the drumroll with which it begins, turns in on itself with subtle tricks of etymological word play and syntactic zigzag (*parārdhyo mahati nṛpakule yaḥ kulottuṃgadevo*, joining what Western rhetoric calls chiasmus and *figura etymologica*), a sort of semantic "rhyme" of synonyms (*-devo, devendra-, surapati-*) and the feigned cancelation of a double negative (*anūne*, "not less than," "not inferior to").

None of this is alien to other modes of Sanskrit *kāvya*, but the combination of these several effects partakes of features of contemporaneous Telugu poetry, and of a peculiarly Andhran register of poetic Sanskrit. This can be seen especially in the play at the syntactic plane between the dense nominal compounding in the first half and the staccato series of syntagma in the second.[61] Here, again the reading in Chellur stands out, and once again it is an improvement, as it corrects a slight metrical flaw in the midst of the long descriptive compound.[62] Again, the reversion to the earlier more imperfect text in Pithapuram is strange; perhaps the compilation of the new conjoint text was out of the Viddaya's control, or the changes in Chellur are owed to another hand or hands.

The verse builds to its final and significant piece of historical reference: it is upon his consecration into the rule over the Coḻa country that the Veṅgī lord earlier only called Rājendracoḍa became Kulottuṅga, a momentous public transformation that this notably grand verse is meant to iconize. Following upon this bravura moment – both serious Sanskrit verse-craft and serious historiography – the three texts substantially diverge. The differences from this point are no longer now simply editorial: the two kings' charters provide alternative accounts. These differences center on the person of the previous Coḻa ruler of Veṅgī, Mummuḍicoḍa/Rājarāja. In Coḍagaṅga's version seen in Teki, this is recorded in three verses:[63]

That bull among kings had many queens, born in the families of famous lords of the earth, ever attentive, passionate, and graceful, just as the sea's queens are rivers, which arise in famed mountain ranges, are always flowing in his direction, full of water and clear.

So the godlike king delights in his many sons, so very like himself and praised by brahmans, the gods among men, that he obtained from these wives: he seems to mock at Śiva himself, who has only a single son.

Setting his sons to several endeavours, as the soul sets the senses upon their objects, he said the following to his son Mummuḍicoḍa –

By contrast, Vīracoḍa's two charters, reading together for the first time, relate over two verses in a longer meter a more detailed account, focusing on only one of Kulottuṅga's queens, "that Lakṣmī born from the sea that is King Rājendra, pinnacle of the solar dynasty, who is known by the name Madhurāntakī,"[64] again indexing the multiple connections that the king and (at least some of) his sons possess to the earlier generations of the imperial line. Vīracoḍa's records go on to suggest that Madhurāntakī bore Kulottuṅga seven sons, to one of whom (here called Rājarāja) Kulottuṅga addresses himself.

Significantly Coḍagaṅga's record elides any direct mention of this final link in the marital chain uniting the Coḻas and the Cālukyas. Presumably the issuing king's own place in the lineage was not served by the mention of Madhurāntakī, his father's Coḻa cousin and wife. It is thus a presumption, though not a great one, to conclude that she was the mother of Mummuḍicoḷa and Vīracoḍa, but not Coḍagaṅga, whose record instead emphasizes his own precedence in birth order, as he is twice said to be the eldest of the brothers (*agrajam*);[65] on this theory, he may have been the product of an earlier marital alliance.

Reverting to simple narrative verse, the three charters relate in unison the imperial father's words to their issuers' brother Mummuḍi-Rājarāja.[66] The reader learns from Kulottuṅga's speech that his paternal uncle Vijayāditya, earlier charged by Kulottuṅga to rule over his possessions in Veṅgī, had died, and that he was entrusting his son with the rule over their Andhra patrimony. After Mummuḍi-Rājarāja's single year of rule, both versions agree that Vīracoḍa was ordered to next rule over Veṅgī. In Coḍagaṅga's record, this is reported baldly; in Vīracoḍa's own version, the result is more elaborate:[67]

Then the emperor addressed [Mummuḍi's] younger brother, the forthright prince Vīracoḍa, who was like the quality of valor embodied:[68] "Setting yourself as the overlord of Veṅgī, just as sun sets itself upon Sunrise Mountain, place your feet, as the sun does its rays, upon the heads of the kings of the earth."

This verse is evidently modeled on the prototype in Teki, but refashions the materials of the earlier charter's prosaic verse into a restatement of the solar theme. From this point onward, the texts issued by the two brothers diverge entirely: Coḍagaṅga's record continues in high literary style, detailing Vīracoḍa's six-year reign in Veṅgī prior to his recall, Coḍagaṅga's own selection by the emperor and his rule in Veṅgī, before switching to an extended passage of complex literary prose, some of it an intensified reworking of the old prose "letterhead" of the Cālukya epigraphic template. It then shifts into the contents of its royal order, given partly in verse. By contrast, in Vīracoḍa's grants, the art-prose is stripped away and we can observe a fascinating process whereby some of the matter, and even the language, of Viddaya's earlier verses on Coḍagaṅga is tinkered with and reworked,[69] as the king's five-year hiatus away from Veṅgī is glossed over as an extended visit to see his loving father.

As in Rājendracoḷa's *mĕykkīrtti*, there was intensely political work performed by the language of these Veṅgī charters. Claims of descent and of the mythopoetics of royal authority are represented in the medium of Sanskrit *kāvya*, transcribing the language of both local and imperial politics into a higher representational key. The shift in all three of the charters from the eulogy to the donative matter continues this still more intensely. In each case, this shift is signaled by the introduction of a version of the prose titulary found in all grants of the Cālukya family. But instead of a strict division between the "poetic" and the "business" portion of the grant, it is better to understand these as united in a common logic.

Throughout, the charters confront the problematic status of Viddayabhaṭṭa's two patron-kings. These Coḻa princes were not secure in their positions, either as the local rulers of Veṅgī or as potential successors to their father in Colamandalam; this is something that the charter's eulogistic narration highlights through its melodramatic amplification of what were certainly real tensions within the imperial family. Coḍagaṅga and Vīracoḍa had Viddaya (and whatever anonymous others) narrate a place for themselves within the family, while attempting to secure a personal, charismatic hold over the newly secured northern salient of the empire. The shifting eulogistic text of all three charters attempts to contain this dynastic instability by figuring it as a moment of spatial and political syzygy – the coming of the sun to Sunrise Mountain – while leaving undisturbed the continuo of the language of Cālukya kingship: both of the princes, Coḻa in their very names, are described as "the refuge of the entire world, Viṣṇuvardhana the great overlord among kings, supreme lord of kings, foremost devotee of Śiva, foremost master, foremost in Brahmanical virtue," as the Cālukyas had been for centuries.[70]

It is worth recalling the nature of these charters as text-artifacts, as works of language recorded in a permanent material substratum, issued to private citizen-subjects or corporate entities, the granting of which was the end result of a spectacular piece of political theater, combining all the excitement of a royal visitation with the extended performance of the literary text which the plates encode. Viddayabhaṭṭa's text represented a literary quantum leap over the earlier annalistic documents of the Veṅgī chancellery, and this leap is equally apparent when the charters are seen as objects: in both their physical size and their textual complexity, these represented a break with the past, an icon of the grandeur promised by the new Coḻa order. The charters' donees, who were presumably the initial possessors of the plates, were heterogeneous: ranging from a cluster of families claiming long service to the Cālukya family to whom Coḍagaṅga confirmed certain customary rights, to Vīracoḍa's donation of a village to a temple patronised by a Brahman subordinate and – finally and most spectacularly – the latter's creation of a new Brahman land grant village, accompanied by the settlement of more than 500 documented colonists from Colamandalam. In each of these, we can see the realization of a very different public project, and can speculate what this may have meant for each of Kulottuṅga's ambitious sons who found themselves in nominal control of Veṅgī.

In Coḍagaṅga's case, the continuity between eulogy and royal order is especially clear: the extended passage of *gadya* art-prose – a single long relative clause in which the king is serially compared to each of the eight guardians of the directions – acts as a bridge between the narrative verses and the narrated fact of his pronouncement. The charter as a whole thus resembles the form of a *campū*, a mixed prose and verse literary composition. In this, we see another Andhra localism at work, as the *campū* is the preeminent genre of the emerging world of Telugu literature in this period.[71] When Coḍagaṅga speaks in the documentary portion, his simple, direct Sanskrit verse mirrors that of his father Kulottuṅga's speech earlier in the text. Indeed, the logic of Coḍagaṅga's royal order itself mirrors the politicking of Kulottuṅga's own preimperial years: in what may be an effort to reproduce his father's successful alliance-building with the people of the Tondai country, Coḍagaṅga elaborately praises the Teliki caste, who in the distant past joined with the ancestral Cālukya Vijayāditya I in emigrating southward from Ayodhyā. The Teliki people, whose subcastes are enumerated with a gazetteer's eye for detail (the grant lists ten, ll. 90–91), are here recognized for their martial qualities in the prerogatives granted to them: the right to ride horses at weddings and ritual prestations like betel-bearing have a long and deep history thoroughout India, especially as the customary rights of *kṣatriya* and later Rajput families. But the Teliki community was not a part of the landed gentry: their traditional occupation was oil-pressing, a quintessentially left-hand vocation.

In direct tension with the eulogy's efforts to link Coḍagaṅga's reign with the coming of the Coḻa sun to its rightful home in Andhra country, the proclamation and its beneficiaries are conspicuously local in character. The seven years prior to Coḍagaṅga's dispatch to Veṅgī saw two of his brothers installed as rulers, only to be summarily recalled. The record, issued when he had barely been in Veṅgī for two years, can be read as an effort to build up a local constituency, a political network resembling the one his father had earlier fashioned in Tondaimandalam. This is by far the most orotund of the three charters, and so there might seem to be a dissonance between the boldness of the assertion of royal glory and the limited nature of this confirmation of local marital customs. Yet to Coḍagaṅga and his court, this strategy of rhetorical assertion mixed with the assiduous cultivation of local elites may have been a prudent way to shore up his position, while connecting himself in words and deeds to the imperial center to the south.

It is unclear whether Coḍagaṅga's local alliance-making failed or was perhaps too successful, thus necessitating his recall. Nevertheless, Vīracoḍa's first surviving pronouncement, issued four years later, hews to a similar but distinct strategy. Again, the donee is from the local Veṅgī elite, though in this case it is a single Brahman, rather than a community of fighting oilmongers, who is singled out for honor. Paralleling the royal eulogy, there is an effort to ground Meḍamārya's pedigree in the deep past, in this case to his founding Brahman ancestor Mudgala, before swiftly introducing his father, "a man of quality, whom the king Rājarāja – knowing quality when he saw it – was delighted to praise by [granting] him the title Rājarājabrahmamahārāja."[72] From this it is clear that Meḍama's family was connected at least in the previous generation with the imperial kings to the south, as the title is a diagnostically Coḻa one.[73] Meḍama had himself been awarded the role of *senāpati* by Vīracoḍa (ll. 91–92, vs. 30), but is otherwise celebrated in the brief *praśasti* which the grant dedicates to him for his piety and religious generosity. The grant, which records support for some repair work undertaken to a Viṣṇu temple in the vicinity of Chellur, appears to be a conspicuous celebration of a Coḻa loyalist, a man with familial connections to the imperial court and with a reputation for religious gifting; further, the record is very clearly directed toward a Brahmanical audience.[74] Again, the immediate consequences of this public celebration of this Brahman grandee are unknown. What is clear, however, is that two years later, Vīracoḍa was to adopt a different strategy, once again centered on the pursuit of Brahmanical alliance.

In the final set of plates, Vīracoḍa inaugurated an altogether new *agrahāra*, bringing together three existing villages; one of these, Ponnatoṟṟam, seems to have been a substantial settlement. The formal declaration of the existence of the new mega-village is preceded by the list of the more than 500 beneficiaries, organized by their *gotra* in descending order of magnitude. The names on the list overwhelmingly suggest these to be colonists from the Coḻa heartland; assuming that each named man served as the *gṛhapati* or paterfamilias of an extended joint family, the number of people imported into the region must have numbered several thousand.[75] This is preceded by another mini-*praśasti*, this time on the virtues of the Brahman order itself (vv. 28–32, ll. 71–80). The appeal to the Brahmanical audience is set out in a starkly instrumental, legitimationist terms: a king – even an awful one, like Triśaṅku – who has even a single Brahman on his side attains heaven, while a very good king like Nahuṣa, who attained the state of Indra in his body, plunges down from heaven should he afoul of even a single man of the order. Even Śiva's destruction of the Triple City hinged upon paying proper reverence to these gods on earth.[76] In a final and pointed reprise of the royal eulogy's solar theme, the king is made to openly reflect on the fact that the sun's ability to overcome the twilight machinations of the *rākṣasa*s and continue its daily protection of the world is all dependent upon Brahmanical power, as embodied in the twice-a-day *saṃdhyā* observance.[77] It is tempting to hear an undertone of slight desperation in this staged poetic self-effacement, with the Coḻa prince perhaps running out of time and options among the different collectivities in the Andhra province, and needing to resort to this openly colonial attempt to shore up his government, both politically and apotropaically.

Throughout Viddayabhaṭṭa's *praśasti*s, there is an ongoing project to imagine a place for his patrons within an unstable conjuncture of local and imperial interests. This is especially evident in its reliance on the doubled dynastic origins of his patrons' father and so themselves. It seems that the coming together of the sun and moon, of Coḻa and Cālukya, was salient within the real social world as well as the symbolic order of the Veṅgī kingdom. By creating through the language of *kāvya* a series of figurative identifications – above all, the coming of the Coḻa sun to Veṅgī's Sunrise Mountain – Viddaya offered his Coḻa patrons a way to lay claim to an august local lineage as well as a privileged place in the distant imperial order. It was this larger project of political metonymy that took as its raw materials the intertwinned history of the Coḻa and Cālukya families over the previous three generations. While we have no reason to doubt the reality of the marital alliances that made this possible, understanding them is only the first step in an interpretation of how these facts were transformed through representation, and to account for their significance within the complex collective project at the intersection of the actions of poet, scribe, audience, and patron in Veṅgī in the 1080s and 1090s.

In the end, Vīracoḍa's efforts to make himself into a viable heir to his father would prove as unsuccessful as his step-brother's.[78] The real decisions as to who would ultimately succeed Kulottuṅga were made far away from their erstwhile kingdom. At some point between 1096 and 1100, the imperial household underwent a major change: the queen referred to in earlier royal pronouncements as Dīnacintāmaṇi ("Wishing-stone for the needy"), Kulottuṅga's chief queen up until that time – likely his royal cousin Madhurāntaki, the mother of Mummuḍi and Vīracoḍa – was replaced by a new *mahiṣī*, publicly named Tyāgavallī ("Creeper of generosity").[79] This was to have far-reaching consequences in Veṅgī. At roughly the same time, another of Kulottuṅga's sons became active in the northern kingdom, evidently in command of the first of Kulottuṅga's two campaigns against Kaliṅga, the second of which would supply the titular subject of Cayaṅkŏṇṭar's *Kaliṅkattupparaṇi*. This campaign is mentioned in Kulottuṅga's twenty-sixth year (1096, SII 3: 72), when Dīnacintāmaṇi (=Madhurāntakī) was still chief queen; from this time onward, this Co͟la prince's career is obscure – there are no records issued in his name in Veṅgī or in Colamandalam – until June of 1118, when he was crowned as Parakesarivarman Vikramaco͟la, the name by which he would rule after Kulottuṅga's death around 1121.[80] The rise to prominence of Tyāgavallī and Vikrama appears to not have been coincidental, and Kulottuṅga's ultimate successor was likely the son of his second chief queen.[81] Besides the rough synchrony of events, the evidence for this relationship is circumstantial but strong: Vikramaco͟la bore the *biruda* Tyāgasamudra ("Ocean of Generosity," a title with strong eastern Cālukya associations), and in turn one of his own queens would bear the name Tyāgapatākā ("Banner of Generosity"); Vikrama's own *mĕykkīrtti*s emphasize his youth during his war against Kaliṅga, suggesting he could well have been the son of a junior queen.[82]

Coḍagaṅga's and Vīracoḍa's inability to effect a transition from ruling the northern kingdom to succeeding their father may ultimately have had less to do with their own alliance-making in Veṅgī and more with the politics of the distant imperial harem: less a matter of a connection with the doubled imperial line that Co͟la–Cālukya royal diplomacy had sought to create, and more to do with intimate access to Kulottuṅga's person. This can be gathered from a final view of the Co͟la–Cālukya conjoint genealogy, seen from the perspective of Kulottuṅga's sons in Veṅgī (see Figure 3.1). Some of the details here remain tantalizingly out of reach: the three queens whom Kulottuṅga acknowledged in his own records almost certainly did not exhaust his wives or concubines, so while it is reasonable to deduce that the woman there called E͟licaivallapi may have been

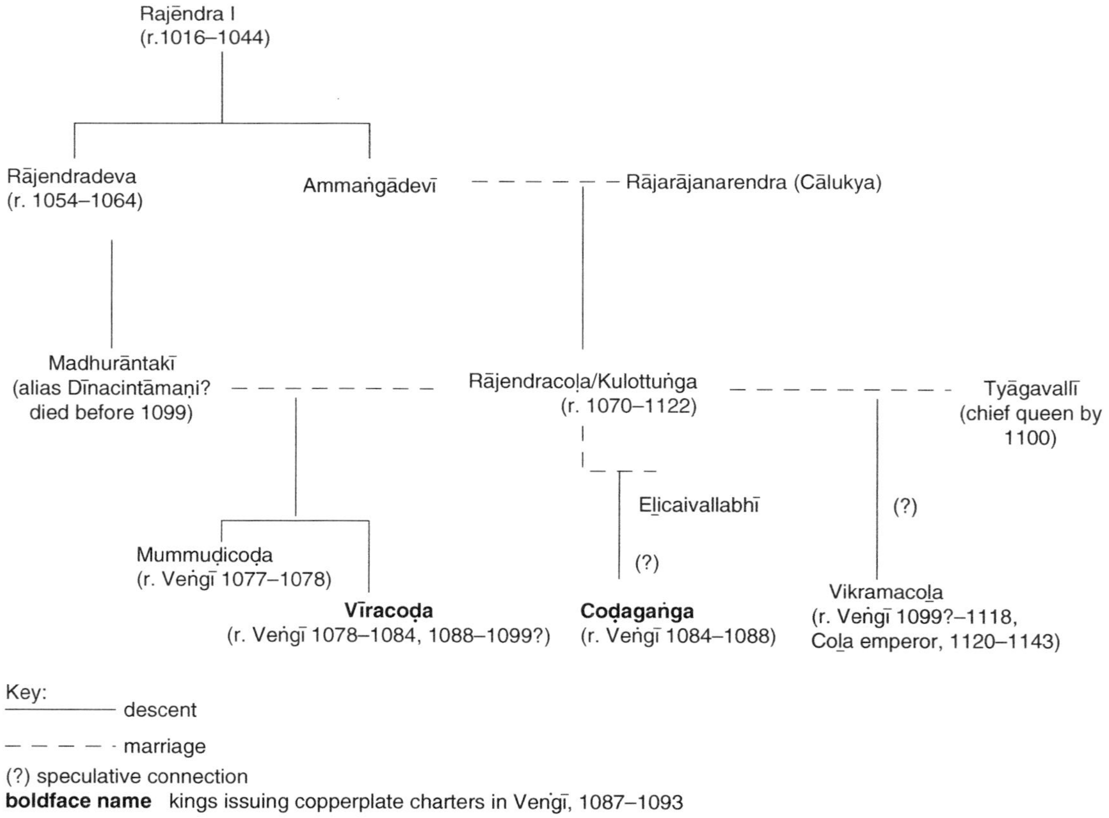

Rajēndra I
(r.1016–1044)
Rājendradeva
(r. 1054–1064)
Ammaṅgādevī
Rājarājanarendra (Cālukya)
Madhurāntakī
(alias Dīnacintāmaṇi?
died before 1099)
Rājendracoḷa/Kulottuṅga
(r. 1070–1122)
Tyāgavallī
(chief queen by
1100)
Eḻicaivallabhī
(?)
(?)
Mummuḍicoḍa
(r. Veṅgī 1077–1078)
Vīracoḍa
(r. Veṅgī 1078–1084, 1088–1099?)
Coḍagaṅga
(r. Veṅgī 1084–1088)
Vikramacoḻa
(r. Veṅgī 1099?–1118,
Coḻa emperor, 1120–1143)
Key:
descent
marriage
(?) speculative connection
boldface name kings issuing copperplate charters in Veṅgī, 1087–1093

Figure 3.1 The Coḻa genealogy, as seen from Veṅgī

Coḍagaṅga's mother, it is not certain. What Coḍagaṅga and Vīracoḍa had sought to realize through triangulation in Veṅgī was to be decided back in the Co<u>l</u>a country, where the shift in Kulottuṅga's mènage seems to have triggered both Tyāgavalli's ascendency and the beginning of the rise in the future Vikramaco<u>l</u>a's fortunes at court.

What is certain is that Vīracoḍa's reign in Veṅgī marked the end of the Cālukya dynasty there: having been effectively absorbed into the Co<u>l</u>a line, when Kulottuṅga and Vikrama were to ultimately lose control over coastal Andhra in the second and third decades of the twelfth century, the long-lived Cālukya family vanished as an effective political force. Instead, the dynasty was to become a part of the little kingdom's political imaginary: the metonymies established by Viddayabhaṭṭa would retain their rhetorical efficacy, but they would become part of the apparatus of rule employed by different families, arriviste gentry warriors of a familiar type. Their own political poetry contained the coda to the Viddaya's dynastic story; it is there that one can catch a glimpse, however fleeting, of the final eclipse of the Cālukya moon in the land of the Sunrise Mountain.

Time Warp and Incarnation

Compared to Bilhaṇa's and Viddaya's works, Cayaṅkŏṇṭār's *Kaliṅkattupparaṇi* contains the most sustained engagement with Kulottuṅga's early history. Composed and initially disseminated in the waning years of the king's long reign, it is an acknowledged masterpiece of the medieval Tamil canon. Its theme was supplied by a successful Co<u>l</u>a campaign against Kaliṅga, ruled by the eastern Gaṅga king Anantavarma Coḍagaṅga, not to be confused with Kulottuṅga's son who had briefly ruled over Veṅgī. The campaign had been conducted at some point around 1112 under the command of the magnate *senāpati* Karuṇākarat Tŏṇṭaimā<u>n</u>. This victory is directly alluded to in the poem's title, "A *paraṇi* offering on Kaliṅga." *Paraṇi*, derived from Sanskrit *bharaṇī* (the name of a triangular asterism contained within the constellation Ares), refers to a battlefield ritual consecrated to the goddess Kālī or her Tamil ectype Kŏ<u>r</u><u>r</u>avai in commemoration of a great victory, one in which myriads of the enemy's elephants were killed. This martial celebration supplied a *point d'appui* for Cayaṅkŏṇṭār's phantasmagoric take on court eulogy, hereafter the *Paraṇi*.[83]

The *Paraṇi* is the earliest surviving integral work of Co<u>l</u>a court poetry, and is the first evidence of the febrile literary creativity of the twelfth century, the seemingly miraculous generations that saw the works of Ŏṭṭakkūttar, Cekki<u>l</u>ār, and Kampa<u>n</u>. It is also the earliest surviving example of its genre, furnishing the standard-setting instance for all of its later elaborations. There are stray references to earlier *paraṇi*s composed in celebration of Rājādhirāja and Vīrarājendra, but no trace of these survives: they might have been strictly occasional entertainments in celebration of particular battlefield victories. While the taxonomy of medieval verse genres contained in the anonymous *Paṉṉiruppāṭṭiyal* supplies an elaborate catalog of the narrative elements of a *paraṇi*, this reads practically like a table of contents to Cayaṅkōṇṭār's poem, and there is little warrant to believe that it preceded him.[84]

There is a near-total lack of information about the *Paraṇi*'s author. Cayaṅkōṇṭār is a total cypher: he reports nothing whatsoever about himself in this, his sole surviving work; another poem, the *Icaiyāyiram*, is lost. Later literary memory has him elaborately rewarded by Kulottuṅga – given a golden coconut for every stanza of the *Paraṇi* – and attributes to him a verse contrasting the unending fame that his poetry will win for him beyond the king's remuneration, a gentler variation on Bilhaṇa's patronage agonistics. There is some suggestion in later literary memory of the poet's origins in Tondaimandalam, corroborated perhaps in his pen-name, with its echo of the Coḻa designation for the region, Cayaṅkōṇṭacoḻamaṇḍalam.[85]

The sanguinary goddess Kāḷi supplies the poem's central focus, recalling the connection between Rājendracoḷa's preimperial court and the goddess in Kolār. This connection is underlined by the form of the *paraṇi*-rite itself, the ritual antecedent whose structure provided the poem's underlying armature. Nacciṉārkkiṉiyar, the wide-ranging scholar of the fourteenth century, described this liturgical background: "By *paraṇi*, a particular custom is meant, in which there is the worship of the goddess who lives in the wild country performed on the day of the *bharaṇī* asterism, through the offering of gruel and the dance called the *tuṇaṅkai*; it is directed towards a particular protagonist, and includes in great abundance utterances given in the martial mode." This was, then, an established form of ritualized performance, the parameters of which would have been known to Cayaṅkōṇṭār's audience. It was, further, markedly gendered: the *tuṇaṅkai* was a dance-mode performed by women. In recasting this ritual form, Cayaṅkōṇṭār deftly transfers it from one social space, that of a more or less independent women's culture, to another, that of the royal court, in principle the exemplary zone of patriarchy and masculinity. This transfer, in turn, supplied the basis for other, even more radical juxtapositions: between the settled, domestic world and the anti-space of the battlefield; and between the human world and that of the horrific, distorted, and deformed realm of the monstrous *pey*s – zombie-like ghouls – who form Kāḷi's retinue.[86]

The world of the *pey*s is expressly figured as a bizarre variation on a royal court, complete with factions, ceremonial comportment, and internal politicking. The parallel with the world of the *Paraṇi*'s first audience is immediate and obvious, and this sort of double play on courtly life is of a piece with the poem's wider fascination with dramatic, narrative, and temporal staging. Throughout, it pendulates between the fantastic and distant (in terms of both space and time) and the immediate surroundings of its initial performance and circulation, narrating a repeated experience of rupture and dislocation, set against a sharply etched portrait of the society surrounding Kulottuṅga. In this, Cayaṅkoṇṭār's poem presents a productive contrast with Bilhaṇa's long work, which eschewed the particulars of the local world in which it emerged. This difference may lie at precisely the divide separating the Tamil *pulavar* from the Sanskrit *kavi*: that is, it may depend on a language "meant not to travel" set against the unbounded world of the cosmopolis. Regardless of these larger structures, however, the realization of these differences calls for a different angle of approach to the *Paraṇi*'s interpretation, which cannot be simply reduced to a common denominator of courtly entertainment and eulogy, however conceived.

Following upon its preliminary invocations, the *Paraṇi* suddenly and dramatically becomes a work of playful, oneiric eroticism: anchored by a repeated, louche exhortation to "open the door" (*kaṭai tiṟamiṉ*, etc.), the women of the Co̲la capital are called to, reminded of their quarrels and lovemaking with their absent husbands, and mischievously taunted for their earlier dalliances with Kulottuṅga himself. The section is usually referred to as the *kaṭai tiṟappu*, "Opening the Doors," and the speaker of these languid independent verses is never named explicitly. While various theories have been argued, these are most likely Cayaṅkŏṇṭār's elegant variation on women's teasingly erotic songs, part of the repertoire of the old custom of the *paraṇi* celebration.[87] Some 500 verses later, the poem concludes a world away: on the blasted battlefield where the Co̲la armies had laid waste to Kaliṅga, with an elaborate cannibal feast by Kāḷi's *pey* courtiers, who cook up a stew (*kūḻ*) from the dismembered bodies that litter the field. These two bravura set pieces, the bookends of the whole poem, significantly occur in reverse temporal order: the mocking songs of the *kaṭai tiṟappu* are said to be sung *after* the return of the Co̲la army from Kaliṅga. The entire poem is thus configured like a Moebius strip: a trick in which Cayaṅkŏṇṭār evidently delights, scattering epicyclic variations of it throughout the work. It is within the *Paraṇi*'s central sections, the trunk of the poem, where its temporal and narrative machinery is at its most intricate; and it is here where Cayaṅkŏṇṭār explicitly reflects on the transformations that followed upon Kulottuṅga's rise to power, structuring his poem around the changing Cōḻa polity from the specific vantage point of his patron-king's own court society.

The perspective that the poet adopts is the single most distinctive feature of the text, as the *Paraṇi* takes its bearings within "a demon's-eye view" of the world.[88] While the bloody business of Kulottuṅga's Kaliṅga war does occupy a major portion of the poem, this properly martial theme comes embedded in a phantasmagoric mixture of eros and cartoonish horror. The initial idyll of the women's songs abruptly ends – in a jarring "jump cut" characteristic of Cayaṅkŏṇṭār's art – and is replaced with a slowly constricting field of vision of the poem's description of the desert wasteland of the *pālai* country, the palace-temple of Kāḷi set within it, and the figure of the awesome goddess and her retinue. It is here that the *paraṇi*'s narrative properly begins, in the midst of Kāli's court of ghouls and *ḍākinī*s, all of them hungering for human flesh. It is from their monstrous perspective that the *paraṇi* recounts the history of the Cōḻa family, of Kulottuṅga's emergence as its culmination, and of his war against his refractory northern neighbor.

To modern ears, this sounds like a strange sort of courtly entertainment, and an even stranger forum for the celebration of the Cōḻa family's past history and present success: the received notion of the court poet as a simple propagandist is entirely inadequate to the material. Throughout the *Paraṇi*, Cayaṅkŏṇṭār reveals a fascination with who says what to whom – this, of course, is an essential and perduring courtly theme. And it is within the inverted world of Kāḷi's horrific assembly-hall that he sets his narration of the Cōḻa lineage, and of Kulottuṅga's place in it. Quite possibly for the first time, the poet uses Tamil as the medium to narrate the family's genealogy: the earlier Cōḻa genealogies that survive are exclusively in Sanskrit.[89] Moreover, this account of the Cōḻa past is introduced through a dazzling, virtuosic piece of narrative staging, a temporal corkscrew within the narrated world of the poem, and arguably Cayaṅkŏṇṭār's boldest experiment with narrative. Set within its whorls, Cayaṅkŏṇṭār transformed recent history in a radical revision of publicly held knowledge; in this, his work resembles the narrative and descriptive project of Viddayabhaṭṭa's Veṅgī text, though exceeding it in its ambitions and achievement.

Central to all of this, and supplying the poem with an organizing conceit, is Cayaṅkŏṇṭār's subordination of the events of Kulottuṅga's reign – and ultimately the entirety of the Cōḻa lineage's history – to the narrative logic of incarnation. The claim that an author's patron fulfills, in however mediated a way, the role of one of the cosmic overlords of classical Indic religion is something met with frequently in medieval court literature, as well as in prescriptive texts dating back at least to the *Manusmṛti.* Cayaṅkŏṇṭār's use of this *avatāra*-topos is unusual: instead of assimilating Kulottuṅga to the figure of god-king Rāma (perhaps the most enduring such prototype, and a figure readily available via the Co<u>l</u>as' place within the solar dynasty) or to a figure drawn from Śaiva myth (as the poem's *śākta* narrative lineaments might suggest), the poet expressly identifies his patron as an incarnation of Kṛṣṇa, especially the uncanny instigator of the *Mahābhārata* war.

This decision took on particular salience within the complex and fractious court society of the later years of Kulottuṅga's reign.[90] We possess no detailed accounts of the everyday workings of this society, outside of the adventitious and highly stylized accounts of royal orders recorded in epigraphy and the testimony of the *Paraṇi* itself, so positing such a strong correlation is risky. It is, however, possible through close attention to the poem's language and structure to sustain this claim. This is especially clear in the way that the poem celebrates several key figures of this court milieu, notably Tyāgavallī, Kulottuṅga's second chief queen – already encountered in discussing the Veṅgī charters – and Karuṇākarat Tŏṇṭaimā<u>n</u>, the warlord responsible for the victory that supplies the poem's theme. The *Paraṇi* is suffused with alternately parodic and stylized representations of roles within court society. In contrast to Bilhaṇa at the Cālukya court, Cayaṅkŏṇṭār was writing for a local audience – local in terms of its language, but also local in its ties to the Co<u>l</u>a court itself. It was this delimited world that the Tamil poet used as part of the raw material of his work, offering up the world of his narrative as a distorting reflection of the cross-cutting loyalties and tensions that characterize court society more generally, and that were peculiarly acute in the waning years of Kulottuṅga's reign.

In a work that delights in proliferating narrative trompes l'oeil, it is best to jump right in: an old ghoul, a *mutupey*, the member of a party that had fallen out of Kāḷi's favor, is ushered trembling back into the goddess's audience hall. Summarily restored to Kāḷi's good graces, the old *pey* seeks to further ingratiate himself by offering the goddess an impromptu entertainment:

> "We are sustained by you kindly showing favor to us. We have learnt by heart a thousand magic tricks, each one as good as the last. Pray, please sit and watch," he entreated.
>
> "Now wait just a moment, and be so kind as to set your two lovely eyes here: Look – in this hand, there are some elephants' trunks. Now, I shift them to this hand and . . . Look! They turn into the heads of bull elephants!

The blood from this elephant's head is drunk up by a goblin, an
alakai, who hoots and gibbers loud as a thunderclap and
staggers around while – look! – headless corpses float by!

And that's not all! Leave all this aside, say long live our Lady
and behold! Behold the great *paraṇi* sacrifice held that
day on the field at Cuttack, where Apayaṉ won his great
victory!" (vv. 161–164)

The ghoul's tricks, and his language, grow more heated and more elaborate from here. So tempting are the scenes of carnage which he conjures up that the other *pey*s of Kāḷi's court are ravaged with hunger, stumbling over themselves and snapping their jaws at his illusions. The assembled troop of monsters takes refuge in their mistress, and pleads that she have the ghoul stop his teasing. When he asks to finish his act, the troop explodes into howls of outrage:

Though he paid reverence, all the *gaṇa*s said, "You wicked trickster! You'll only torture us further! Let Queen Aṇaṅku command!" And Aṇaṅku then said, "Put a stop to these, now: where did you learn them?"

"Fearing your wrath, and the wrath of Curakuru, too, I thought that this place had become too risky, so I set out for the Himalayas. There, a lady gave to me a great deal of *mantra*s and spells, telling me that 'Her wrath and his will be stilled by these.'

She was the divine Rudrayoginī, the servant of your ancient servants. She told me, 'There is yet more for you to learn; remain here.' And so I stayed a while. One day . . ." (vv. 175–177)

There is much here that is distinctive of the *Paraṇi*, above all the boldness of the poet's imagination, and his ability to frame the everyday Tamil of his time into rhymed, rhythmic verse: the ghoul's mountebank brag, punctuated by the simple command *pār* ("Look!"), is marvelously direct. There is also the light-handed irony with which he portrays the unctuous courtesy of Kāḷi's functionaries and hangers-on. Throughout this passage, there is a recurrent gesture toward the elaborate prestations of the Coḻa chancellery and of the protocols of the court ceremonial, transferred and inflated into knowing caricature, as when the goddess's "gracious thought" (*tiruvuḷḷam*) is solicited, and her favor (*aruḷ*) gratefully acknowledged. At the heart of the scene, however, is the *pey*'s prestidigitation. The published editions all adopt this as the title of the whole section, *intiracālam* or "The Magic Trick." It is easy enough to see Cayaṅkŏṇṭār inserting himself into his work in the suitably (if transparently) disguised form of the ghoul-magician, prefiguring the verbal magic of its later sections, especially the poet's skill with metrical tricks and phonaesthesia. Cayaṅkŏṇṭār's magician's gambit then takes a vertiginous turn:

Once, whip in hand, Karikālaṉ was pleased to turn the great peak of the Himalaya about on its axis, and there, with the words, "Let it stand there as it once did," again carved the wide-jawed tiger-emblem on its slope, and set it back the way it had been. It was then

That the one called Nārada, divine sage of the Veda who comprehends all three times, came there. "In the whole of the sea-girt earth, there is no king like you," with this benediction offered, he said: "There is something I must tell you. Listen to me, king:

Long ago, as Parāsara's son proclaimed the Bhārata tale, Gaṇapati, his face a wild bull-elephant's, took in his hand one of his broad tusks and wrote it upon one side of Meru's peak. It is hard to describe this, this fruit of the earth's *tapas*.

The Bhārata's purifying story contains the fine deeds of my Lord: it is nothing less than the four true and ancient Vedas themselves. Now, as I tell you something equal to this, write down what I say on this tall mountain: this story will prove to be a fitting one." (vv. 178–181)

Over this series of enjambed verses, the narrative tumbles into the distant past, to the Co̱la culture-hero Karikālaṉ and his sojourn to the far north, a sudden shift of temporal focus that is neatly iconized by the appearance of the omniscient Nārada, "who comprehends all three times" (*kālamummaiyum uṇarnt'aruḷum*). Like this sage – himself a proverbial troublemaker – the poet is able to move freely into the past, present, or future within the world of his poem. The recursion here is bound up with well-aimed glances at earlier works of the Tamil literary canon: the Co̱la's Himalayan tiger-graffito is an obvious borrowing from the *Cilappatikāram*, while the story of Gaṇapati's copying of the *Mahābhārata* onto the mountain-side alludes to the invocation to Pĕruntevaṉār's *Pāratavĕṇpā*.[91] The second of these is especially significant: this was a work of Pallava court culture and, to judge from the late testimony of Paṭikkācuppulavar's *Tŏṇṭaimaṇṭalacatakam*, one that long remained associated in literary memory with the northern Tamil country. This marks the poet's first gesture toward Tondaimandalam: significantly, this localism intertwines with Cayaṅkŏṇṭār's invocation of the *Bhārata*, the preeminent charter-myth of the lunar dynasty.

In these few scene-setting verses, the poet briskly summons into existence an elaborate machinery of temporal and narrative staging. Nārada is telling a tale to Karikālaṉ, which he writes on the mountain side, which the *yoginī* will later learn, which she will teach to the old ghoul, who will ultimately teach it to Kāḷi and so to Cayaṅkŏṇṭār's dazzled audience.[92] The tale is the future history of the Co̱la kings, told under the sign of the Bhārata clan and pointedly *not* Rāma's or Manu's solar line. But from its very beginning, it is clear that Cayaṅkŏṇṭār has more in mind than simply retrojecting his patron's family's past into prophecy (vs. 182):

ataṉ mutaṟkaṇ varum ātimutaṉ māyaṉ ivaṉe
aprameyam ĕṉu' mĕy priyam at' ākav uṭaṉe
patamum ippatam vakukka varu pātam atuvum
pātamāṉa cila pār pukaḻ vantav avaiyum

It is this one, Māyaṉ, who always comes at the beginning of that, who is the primordial cause. As soon as that reality called the Immeasurable becomes desired, there is the word, and as this word is itself divided, there comes the line of verse, and of these lines, there are some that achieve fame in the world.

Cayaṅkŏṇṭār's audience suddenly find themselves thrust into the middle of an emanatory ontology of language. The verse is obscure, and likely deliberately so: Viṣṇu, here given his classical Tamil title *māyaṉ* ("the dark one"), is ever at the "beginning of that," *ataṉ mutaṟkaṇ*, though the referent of "that" is undetermined: is it the Bhārata story? The Coḻa lineage that Nārada is about to narrate? Or does this subtle trickster god lie behind every word ever uttered? The next few words do not give an answer – with his marked Sanskrit lexis here (*aprameyam, priyam, patam, pātam*), Cayaṅkŏṇṭār seems intentionally orotund, and frustratingly vague: Is Māyaṉ himself the unknowable truth, or is it he who does the desiring? The poet is not a metaphysician, and his point seems to be something like: words spill out of a primordial unknown, they find articulation in verse, and some verses go on to worldly reknown.[93]

Cayaṅkŏṇṭār next declares that it is the Veda, which he had earlier compared to the Bhārata story and to his own king-list, that is the end product of this emanation: *ṛk*s and *varga*s and *aṣṭaka*s and *saṃhitā*s, all articulating themselves out of Viṣṇu's singularity. Then another jump-cut: the Coḻas, Nārada tells Karikālaṉ, have their origin in Brahmā, the god born from the lotus, and in that family, there is a long line of valiant kings (vs. 184 *kamalayoṉi mutalāka varum uṅkaṇmarapiṟ kāvaṉmaṉṉavarkaḷ āki varukiṉṟa muṟaiyāl*). For this reason – origins in Brahmā coupled with unbroken transmission over the generations – the Coḻas are themselves like the unblemished Veda. Just as the Veda has its sum and conclusion in its final section, the *vedānta*, the Coḻas have as their apex (*āraṇanilattu*, "in the place of the Āraṇyaka") that same perfect one with whom it all began, who will come as Apayaṉ (*amalaṉey apayaṉāki varuka*). This is the poet's crowning touch, the trick he reveals with a flourish: his patron is shown, through the imagined testimony of his ancient ancestor, to be none other than Viṣṇu himself. The end becomes the beginning, and the story of the Coḻa *vaṃśa* finds its fulfillment in Kulottuṅga.

Amidst all of this multiplying and mischievous ambiguity, Cayaṅkŏṇṭār embeds an arresting piece of verbal gamesmanship, centered on the different temporal and modal inflections of the verb *varutal*, "to come." Playing upon his narrator Nārada's transtemporal point of view, Cayaṅkŏṇṭār exuberantly mixes together the various tense and aspect-inflected forms of the verb. He has the sage arrive on the scene (*vantu*, perfective, vs. 179) and tell of Viṣṇu, who comes (*varum*, usitative future, vs. 182) "at the beginning of that," and of the verse-lines that emerge (*varu*, untensed root-form, *ibid.*) from the primordially available word, some of which have already come (*vanta*, again perfective, *ibid.*) to be famous. Both the Ṛgvedic *varga*s and *aṣṭaka*s have derived (*vanta* ... *vanta*, vs. 183) from this matrix, while – in the enforced yet explicitly violated order of the simile – Karikālaṉ's family tradition eternally derives (*varum*, usitative, vs. 184) from Brahmā, which in the unfolding process of orderly coming down through the generations (*varukiṉṟa muṟai*, imperfective, so-called "present" tense, *ibid.*) is yet to result – we hope – in the birth of Apayaṉ/Kulottuṅga (*varuka*, optative, *ibid.*).[94]

In relying on this scrambled verbal paradigm to supply the armature to this passage, Cayaṅkŏṇṭār perhaps gestures toward an unmentioned term of art, *varalāṟu*, a "sequence of events" or "set of circumstances," a noun deriving from this same root, and a word that speakers of Tamil would come in time to adopt as their equivalent to "history." Cayaṅkŏṇṭār never uses the word himself, and its own early history (that is, *varalāṟu*'s *varalāṟu*) is difficult to trace: it may be only a mirage of retrospection that sees this lying behind the poet's cunning bit of verbal legerdemain.[95] This trace of *varalāṟu*, of a more or less full account of the past, as enunciated by the all-seeing Nārada, impresses itself upon any reading of the *Paraṇi* that sees in it an effort to refashion the past into the stuff of poetic representation. From the perspective of the back-and-forth wavering between the accomplished fact and its imaginative supplement – a movement that Cayaṅkŏṇṭār's poem reflects on repeatedly – the playing out of this temporal whorl and the marshaling of mythic antecedents (Karikālaṉ, Viṣṇu, the protagonists of the Bhārata war) at its outset appears very deliberate.

Karikālaṉ goes on to record the future history of his lineage, from his own time onward until the imperial achievements of Rājarāja, Rājendra, and their successors. This is set forth in a straightforward, annalistic register of plain rhymed verse, up to and including Vīrarājendra.[96] The report of Karikālaṉ's long Himalayan inscription concluded, the assembled *pey*s of Kāḷi's court go on to entreat the goddess to end their great hunger, when she receives an envoy informing her of the great Coḻa victory in the war against Kaliṅga. Thus yet another time-warp: the great battle of the latter sections of the poem has *already happened* at this point in the narrative, set in the court of Kāḷi, just as it would of course have already occurred for the Kulottuṅga's courtiers who formed Cayaṅkŏṇṭār's first audience. Could it be, the hungry ghouls ask, that the feast there could be as great as it had once been after Rāma's war in Laṅkā?

Yes it is, Kāḷi replies, beginning the section modern editions dub *avatāram*, "the incarnation." The two wars, along with the one in Kurukṣetra, are closely linked:

> The very one who once warred in Laṅkā and left it in ruins,
> brought the Bhārata war to an end and then arose
> as Vijayadhara, whose bright war-quoit brings victory.
> Listen, as I speak of him. (vs. 232)

Alert to how the play between the solar and lunar dynastic tropes informed the Veṅgī charters, it is easy to read this verse along with others scattered throughout the *Paraṇi* as variations on a similar theme. The success of the *sūryavaṃśin* Rāma's campaign against the *rākṣasa*s, and Kṛṣṇa's stage-managing of the *somavaṃśa*'s civil war both act as mythic prototypes that are realized in the birth of the Coḻa king, called Vijayadhara, the Victory-bearer, here and elsewhere. But for all that Rāma's ethos of just war had already been explored by Coḻa court poets, it is again the powerful, uncanny figure of the *Mahābhārata*'s Kṛṣṇa that Cayaṅkŏṇṭār insists upon as Kulottuṅga's underlying divine identity. Here at the outset of his incarnationalist account of his patron's life in the world, the poet stresses luni-solar syzygy: for all that the king bears Kṛṣṇa's ensign of the *āḻi* or war-quoit, he is pointedly said to have arisen, *utittāṉ*, a Sanskrit *tadbhava* loan evocative of the sun, as in *udayagiri*, Sunrise Mountain.[97]

But it is Kṛṣṇa who provides the dominant element of the implied mythic comparison. Kṛṣṇa is the cross-cousin to the *Mahābhārata*'s Pāṇḍava heroes; in venturing this identification, Cayaṅkŏṇṭār integrates a knowing gesture toward Kulottuṅga's dynastic origins, while underplaying it in the patent account of his accession. Like a magician simultaneously performing a sleight of hand while showing his audience how they are being tricked, he rewrites his patron's history while alluding to it through this recurrent structuring device of the narrative. The connection with Kṛṣṇa is again made explicit in the following verse, referring to the form of Māl/Viṣṇu who took birth as the son of Vasudeva and Devakī. This supplies a transition for a return to the historical-referential mode:

He, who had descended on the banyan leaf, appeared once more
in the blessed womb of the cherished Lakṣmī of Rājarāja,
she from the family of the glorious, all-conquering sun,
a queen to a scion of the family of the moon, dispeller of darkness. (vs. 234)

From other sources, above all, Viddaya's eulogies, this verse is easily interpretable, but shorn of a proper name for the king's mother and of all but the most generic of titles for his father, the generational intertwining of the Co̱la and Cālukya families remains unspoken here. A combination of the sentimental and the miraculous follows directly upon this condensed genealogical *mise en place*:

A shower fell, of gold and blossoms.
The queen of the Co̱la who once seized the Gaṅgā saw this,
and raised up in her lotus-blossom hand the noble son
born to a daughter of her own family.
And seeing that he bore on his body
all the marks of Indra the citadel-burner
among the lords of the earth, she declared
"This boy, our own son, is fit to bear
the burden of the solar line."
"This little child of the Moon is a mighty hero."
"This child of the haloed sun is a master."
It is as if the fruit of each single act of austerity
by every king of both families, delighting in themselves,
had come together and to a good end. (vv. 236–8)

All of this is sketched in briefly and economically: there are none of the referential and temporal-aspectual games in which Cayaṅkŏṇṭār delights elsewhere in the poem. Even the requisite and stereotypical reference to the miraculous shower of gold and flower petals sent by the gods is quickly told, and swept past in an alliterative rush that ends with the future Co̱la emperor taken up in the arms of the queen, at once his great-aunt and grandmother. Whether the supposed "adoption" described here was a historical fact has occasioned a great deal of debate, so much historical embroidery spun from the single, slender thread of this verse.[98]

But whatever the nature of Kulottuṅga's early connection with the members of his matriline, Cayaṅkŏṇṭār's account is scrupulous to balance this against yet another appeal to his conjoint ancestry. For all that it lacks the specificity of the Andhra charters, the poet is careful to retain a similar mythopoetics. This connection, moreover, is disconnected from the line of male descent that had structured Karikāla̱n's history of the future: here the animating force of the Co̱la lineage is pronouncedly feminine. While this is an incorrigible fact of

Kulottuṅga's place in the Cōḻa family line, its emphasis by Cayaṅkŏṇṭār is significant: from the narrative frame of Kāḷi's court, through to the erotic women's songs with which it begins, the *Paraṇi* is suffused with modes of feminine authority and power.

The poem moves on to a rapid account of Kulottuṅga's wonderfully auspicious childhood, prefiguring what would later come to be the *piḷḷait-tamiḻ* ("child's song") genre. Throughout, there is continued reference to the incarnational backstory: the amulets the young boy possesses are none other than the five weapons of Viṣṇu, as "it became all the more clear that this one was Māyaṉ himself, who has once been Vasudeva's son, here to purge all the troubles of Lady Earth," while his sacred thread is likened to the wedding-necklace of Lakṣmī "as it rests on Viṣṇu's lovely chest."[99] Once the incarnational motif is established, the play between the lunar and solar themes recedes from the *Paraṇi*'s narrative. With this conspicuous silence, the story becomes one of the Cōḻa dynasty's finding its prophesied fulfillment in the current king. Kulottuṅga's childhood abruptly ends with his assumption of royal power:

> Far-famed Apayaṉ, who had seized the victory-banner, installed him as junior king over the earth. A royal command was allotted to him, to draw what duty was owed by the kings of the borderlands. (vs. 249)

"Apayaṉ" here refers to Vīrarājendra: it is a title echoed in in his own inscriptions and elsewhere in the *Paraṇi* (vs. 206), though confusingly it is a name which Cayaṅkŏṇṭār also uses for Kulottuṅga. As in his annalistic version of the Cōḻa lineage, Cayaṅkŏṇṭār again shifts into a straightforward narrative style: the account of the king's early deeds maps onto his earliest *mĕykkīrtti*, embellished with the rhetorical conflations and antitheses. Notably, there is no reference here, as there was not in the king-list, to Adhirājendra. Kulottuṅga's cousin is effectively written out of the poem's vision of the past: the death of Vīrarājendra simply opens the way to his succession. But first, there is a complication: upon the old king's departure for heaven, Cayaṅkŏṇṭār turns directly to his audience and pregnantly says, "let us now speak of what came to pass in the South," allowing him to draw upon a rich vein of stylized cataclysm:

> Brahmans' sacrifices went wrong, the precepts of Manu decayed,
> as did all six disciplines, and the sound of the Veda fell silent.
>
> Castes mixed together, each one with another, and the good measure
> of the duties taught to all men became unsteady and was forgotten.
>
> Men seized other men as slaves, and the temples of the gods grew lax,
> Lax too grew women's virtue, and defenses weakened.

As the darkness of Kali spread abroad,
like the Sun arisen from the the roaring sea to obliterate the great dark,
he came, to rescue the world. (vv. 257–261)[100]

Over this series of swiftly sketched verses, the imminent collapse of their entire way of life is set out for his audience, and a solution proposed in the figure of Kulottuṅga, in full-on solar dynastic regalia. The contrast between the *Paraṇi* and the two earlier renditions is instructive. Bilhaṇa figures the convolutions of the Cōḻa succession as a personal tragedy for Vikramāditya, a series of deaths in the family dangerously ratcheting up the tensions with his brother; Viddaya, innocent of the politics of Colamandalam, neglects to mention it entirely. For Cayaṅkŏṇṭār, the death of Vīrarājendra leads to a generalized crisis, a potential collapse of civilization as a whole. Indic court poetry, celebratory of its patron and its patron's family, regularly sets out a vision of the ruling order as a break with the past. And this is often constructed around an appeal to the theory of the cyclical decline of the ages of the world, a quasi-natural process that the reign of a good sovereign is able to disrupt, restoring his kingdom to the golden age of the *kṛtayuga,* while the rest of the world is left to languish in the depravity of the *kali* age. This is a model of time and the social cosmos that contains significant presuppositions about history and historical change; Cayaṅkŏṇṭār participates here in this older discourse on royal power, cyclical crisis, and renovation.[101] But this also contains traces of what was certainly the living memory of the events of the early 1070s, when Cōḻa rule in the Kāveri heartland appears to have temporarily disintegrated, and power to have devolved onto local lords and caste-associations.[102] Though the traces of it are few and far between, they suggest that this was the most general crisis that the mature Cōḻa political system had faced since its inauguration under Rājendra I. For all the deeply conventional character of this passage – the symptomatic concerns of miscegenation, decay of Brahmanical ritual, and disintegration of patriarchy – there is no reason to doubt that Cayaṅkŏṇṭār played upon real anxieties, and real memories, of the period leading up to Kulottuṅga's imperial enthronement.

Following two verses describing Kulottuṅga's coronation, the account of his coming to power effectively ends. The *avatāram* canto, however, does not; instead, its narrative momentum seems to unwind itself. Cayaṅkŏṇṭār gives a series of chiming verses full of wordplay depicting the happy realm constituted around the new Cōḻa king, structurally mirroring the earlier dystopia.[103] Nothing much happens in the paradise that is Kulottuṅga's kingdom, and this seems to be the point. The poem shifts from the time of past events, of *varalāṟu*, into what seems to be the eternal present of the life of the court: cultured, erotic, and prosperous.

The *Paraṇi*'s forward movement resumes with the beginnings of a royal progress: although there is no effort whatsoever to locate this in time, the description of courtly stasis passes over decades of Kulottuṅga's reign. From the heart of his domains along the Kāveri, the king – in one of the rare moments in the poem that he is made to speak – orders his court "to hunt on horseback near the lovely banks of the Pālāṟu," deep in Tondaimandalam. In the larger design of the narrative, this leads to a holding of court in Kāñcī, where Kulottuṅga receives the tribute-bearing delegations of kings subordinate to him. It is there and then that his officials realize that the Kaliṅga king is two years in arrears, leading to Kulottuṅga's dispatch of his armies on their punitive campaign.

The spatial transition on which this depends is deeply significant, though easily overlooked: the Tŏṇṭai poet has the action of his story quicken into life as his patron moves northward. He passes in review over the great elephant corps that conveys the court there; at the head of this description we find the verse with which this book began, joining the sun and moon over Sunrise Mountain in picturing the king atop his royal tusker. To the acclamation of the assembled crowds, Kulottuṅga gets under way, closely followed by one and then another of his queens:

> Hail! Riding atop the king's elephant, never separate from him,
> like the sweet flute to the music made by that pinnacle of the Coḻa line,
> came the queen, this lady skilled in music,
> she who rules alike over the seven worlds
> and the seven notes of the gamut.
>
> All around the queens of other kings come atop cow-elephants,
> now intent on making necklaces of gold and flower-garlands.
> And close at hand comes Tyāgavalli, with her spectacular fortune:
> the queen who by right gave commands
> that were equal to the Coḻa's own. (vv. 285–286)

The first of these verses embeds through elegant periphrasis the name of Kulottuṅga's queen Eḻicaivallapi, surnamed Eḻulakuṭaiyāḷ, "the mistress of the seven worlds," who had been associated with him since early in his reign.[104] Though not given pride of place, Tyāgavalli is said to have *cĕṉṉiyāṇaiyuṭaṉ āṇaiyai naṭattum urimai*, the right to promulgate orders along with the Cĕṉṉi (that is, the Coḻa) himself. Appeal to *urimai* ("right, property") is key to the claims of sovereignty more generally in the language of Coḻa politics, and this is thus an extraordinary and wholly unprecedented claim. Though limited to just this reference, the anomaly of Tyāgavalli's courtly status hangs over the courtly order summoned into existence by Cayaṅkŏṇṭār.

The northward course taken by the royal progress wends through the paradise of the Kāveri region, its abundant geese, carp, and plantain trees, all luxuriantly reminiscent of the idealized female body. By contrast, the passage into Tŏṇṭai country is marked by its civilization: the court passes rapidly through the temple centers of Cidambaram and Tiruvatikai before arriving, after easy stages, at Kāñcī. Cayaṅkŏṇṭār then returns to the outer frame of Kāḷi's court, with the arrival of a ghoul-messenger (in another jumping time-loop), reminding the audience of the corpse-strewn battlefield that awaits her and her retinue. But this interruption of the narrative only serves to highlight the shift into the clearly set out domain of the northern country: as if emerging out of a dream, the real world of Tondaimandalam draws into focus.

Though still filled with the language of conventional hyperbole, much of the *Paraṇi*'s version of Kulottuṅga's court participates in this heightened sense of the specific and the actual: court is held in "the southwest corner" of a palace in Kāñcī (albeit one made entirely of gold), while an official of the chancellery, a *tirumantiravolai*, oversees the conduct of the offerings of tribute (albeit offered by most of the kings of the known world).[105] Despite this specificity, all of this remains set within a conversation taking place in Kāḷi's reeking abattoir-palace, now taken up by the recently arrived *pey*: Cayaṅkŏṇṭār remains a step ahead of his audience, in his studied collision of the actual and the fantastic.

It is at this uncanny point in the narrative that Karuṇākarat Tŏṇṭaimāṉ enters the scene. Reckoned as the "first among the councillors" of the court, he is the "lord of Vaṇṭai," a descendent of the Pallava kings, and of course a great war-leader. This finds some thin confirmation in epigraphy: the wife of one Karuṇākaraṉ, alias Tŏṇṭaimāṉār, described as a man of the gentry (*veḷāṉ*) and as a landholder in Vaṇṭāḻañceri in Tirunaṟaiyūr nāṭu (near Kumbhakonam), made a lamp donation to the Aruḷāḷapĕrumāḷ temple near Kāñcī in 1113–1114, right around the time of the Kaliṅga campaign. This appears to be the same man, though his social profile is in several ways unusual. He was based, first of all, not in the Tŏṇṭai country but in the Kāveri heartland: the *Paraṇi*'s Vaṇṭai is a truncation of Vaṇṭāḻañceri (a typical Tamil habit with place names, then as now). The man's social identity in the record is not tied to any Coḻa title of honor or officialdom, and he is expressly identified as a Veḷḷāḷa. On the other hand, his wife's high titles – she is referred to as *teviyār* and *āḻvār* – indicate a place in the upper echelons of the kingdom's elite.[106] Given the continued connection with an important Tŏṇṭai temple site, it is plausible to see Karuṇākaraṉ as one of the new men who began to emerge in the years before Kulottuṅga's accession: warriors from outside the Delta who transformed themselves into private landholders and kingmakers in the central part of the kingdom. Extrapolating from the (admittedly slight) testimony of the Kāñcī inscription, Karuṇākaraṉ appears to be an example of the possibility of social mobility available to members of the gentry possessed of a talent for organized violence, men who crossed over into the magnate ranks.

There are some more traces in the *Paraṇi* where the text appears to make contact with the bedrock of social referentiality that suggests similar conclusions. This can, however, be difficult to trace, owing to the the poet's habit of wordplay. As the Coḻa army is marshaled for its march to Kaliṅga:

taṇṇāriṉ malarttiraṭoḷ apayaṉ tāṉ eviya ceṉai taṉakk'aṭaiyak
kaṇṇākiya coḻaṉa cakkaramām karuṇākaraṉ vāraṇameṟ kŏḷave

tŏṇṭaiyarkk' araciṉ muṉvaruñ curavi tuṅkavĕḷviṭaiy uyartta koṉ
vaṇṭaiyarkk' aracu pallavarkk'aracu mālkaḷiṟṟiṉ micai kŏḷḷave

vāci kŏṇṭ'aracar vāraṇaṅ kavara vāṇakovaraiyaṉ vāṇmukat
tūci koṇṭu muṭikŏṇṭacoḻaṉ ŏru cūḻi veḻamicai kŏḷḷave

(vv. 363. 364, *365[107])

As Apayaṉ, his thick shoulders adorned with a cool garland, gave the command, the army's eye, Karuṇākaraṉ, the Coḻa's discus-weapon, mounted upon his elephant.

The king of Vaṇṭai, Pallava king, the lord who raised up the lofty white bull, the wish-giving cow that ever runs before the king of the Tŏṇṭaiyar, mounted his great tusker.

In order to snatch away the defenses of horse-riding kings, Muṭikŏṇṭacoḻa Vāṇakovarayaṉ, took up position at the van full of sword-blades, and mounted upon his own armored elephant.

These verses are difficult, and different emendations have been proposed. We see here two figures, Karuṇākaraṉ and another man bearing a royal as well as a magnate title: this Vāṇakovarayan is also attested in epigraphy and merits a mention in Ŏṭṭakkūttar's *Vikramacoḻavulā*. The first two verses, on Karuṇākaraṉ, essentially convey the same message twice (for this reason it has been suggested that they refer to different men); on my reading, the second of these appears to convey further specifics about the Tŏṇṭaimāṉ warlord: he evidently bears the title *pallavaraiyar* (such seems to be implied in Cayaṅkŏṇṭār's periphrasis *pallavarkk'aracu*), and to have associated himself with the royal glamor of the old Pallava lineage through adopting a bull-standard. This perhaps lends further support to the hypothesis linking Karuṇākaraṉ with the north of the kingdom, with its long imperial memories.[108]

The point is not that the major interest of Cayaṅkŏṇṭār's poem lies in these scant prosopographical details. Instead, what is of significance is that this wildly ludic phantasmagoria bothers to include them at all. This may be contrasted, once again, with Bilhaṇa's poem. The *Carita* was meant to travel far beyond the world of the Cālukyas: this seems to be the implicit condition of Bilhaṇa's employment, the reason why his patron was willing to put up with him. For a text that was meant to be consumed in the confines of the Co̲la court, there was much to be gained in specificity. The *Paraṇi* was not meant to give distant future readers a glimpse of court life – of who was in and who was out – but rather it sought to anchor itself within the social world surrounding Kulottuṅga: it was *this* queen and *that* lord whose doings were bound up with the events of the poem.

We may join this courtly specificity to the presence of feminine power that runs throughout the text, and see this as an equivocal gloss on Kulottuṅga's court during Tyāgavalli's ascendency. The evidence of this courtly-political conjunction is slender, but there is enough to permit some hypotheses. The queen emerged around 1100 as the king's favorite, and her rising fortunes coincided with those of a prince who was likely her son, who would reign as Vikramaco̲la. Vikrama, however, was only one of several potential heirs, and Tyāgavalli's ultimate success, from its beginnings in the harem, could only be realized beyond the king's domestic circle. The Tŏṇṭaiyar lords and the magnate families of the expanded Jayaṅkŏṇṭaco̲lamaṇḍalam had played a conspicuous part in Kulottuṅga's imperial accession, and their role in ruling over the Co̲la kingdom continued throughout his reign. By the time of the second campaign against Kaliṅga around 1115, Kulottuṅga had been ruling for more than four and a half decades, and he could well have been a senile invalid in the final years of his life and reign. Tyāgavalli's position as a queen who "by right gave commands that were equal to the Co̲la's own" made her a formidable presence at court: above all, she was likely concerned with ensuring her son's succession in the face of the competition of his half-brothers. The complex triangulations between the ascendant Tŏṇṭaiyar lords and Tyāgavalli and her household were thus likely inevitable.

Enter Cayaṅkŏṇṭār. He was himself a man of Tondaimandalam, and although we lack a biographical sense of him, his work suggests a fascination with verbal and narrative sleight of hand. In the ritual and performance form of the *paraṇi*, he found a ready-to-hand template for martial celebration, and a social form with its taproots in women's culture. It is impossible to know what he may have taken over from earlier examples of the *paraṇi*; it is not even possible to know whether these were discrete, formalized literary compositions or only partly scripted occasional performances. Presuming, however, that what we see in the *Paraṇi* draws to a significant degree on his particular literary imagination, the decision to embed within this war-poem his ingenious presentation of the Cola past and present becomes all the more significant. In the overarching figure of Kāḷi, there may have been a mediated reflection on the significance of the martial goddess of Kolar to Rājendracoḷa's transformation into Kulottuṅga: recall that it was Tŏṇṭaiyar officials who oversaw the public recruitment of that temple's goddess to Rājendracoḷa's cause.[109] But the figure of the awesome, all-powerful goddess surrounded by a retinue of servile courtiers may just have had a target close to hand, in the society around Tyāgavalli herself.

The elaborately staged and deeply ambiguous presentation of both the Cola *vaṃśa* and Kulottuṅga's place in it thus becomes even more sharply set out from the rest of the poem. Only giving passing acknowledgment to the anomalies of the king's ancestry – and notably shifting from a classically patriarchal account of the family's descent through time to the boy-king's supposed adoption into the main line by his grandmother – the poem codes Kulottuṅga's succession as salvation from universal crisis, repurposing the logic of *avatāra* not just for royal eulogy, but as a way to narrate historical disjunction. As the epic incarnational theology has it, God enters into a world out of joint in order to set it right, and to remake time. Kulottuṅga's reign reset the tottering Cola realm, but the courtly world that followed from this renovation was a substantially different one, filled with unprecedented actors. Cola court literature as such can even be said to emerge with his reign, in this very text. The irruption of the chaos of Kāḷi's court in the poem suggests a playful acknowledgment of this new, or newly transformed, space: in the hooting, gibbering, orally fixated ghouls surrounding the goddess, the courtiers in the audience were meant to see their own worst selves. In the midst of this spectacular display – and in the bravura description of the battlefield and its gory sequel in the ghouls' kitchen – the real workings of the court could be openly addressed.

It is this conjunctural setting of the *Paraṇi* in the final years of Kulottuṅga's court that accounts for the gradual disappearance of the king from the poem's latter sections. Kulottuṅga entered into time and history to make right the irruption of the Kali age; having done so, his moment of active agency in the poem effectively ends. While the reveries of the *kaṭai tiṟappu* continue to figure him as an erotic afterimage of royal potency, Kulottuṅga's place as the source and summation of the Cola lineage is superseded in the narrative by the cultured eternal present of the court society that was the result of his intervention. That this court society is doubled by its horrific *pālai* counterpart is, of course, the point. The *Paraṇi*'s supersession of the historical moment of the accession is not a case of historical teleology, where the earlier events are fulfilled and overridden by the resulting end-state. Instead, the sense of rupture seen in the near-collapse of the Co<u>l</u>a state is reinscribed within the new courtly order. The heroic ideal of Kulottuṅga-as-Viṣṇu's predestined entry into the Co<u>l</u>a line is replaced by a strange and uncertain world, one whose absurd shadow-self is always just on the verge of emergence. It is easy – intentionally so – to see in this a resonance with the court society during what everyone involved must have known to be the waning years of Kulottuṅga's reign. He had reigned for nearly two generations, and the future must have seemed uncertain indeed. When the current reigning king is the sum and fulfillment of his family's career on earth, what happens next? We all know what happened when Kṛṣṇa died: it marked the beginning of the Kali *yuga*. Far, then, from being a straightforward celebration of Kulottuṅga's rule, and a propagandistic effort to suture him into the Co<u>l</u>a lineage in which he was otherwise only a nephew and a son-in-law, Cayaṅkŏṇṭār's poem leaves unanswered a great many of the troubling questions it so insistently raises.

Conclusions

In considering these three very different renditions of Kulottuṅga's accession, it is helpful to return to the trio of organizing rubrics – history, politics, and philology – that structured this book's introduction. First of all, there is the difficult, if by now rather tired, question of the degree to which it makes sense to assess Indic literary texts by the criteria meant to judge the historical and historiographical works of other times and places. Certainly, none of these works aspired to the identification and synthesis of earlier source materials (that is, to the writing of history) or to the assessment of claims made by earlier attempts at such synthesis (that is, to historiography). But all three do present interpretative, perspectival accounts of the events of a commonly acknowledged past. Of these, the synoptic text of Viddayabhaṭṭa partook of at least one feature usually considered to be diagnostic of historical writing, in that it is indexed to the epoch of the Śaka kings. This gave modern scholarship some purchase on the events surrounding the joining of the Co<u>l</u>a and Cālukya royal families; and this annalistic dimension of the Veṅgī charters sets them apart from the stock temporal references scattered throughout the *Carita* or the topsy-turvy conundrums of the *Paraṇi*.

Cayaṅkŏṇṭār's poem contains the most detailed list of Co<u>l</u>a kings that had ever been composed in Tamil, but it does so in a way that conspicuously lacks any external temporal referent (none of the kings even have the length of their reign specified), and in any case embeds this linear account within its rococo chronotopic structure, curving the path of time's arrow by surrounding it with funhouse mirrors. In this, the *Paraṇi* recapitulates the chronological habits of its surrounding court culture, as the Coḻa royal center was curiously disinterested in recording dates according to any measure more objective than the regnal years of the current king. But Cayaṅkŏṇṭār used the occasion of his virtuoso entertainment to reflect on the sense of disjunction that set Kulottuṅga's reign distinctly apart from its predecessors, implying a sense of historical consciousness etched more strongly into the fabric of the work than Viddayabhaṭṭa's reflections on the distant events in the Tamil country. Compared to these two precocious accounts of political transformation, Bilhaṇa's poem appears the least invested in any sort of positive or interpretive history. The *Carita* depends on the flattening out of any vision of historical specificity, adopting the figure of Rājiga/Kulottuṅga as a general type of tyrannical grotesquerie. For Bilhaṇa, the value of this cynical image of unchecked royal power depended precisely on its being generalizable and exportable. That it could be unmoored from its historical referent and applied to the Kashmirian's own patron is only the most immediate of its advantages.

It is only Bilhaṇa, with typical élan, who engages with the classical language of politics inherited from Kauṭalya, and his flattening out of historical reference appears to have been deliberately keyed to an attempt to articulate an independent judgment on the nature of royal power. Yet in two seemingly contradictory, deeply interrelated ways, the political vision of the *Vikramāṅkadevacarita* is eccentric. First, the very independence of judgment that so distinguished the work is ultimately subordinated to the poet's own project of self-fashioning. This subordination was at once conceptual and structural: the *Carita* never rises to the level of all-out polemic against the world of the court, of the sort sketched in centuries earlier in Bhartṛhari's epigrams, simply because it depended so absolutely on Bilhaṇa's own game of brinksmanship with his royal patron and with the wider institutions of courtly life. Its acid humor could only flourish in the medium against which it reacted. Bilhaṇa's skepticism was perhaps so thoroughgoing that he could not attach himself to another source of value – say, renunciation, as in Bhartṛhari, or a sedate devotionalism, as in his Vaiṣṇava countryman Kṣemendra. So, in the overall architectonics of the *Carita*, the broadside of its sixth *sarga* gives way to many hundreds of verses of heroic, erotic, and otherwise courtly poetry that is never dully conventional, but nevertheless committed to a recognizable courtly standard. It is only in its conclusion, with its imagined return to Kashmir and its celebration of its author's hard-won and fiercely protected autonomy, that the *Carita* again marks such a radical departure from courtly norms.

But if the politics of the *Carita* were inextricably tied up with the career of its author, it was equally connected to the hugely expansive world of the Sanskrit cosmopolis. That a work of art could be so bound up with both the idiosyncrasies of its maker and such a timeless, placeless standard of culture appears contradictory. Yet Bilhaṇa was the greatest single example of the footloose intellectual of the cosmopolitan order at its height; for all his appeal to Kashmirian chauvinism, he was equally engaged in a work of self-universalization as the quintessential cosmopolitan *kavi*. It is this imperative that motivated the evacuation of historical detail from his account. Vikrama's struggle with his brother and with Rājiga makes sense in the terms intelligible to the aesthetic and moral categories available everywhere in the horizonless world of Sanskritic culture. The difference with Viddaya and with Cayaṅkŏṇṭār is stark. Both the Veṅgī charters and the *Paraṇi* participated in the cosmopolitan order: the Sanskrit charters in their language and form, the Tamil poem by its range of literary and cultural references. Nevertheless, each is pronouncedly rooted in its local world, and it is in these particular contexts in which each was meant to make a difference. The Veṅgī charters at once recapitulated the long history of Cālukya public pronouncement and intervened into the conjunctural instance of the newly established Coḻa-dominated court. As works of *kāvya* and legal documents both, they attempted to intervene into the local political settlement, in which elements of the rhetorical and practical ("worldly") strategies earlier employed in Kulottuṅga's court were repurposed by his sons. The failure of these strategies for both Coḍagaṅga and Vīracoḍa seems to have depended largely on the changing circumstances of the Coḻa imperial court, the precise context of the *Kaliṅkattupparaṇi*'s own ambivalent political gamesmanship. Unlike Viddaya's charters, the *Paraṇi* did not possess any explicit practical project, nor did it engage with a normative model of kingship like Bilhaṇa's *mahākāvya*. Instead, it took as its point of departure the situation of the Coḻa court in the waning years of Kulottuṅga's reign, effecting a bravura transplantation of the court's social energy into its wild, alternately mythic and folkloric reimagination of the Kāḷi-cult.[110] This process was only intelligible through Cayaṅkŏṇṭār's embedding recognizable references to the real world of his poem's first publication, in the mention of actually existing figures like Karuṇākaraṉ and Kulottuṅga himself, and possibly in the homology between the goddess and the emperor's chief queen. If in fact Tyāgavallī did emerge as the leading figure of the court society in the early years of the 1100s – and the situation in Veṅgī certainly suggests that this may have been the case – then the *Paraṇi* may contain a glimpse of a singularly important event of consequential court politics.

Each of the three renditions was an internally complex work of verbal art embodying and responding to extrinsic generic codes, and subject to change through the vicissitudes of its dissemination and transmission. As such, each has provided an occasion for philology, both in the work of earlier scholarship and in the interpretations offered here. But the degree to which the three renditions call for different philological modes is worthy of note. The redaction history that can be reconstructed across the three Veṅgī charters provides important evidence of their distinct worldly projects. Critical exegesis on just a pair of verses of Bilhaṇa's *Carita* – a text-place that has preoccupied the poem's interpreters for more than a century – supplies an angle of vision on the poet's characteristic ambiguity, and the key note for his denunciation of royal power, precisely that element of the text that earlier scholars have most misrecognized. The case of the *Kaliṅkattupparaṇi* is perhaps the most intricate, as it is only through attention to its grammatical and narratological tricks that we can gain an accurate sense of what the text in fact was about, while it is only through prosopographical study that its embeddedness in the world of Kulottuṅga's court can be made visible. It is thus only through getting inside the contingent particulars of each rendition – of seeing how each works as a sustained piece of language – that any sort of understanding of their historicality, literary quality, and referential value can be ventured.

Summary

The texts of Bilhaṇa, Viddayabhaṭṭa, and Cayaṅkōṇṭār differed in language, genre, and medium, but all were united in the shared fact of their literariness, the yoking of artfully constructed language to expressive ends. They were further united by each containing a rendition of Kulottuṅga's rise to imperial prominence, however much they differed in their interpretation of that event. Whether figured as Machiavellian coup d'état, the realization of family destiny, or the intervention of the divine into human affairs, the accession of the Coḻa king was a central feature of the poems' narrative and imaginative logic. Scholars of the nineteenth and early twentieth centuries had excavated these texts in their effort to understand what exactly happened in the murky events of 1070. While these texts supply valuable information about this not available otherwise, their real value as historical evidence lies in their work of interpretation and judgment.

Another feature that unites these three different literary works is their common worldliness. This is as much a feature of the interpreter's gaze upon them as it is a peculiar feature of these texts. Each took shape within a determinate social and cultural setting; unusually for early Indian texts, these settings can be reconstructed with a reasonable amount of precision. The interpretative gaze on the Kulottuṅga narrative in all three thus becomes doubled: focusing sequentially on the internal logic of the narrative and the work that it does within the text's wider intervention into its context. As all three were the product of the royalist cultures of different court societies, the story of a man becoming paramount king captures important presumptions, tensions, and statements of value.

However, these texts were more than just the reflection of the circumambient courtly worlds: each was also the product of the particular literary intellect of their authors. This is even in the case with Viddayabhaṭṭa's *praśasti*, the composition of which was in certain ways distributed and "socialized." In the two, more conventionally textualized works of Bilhaṇa and Cayaṅkŏṇṭār, the particularities of the poet's thought and voice proved consequential as exempla for later poets and as standard-setting models for readers. These texts made history, in that they provided a narration of events of their recent, meaningful past, but also in the ways they created and foreclosed future modes of thought and action.

4 The Emperor of the Three Worlds and the Lord of the Little Shrine

Introduction

A great deal happened in the course of Kulottuṅga's reign. Over its unprecedented five decades, the territories claimed by the Coḻa center underwent a sharp contraction: by the end of the 1110s, Kulottuṅga had abandoned claims over Sri Lanka, Gaṅgavāḍi, and, significantly, his natal kingdom of Veṅgī. In Nilakanta Sastri's words, by the close of his reign, "the Cōḷa empire became more or less a purely Tamil power."[1] The Coḻa martial and dynastic presence in Sri Lanka had at no point been either intensive or extensive; its withdrawal occurred at some point between 1070 and 1073, in the period of pre-imperial rule by the future Kulottuṅga. The Coḻa reversals in the Kannada-speaking region would only prove temporary – Vikramacoḻa would later issue inscriptions there – but the ultimate inability of the Coḻa state-system to establish a lasting hegemony over Veṅgī was evidence of the absolute limits to its effective power.

So during the period 1074–1120, the settled space of the Coḻa polity came to be increasingly co-extensive with Colamandalam and Tondaimandalam, while control over the territory to the south was increasingly contested by the renascent kings of the Pāṇḍya lineage. Within the settled area of the core territories, there was an effort at reorganization of the fiscal and political order: the *puravuvaritiṇaikkaḷam* under Kulottuṅga conducted the first cadastral surveys since Rājarāja's time, one during his sixteenth year and another in his fortieth. Unsurprisingly, this saw the extension of the system of *vaḷanāṭu*s into Tondaimandalam. Lacking the skills of an economic historian, I can only assume as a working hypothesis that the *tŏṇṭaiyar* magnates, gentry, and Brahmans benefited from this extension of the land tenurial order of the Coḻa heartland to their native territories.

There is much to be said of these military-political and economic results of the five decades of Kulottuṅga's imperial rule. Yet this chapter will look elsewhere for the long-term effects of his reign, at its semiotic or representational, as well as its practical, consequences. These consequences were unintended by Kulottuṅga or by his court society; nevertheless, the initiating events of the reign – the transformation of the lunar Cālukya prince into the solar Coḻa emperor with which this book has been concerned – continued to frame further acts of narrativization, memorialization, and political imagination. The case studied here is limited to the effect of such consequences in a single, albeit significant, location: the temple city known variously as Tillai, Puliyūr, and Cidambaram. While Kulottuṅga's court undertook no great *ab initio* construction projects like the Tanjavur or Gaṅgaikŏṇṭacoḻapuram complexes, his reign saw the beginning of a dramatic and consequential reorientation toward this ancient Śaiva holy place. The Cidambaram temple is today understood as the centrepiece of the high culture of the Coḻa period, and its central image of Naṭarāja as closely linked with the received idea of the dynasty as the Taj Mahal is with the Mughals. As we saw in the opening tableau of Kulottuṅga's earliest imperial record of 1074, the Emperor of the Three Worlds sought to conspicuously connect himself with the temple town. Nevertheless, large-scale courtly interest in the temple and its surrounding region only becomes visible decades later. In the early decades of the twelfth century, at the very end of Kulottuṅga's reign, Cidambaram became the scene of an ambiguous series of public pronouncements and grandiose gifts recorded in the temple's epigraphic archive. This intensified elite involvement was interbraided with the emergence of the region's new and anomalous Brahmanical ruling society, and perhaps the first stirrings of the present-day temple complex's unique liturgical and tenurial arrangement. The regional Brahmanical hegemony that emerged there produced an account of itself in a collection of temple legends in Sanskrit narrative verse. This drew upon the resources of Kulottuṅga's narrative, but did so in the service of a political and social project sharply distinct from that of his royal court.

It is this distinction from the cluster of institutions, networks of persons, and schemes of representation centered on Kulottuṅga and his court society that suggests that the case of Cidambaram be considered separately from the renditions studied in the previous chapter. While the three renditions were, as I have suggested, crucially parts of "what happened" rather than reports or reflections of the events of the accession, here we will be dealing with second-order occurrences, which were less part of what happened than its further ramifications.

Around the Little Shrine

In the popular and scholarly imagination, the great Śaiva temple city of Cidambaram has long been closely linked with the kings of the Coḻa dynasty, while modernity has seen the adoption of the temple's central image of Naṭarāja, Śiva the Lord of Dancers, as an icon – practically a trademark – of Hinduism as a whole. Despite its densely populated sacred landscape, for Tamil Śaivas the complex at Cidambaram is simply called *koyil*, "*the* temple." This ubiquity and centrality is illustrated by a range of anecdotes: it was from the *koyil*'s storerooms that the moldering manuscripts were recovered that supplied the basis for the redaction of the *Tirumuṟai*, the Tamil Śaiva canon, and seemingly every learned Śaiva divine hailed from or was educated in Cidambaram or its environs, from Aghoraśiva in the twelfth century to Umāpaticivaṉ in the fourteenth to Arumuga Navalar in the nineteenth. Every Śaiva manuscript that has come down to us, every print edition in modern times, and every recitation of Śaiva texts down to the present begins with the invocation "*tiruciṟṟampalam*," the name of the temple complex's heart, the Little Shrine.

It is difficult to escape the weight of all of this significance, and so to rethink what we think we know about the temple and its surroundings. The temple and its surroundings have accordingly attracted a large scholarship, though one beset with problems that are both particular to the place and more general. Cidambaram's outsized significance for modern Tamil Śaivism (and modern global Hinduism) is the source of some, but not all, of these. Much of this literature draws extensively upon hagiographical sources celebratory of the temple's sacrality; this has at times occasioned efforts at overzealous revisionism. Even those studies reliant upon the "harder" evidence preserved in epigraphy are faced with particular challenges for the site. One can only sympathize with the *cri de coeur* of the early-twentieth-century epigraphist, who lamented that the pious charity of some (the Nattukkottai Chettiyars were especially singled out) had been inadvertently responsible for the eradication of much of the historical fabric of "the ancient Śiva temples of South India," especially the loss of the records from major sites in Kāñcipuram, the island of Śrīrangam, in the Coḻa heartland of Tanjavur district. Cidambaram goes unmentioned in this reckoning, but this habit had been and continues to be especially acute there, leaving a modern structure that is even more of shambolic than other medieval temple complexes.[2]

Even the name of the temple town is unstable. In early sources, the place that I will refer to as Cidambaram is variously called Tillai, Puliyūr, Pĕrumpaṟṟapuliyūr, or Puṇḍarīkapuram. Even its most recognizable name contains within it multiple possibilities: the etymon here is certainly the Tamil *ciṟṟampalam*, "the Little Shrine," a reference to the earliest part of the now-sprawling temple complex. Transposed into Sanskrit, this became *cidambaram*, "the sky (or space) of consciousness." The semantic distance between its humbler earlier name and its subsequent reimagining speaks volumes about the long-term history of the place, in which a small and inaccessible site of worship came to be promoted into a place of transregional, and indeed cosmic, significance. The central passage of this transformation occurred under Kulottuṅga and his successor; as we shall see, this was a process that was imagined by contemporaries to be a consequence of the king's rise.

An earlier centuries-long history of the site centered on the Little Shrine is marked by gaps and post facto reimaginings. Another of the place's many names provides a clue here: Tillai, probably the earliest name of the settlement, is borrowed from the name of a local plant, the poisonous milky mangrove (*Exocoecaria agallocha*) that is endemic in the salt wetlands surrounding it. In contrast to the settled, densely cultivated and beneficent temple landscape of the Kāveri, with its paddy fields, bananas, and areca palms, Tillai was set in forbidding terrain, at the northern edge of the delta's coastal fan: it fell into the vaguely defined internal borderlands of the Coḻa landed imagination, in *naṭuvil nāṭu*, the "country in the middle" between the Kāveri country proper and Tondaimandalam. There are some references to Tillai or to Puliyūr in the canons of the Śaiva and Vaiṣṇava *bhakti* hymnists of the final centuries of the common era's first millennium, along with its most famous residents, the 3,000 Brahmans of Tillai (*tillaimūvāyiravar*). Intriguingly, the most detailed of these references are those found in Tirumaṅkai's contributions to Vaiṣṇava hymnal; these connect the temple with the Pallava kings of the Tondai country, and specifically mention the 3,000 Vedic Brahmans who worship there.[3] The overriding impression of the earliest history of the place is that of a *tapovana* or penitential retreat, an image that doubtless made it attractive to ascetics and the odd pilgrim. There is, however, no mention of it as a major feature of the religious or cultural landscape.

The growth of the site into a temple city of great importance is generally linked with the fortunes of the Coḻa kings, although this connection remains highly anomalous. Parāntaka I (r. 907–955) was allegedly responsible for the paradigmatic act of royal charity to the temple, the gilding of the roof of the *ciṟṟampalam* shrine, an event celebrated in the twentieth *patikam* of the *Tiruvicaippā*, a hymn attributed to his son Gaṇḍarāditya. While this claim became a topos in later eulogistic writing, it is problematic as history. There is only a single record dated in Parāntaka's regnal years to be found anywhere in Cidambaram, and the Śaiva hymnist Appar – the earliest of the *Tevāram* poets, usually dated to the first half of the seventh century – already sings of the gilding.[4] With the noontide of Coḻa power in the eleventh century, royal and elite interest in the growing temple site and the habitations that had emerged around it seems certain, though even this is difficult to substantiate based solely on local architectural or epigraphic traces. That the imperial kings of the dynasty were devotees of Naṭarāja is widely accepted, despite the exceedingly thin basis of this claim. Rājarāja is often said to have taken the Cidambaram Śiva as his *iṣṭadevatā* or personal deity solely on the strength of the title *śivapādaśekhara* ("he who is crowned by Śiva's foot") found in inscriptions commemorating his construction of the Bṛhadīśvara temple in Tanjavur. While that great royal temple did incorporate a shrine to Naṭeśa, it was only one among many others subordinated to the central massive *liṅga* shrine and to an iconographic program centering on the martial figure of Śiva in his heroic form as Tripurāntaka. There appears to be no evidence at all to suggest that the Cōḻa coronation ritual or *rājyābhiṣeka* was held at Cidambaram prior to the time of Kulottuṅga II's in 1133.[5] Again, little trace of this interest can be found in Cidambaram itself: of the hundreds of inscriptions recorded in the temple's precincts, only a handful can be dated before the 1100s.[6]

Among these, there is one outstanding and detailed record dated to the twenty-fourth year (*ca.* 1036) of Parakesarivarman Rājendra's reign. The royal order, directing resource flows in cash and produce in order to support parts of the temple's festival calendar, supplies details of the commercial and residential infrastructure that had developed in the micro-region by that time: as such, it has been understood to document Cidambaram's status as an "economic center" of its region.[7] Though the evidence for this strong claim is equivocal, the record certainly attests to an effort in Rājendra's time to integrate the Cidambaram micro-region into the Cōḻa landed order, in a significant and unusual way. In it, Pĕrumpaṟṟapuliyūr is classed for the first time as a *taṉiyūr* or "autonomous settlement" within the sprawling Rājendrasimha-*vaḷanāṭu*. While the *taṉiyūr* had been a part of the Cōḻa territorial imagination since Parāntaka's time, these had been exclusively centered on *brahmadeya* complexes of long-standing, and had been a characteristic feature of Tondaimandalam, in the northern part of the kingdom.[8] To name Cidambaram as a *taṉiyūr* was practically a category error in Rājendra's times, as was the location of this Tondai-specific institution within the imperial system of the *vaḷanāṭu*s. Cidambaram was one of the two most southerly such places; only Uḍaiyārkuṭi, about ten miles up the Kollidam river, was located as far to the south, and this thriving, ancient Brahman estate was itself a Pallava foundation, a salient of Tondai high culture set at the northern fringe of Colamandalam.[9] This suggests two features of the emerging temple town: first, despite the absence of a *brahmadeya* foundation, it possessed its own localized Brahman subculture, something that accords with the long-standing if vague association of the place with the 3,000 Brahmans. Second, it was a place oriented toward the Tondai north instead of the Kāveri delta.

Rājendra's royal order, which was conveyed through a royal "female intimate" (*aṇukki*), one Nakkan̲ Pāvai, attests to an institutional complexity extending beyond the temple precinct itself. Assuming the record to be reliable, already in 1036 Cidambaram possessed a cluster of satellite settlements or *piṭākai*, five of which are listed by name in this record.[10] These appear to be principally Brahman habitations by their names, though they evidently possessed a range of service castes and, in one case, an ascriptively diverse mercantile assembly. Thus despite the thin inscriptional presence of royal investment prior to the end of Rājendra's reign, Cidambaram had become a significant, if anomalous, part of the religious and institutional landscape, dominated by Brahmans and increasingly falling within the purview of the Co̲la state apparatus. But there is no evidence of direct royal involvement, still less of a sense of the temple as the center of a state or royal family cult; nor is there any sense at all of Cidambaram as a theologically or ritually distinctive place: the main deity is simply referred to, like any other Śiva, as the temple's *uṭaiyār*.

It is difficult to get any sense of what the main temple was like in this period, whether as an architectural or as a cultic fact. The Little Shrine itself certainly existed, its roof shingled in bright gold, but otherwise there is little that can be said. It was already much changed from its earlier history as an inaccessible ascetic retreat surrounded by mangrove jungle: the region supported a flourishing network of residential villages centered on the temple, yet it still retained the character of a marginal site when seen from Kāñcī or from the delta. The best reconstruction of the physical surround of the temple complex is that of Paul Younger, who proposes that it was precisely in Kulottuṅga's period that the temple began to take on the outlines of its present form.[11] These changes to the built environment seem to have been sudden and dramatic, and catalyzed by the royal court's interest. Already in the late 1060s, Vīrarājendra had claimed in his Sanskrit *praśasti* to have made the conspicuous donation of a fabulous gemstone to the Cidambaram Śiva, but neither he nor his agents left any epigraphic trace whatsoever in the temple's vicinity.

Courtly Donors of Kulottuṅga's Time

In the closing decade of Kulottuṅga's reign, by contrast, there are three donations made by prominent figures of the royal court. Two of these are made in the name of the emperor's younger sisters, Kuntavaiyāḻvār and Maturāntikiyāḻvār, neither of whom had any previous records. Kuntavai's donations are dated to 1114 and were professedly made at Kulottuṅga's behest. Interestingly, he is publicly referred to there as "Rājendra" for the first time in decades. The gifts are grandly ornamental: besides what seems a symbolic claim (made in verse) to gilding the temple's shrine, the Coḻa princess presented the god with a golden water-pot, a mirror, and a "stone that had been presented as a wonder to Śrīrājendracoḻa by the king of Kamboja," to be set in the *ĕtirampalam* or "facing shrine." In Maturāntikiyāḻvār's donation, dated insecurely to two years later, the princess is said once again to enact the king's will, but only to oversee the transfer of land for the establishment of a temple garden and hospice to feed Śaiva devotees. This donation is enacted in the name of a local Brahman, one Vācciyan̲ Iravi Tiruccir̲r̲ampalamuṭaiyān̲.[12] Alongside these detailed local donations, there is also a short verse inscription, in Sanskrit, on the eastern face of the same wall, celebrating Kulottuṅga's victories over the Pāṇḍyas and Ceras, and his erection of a pillar of victory on the west coast; this undated record, however, contains nothing that links it or its subject to the temple.[13]

A record of another figure from Kulottuṅga's court was incised in the same places as the grants of the two royal sisters, on the northern face of the inner *prākāra* wall. The figure it memorializes was not a part of the Coḻa royal family, but instead a member of Tondaimandalam's aristocratic elite, who has become known to modern scholarship as Naralokavīra. This was just one epithet borne by this figure, whose civic name was Arumpākkiḻān̲ Maturāntakatevan̲ Pŏn̲n̲ampalakkūttan̲, and who hailed from Maṇavir̲koṭṭam on the southern banks of the Pālār river.[14] His given name (*iyar̲pĕyar*) Pŏn̲n̲ampalakkūttan̲ ("Dancer in the Golden Hall") suggests a special connection with Cidambaram; but while his donations there were massive, these were only the most important node in a wider network of his benefactions, extending throughout the northern part of the Coḻa kingdom, concentrated in a rough arc connecting Tiruvatikai, Siddhaliṅgamaṭam, and Cidambaram. The constructions and endowments with which he was associated in these three sites represented an enormous inflow of capital and marshaling of labor power, most conspicuously so in Cidambaram, where the constructions to which he lays claim utterly transformed the built environment.

The major surviving trace of his public life, Naralokavīra's Cidambaram *praśasti*, consists of thirty-one Sanskrit verses in various meters and thirty-seven Tamil *veṇpā*s. It has been published several times, though never satisfactorily, and the original record is not at present accessible in situ. Already in 1888, when first noticed in the *Annual Report* *of Epigraphy*, Hultzsch described it as "defaced"; whether this was the result of accidental damage or deliberate vandalism is unclear. Features of the published Sanskrit text suggest hasty or uncautious engraving, while the Tamil verses would be all but uninterpretable except for their conjectural restoration by the great philologist Mu. Irākavaiyaṅkār.[15] While much remains unclear, some cautious judgments can be ventured. There is, first of all, the *praśasti*'s departure from the Co̲la chancellery standard: the record contains no dating, regnal or otherwise, and practically no reference to the ruling king. The whole of the record is focused on the figure of Naralokavīra: in this, its poets seemed to have learned from the example of the *mĕykkīrtti* composers, but otherwise there is little trace of their influence. While the two halves of the text overlap in many of their details, except for a few benefactions mentioned solely in the Tamil, they strongly differ in their emphases. Both resort to the regimen of figurative language typical of their genre, but the Sanskrit verses remain tied to the immediately local world of the temple compound. While Naralokavīra's donations are elaborately detailed, the man himself is all but absent, swallowed up in the grandness of his donative gesture. The Tamil *vĕṇpā*s, by contrast, contain a subtle but significant argument about the person of the magnate donor, whom they situate in a series of wider regional and dynastic contexts, and about whose claims to lordship they present a series of arguments.

Naralokavīra's *praśasti* embodies a significant departure from the cosmopolitan standard, where Sanskrit is allotted the interpretative function and the vernacular the burden of documentation. Here both languages are directed toward memorializing the specifics of the donations, while retaining their expressive and poetic capacities. The horizons, however, of the Tamil verse extend beyond those of the Sanskrit, which is limited to a series of versified statements of fact about the immediate environs of the Cidambaram temple, by means of the hyper-real expressive potentialities of Sanskritic praise-poetry.[16]

The opening of each section is illustrative of these larger tendencies. The first verse of the whole eulogy begins, in Sanskrit, with a statement directed toward the text's audience:

> Listen to me carefully, now, to the things that were done for the Lord of the Assembly, who performs the supreme dance for the benefit of the three worlds, by that Mānāvatāra, Pride Incarnate, whose mind is set solely on Him. Creatures joyously wander both heaven and earth with mouths that are the abode of that praiseworthy man.[17]

The Sanskrit then dives headlong into the details of Naralokavīra's donations of gold and ritual accoutrement, and of the buildings whose construction he himself performed (as the language of the eulogy insists, using simplex instead of causative verbs). The audience learns of the street lamps he himself erected, the water-pots he donated, areca palms he planted, *maṇḍapams* he constructed, and on and on in this vein for another thirty verses.

The opening gambit of the Tamil is strikingly different:

> In times long past, there was a generous man, who gilded the Little Shrine with all the treasure that had allured the hostile kings stretching all the way to the bordering ocean, in order to check the pride of powerful Kali: He was surely a dancer with his spear.
>
> They say that he covered the golden shrine of Tillai with bright gold [and thus] gilded the horizons. But what of the Tŏṇṭaiyar, the parasoled kings who take up a spear in order to seize all the treasure of the powerful kings of the north?[18]

Where the Sanskrit verses set all of Naralokavīra's donations in the narrative past, the Tamil begins further still back in time, as marked expressly by the word *tŏllai* ("[in] times long past"), made even more emphatic by its place in the first *vĕṇpā*'s metrical structure and rhyme scheme.[19] Though neither he nor his family are explicitly named, the ancient patron referred to here is surely Parāntaka, in the paradigmatic case of the gilding of the Little Shrine. It is this founding act that made possible the subsequent history of religious charity at the temple; in the case of Naralokavīra, in his civic life as Pŏṉṉampalakkūttaṉ ("Dancer in the Golden Shrine"), this act was in a real sense constitutive of his social self. In the second verse, unusually united by rhyme with the first, this is allowed to set up an explicit contrast: the (again unnamed) Coḻa king became famous throughout the world for this act, but what about the lords of Tondaimandalam, the region with a much stronger link to Cidambaram?[20]

A close reading of the rest of the eulogy bears out this disjunction between the royal center and the world of the Tamil-speaking north. While variations on its honoree's given name are used throughout its early verses – he is Pŏṉṉampalakkūttar in vs. 4, Vāṭkūttar ("Kūttar with a sword") in vs. 5, and Naralokavīraṉ in vs. 7 – these epithets increasingly give way to descriptions of him as the *ko*, *maṉ* (both mean "king") or *eṟu* ("bull") of the *tŏṇṭaiyar*, while repeatedly emphasizing Naralokavīra's warrior bona fides. This appeal to regionalist identity recurs throughout the Tamil verses, conspicuously coloring the eulogy's two (and *only* two) passing references to Kulottuṅga as Naralokavīra's overlord: "the king of the Tŏṇṭaiyar feels joy in his heart once he had royally set the lady Earth, with her ancient seas, beneath the moon-like parasol of his king"; and "The Tŏṇṭaiyar king conquers the limits of the earth, where the waves of the roaring sea crash constantly, so that it might belong to Apayaṉ alone," referring to Kulottuṅga with the name also favored by Cayaṅkŏṇṭar in his *Kaliṅkattupparaṇi.*[21] The martial details of Naralokavīra's victories are detailed in the Tamil version, where we read of victories in Kollam, Kalinga, and the Pāṇḍya country. The eulogy's implicit argument, at every step, is of the autonomy of the man it honors, and of his and his people's all-important connection with Cidambaram's dancing Śiva.

To be certain, this does not suggest a rebellion or a rejection of Coḻa sovereignty: the language of the Tamil political poetry is subtler than this.[22] It represents instead a deliberately staged political ambiguity, where assertions of independence and appeals to regional charisma are juxtaposed with references to loyal service to Kulottuṅga. A dramatic instance of this can be found late in the Tamil section, in a donation significantly unparalleled in the Sanskrit text:

> The king of the Tŏṇṭaiyar who took away the troubles of the people of the earth, made tax-free the boundaries of . . . twenty-five [?] . . . [under the name of] Tillai Tyāgavalli, and he arranged a hospice of the street of the Brahmans of Tillai, who bring the Veda to fruition.[23]

This creation of a land grant in the name of Kulottuṅga's final chief queen connects Naralokavīra and his Cidambaram benefactions with the world of the court in the king's final years that is summoned up in hallucinatory detail by the *Kaliṅkattupparaṇi*, with which the Tamil *vĕṇpā*s possess further thematic and verbal affinities.[24] Like Cayaṅkŏṇṭār's poem, with its triangulations between king, chief queen, and the Tŏṇṭaiyar party at court, the Tamil eulogy took shape in the final years of Kulottuṅga's very long reign, in the midst of a lingering ambiguity as to what was to come after the old king. Recall that Naralokavīra's eulogy, incised on the northern side of the main shrine complex's *prākāra* wall, was directly juxtaposed with the donations of Kulottuṅga's royal sisters Kuntavai and Maturāntaki: the royal court in the final years of Kulottuṅga's senescence seems to have been dominated by the female members of the dynasty, especially in the absence of a clear male heir. The Tamil eulogy's complex reflection on loyalty and independence appears to have been attuned to capitalize on some of the uncertainties of this conjuncture.

The contrast with the earlier, Sanskrit section of the eulogy is stark. Instead of the courtly and regional vision of the *vĕṇpā*s, the Sanskrit verses focus relentlessly on the scene in Cidambaram; the rare martial topoi given there are completely formulaic, with Naralokavīra called, for instance, "he who clothed the wives of his enemies solely in the smoke of forest fires."[25] The poet responsible for the Sanskrit verses was above all concerned with the transfiguration of the local world of the temple. There is no mention of the donor's place of origin or any specifics of his wider career; instead, a pleasure garden that he had "devoutly arranged ... swallows up the horizon in its ocean of white flowers, its margins filled with the ritual calls of the best of Brahmans, come to see the dance of Three-Eyed Śiva."[26] Instead of grotesqueries drawn from courtly fashion, the environs of the Little Shrine are transformed into a sub-Kālidāsan idyll, with clouds clinging to the heights of the temple compound's outer retaining wall, "at whose thunderings the Goddess' pet peacocks dance."[27] Another verse details the construction of what is evidently the very wall on which the inscription is located:

> This same man, Sabhānaṭa, the initiatory guru in the destruction of the cities of his enemies, has made in this same place the great wall for the Lord that is called "Naralokavīra." The flag-banners mounted on the top of this wall, heated by the sun now so much nearer, lap up the cool waters of the celestial Gaṅgā, as if they were [the mythical serpent] Takṣaka [?].[28]

Beside the figuration of the temple flags, consistent with the style of the rest of the Sanskrit verses, and the historical datum of the naming of the wall, the poet here significantly stages a fusion of the temple's god and the magnate devotee: both are Sabhānaṭa, the "dancer in the assembly," the Sanskrit hypernym of Naralokavīra's given name.[29] The poet extends this identification by calling the man *parapurapradhvaṃsadīkṣāguruḥ*, "the initiatory guru in the destruction of his enemies' cities." There are several levels of poetic and theological reference in this description. First of all, it brings to mind Śiva's form as the destroyer of the anti-gods' triple city. At the same time, this compound noun recalls the crucial mediating role of the teacher in the Śaiva ritual of initiation. It is only through the actions of the *dīkṣāguru* that the initiand's three inherent limitations of indwelling impurity, the working of *māyā,* and the actions of his prior karma can be destroyed. These three theological terms thus act as the implied standards of comparison for the enemies' cities, playing upon the fact that the cities of the *asura*s are three in number. Further, since this fundamental Śaiva ritual depends on the explicit consubstantiation of god and preceptor ("to worship Śiva, one must first become Śiva"), the verbal equation of the two Sabhānaṭas possesses a further, metaphysical dimension.[30] This signals something important about the intended reception of Sanskrit text. The *praśasti* is meant as an argument not for the court or the other leading figures of the kingdom, but for the Sanskrit-knowing Śaiva Brahman society centered on the temple. It was precisely this audience for whom the verbal transfiguration of the environment of the temple complex would have possessed any significance, and it would have contained men familiar with the tantric ritual theory on which this verse depends. This group would have also been receptive to the nuances of the Tamil verses, especially the way that their complex poetic texture distinguished them from the unchallenging literary style of the royal *mĕykkīrtti*s.

Naralokavīra's actions in Cidambaram were to feed back into the wider sphere of dissemination of the royal eulogy when, from his eleventh regnal year in 1129–1130, Vikramacoḻa's inscriptional preamble began to include an additional passage:

> from the heap of pure gold that was gathered together and poured out before [him] by the lords [of the kingdom] of the abundant tax revenues of his tenth regnal year, he gilded the beautiful enclosure that surrounds the hall of fine gold where his family deity performs the *tāṇḍava* dance, and the hall along with the temple-gateways, such that it appeared as if the shining mountain range which encircles the earth had been joined with the mountain of the sunrise.[31]

Among the many other gifts the revised *mĕykkīrtti* goes on to detail, several (renovations to a temple car, a donation of pearls, a ritual trumpet) accord so closely with those found in Naralokavīra's *praśasti* that it is clear that the now-established king is claiming credit for the Tŏṇṭai lord's donations. This is unusual: the contents of all earlier *mĕykkīrtti*s had been overwhelming martial in content. Vikrama was the first Coḻa king whose public text devoted such close attention to religious patronage, and certainly the first to claim that the Cidambaram Śiva bore a special relationship with the dynasty, as its *kulanāyaka* or tutelary deity.[32] Even more novel is royal eulogy's conclusion to this insertion:

> this along with many other such donations, the king was pleased to accomplish in his tenth year, on the Sunday that marked the thirteenth *tithi* of the bright half of the month of Cittirai, as the moon was in Hasta, so that he might make flourish the entire world beneath the shade of his singular royal parasol.[33]

The information given here translates to April 15, 1128: remarkably, this is the only exact date given anywhere in the corpus of Coḻa *mĕykkīrtti*s.[34] This then marks the exact point when the circulating social energies constituted by Naralokavīra's actions in Cidambaram were taken up into the court's projected image of royal piety and lawful rule, when the Coḻa king became for the first time the god's foremost devotee on earth. Underlying this declaration, we can imagine the complex negotiations of the senior female members of the dynasty and Naralokavīra, and the Tŏṇṭaiyar lord's own complex pull between independence, loyalty, personal devotion, and public aggrandizement. Vikrama's public adoption of the Cidambaram donations did not portend a fall from royal favor for Naralokavīra, who is reckoned among the list of Vikrama's leading courtiers in Oṭṭakkūttaṉ's *ulā,* written a generation later.[35] The transfer of institutional charisma from Tŏṇṭaiyar lord to Coḻa king, then, seems to mark the successful working-out of the newly forged political order in the wake of Kulottuṅga, a new order in which royal devotion to Naṭarāja became one of the hallmarks of the dynasty.

Beyond the Three-Thousand: Cidambaram's Brahman Subculture

But for all that the Coḻa kings would from Vikrama's time compete to announce themselves as the Cidambaram Śiva's greatest devotee, and for all that the temple town remained a stopping point on the court's interminable progresses throughout the kingdom, the long-term story of the micro-region centered on Cidambaram is one of its increasing insularity. Some of the rhetorical force of the Sanskrit verses in honor of Naralokavīra was likely directed toward the Brahmans connected with the temple's observances; the descendants of these Brahmans were to densely settle in the surrounding agrarian regions and retain their tantric Śaiva traditions. We have seen how the temple and its surrounding patchwork of residential hamlets were already in the early eleventh century anomalously classified as a *taṉiyūr* or independent settlement, an institutional form usually reserved for Tondaimandalam's large *brahmadeya* complexes. Answering to this is the demographic slant evident in Cidambaram's epigraphic archive: the figures mentioned in the temple's records tend disproportionately to be Brahmans (about half of the 1,600 individuals).[36] The impression that emerges of the Cidambaram Brahmans is not of just temple functionaries, much less of a single homogenous group like the legendary Tillai 3,000, but of a substantial and powerful landed elite.

This local Brahmanical society distanced itself from the management of the temple over the course of the next century, transforming into a rentier class resident in the town's surrounding *piṭākai*s. While twelfth-century records witnessed members of Brahman assemblies variously described as *sabhaiyār* or *mūlaparuṣaiyār* taking an active role in temple governance, by the 1200s, when "by far the largest number of inscriptions" is recorded in the temple, the *mūlaparuṣai* continues to be active in land transactions, but not temple affairs. By the latter half of that century, individual Brahmans of the region appear just as the beneficiaries of land sales to the temple complex, which was by that time enormous and possessed of its own complex system of independent managerial committees. The rising fortunes of these landed Brahman groups are more significant given their anomalous status. Most of the named Brahman figures are united by their unusual *gotras* or Brahmanical descent groups. Of the *gotra* names encountered most frequently, only one, Kavuciyaṉ, possesses a transregional distribution as well as a pan-Indic equivalent (Kauśika). The other two major Brahman *gotras* claimed by Cidambaram Brahmans,Vācciyaṉ and Uḻaiccaraṇaṉ, are closely associated with the temple town; the last and most anomalous of these being by far the most frequently encountered there.[37] This suggests as a hypothesis a period of rapid Brahmanization, where local communities possessed of elite ritual status assumed a place within the genealogical ideal of the pan-Indic caste hierarchy, but had yet to completely assimilate their collective identities to translocal norms. There is strong evidence that something similar took place among the nearby Pāñcarātrika Vaiṣṇava groups claiming Brahman status in the mid-eleventh century; the Brahmanization of Cidambaram may have simply taken place in obedience to a slightly different temporal rhythm.[38]

The maneuverings of Kulottuṅga's sisters, Tŏṇṭaiyar war-leader, and heir thus occurred at an early stage of a massive process of social differentiation and change in the landed order in the region. This was a process of a centuries-long duration. At some point, members of this local Brahmanical order came to reflect on the connection between Cidambaram and the events of Kulottuṅga's reign, and derive from this reflection an account of their place in the world. It was the community of literate Śaiva Brahmans, settled in the region and devoted to Naṭarāja but likely not a part of the temple's cadre of ritual functionaries, that produced our final narrative of Kulottuṅga's coming to power and his special relationship with the temple town. This is contained within a cycle of purāṇic legends called the *Cidambaramāhātmya* ("On the Magnificence of Cidambaram"). The historian Hermann Kulke has drawn attention to the similarities between the cycle's concluding account of a king it calls Hiraṇyavarman and the historical events of Kulottuṅga's imperial accession.[39] Kulke's identification of the context of the *māhātmya*'s production and its relationship to Kulottuṅga is in important ways similar to the sort of historical reading that has been practiced throughout this book; his methods and their conclusions also significantly differ from those argued for here. As such, it is worth lingering over his interpretation.

For Kulke, the final section of the *Cidambaramāhātmya* (hereafter CM), consisting of its nineteenth through twenty-sixth *adhyāyas*, represents the basic details of Kulottuṅga's accession in a heavily reimagined, mythicized form. Significantly, this discrete narrative also forms the major part of the final "layer" of what he hypothesized to be the composite text of this local mini-*purāṇa*. The story is of an eastern prince, originally named Siṃhavarman and, in keeping with his name, possessed a lion-like appearance. After a peregrination through southeastern India, and healed of this affliction by the waters of the Śivagaṅgā tank in Cidambaram, the prince – now renamed Hiraṇyavarman – becomes a disciple of the place's two tutelary sages Patañjali and Vyāghrapāda, who reveal to him Śiva's *ānandatāṇḍava* dance. Hiraṇyavarman, initiated into kingship and gifted a tiger banner by Vyāghrapāda, settled the legendary 3,000 Brahmans in the vicinity, constructed a miraculous and extensive temple for Naṭarāja, and established its annual festival calendar.

In this account of the temple's founding royal patron, Kulke detects enough "vague allusions" to events of Kulottuṅga's public life to suggest that it supplied the historical template for the mythic account. Among these "politically conditioned" details are Hiraṇyavarman's northeastern origins, the transfer of the tiger flag – the Coḻa royal crest – from the sage to the *bhakta*-king, and such otherwise inexplicable details as the reference to Hiraṇyavarman's ancestor as *bhāgīrathīpūraparipanthin* or "enemy of the Gaṅgā," taken as a Sanskrit calque of Rājendra's epithet *gaṅgaikŏṇṭa*.[40] In Kulke's view, the confection of this narrative, especially the sage's endorsement of the new king, reflects an effort at the legitimation of Kulottuṅga's disruption of the direct line of Coḻa succession through his association with the religious charisma of the Cidambaram temple and its Brahmans. He goes on to suggest that the reference to the importation of the 3,000 Brahmans, from what the text unambiguously describes as the *antarvedī* of the Ganges–Yamuna doab, may have reflected the importation of Veṅgī Brahmans into Cidambaram, as "[for] an usurper [*sic*] of the Cōḷa throne, the presence of priests owing allegiance to him in the sacred center of the empire must have been of great significance." Although Kulke readily admits there are no epigraphic or other evidence to support this hypothesis, it has been repeated by others as an established fact.[41]

There is much to be admired in Kulke's bold hypothesis, in his correlation of the details of the myth-cycle with other textual and art-historical materials, and in his effort to theorize the antecedents and consequences of such a literary representation of events of political culture. In this last aspect, Kulke acknowledged the influence of the historian of Java C. C. Berg's theories of the "optative character" of certain literary texts from classical Indonesia; in his focus on the legitimation of political authority, he owes a much greater debt to Weber's historical sociology.[42] Further, the guiding presupposition of Kulke's larger study of the CM – that it consists of multiple compositional layers that can be analytically differentiated – is broadly convincing, as the text evidently incorporates multiple registers of Sanskrit writing within it, and so potentially was the product of multiple hands. And the effort to understand this stratified text to be serving a coherent political project, rather than just being an accidental accretion of the religious imagination, is commendable. But there is a rather different and more complex story that the CM's Hiraṇyavarman myth-cycle can tell. Elements of this narrative certainly depended upon the events of Kulottuṅga's accession and their consequences. But by restoring some of the complexities that Kulke's "optative" reading suppresses, this text can be made to articulate with the other renditions, remountings, and echoes that have been traced in this chapter and earlier. In fact, the CM possesses only the most tenuous connection with the events of the accession, but this itself can tell us significant things about the wider transformations that Cidambaram experienced as a consequence of Kulottuṅga's half-century of rule.

The *māhātmya*'s Hiraṇyavarman cycle was the product of a talented composer of Sanskrit narrative verse, and its transmission and composition raise tantalizing questions that must remain unexplored here.[43] Instead, I will concentrate on three episodes: its opening passage (20:4–33), which sets the narrative within a larger metaphysical and political-theoretical context; parts of the cycle's central narrative of Siṃhavarman's origins, his coming to Cidambaram, and his diffident relationship to royal power (20: 38–49, 22:1–13, 31–39; 25:4–31); and the description of his construction of an imagined version of the Cidambaram temple complex, and his settlement of its community of 3,000 Brahmans (24.54–90; 25:32–48)

Kulke finds little of interest in the cycle's opening; for him it just supplies "a creation myth" composed "in the style of the *purāṇa*s."[44] He leaves unasked the question of why the text's author-compilers felt the need to return to the beginning on the universe before starting to tell their story, or of what materials, purāṇic or otherwise, they may have created this account from. A closer look at the passage proves there to be much that is of significance in it:[45]

During the great period of the dissolution, Śiva adopted the form of Rudra and himself performed his furious *tāṇḍava* dance. Though completely free, God was impelled by the Power of his Volition in the final period of the dissolution and established the created world on the basis of his own Powers; manifesting the great *māyā*, the lord of the worlds produced upon that marvellous collection [of his Powers] the five realities, beginning with *nāda*, the subtle precursor of sound; from that he created the whole of the Pure Universe and likewise language, in its four parts; from the fourth of these sources, Śankara created the phonemes: of these, he first created the self-luminous OM, consisting of three parts and connected to the [three] cosmogonic acts beginning with the creation. From this God immediately created the three ritual cries [*bhūḥ, bhuvar, svar*] and from these the *gāyatrī mantra*, the mother of the Veda, and then all of the Vedas. From these God created the seventy million great *mantra*s, and from these he created the lesser *mantra*s, in the same number. Then, from the other *māyā* he created the set of realities from Time down to Earth, and with them all things moving and immobile.

The major elements of this emanationist cosmos are not purāṇic at all, as Kulke had supposed, but are instead tantric, drawn from the ritual and speculative corpora of Śaiva initiates. Much of the terminology is doctrinal boilerplate, held in common by all Śaivas: thus the uppermost reality levels (*tattva*s) evolve out of a "great" *māyā* and consist of purely sonic phenomena, beginning with the subtle reverberation or *nāda*; the subsequent emergence of the world of everyday experience comes from another, lower level, also called *māyā*. This would be immediately relatable to the majority tradition of the Śaivasiddhānta, represented in the works of Aghoraśiva (active mid-twelfth century, likely in Cidambaram). But there are traces here of the more goddess-centered, non-dualist Śaivism, as in the centrality accorded here to Śiva's *icchāśakti*, or Power of Volition. The passage is also ambiguous on major issues of metaphysics: instead of a clear statement as to the identity or difference between Śiva, his Powers, and the world – the central issue dividing the dualist Siddhāntins from their non-dualist coreligionists – it only speaks of a loose imposition of the created world onto the substratum of Śiva's Powers (*sargaṃ sthāpya svaśaktiṣu*).[46]

The CM's author-compilers were thus eclectic in their sources, drawing upon both the dualist doctrinal "right" as well as the non-dualist "left." To this they grafted several references intelligible to a less sectarian audience, including a *locus classicus* known to any Sanskrit literate, while centering the account of both sonic and material creation upon the emergence of the Veda, in the service of a Śaiva-Brahmanical synthesis.[47] This synthesis continues, as the text has Śiva look out upon his creation: the god had created the *mantra*s of the Veda in order to empower the sacrifice, Brahmans to learn the *mantra*s and perform the rites, and cows to provide the raw material for fire-offerings. Sacrificers such as these gain heaven, while a series of desirable afterlives is delineated for other devout Brahmans, whether Śaivas or Vedāntins.[48] Śiva then introduces a complication into this scheme; it is here that things get interesting:[49]

And as for those evil men who do not abide by either the ways of ritual or secret insight [*brahma-*] that have been taught in the Vedas and the [Śaiva] *āgama*s, they are to be chastised by the four classes of punishments that have been taught in the authoritative texts. So it is in this world that it is the king, consecrated for the protection of his subjects, who is able to make those who are capable and ritually qualified grasp the meaning of the authoritative texts, and who is able to encourage these to act, and as a result to establish moral actions [*dharma*]; to turn those unworthy and unqualified away from us, and also to discipline those who have embarked upon unlawful ways. The king disciplines the wicked; the king is the instrument of Time. Thus the Moon-crested Lord considered in his mind, and he reflected on someone who would be capable of ruling over the entire world. Thereupon he summoned the two righteous sons of Savitṛ, the sun-god: to one of them, the blessed Lord of the Worlds gave a staff and made him the guardian of the southern direction, able to roam the entire triple universe; and he made the other into the diademed leader of kings.

The machinery of Śaiva doctrine is thus made to support a novel theory of kingship. The world needs a king so that the orderly practices of Vedic and Śaiva ritual may reliably deliver their practitioners to their postmortem destinies. The CM borrows lightly from *dharmaśāstra* (its "four punishments" is a cliché found in the *Manusmṛti* and elsewhere) and from the Epic's many paeans to royal power.[50] But the text is distinctive in what happens next: this combination of these disparate elements leads to a slightly uncanny reminder of the kinship between Manu and Yama, the death-god – both are sons of the Sun, like the Coḻas themselves.

This metaphysical and political amalgam seems keyed to a particular audience, the unmarked silent majority of Brahman householder-ritualists, whose own practices were at once Veda-congruent and connected with the various strands of tantric Śaivism. The CM reveals itself to be akin to another Cidambaram work of purāṇic Sanskrit, the longer, rangier, and more doctrinal *Sūtasaṃhitā*, which was equally directed to this middle ground of Śaiva brahmans, and toward a textual reconciliation between Vedic orthodoxy and Śaiva esoteric traditions.[51] This preamble addresses itself to this very specific audience, placing their own particular concerns with religious practice and its promised consequences as the central theme to the history of the universe.

It is to this implied audience of local Śaiva Brahmans that the text relates the central events of Siṃhavarman's transformation into Hiraṇyavarman, and his special devotion to the site's Dancing Śiva. The most significant traces of a historical Coḻa prototype that Kulke detects here bracket the major actions of the narrative. At its outset, the text describes the then-Siṃhavarman's father as *bhāgirathīpūrapratipanthiyaśoṃkura*, "an offshoot of the fame of the one who opposed the swell of the Bhāgirathī," in which Kulke sees a reference to Rājendra and his "conquest" of the Gaṅgā.[52] Some 200 verses later, as the Cidambaram sages stage an elaborate consecration of the now-Hiraṇyavarman in the presence of the 3,000 Brahmans, Vyāghrapāda conveys to the new king a *vyāghradhvaja* or "tiger flag," bearing the Co̱la family emblem, immediately upon completing his consecration.[53] To understand these to be deliberate references to the Co̱las seems very plausible. But understanding these isolated elements as determinative of the referential or figurative burden of the narrative as such is a much greater interpretative leap. Taken on its own terms, the Simhavarman–Hiraṇyavarman narrative is variation on one of the most enduring tropes in Indic literature, familiar already in the epics, of the "disqualified eldest."[54] Simhavarman is the eldest son of a king of the solar line, the fifth in descent from Manu. Born for unexplained reasons "bearing the form of a lion" (*siṃharūpadhara*), he should be barred by this disfigurement from the kingship, and it should instead devolve onto one of his younger brothers, called Sumati and Vedavarman (20.37). In a deliberate reversal of this commonplace, however, it is the eldest brother who repeatedly wishes himself to be disqualified, in order to fully devote himself to worshipping Śiva, and his father who proclaims him fit to rule, a sentiment explicitly echoed later in the story by the sage Vyāghrapāda, himself the subject of a feline deformity (the name means "Tiger foot"), and later to become the prince's adoptive father.[55] In another reversal, the prince's wanderings are not motivated by exile from rule, but by attraction to *tapas* and Śaiva worship, and a self-willed flight from the royal power his father wishes to give him. His wanderlust lands him up in the wild country around Mount Kālahasti, and in the company of forest-hunter, a Kirāta, who introduces him to a host of wonders and, eventually, guides him to Cidambaram. In a final twist, the prince's miraculous healing in the waters of the Śivagaṅgā tank and his emergence as Hiraṇyavarman remove the obstacle from his ability to rule, but only increase his predicament: although he is now qualified to rule, he has no desire to abandon Cidambaram and its dancing Śiva.

The prince's career begins somewhere off to the east – he refers to himself once (and only once) as "the son of the king of Gauḍa," and his early peregrinations take him through Vaṅga, Oḍra, and Āndhra before his arrival at Kālahasti, and his establishment in the south does occasion a change of name, but otherwise there is little to connect the Hiraṇyavarman cycle with the dynastic change brought about by Kulottuṅga.[56] There is no intimation of a failure of succession, no real crisis, and thus no real solution, in the CM's narrative; nor does the narrative of the deferral of royal power in favor of devotion resonate with other public renditions of the life of the Co̱la king. Neither the two younger brothers nor their and Simhavarman's father – whose name lies concealed beneath a textual corruption – appear to have any sort of historical counterpart; the two names borne by the cycle's protagonist, in turn, appear to be dim recollections of parts of an old Pallava king-list.[57] This last detail suggests another linkage between Cidambaram and Tondaimandalam, but it does little to support the sort of thoroughgoing political allegoresis that Kulke's "optative reading" requires. Instead, for all its occasional literary polish, the story of Hiraṇyavarman seems to be a work of narrative bricolage of a familiar purāṇic sort. This is evident in the frankly (and one suspects, deliberately) silly name-as-destiny device of a lion-faced Siṃhavarman becoming a golden-hued Hiraṇyavarman through the intercession of the tiger-footed sage.

Kulke's adoption of Kulottuṅga's reign as a *terminus a quo* for the creation of the final version of the CM certainly seems correct. Yet a reading of the text's closing chapters on Hiraṇyavarman's establishment of the organized Śaiva cult at Cidambaram suggests further inflections to his narrative. In Kulke's reading, the mythic king's implantation of the temple town's famed 3,000 Brahmans reflected the emigration of Veṅgī Brahmans to plug the gap in the "foreign" Kulottuṅga's legitimacy. While such Brahmanical colonizations were certainly possible (recall the testimony of Vīracoḍa's Pithapuram plates, discussed in Chapter 3), there is no other evidence to support this claim, and much to suggest otherwise.[58] In what Kulke supposes to be an awkward interpolation, the arrival of these Brahmans is in fact a return to their ancient native place. Immediately prior to the story of Simhavarman/Hiraṇyavarman proper, the CM includes a brief mythic aside about their emigration at Brahmā's request to the *antarvedī*, the Ganga–Yamuna doab.[59] In light of what we know of the social history of the Brahman communities based in and around the temple city, it might be better to see this as an effort at the recuperation of historical memory. References to the 3,000 Brahmans are vanishingly rare in the epigraphical remains of the eleventh and twelfth centuries. Despite the certain antiquity of the name, there is only a single mention, no doubt as a literary flourish, in the concluding verse of Naralokavīra's Tamil eulogy. The CM author-compilers may thus have self-consciously sought to reintroduce the term as a form of collective identity of the region's emerging Brahmanical ascendency.[60]

Something similar seems to be the case with Hiraṇyavarman's "coronation" at Cidambaram (25.4–20) and his subsequent building project. The narrative inconsistency that can be seen in the foreign prince assuming his "ancestral throne" (27cd: *siṃhāsanaṃ ... paitṛkam*) in Cidambaram points to the local dynasty as directly as the invocation of the tiger banner. Recall that Kulottuṅga's earliest imperial order was issued from "the Cetirāja hall in his palace at Perumpaṟṟapuliyūr";

the CM may in fact contain a distant echo of the early 1070s. But the real significance of this detail was likely more prospective than retrospective. When subsequent generations of Kulottuṅga's successors grew ever more closely associated with the Cidambaram temple, or when the resurgent southern king Sundarapāṇḍya was to hold his own *vijayābhiṣeka* or "victory consecration" there to announce his ritual independence from the Cola̱ imperium, they may have precisely been enacting the script first set out by the makers of the CM.

Following upon his consecration, Hiraṇyavarman is seized with the desire to "renew" Cidambaram, and to found "ample hermitages" in its environs for the assembled sages.[61] The miraculous construction of the temple – with the gem-encrusted opulence familiar from the Sanskrit literature of the fantastic – would only have made sense in the wake of the public negotiation between Naralokavīra and Vikrama; in the equally wondrous nature of the sages' ashrams we may detect a mythic transposition of the real process of Brahmanical settlement that was the generations-long outcome of landed transfers to the temple's accounts. The text then shifts into a noticeably rougher register of Sanskrit as it details a festival calendar inaugurated by Hiraṇyavarman. It is, however, the autonomy and independence of this Brahmanical world centered on the Cidambaram temple that the text everywhere seeks to magnify. It is in this context that the never-resolved double consciousness of its royal protagonist makes sense: the king is attracted to worshipping at Tillai because – we are assured – doing so is the most precious thing in the universe. Yet this Śaiva paradise is only possible if there is a king to make it so, and Hiraṇyavarman' desire to renounce must always be deferred – first by his father, later by Vyāghrapāda, and ultimately by Śiva – so that things can continue as they should. The text asserts that it is a wonderful thing to have kings who are good Śaivas and especially devotees of Naṭeśa; but it is the Brahmans, at once Śaivas and Vaidikas, who really matter. The *Cidambaramāhātmya* is not a royalist text at all, either in authorship or in intended audience.[62]

Thus it is that the difference between my own and Kulke's interpretation of the text depends less on philology than on social theory. For Kulke, the only account of the text's creation that makes sense is one in which someone commissioned the text's creation, in order to supply "an additional legitimation" to Kulottuṅga's *ex hypothesi* illegitimate rule. The argument insists that this text and others like it sought to create a "new legendary reality" to patch over the messy bits of the past. These can only obtain in an *ex post facto* relationship with the actions of historical actors, and their task is to obfuscate those actions, and to cause some (presumably passive) audience to misrecognize them in the service of some larger political end. The interpretation advanced here suggests first of all that we see the text taking shape within a wider social process of Brahmanization and regional settlement, and see it as articulating a prospective vision, indeed a sort of charter, of this new form of local collective life. The story of the eastern king coming to rule in the Tamil south was one of the several textual strands that the *māhātmya* text wove together, and it did so in a social world that was bound up with the consequences of Kulottuṅga's reign. But it did so in the service of a project to summon into being a new form of local solidarity configured around the much older idea of the 3,000 Brahmans of Tillai.

Viewed in this way, the *Cidambaramāhātmya* should be understood as a political text, but in a way that can be sharply distinguished from its "political" conditioning as it is conceived by Kulke. It was a work that was intended to intervene within a set of material and symbolic relations among persons and institutions, and to present an argument for how this order should be maintained. In it, the narrative of Kulottuṅga was unmoored from its initial contextual setting and from the networks of significance that it there possessed. Despite its distance from the world of the Cōḻa court, and the different world of Śaiva Brahmanical values that it sought to enact, the *Cidambaramāhātmya* was not disinterested in the political; indeed, it might have been the single most consequential political text of any of the renditions of Kulottuṅga we have seen. The text's complex meditation on the place of the king in a Śaiva cosmos as a figure at once necessary and subservient to the maintenance of ritual and socio-moral order was perhaps the closest thing to an original contribution to the theory of kingship made in the Cōḻa period. It was an isolated and generically conditioned piece of political thought, in the midst of much political thinking and doing. Theories can, of course, exert a real influence on events. Unique among the temples of Tamilnadu, the Naṭarāja temple remains the collectively held property of the endogamous group of its Brahman officiants, now called the Dikshitars: efforts by the state government to assume the administration of the place have been rejected, most recently in January 2014. The *Cidambaramāhātmya*'s argument for the necessary yet necessarily accessory nature of political authority retains something of its currency, even in our own times.[63]

Conclusions

It is possible to write a history of any of a number of later reimaginings of the story of Kulottuṅga. In postimperial Veṅgī, around the turn of the thirteenth century, rival lineages of local lords serially attempted to connect their families with the still-living memories of Co̱la rule.[64] Another account might be found in the biography of King Uttuṅga in the Vīraśaiva poet Pośeṭṭi Liṅgaṇa's (late fifteenth century?) Telugu work, the *Navacoḷacaritramu*. Memories of Kulottuṅga provided the starting point for Virūpākṣakavi's *Coḷacampū* from seventeenth-century Tanjavur; close to our own times, earlier historical writing suggested the plot to Shandiliyan's 1967 historical novel *Kaṭal puṟā*.[65] It is possible to tell a story of Kulottuṅga as furnishing an occasion for narrative, as it became increasingly disconnected from the events that the early chapters of this book have traced. There are notable examples of this sort of scholarship – one thinks of Thapar's fine work on Somanātha – yet this is not the sort of study attempted here. If, as I have urged, we understand the literary renditions of Kulottuṅga's coming to power as a part of "what happened," then the events in Cidambaram are perhaps best understood as "what happened next." The two chains of events were serially connected but each possessed its own inner logic.

In twelfth-century Cidambaram, the real memory of Kulottuṅga and his family was ready to hand, and was remade in the service of Naralokavīra's diffident assertion of autonomy. Still later, it influenced the anonymous Brahman composer(s) of the *Cidambaramāhātmya*, which can be understood in light of the wider fissiparous politics of its period, along with the wider social processes of Brahmanization and land settlement, which subtended the text's production. The memory, image, or latent evaluation of Kulottuṅga's imperial emergence made a difference in Cidambaram: it was interpretable within the particular cultural frameworks of its social or sociotextual collectives. Simply put, the story of Kulottuṅga meant different things to different people in this same context. But – in marked contrast to, say, the destruction of the Somanātha temple – it later came to mean not very much at all. At a certain point, as the long twelfth century gave way to the long thirteenth, the story of Kulottuṅga ceased to make a difference, at least in the Tamil country (Andhra, it appears, was another matter). Not until historians first recovered the scattered details of his reign late in the nineteenth century could its many valences, the many ways it once made a difference, begin to be reconstructed.

In speaking of "making a difference," I am gesturing ahead to the next chapter, where I will suggest that an available model for thinking about structure, event, meaning, and change might be of some use in the kind of historical reconstruction this book has offered. For now, it will suffice to see this complex local reimagining of the unlikely Co̱la king as an opportunity to reflect on the limits of the endurance of historical meaning. That historical events can matter very much indeed and then can come over time to matter not very much at all might seem like a small point. It makes the first of our guiding questions – what actually happened? – all the more interesting and appealing, at least to certain sorts of historians or readers of history. But it serves a salutary purpose for the second of our questions, too. We should care about even the disremembered past not just out of some humanist impulse to the curatorial but to be reminded of the ways in which the formation of historical understanding is itself, of course, historical, is subject to adaptation and transformation, and possesses its own limits of intelligibility.

Summary

This chapter charted the long-term ramifications of Kulottuṅga's emergence in a single local society. Cidambaram presents an atypical case, and what transpired there cannot be taken as a model for other places. Yet the great temple city's rise to regional prominence began precisely with the Coḻa court's reorientation toward it in Kulottuṅga's lifetime, and texts produced and circulated there returned both obliquely and explicitly to his reign as a narrative resource. Initially, the new courtly interest in the site can be seen in the donations of members of the royal family. This is perhaps explicable in terms of the temple's place within a Tondaimandalam-centered religious landscape. As northerly magnates, gentry, and Brahmans became significant kingdom-wide actors under Kulottuṅga and his immediate successor, the court may have sensibly took an interest in the ancient Śaiva holy place in Tillai. This interest turned into massive investment with the donations of the Toṇṭaiyar warlord Naralokavīra, one of the martial new men who exercised an outsized influence in the early 1100s. His complex Cidambaram *praśasti* rewrote many of the inherited norms of Tamil and Sanskrit public praise, in the service of deliberately ambiguous claims about autonomy and regionalist solidarity. Evidently, Naralokavīra managed to successfully negotiate his claim with Vikramacoḻa's own declarations of public Śaiva piety; whatever tensions there may have been are not reflected in the record.

Over a longer period of several generations, the local Brahman hegemony consolidated the gains it first achieved under Kulottuṅga's rule, coming in time to form an independent Brahmanical micro-society, domiciled in the environs of the temple. A work of local Sanskrit, the *Cidambaramāhātmya*, articulated a version of this society's public self-conception, through a final rendition of Kulottuṅga's story, now translated into purāṇic myth. Cidambaram, a quintessential center on the margins, was productive of independent public lifeways; this finds a reflex, unexplored here, in the Naṭarāja temple's deeply idiosyncratic liturgical order. Although it was disjunct from the workings of Coḻa court propaganda and ideology, and although its links with this one Coḻa king and his court were long forgotten, the localist social and religious order centered around the Dancing God in his Little Shrine was perhaps the most enduring consequence of the political transformation which began in the early 1070s.

Conclusions

In June of 1070, an unexpected thing happened: a man was initiated into the line of the Co<u>l</u>a kings, who ruled what was at the time the most powerful kingdom in southern Asia. Though the man was closely related to the ruling line, he was in many ways an outsider, an émigré prince from the kingdom of Veṅgī to the northeast, the land of Sunrise Mountain, and the circumstances of his coming to power were unprecedented. The institutional arrangements and aleatory successes that had brought the Co<u>l</u>a family and its kingdom to their then-eminence had also brought a host of unforeseen troubles. The necessity for continued martial and agrarian labor recruitment, the increasingly far-flung extent of Co<u>l</u>a territory, the need to enlist landed elites from beyond the empire's deltaic core, the overelaboration of the formal mechanisms of a revenue and executive state apparatus, the parcellization of regional rule, and the fractious nature of internal family conflict: as the 1060s drew to a close, all of these several problems reached the point of crisis.

The Veṅgī prince consecrated as Rājendracoḷa entered into these circumstances at an apparent disadvantage. Though ruling independently, he was one of a trio of kings; his court was in the main confined to the northern territory of Tondaimandalam and its adjacencies; and he lacked both the claim of patriliny and the control over dynastic retainers and resources possessed by his cousin Adhirājendra. Their period of corule, especially after the death of Vīrarājendra, the senior member of the triumvirate, appears to have coincided with the temporary collapse of the dynasty's authority in its central territories, and to have set off a scramble by both court societies to lay claim to the loyalty and the revenue of the northern limits of the Tamil country. Both courts attempted to recruit or cajole the northern Tamil elites through material inducement, and both courts issued carefully crafted political appeals in their official *mĕykkīrtti* eulogies. Adhirājendra's major text blended allusions to the eulogies of his father and paternal uncles into an explicit argument about dynastic continuity, while Rājendracoḷa's broke new ground in its appeal to his conjoint dynastic origins, figured around dynastic symbology, purāṇic myth, and his martial bona fides.

The political work accomplished by these texts was certainly real, however difficult it is to gauge their practical results from this distance. Rājendracoḷa's most dramatic actions were broadly congruent with the rhetorical program of his *mĕykkīrtti*. These took place in the environs of Kolar, a dry-tract territory on the Kannada-speaking fringe of Coḻa imperial territory. A member of his court society was involved in the assertion of particularist rights made by a sodality of Tamil soldier-colonists, who had settled in the region two generations earlier. Rājendracoḷa's public face as warrior-prince and at once Coḻa insider and northern outsider seems uniquely well-suited to have appealed to men such as these. Yet more dramatic was the reorganization by other men loyal to him of the ritual and social disposition of the temple to Kolar's martial goddess. This may have been the earliest of the king's public acts; it was among the most consequential. This too was closely bound up with the Rājendracoḷa's public presentation as a warrior and, with his court's use of a mythopoetic register, different from earlier Coḻa courts. But this propitiation of the Tantric deity of the dry uplands was not simply a matter of legitimatory representation, but an effort to participate in the cultural fact of the goddess' power, and her ability to affect outcomes through her action in the world.

Through whatever combination of rhetorical suasion, astuteness of mobilization, and divine intervention, Rājendracoḷa was successful, increasingly so in the wake of his cousin's death in 1072–1073. The circumstances of Adhirājendra's end remain unclear: disease, political unrest, misfortune, sorcerous murder, or some other machination on Rājendracoḷa's part could have been responsible. But being the last man standing did not itself guarantee Rājendracoḷa's success. The reasons for this lay instead in the adroit extension of his court's political network. This success was iconized by the transformation of the now-paramount king's public identity: by the middle of 1074, he came to be styled as Kulottuṅga, Lofty in his Family, and proclaimed as *tiripuvaṉacakkiravarttikaḷ*, the Wheel-turning Emperor of the Triple World. He was the first Coḻa king to change his regnal name, and the first to claim such an imperial title.

This certainly came as a surprise to some. A reflex of this surprise is seen in the earliest literary rendition of these events, in Bilhaṇa's *mahākāvya*, the *Vikramāṅkadevacarita*. Though he wrote a decade and a half after Kulottuṅga's emergence as emperor, the Kashmirian poet's long work still registers a sense of shock. Bilhaṇa seems to echo the conventional wisdom of his patron's court in Kalyāṇa: this had spoiled

Vikramāditya's own chance to enter into the Coḻa family through marriage, and the disappointment still rankled. This reversal of fortune, suggestive of the parallel lives lived by the Cālukya and Coḻa kings, supplied perfect material for the poet's double game in his subversive eulogistic poem. Of little use to the positivist historian – it compresses years into weeks, and rewrites complex events as lurid melodrama – the *Vikramāṅkadevacarita* is invaluable for its dissident reflection on the whole structure of royal politics in the medieval South. Bilhaṇa's Rājiga is a product of the antimonies of his poem's sardonic logic, a foil against its ostensible Cālukya hero. The events that took place far to the south and years earlier supplied raw material that the poet could use in his own agonistic literary game with his patron.

It was in Veṅgī, the patrimony of Kulottuṅga's father's family, that the story of his southern accession retained its greatest interest and continued salience. The successive issues of Sanskrit charters by two of Kulottuṅga's sons showed an annalist's eye for date and detail: this derived equally from the local particularities of historicality and royal self-presentation, and from the unstable conjuncture in which these Veṅgī princes found themselves. Without the shifting text of these charters' eulogies, it would not have been possible for modern scholarship to reconstruct the series of royal marriages whose result had been Kulottuṅga. But these texts were not written with later historians in mind; they each argued a case for one of Kulottuṅga's potential heirs as a virtuous inheritor of this doubled royal charisma, at once solar and lunar, Coḻa and Cālukya. This was nowhere nearly so significant as it was in Veṅgī, though the reasons for this are not entirely clear. Was it a source of regional pride that the southern emperors had joined themselves to their own local dynasty? Or did the Brahman and warrior elites of the little Andhra kingdom see their Coḻa overlords as foreign interlopers, the security of whose rule relied on the importation of settler colonists? It is perhaps most likely that both of these were the case, necessitating the three charters' complex triangulations and revisions.

But the most enduring resonance of Kulottuṅga's imperial success was found closer to the Coḻa heartland. Cidambaram, long a significant but eccentric site of Śaiva devotion and ritual discipline, was transformed in the wake of the dynastic transition into a major hub of regional religion; Kulottuṅga's successor decreed its Naṭarāja to be a dynastic palladium, beginning the temple's ascent to its present eminence as one of the central icons of modern Hinduism. Kulottuṅga showed an interest in Cidambaram as a stopping-point for royal progresses and a site for holding court; its location and earlier history linked it with the

Tondaimandalam ascendency on which his reign depended. But its transformation depended more on other figures at court – preeminently royal women and Tŏṇṭaiyar warrior-magnates – who seem to have dominated its politics in the end of his reign.

This was the identical balance of elite social actors critical for the poet Cayaṅkŏṇṭār's reinvention of literary Tamil in his *Kaliṅkattupparaṇi*. The poem and the flourishing cult at Cidambaram were equally linked in their syntheses of their local world with the pan-Indic forms of high culture; the *paraṇi*, decades after the events, reconfigured Kulottuṅga's coming to the Co<u>l</u>a country as the central moment in an incarnational drama on a cosmic scale, with the Co<u>l</u>a emperor cast as Kṛṣṇa-savior. In its interest in both the narration of the Co<u>l</u>a genealogy and its place within its particular court society, the poem self-consciously represented a break with the past, ushered in by the dynastic shift inaugurated by its patron-king. Similarly, the massive Cidambaram construction project memorialized by Naralokavīra's inscriptional eulogy marked another such break, albeit one far more ambivalent toward the dynasty. This Tŏṇṭaiyar lord's reintegration into Vikramaco<u>l</u>a's court society showed that ad hoc solutions remained available to the royal center when faced with assertive subordinates; later Co<u>l</u>a kings were to find this increasingly difficult.

This dimunition of Co<u>l</u>a central authority, which earlier historians have identified as the leading theme of the dynasty's final century, played out in more than just the arena of courtly high politics. The reverberations of Kulottuṅga's story discernable in the *Cidambaramāhātmya* were not an appeal to royal legitimacy, but the result of the local society's desire to narrate its own claims to autonomy. Paradoxically, royalist investment in the temple city enabled its Brahman ascendancy to craft their own, non-royalist vision of themselves. Over the same period, a stratum of lordly figures from Tondaimandalam would come to dominate Colamandalam's courtly and martial upper echelons, and it would be the descendants of these men who would undo the Co<u>l</u>as' hegemony in the later twelfth and thirteenth centuries.

The consequences of Kulottuṅga's and his court's maneuverings ramified far beyond the domain of intradynastic jostling for supremacy. More than just a successfully negotiated irregular succession, the making of Kulottuṅga was the central occurrence about which a series of other transformations were arrayed. To return to the first of this book's two guiding questions, then, "what really happened" comprised both the story of the pivotal conjuncture of the period 1070–1074 and the long series of reverberations, reimaginings, and unintended consequences that can be traced back to, or which reflected on, this conjuncture. An initial answer to the second guiding question – why should we care? – can be found in this view of things: the ways in which members of a long-vanished society sought to make sense of their own world, and to intervene meaningfully within it, make a claim upon us, as fellow humans faced with similar predicaments.

Perhaps this appeal to a humanist historicism is appealing enough on its own: anyone still reading this, I imagine, must feel at least a tug upon her sympathies. The remainder of this chapter will be devoted to developing a more nuanced gloss on this appeal. Specifically, I will link the argument developed over the course of this book with an existing theoretical conversation, which I find to be especially suggestive in the ways it connects with the book's three informing rubrics of history, politics, and philology. In the Introduction, I suggested that a model for these rubrics could be found in the studies of European political language associated with Cambridge. This final theoretical adjunct is just as strongly associated with the University of Chicago. This is the reflection on the nature of the event and the "possible theory of history" developed by the anthropologist Marshall Sahlins and the historian William Sewell.

The theory emerged from Sahlins's controversial interpretation of James Cook's death in Hawaii in 1779. Sahlins argues that Cook's second visit to the island that year at the start of the Hawaiian rainy season coincided with the beginning of the temporary rule of the god Lono, with whom Cook, by virtue of this accident of timing, came to be identified. The mechanism here is crucial: the Hawaiians, Sahlins claims, interpreted the arrival of the English ship through their preexisting cultural structures, including the Saturnalian reversal of the regular order of kingship during the period of Lono's ritual reign and the wider Polynesian mythos of the stranger-king, the figure come from over the horizon to renew the island's social and political orders. Cook's departure from the island coincided with the end of Lono's Makahiki festival, and was thus equally interpretable within the Hawaiian scheme of things. The same cannot be said of Cook and his crew's return a few days later, after a mishap at sea necessitated repairs to their ship, the *Resolution*. The return of Cook/"Lono," instead of smoothly meshing with Hawaiian conceptions of time, kingship, and divinity, produced a cognitive and cultural dissonance among the Hawaiians, not least because the Makahiki season was habitually closed by the dismantlement of the image of Lono, understood as a kind of recurrent death. This dissonance resulted in a series of escalating conflicts between the locals and the Europeans and, eventually, to the affray that ended with the killing of Cook.[1]

This interpretation was the subject of a memorable polemic between Sahlins and Gananath Obeyesekere, which I will not enter into here. I am less interested in the empirical detail of Sahlins's account – or in its ethical entailments, as was Obeyesekere – than I am in the heuristic categories that Sahlins developed in the service of his interpretation. Though Sahlins's case was built around the unrepeatable situation of culture contact – what the late novelist Iain Banks dubbed an "outside context problem" – the extremity of the case brings to light certain generalizable features of cultural life and historical change. The theory rests on two propositions. The first of these, as aphoristically put by Sahlins, is that "the transformation of a culture is a mode of its reproduction." Glossing this, Sewell describes how "unexpected happenings – like expected happenings – are appropriated and can only be appropriated and acted upon by people in terms of their existing cultural categories"; here both Sahlins and Sewell presume, as do I, that such categories exist, and can be made available to the analyst through their expression in language and practice. Existing systems of belief and of evaluation, along with their accompanying and ratifying practices, supply the raw material through which intersubjectively available experience can be interpreted and rendered meaningful.[2]

Sahlins's second proposition follows from the first: for all that the working of cultural categories is always and everywhere the case in human life, the world is under no compunction to conform to the arbitrary scheme of any given culture. It is here that the possibility of change comes into play. Sahlins writes that "in action in the world – technically in acts of reference – the cultural categories acquire new functional values. Burdened with the world, the cultural meanings are thus altered."[3] Sewell emphasizes an important example described by Sahlins that perfectly captures this: Cook's surprising postmortem career on Hawaii. Adopted as a tutelary deity by the ruling line of chiefs, Cook's political charisma was to be transferred in time to Kamehameha, the first paramount chief of the entire archipelago. The direct empirical effect of Cook's *mana* on Hawaiian political history is difficult to properly measure; but this was to have long-term effects on the Hawaiian economy and its culture of royal sumptuary comportment, as the central cultural notion of *tabu* was revalued as a chiefly monopoly upon Western trade goods, precisely due to the paramount chief's connection with England via the apotheosized Cook. Muskets, linens, cutlery, and plate thus came to be coded as subject to royal *tabu*, giving rise in the process to a controlled economy of royal grandeur connecting Hawaiian cultural logics to European manufacturing and the circulatory spaces of the early modern world system.

This emphasis on long-term practical, cultural, and cognitive transformation, and on the need to account for different levels of scale, is in keeping with Sewell's critical modification of Sahlins's theory. First of all, Sewell rightly insists that there is a multiplicity of structures or schemes that may be differentially invoked depending on a given agent's place in a particular social and cultural order. Commoner Hawaiian women, their practical lives set within routines of work, modes of reckoning kinship, sexual habits, and structures of affective life distinctively their own, invoked different cultural schemes in their ongoing "appropriation of specific percepts by general concepts" than did chiefly males, embedded within their own practical ensembles. "For any given geographical or social unit," Sewell contends, "the relevant structures would always be plural rather than singular." This implies that structures aren't necessarily automatic in their application; even more importantly, structures "overlap or interlock in more than one way ... and they coexist in and hence inform the subjectivities of the same persons."[4] This pluralism and perspectivalism bring out one of Sahlins's theory's most suggestive elements, its conjoining of interest and risk: along with the "objective risk" of categories in action – that the world is under no compunction to conform to them – there is a further subjective risk, that of "the possible revision of signs by acting subjects in their personal projects." Cultured action is in this way always interested action, and the value of a given element in a cultural system can be contested or negotiated, and this value can be transformed as a result.[5] Further, these essentially immaterial – because cognitive and linguistic – schemas must be seen as operating within, but not reducible to, schemes of material and human resources. These are themselves subject to constraints other than the purely cultural, as Sahlins's phrase "burdened with the world" suggests: existing cultural categories can encode certain things as resources, but resources are not the *ex nihilo* productions of a cultural imaginary.

With this idea of a recalcitrant and contingent materiality firmly in place, along with a notion of the multiplicity of cultural schemas, the interpreter can understand how an effort to appropriate a given percept under a certain concept can creatively misfire, and how the cascading consequences of such an act can come to transform a given cultural, social, and material order, and so may come to constitute a historical "event," so called. The application, extension, and diachronic change of cultural categories is an ongoing process throughout human social life, but only some subset of instances of this process demarcates events, when the cultural schemes and material and human resources are transformed in the act of their invocation. "Events," writes Sewell, "are the transformations of structure, and structure is the cumulative outcome of past events." How this works in empirical practice – why some sequence of human acts ramify into events, while most do not – is something the theory does not attempt to predictively determine. Sahlins speaks instead of the "structure of the conjuncture" as a discernable balance of forces, in which a plurality of preexisting structures and particular intentional projects come into contingent alignment and, so to say, history is made.[6] The coming of Cook to Hawaii, his identification with the local god Lono, and his subsequent death are the conjunctural locus of one such event; the taking of the Bastille in 1789 is another. So too, I would suggest, is the emergence of *tripuvaṉacakkiravarttikaḷ* Rājakesarivarman Kulottuṅga Coḻa.

Of course, Kulottuṅga's accession appears to be an "event" in the ordinary sense of the term in that it was a punctual, unrepeatable occurrence; it may also be so called in the lay-historical use of the word, in that it "changed the course of history," at the very least the dynastic history of one corner of South India. But these theoretically naïve senses of the term fail to capture significant features of the "event" that have been detailed here. In the first place, it is chimerical to try to isolate a single occurrence as decisive in the historical becoming of Kulottuṅga: Was it one of his two *abhiṣeka*s? Or a specific moment of intended or unintended success, such as his alliance with the Kolar goddess, or the death of his cousin? If, as I have insisted, the literary renditions are understood as internal to this historical sequence, then the event of the accession and its subsequent interpretations together possessed a temporal extension of some decades; it is precisely the consequences of this unexpected happening beyond the royal succession that mark it as an event in the expanded sense of Sahlins and Sewell.

The Sahlins–Sewell theory further recommends itself in its resonances with the three rubrics of history, politics, and philology that have organized this book. The first of these is the most obvious, as the theory provides for its author a "possible" theory of history, one which, in Sewell's appreciation, provides a "generalizeable, fruitful, and open-ended theory of historical change."[7] The brilliant historical scholarship on the Coḻas over the last several decades has been profoundly allergic to events; one of the guiding intentions of this book has been to serve as a corrective to the tendency to produce models of the South Indian past that are all structure and no agency, where long-term patterns of change appear as the result of quasi-natural processes of social evolution and decay. This theory reminds the Coḻa historian that the period's surviving evidence was the result of innumerable human actions, in pursuit of particular individual and collective ends, subjected to material and imaginal constraints, enmeshed within a range of unforeseen consequences.

In its central concern with "acts of reference," the embeddedness of these within a multitude of cultural structures, and the potential for their innovation, reinvention, or misprision, the theory introduces the workings of language and so of consciousness as a central concern for the historian. It is for this reason that I understand the Sahlins–Sewell theory of the event to be inherently philological in orientation. Admittedly, this might come as a surprise to its cultural-anthropologist and social historian originators. This is not to say that its use is limited to cultures known primarily or exclusively through written texts, though this is the case for their empirical demonstrations from Hawaii, Fiji, and revolutionary France. Philology, properly understood, is precisely the discipline that operates at the intersection of language-as-text, the shifting codes and structures of given culture, and the differentially realized intentions of a text's authors and audience.

But it is with the third of the book's rubrics that the theory finds its greatest resonance. This makes a good deal of sense, as Sahlins and Sewell are both expressly interested in political practices. Sewell's particular attention to the dialectical interactions of material and human resources with Sahlins's structures of cultural meaning is vital here: any theory of politics must account for the work performed by language ("acts of reference"), and any such theory must presume the scarcity of resources and the singular and collective intentions of political agents and patients, while acknowledging the fact of an inescapeable, global contingency. All of this I think the Sahlins–Sewell theory does, and does well, while retaining an openness to a wide spectrum of possible politics seen in a range of social formations. It also insists on the necessity of understanding semiotic practice as dynamic, contested, and subject to change, and on tracing out the ways in which these changes and contestations made a difference to their agents and their worlds.

It is not that I think this an all-powerful Theory of Everything. Sahlins, immersed in the details of Cook's would-be apotheosis, writes with a lyrical brio but without great analytical rigor; Sewell's purely theoretical work is wonderfully lucid, but his attempt to mount his own empirical demonstration around the taking of the Bastille lacks the force of Sahlins's example. Their "possible" theory – its tentative character is for me a part of its appeal – merely provides some useful conceptual scaffolding with which to frame the event of Kulottuṅga's emergence and its entailments. What might this look like? I will touch on three significant and interlinked waypoints in the book's narrative: the underlying conditions of possibility for Rājendracoḻa to be a candidate for the Coḻa succession; his court's interactions with the Cāmuṇḍeśvarī temple in Kolār; and the series of projects brought to fruition, decades later, in and around Cidambaram.

First of all, the theory helps to expose the cross-cousin model of Kulottuṅga's eligibility for its inadequacy: static, overly reliant on a single explanatory logic, structuralist in a bad way. The situation, dynastic as well as more broadly socio-political, of the period 1068–1070 emerges instead as a tangle of overlapping cultural schemes, aleatory happenings, and resources unclaimed by any regnant conceptual system; that is, it forms what Sahlins calls a structure of the conjuncture. The norms of Dravidian kinship, and the pent-up tensions of the preceding generations of elite dynastic marriages were only one such cultural scheme; among these were the epic stereotypy of the solar and lunar dynasties and the growing centrality within the Co̱la core of the *arriviste* men possessing martial values different from the *kṣatriya* codes of the ruling families. To these we may add a set of more political-structural circumstances: the still-recent subsumption of the old magnate polities into the Co̱la *vaḷanāṭu* system, the ambiguous place of Tondaimandalam in this expanded landed order, as well as the purely adventitious facts of Vīrarājendra's advancing age, the seemingly spectacular success of his political *coups* in the two Cālukya kingdoms to the north, and the uncertain health of his own son and direct heir. The triarchy of 1070 was less a new articulation of structures arising at this conjuncture than a ratcheting up of its then-seemingly irresolvable tensions. From the jaundiced retrospective view of Bilhaṇa's *Vikramāṅkadevacarita*, an equally possible outcome could have seen Vikramāditya VI acting as kingmaker, or he himself crowned as the new Co̱la emperor.

But things didn't work out this way. In the midst of this concatenation of dynastic possibilities, the poorly documented but evident instability of Co̱la authority in the Kāveri region created a significant arena for political action in Tondaimandalam, something to which the epigraphical footprint, rhetorical arguments, and the practical enactments of Rājendracoḷa and Adhirājendra's epigraphs all attest. The value of the leading men of the Tondai region was thus recoded; the recognition of this human resource occasioned the redirection of material resources – gold, paddy – and other, immaterial ones – honor, divine favor, legal claims to property – into the region. The Tŏṇṭaiyar elite preexisted the conjuncture of 1071–1073, of course; and their rising eminence may have been the case whatever the outcome of the succession. But the course the events took created the conditions of this deeply consequential reorganization of the varieties of elite power, and this would produce ever-expanding effects for another century of Co̱la rule. Conceived as resources and thus as patients within the overlapping designs of the two court societies, the Tondai lords would come to overcome the conditions of their patiency, and to assert themselves as a coherent class of political actors.

The evidence from Kolar precisely demonstrates the central dynamic of the transformation of cultural structures. The creation of the goddess temple's new ruling society and the discovery of her āgamic identity as the deity of the *Brahmayāmala* were two coordinated projects that came to fruition in Rājendracoḷa's inscription of around 1071–1072, one at the level of social organization and the other within the idealities of the ritual cult. At the intersection of these two articulating structures, material resources – pots, ghee, gold, blood, toddy, cloth – combined to produce a new encultured entity, the goddess Cāmuṇḍeśvarī, whose efficacy was taken as a given by still other circumambient cultural structures. Above all, acts of reference about the goddess entailed notions of her ability to grant victory to her leading royal devotee, in this case Rājendracoḷa. A reflex of this reappears decades later in the *Kaliṅkattupparaṇi*, with goddess and king explicitly placed in alignment. This does not exhaust the complex workings of the court poem; the reimagined figure of the goddess was only one among a spectrum of complex signs manipulated by Cayaṅkōṇṭār, his own interested project involved in its own several contexts. But the poem is significantly infused with a second-order reflection of the goddess's efficacy as a martial and political agent, recoded as wild satire and courtly *poème à clef*.

The temple city of Cidambaram was the scene of the projects of multiple courtly actors, alongside the local imagination of a new Brahmanical hegemony. In Naralokavīra's gambit, the rhetorical arguments for Coḻa sovereignty were refracted through a regionalist lens; as a result of the subsequent public triangulations with the members of the dynasty, the Coḻas and the temple's Śiva were linked together. Seemingly for the first time, Naṭarāja became the king's family god; the linkage, further, became naturalized as the way things had always been. This intersection of royal and magnate investment in temple supplied the anonymous author(s) of the *Cidambaramāhātmya* with the narrative materials for a revision that recoded the connection between king and god into a sustained argument about collective Brahman autonomy. The realignment occasioned by the last years of Kulottuṅga's reign thus catalyzed the Dancing God's ascent to global eminence, as well as the modern temple's distinctive ritual culture and proprietary rights, in a way that blends the cultural, practical, and material dimensions of the site into a unique amalgam.

It may well be that the historical record furnishes few occasions from medieval India like the accession of Kulottuṅga. Both in quantity and quantity, the evidence from the eleventh- and twelfth-century Tamil country is of a different order than that surviving from elsewhere. Yet the sheer richness and heterogeneity of the South Asian textual and material–cultural archive from these centuries suggests that there are other cases that await their interpreter. At the least, the rare survival of the trace of events like this can remind the historian of the worlds of interested projects, contestation, and unforeseen consequences that always underlay the production of polity, social formation, works of art, religious culture, and lived landscape in the period. The sort of readerly, philological reconstruction practiced here is not meant to supplant other methods for the study of the past, but to complement them. Cases in which such reconstructions can be carried out are therefore worth being sought out.

The exercise of reexamining this case, as I have over the last few pages, within an exogenous explanatory framework might strike some readers as unnecessary. As already mentioned, the work of Sahlins and Sewell suggested itself as one possibly useful idiom in which to translate my results. But I am unwilling to abandon the particularity of my evidence, for reasons of both personal predeliction and disciplinary location. As a practitioner of a discipline as specific as Indology, what Richard Rorty once styled "a connoisseur of diversity," it is my obligation to bear down upon the details, for it is there that I have the best chance of discovering something new or something of interest.[8] Something similar may be said for my invocation throughout of the category of the political. Whether in the first-person-plural announcements of a *sabhā*, in the diffident maneuverings of the women of the royal family, or in the arch reimaginings of a court poet, we are faced with multiple, partly overlapping conceptions of political authority and practical power. We can glimpse their presuppositions about time, agency, legitimacy, and virtue, but only if we are prepared to engage with them in the terms of their own time and place.

Starting from there, it becomes possible to place these materials within a wider conversation about the global history of political forms and political practices, which does not presume a triumphalist Western monopoly on thinking, but neither does it collapse into a well-intentioned but vapid relativism. This book has been researched and written over a period of some six years, and in three countries: India, Britain, and the United States. In all three, the urgencies and the frustrations of political life of the modern liberal–democratic sort have been eminently on display; elsewhere, much of the rest of the world has in that time lurched from catastrophe to catastrophe, much of it the product of political action or inaction, whether war, state collapse, climate change, or epidemiological disaster. Politics seems everywhere. It is perhaps unsurprising, then, that the political presents itself as a category with which to think of the past, even the distant and exotic past of the medieval Tamil country. But this suggests the troubling possibility this might be a retrospective illusion, a backward projection of one's own concerns. It is my strong belief that this is not the case, and that the political, like its cousin the historical, is a domain that a global humanism must be prepared to search out in very different times, places, and societies than our own. We do not need to learn how to speak the languages of medieval Indian politics, but there is much to be gained in learning how to listen for them.

Notes

Introduction

1. *Kaliṅkattupparaṇi*, ed. A. V. Kaṉṉaiya Nāyuṭu (Cennai: P. N. Accukkuṭam, 1944), vs. 282.
2. This is a truncated translation of ll. 3–15 of ARE 68 of 1921, with a great deal of additional information, especially onomastic toponyms, excised.
3. A sketch of the history of the discipline, especially as it coincides with the history of South Indian epigraphical study, can be found in Y. Subbarayalu, *South India under the Cholas* (Delhi: Oxford University Press, 2012), pp. 16–26.
4. K. A. Nilakanta Sastri, *The Cōḷas* (2nd edition, Madras: University of Madras, 1955), p. 447, cited, whether supportively or skeptically, in practically every study thereafter.
5. See e.g. Noboru Karashima, *South Indian History and Society: Studies from Inscriptions, A.D. 850–1800* (Delhi: Oxford University Press, 1984), pp. 21–35; and Noboru Karashima, Y. Subbarayalu, and P. Shanmugam, *Land Control and Social Change in the Lower Kaveri Valley from the 12th to 17th Centuries* (Tokyo: Institute for the Study of Languages and Cultures of Asia and Africa, 1980).
6. Subbarayalu, *South India under the Cholas*, p. 18.
7. Nilakanta Sastri, *The Cōḷas*, pp. 662–692.
8. Nilakanta Sastri, *The Cōḷas*, p. 536; Karashima, *South Indian History and Society*, pp. 69–105 ("Revenue Terms in Chola Inscriptions" and "Land Revenue Assessment during Chola Rule"); Subbarayalu, *South India under the Cholas*, pp. 100–115 ("Quantifying the Land Revenue of the Chola State").
9. See Jan Gonda, *Ancient Indian Kingship from the Religious Point of View* (Leiden: Brill, 1966). This pair can be (and have been) mapped upon a purely Dravidian dyad, *maṟam/aṟam*: see George Hart and Hank Heifetz, trans., *The Forest Book of the Rāmāyaṇa of Kampaṉ* (Berkeley: University of California Press, 1989).
10. The inverted commas are meant to signal my dissatisfaction with Stein's choice of terms: see the longer critique, pp. 81ff.
11. Here and more widely, compare Inden's fine critique of Stein's argument. Ronald Inden, *Imagining India* (Oxford: Basil Blackwell, 1990), pp. 206–211.
12. *Cf.*, however, Cohn's intelligent critique of Africanist theory in Indian history (Bernard Cohn, "Indian Histories and African Models," in *An Anthropologist among the Historians and Other Essays* (Delhi: Oxford University Press, 1990), pp. 200–223).

13. An excellent survey of this tradition's most independent thinkers is Brajadulal Chattopadhaya, *The Making of Early Medieval India* (Delhi: Oxford University Press, 1994).
14. Max Weber, "Politics as a Vocation," in *From Max Weber: Essays in Sociology* (New York: Oxford University Press, 1946), pp. 77–128. The brief discussion on Kauṭalya is on pp. 123–124; Weber probably knew of the text through the work of Alfred Hillebrandt (see his *Kleine Schriften* (Stuttgart: Steiner Verlag, 1987)); it is possible, though unlikely, that Weber had access to Shama Sastri's 1915 translation.
15. *Cf.* Hartmut Scharfe, *Investigations in Kauṭalya's Manual of Political Science* (Wiesbaden: Harrassowitz, 1993), pp. 78–101; he rejects the frequently argued point that the text's lexis suggests preclassical composition. A fine recent introduction to the text is Patrick Olivelle, *King, Governance, and Law in Ancient India: Kauṭilya's Arthaśāstra* (New York: Oxford University Press, 2013).
16. A similar critique of what I term the "lexicalist" approach has also been ventured in the arena of European political thought by Quentin Skinner ("The Idea of a Cultural Lexicon," in *Visions of Politics*, vol. 1 (Cambridge: Cambridge University Press, 2002), pp. 158–174).
17. Upinder Singh, "Violence, Politics, and War in Kāmandaka's *Nītisāra*," *IESHR* 47 (2010): pp. 29–62.
18. See pp. 128ff.
19. Louis Dumont, "The Concept of Kingship in Ancient India"; I cite the version that appeared in *Religion, Politics, and History in India: Collected Paper in Indian sociology* (The Hague and Paris: Mouton, 1970, p. 78). The same essay is also reprinted as "Appendix C," in Dumont, *Homo Hierarchicus: The Caste System and Its Implications* (Chicago and London: University of Chicago Press, 1980), pp. 287–313.
20. Dumont, *Homo Hierarchicus*, p. 310, n. 73b, *cf.* Dumont, *Religion, Politics, and History*, p. 88.
21. Dumont, *Homo Hierarchicus*, pp. 167, 183.
22. Inden, *Imagining India*, p. 28, drawing on central sections of Collingwood's *The New Leviathan, or Man, Society, Civilization and Barbarism* (Oxford: The Claredon Press, 1942).
23. Among these were John F. Fleet, B. Lewis Rice, and, a generation later, Lionel Barnett and D. R. Bhandarkar. An excellent survey of the history of Indian epigraphy can be found in Salomon's handbook to the subject (Richard Salomon, *Indian Epigraphy: A Guide to the Study of Inscriptions in Sanskrit, Pali and Other Indo-Aryan Languages* (New York: Oxford University Press, 1998), pp. 199–225).
24. See especially Sheldon Pollock's "Future Philology? The Fate of a Soft Science in a Hard World," *Critical Inquiry* 35, 4 (2009): pp. 931–961, intervening into a wider but diffuse discussion (as Pollock bemusedly notes, there have been three different articles entitled "A Return to Philology," by a mutually discordant group of scholars: Lee Patterson, Paul de Man, and Edward Said). See also Pollock's "Indian Philology and India's Philology," *Journal Asiatique* 299, 1 (2011): pp. 423–442, a review article of Gérard Colas

and Gerdi Gerschheimer's *Écrire et Transmettre en Inde Classique* (Paris: École française d'Extrême-Orient, 2009).

25. Following the terms laid out by Alton Becker, "Aridharma: Framing an Old Javanese Tale," in *Beyond Translation: Essays towards a Modern Philology* (Ann Arbor: University of Michigan Press, 1995, esp. pp. 137–140). It is ironic that Becker's wonderfully astute work in an impressive range of texts and source languages should depend on such a specious distinction.
26. Pollock, "Future Philology," p. 934; see also pp. 950–956 for his remounting of the classical Buddhist śāstric distinction *vyavahārika/pāramārthika sat* (conditional and absolute truth, or here "contextual" and "textual" meaning) in the philological study of history. This distinction, seen as a set of dialectically related rather than opposed terms, neatly captures the wide ambit that I attribute to philology here.
27. See the now-classic account in Sheldon Pollock, "Mīmāṃsā and the Problem of History in Traditional India," *JAOS* 109, 4 (1989): pp. 603–610.
28. This shares in the concerns voiced by Pollock ("Crisis in the Classics," *Social Research*, 78, 1 (2011): pp. 22–48); on the unforeseen consequences of the quantitative turn in Co̱la historical studies; see Sanjay Subrahmanyam, "Whispers and Shouts: Some Recent Writings on Medieval South India," *IESHR* 38 (2001).
29. For the sort of reader who feels compelled to check this note, I would suggest a second bookmark. Go ahead: I'll wait. There are two major exceptions to the book's efforts at transparency in its handling of evidence. For textual materials that are available in readily available editions, and especially where the texts of these editions are available online at the time of writing (2016), I have only cited the original-language text when its constitution or verbal texture is directly relevant to the discussion. Also, I have not reproduced the text of the transcripts of unpublished inscriptions that I was able to consult in the Mysore offices of the Archaeological Survey of India. The scholars working there are committed to the long-term project of the edition of all of their holdings; like all researchers interested in the period, I depend upon their expertise, and I eagerly await the published results of their labors.
30. Representative works include J. G. A. Pocock, *The Machiavellian Moment: Florentine Political Thought and the Atlantic Republican Tradition* (second edition, Princeton University Press, 2003), *Political Thought and History: Essays on Theory and Method* (Cambridge University Press, 2009); Quentin Skinner, *Visions of Politics*, 3 vols. (Cambridge University Press, 2002), *Machiavelli* (New York: Hill and Wang, 1981).

Chapter 1

1. The quotations are from John Faithful Fleet, "Eastern Chalukya Chronology," *Indian Antiquary* 20 (1891): p. 277; Murari Lal Nāgar, introduction to *Vikramāṅkadevacarita* by Bilhaṇa (Benares: Vidya Vilas Press, 1945), p. 27; T. V. Sadasivapandarathar, *History of the Later Cholas*, vol. 2 (Annamalainagar: Annamalai University, 1958), p. 1; Fleet again; Hermann Kulke, "Funktionale Erklärung eines südindischen Māhātmyas: die Legende

Hiranyavarmans und das Leben des Cōḷa-Königs Kulottunga I," *Saeculum* 20 (1969), p. 417 [*cf.* the English rendering in Hermann Kulke, *Kings and Cults: State Formation and Legitimation in India and Southeast Asia* (Delhi: Manohar, 1993), p. 200: "assumed power by a *coup d'etat*"]; Thomas Trautman, *Dravidian Kinship* (New York: Cambridge University Press, 1981), p. 387.

2. See "The Accession of Kulōttuṅga," chapter 12 in Nilakanta Sastri, *The Cōḷas*, pp. 285–300, esp. pp. 294–295 (with an unacknowledged quotation of Bühler), p. 297.
3. Following the account of N. Venkataramanayya, *The Eastern Cāḷukyas of Vēṅgi* (Madras: Vedam Venkataraya Sastri, 1950), pp. 203–211.
4. On the Koṭūmpāḷūr "chieftains" see K. V. Subrahmanya Aiyar, *Historical Sketches of Ancient Deccan* (Madras: Modern Imprint, 1917), pp. 195–208, as corrected by M. S. Govindasamy, *The Role of Feudatories in Later Chōḷa History* (Annamalai Nagar: Annamalai University, 1979), pp. 6–23 and *cf.* Thomas Trautmann, *Dravidian Kinship* (Cambridge and New York: Cambridge University Press, 1981), pp. 391–392.
5. See the superb discussion in Trautmann, *Dravidian Kinship*, pp. 357–358 and esp. pp. 431–433.
6. For the details of these sources, all of them found only in Veṅgī, see Chapter 3, "Moonset on Sunrise Mountain."
7. Pierre Bourdieu, *Outline of a Theory of Practice* (Cambridge and New York: Cambridge University Press, 1977), pp. 30–71, is typically dense both in ethnographic detail and in theoretical argument. A useful summary statement is the following (p. 37):

   When the anthropologist treats native kinship terminology as a closed, coherent system of purely logical relationships, defined once and for all by the implicit axiomatic of a cultural tradition, he prohibits himself from apprehending the different practical functions of the kinship terms and relations which he unwittingly brackets; and by the same token he prohibits himself from grasping the epistemological status of a practice which, like his own, presupposed and consecrates neutralization of the practical functions of those terms and relationships.
8. David P. Henige, "Some Phantom Dynasties of Early and Medieval India: Epigraphic Evidence and the Abhorrence of a Vacuum," *BSOAS* 38, 3 (1975): pp. 541, 549.
9. See Chapter 4, "Courtly Donors of Kulottuṅga's Time."
10. Certainly the sort of conflicts that drove the dynastic troubles of the Coḻa and Cālukya families – which tended to constellate around the fractious relationships between brothers and cousins and nephews – was not the monopoly of these southern dynastic polities. As Salomon's richly detailed synthesis indicates, *every single* succession of the imperial Guptas of the late fourth and fifth centuries seems to have been contested along similar lines ("The Men Who Would Be King: Reading between the Lines of Dynastic Genealogies in India and Beyond," *Religions of South Asia* 5, 1 (2011): esp. pp. 274–275). *Cf.* also the account in Michael Willis, "Later Gupta History: Inscriptions, Coins and Historical Ideology," *JRAS* 15, 2 (2005): pp. 131–150.

11. See e.g. Nilakanta Sastri, *The Cōḷas*, p. 177 (and *cf.* his *A History of South India from Prehistoric Times to the Fall of Vijayanagar* (Madras: Oxford University Press, 1955), p. 181); Pollock (*Language of the Gods*, pp. 159–160) suggests that extra-regional control over Veṅgī may be relevant to the understanding of changes to western Cālukya dynastic self-presentation in Vikramāditya's Kauṭhem plates, issued in 1009.
12. Here I adopt as the most plausible account Venkataramanayya's masterful synthesis (Venkataramanayya, *Eastern Cāḷukyas*, esp. pp. 212–218).
13. Sylvain Brocquet, "Une Epopée epigraphique," *BEI* 22 (2007): p. 75: "les panégyriques épigraphiques ... se donnent comme des fragments épiques, participant d'une épopée implicite, celle du souverain et de sa lignée. Cette dimension de la *praśasti* révèle sa fonction, qui est de proposer une lecture épique de la réalité historique, et, par là, de contribuer à l'action transformative qui fonde la royauté." *Cf.* also his conclusions (p. 99): "nous percevons ... la silhouette d'une implicite épopée, répétition actuelle des grands cycles immémoriaux. Le roi y apparaît comme la duplication du héros épiques, il met en acte les mêmes valeurs, et entretient la même relation avec le mythe."
14. As Pollock has eloquently argued. See Sheldon Pollock, "*Rāmāyaṇa* and the Political Imagination in India," *JAS* 52, 2, p. 283: and Pollock, *Language of the Gods*, pp. 225ff.
15. See especially Velcheru Narayana Rao, "Multiple Literary Cultures in Telugu: Court, Temple and Public," in *Literary Cultures in History. Reconstructions from South Asia*, ed. Sheldon Pollock (Berkeley and Los Angeles: University of California Press, 2003), pp. 390ff.
16. Translation from David Shulman and Velcheru Narayana Rao, ed., *Classical Telugu Poetry: An Anthology* (Berkeley and Los Angeles: University of California Press, 2002), p. 59.
17. Summarized in Nilakanta Sastri, *The Cōḷas*, pp. 245–275, drawing especially on Hultzsch's reconstructions in the third volume of *South Indian Inscriptions* (SII).
18. Rājādhirāja appears to have assumed this alternate title to commemorate his successful siege of Kalyāṇa in *ca.* 1048 (Nilakanta Sastri, *The Cōḷas*, p. 247).
19. The clearest formulation is that of the Tiruvālaṅkāḍu plates of Rājendra's time (SII 3: XX, vs. 32): *tataḥ prabhṛti coḷānām abhiṣekakramād ime | nāmanī parivartete rājñām ājñābhidhāyinī* | |, "From the [time of these two] onwards, these names would continue to announce the rule of the Cola kings, in the order of their coronation."
20. Nilakanta Sastri, *The Cōḷas*, p. 332; the text shared by the Chellur and Pithapuram copperplates of Kulottuṅga's son Vīracoḍa establishes her relationship to the main Co̱la line; see p. 146.
21. I depend here on Nilakanta Sastri's *The Cōḷas*, which is unlikely to ever be surpassed as a narrative synthesis of the dynasty's political history. But it needs be registered that this work depends fundamentally on the epigraphic editions and interpretations of a number of earlier scholars, prominently Eugen Hultzsch, J. F. Fleet, V. Venkayya, and H. Krishna Sastri, and on the chronological calculations of Franz Kielhorn; all of these are spread throughout years of *Indian Antiquary* and *Epigraphia Indica*, as well as the early volumes of *South*

Indian Inscriptions. This underlying armature to Nilakanta Sastri's text is worth emphasizing, as he tended only to register his disagreements with prior scholarship, and his indebtedness to it is not always apparent.

22. The quote is from Burton Stein, *Peasant State and Society in Medieval South India* (New Delhi: Oxford University Press, 1980), p. 104.
23. The crucial reference for significance of the *nāṭu* for medieval Tamil history is Y. Subbarayalu, *Political Geography of the Chōḷa Country* (Madras: State Department of Archeology, 1973).
24. Refer to Subbarayalu, *Political Geography*, pp. 72–81 and Map no. 12, and Kesavan Veluthat, *The Political Structure of Early Medieval South India* (New Delhi: Orient Longman, 1973), pp. 106–136.
25. On the titles borne by the lords of Milāṭu, see Veluthat, *Political Structure*, p. 123 (citing *Concordance*, nos. 3325, 3623); the lengthy praise-poem, quite distinct in its idiom from the Coḻa style of *mĕykkīrtti*, was first published in SII 7: 863; it is presented with metrical lineation and commentary in *Mĕykkīrttikaḷ*, ed. Pū. Cuppiramaṇiyam (Ceṉṉai : Ulakat Tamiḻārāycci Niṟuvaṉam, 1983), pp. 13–20 (no. 2; typically, Cuppiramaṇiyam classes it among Rājarāja I's eulogies). See also Nagaswamy's edition and commentary of the text ("*Tirukkovalūrppāṭṭu*," in *Cŏlmālai* (Chennai: Tamil Arts Academy, 2000, pp. 75–90) and his brief English-language discussion of it, "Sangam Poetic Traditions under the Imperial Cōḻas," in *South Indian Horizons* (Pondicherry: IFP/EFEO, 2004), pp. 487–494.
26. The characterization of gentry–Brahman condominium derives from Stein, *Peasant State*, pp. 63–89, *et passim*, what he refers to as the "Brahman-dominant peasant alliance." This captures a central dynamic of medieval agrarian order in South India: it is worth noting that, for all the elements of Stein's historical thesis have been disavowed by later scholarship, this central tenet of his model has not been strongly challenged (Veluthat, *Political Structure*, p. 232 offers only a desultory critique). There are nevertheless problems of terminology and of detail, starting with the use of the term "peasant" itself. "Peasant," insofar as it connotes a direct agricultural producer, one who cultivates primarily for household subsistence (what may fairly be termed its meaning in everyday modern English; compare its use as a technical term in Chris Wickham, *Framing the Early Middle Ages: Europe and the Mediterranean 400–800* (Oxford and New York: Oxford University Press, 2005), p. 387), fails to capture the elite landholding actors characterized by Stein. Faced with this, his further qualifications as "dominant" peasant (Stein, *Peasant State, passim*) or "controller of localities"/"dominant land controllers" (p. 104) only draw Stein further away from either a common or a technical meaning of what a "peasant" in fact is. As a result, I adopt here the use of "gentry" as used by David Ludden, *An Agrarian History of South Asia* (Cambridge: Cambridge University Press, 1999). While Ludden notes the exogenousness of the term in writings on South Asian agrarian studies, it has the advantage of capturing the elite character of these historical actors, who "consist of relatively high-status local land-owing groups that marry their own kind and form alliances with other high-status families to expand their horizons as they redefine their ties to the land" (p. 76). As an English

collective singular, "gentry" has a further advantage in the present context of capturing the group identity (as the *nāṭṭār/nāṭṭom*) in which these rural dominants are most frequently encountered in our epigraphic sources. I also owe my invocation of the category of "patriarchy" to Ludden's elegant presentation.

Stein's account of "alliance" (Stein, *Peasant State*, esp. pp. 83–89) is further limited by both his weakly functionalist explanation of the "shared interests" uniting Brahmans and "peasants" and his jejune historical account of the relationship's origin. Stein brings in the often-invoked "Kaḷabhra interregnum" as the *explicans* here: non-"peasant" in social character, non-Vaidika in religious observance, the mysterious Kaḷabhras supply for him an enabling rationale for the forging of this transregional, centuries-long relationship of mutual protection and benefit. All these do not detract from the utility of identifying this dynamic as supplying the enduring core of rural social power in medieval times; also sound is Stein's insistence that this condominium dates to pre-Co̱la, even pre-Pallava, times, and thus supplies a pregiven state of social affairs with which the Co̱la state project had to come to terms.

27. Orr, *Devotees, Donors and Daughters of God*, p. 31, expresses understandable caution in projecting the term's later acceptation into medieval times, drawing on Bayly's recognition of the instability of the category in the eighteenth century (*Saints, Goddesses and Kings: Muslims and Christians in South Indian Society, 1700–1900* (New York: Cambridge University Press, 1989), p. 411).
28. The shared quality of lordship is key to James Heitzman's analysis (*Gifts of Power: Lordship in an Early Indian State* (New Delhi: Oxford University Press, 1997), esp. pp. 202–205, 223–237); see also Inden, *Imagining India*, pp. 239–244.
29. On Uttaramerūr, see K. A. Nilakanta Sastri, *Studies in Chola History and Administration* (Madras: University of Madras, 1932), pp. 96–175 (the best philological account of the records); François Gros and R. Nagaswamy, *Uttaramerūr: Légende, Histoire, Monuments* (Pondichéry: Institute Française d'Indologie, 1970) and the discussion in Stein, *Peasant State*, pp. 146ff. Also worthy of note is the learned but highly eccentric early account in R. Sathianathaier, *Studies in the Early History of Tondamandalam* (Madras, 1944), pp. 32–40 (a paean to what he calls "democratic Brahmanism").
30. The characterization of the *brahmadeya* temple as the Brahman village's "nerve-center" is borrowed from Veluthat, *Political Structure*, p. 202; the focus on *brahmadeya*s as central-place institutions is indebted to Heitzman, *Gifts*, esp. pp. 107–116.
31. The focus on Brahmans as exclusively professional *religieuses* (and the reference to them en bloc as "priests") is a telling slippage on Stein's part, who sees the cultural expression of his "alliance" in the bhakti cult driven by Tamil hymnody fitted out with Sanskrit liturgical filigree: see Stein, *Peasant State*, pp. 86–88. Within the ascriptive hierarchy of those possessed of Brahman *varṇa*, priestcraft was a specialist (and generally a socially inferior) calling; see Alexis Sanderson "The Śaiva Age: The Rise and Dominance of Śaivism

during the Early Medieval Period," in *Genesis and Development of Tantrism*, ed. Shingo Einoo (Tokyo: Institute of Oriental Culture, 2009), pp. 276–279 for references to the Ādiśaiva subcaste of temple officiants.

32. George W. Spencer, "Temple Money-Lending and Livestock Redistribution in Early Tanjore," *IESHR* 5 (1968), pp. 286–287, and see especially the discussion in Heitzman, *Gifts*, pp. 128–134. The best evidence of *brahmadeya* capital investment is found in the admittedly exceptional inscriptional corpus of the Bṛhadīśvara temple in Tanjavur. Here the investors are conspicuously members of the most elite levels of society: see *e.g.* SII 2:6, which records Rājarāja's sister Kuntavai's deposit of a total of 2,936 *kācu* to the *sabhā*s of ten different *brahmadeya*s; or 2:10, a leveraged investment by the temple treasury, including monies previously deposited by a Śaiva *guru*, an entitled official, and the members of "the ancient army of the Right Hand" (*valaṅ-kaippaḻampaṭaikaḷilar*). The formalities of such an investment – including both the legal fiction of deposit with the Śaiva demigod Caṇḍeśvara and the promised rate of return of one-eighth or 12.5 percent per annum – appear to be conventional.
33. On *kaṇakku* literacy, see Leslie Orr, "Words for Worship: Tamil and Sanskrit in Medieval Temple Inscriptions," in *Bilingual Discourse and Cross-cultural Fertilisation: Sanskrit and Tamil in Mediaeval India*, ed. Whitney Cox and Vincenzo Vergiani (Pondichéry: Institut Français de Pondichéry/Ecole française d'Extrême-Orient, 2013), on the mixed orthography of inscriptional Tamil. The later colonial history of these professional communities is central to the recent study of Bhavani Raman, *Document Raj* (Chicago: Chicago UP, 2011). The Brahman "mobility" mentioned here is to be distinguished from the "migrations" that are incessantly referred to in secondary literature, often on very weak evidentiary grounds (e.g. Mahadevan, "On the Southern Recension of the *Mahābhārata*" (*Electronic Journal of Vedic Studies*, 15 (2), 2008)). Cox, "Scribe and Script," contains a case study of Brahman professional mobility in the Cālukya kingdom.
34. The record is EI 16, no. 11a. Subbarayalu notes the militarization of the Colamandalam society (*South India under the Cholas*, pp. 168–170, 228–231 and 238). The sources for the military history of the eleventh century are very poor: there is little evidence outside of the much-discussed "regimental" titles attested in the Tanjavur temple records (see SII vol. 2, Introduction, pp. 8–10), and the corresponding status of the title *veḷaikkāṟar* found there and elsewhere, especially in the Tamil inscriptions of Polonnuruwa; the latter has been the subject of incessant debate, largely turning on decontextualized attempts to capture the semantics of *veḷai* ("occasion"?).
35. On the catalytic effects of loot on the landed society of the central regions, see Karashima, *South Indian History*, pp. 27–30, who argues that the secular rise of private landholding in this period can be in part attributed to it. The earlier scholarly fixation on this plunder as the sole source of revenue for the Coḻa royal center (e.g. Stein, *Peasant State*, pp. 333ff. and Spencer, "Politics of Plunder," *JAS* 35 (1976): pp. 405–416) has been effectively refuted by more thorough studies of the revenue system: see especially Shanmugam, *The*

Revenue System of the Cholas 850–1279 (Madras: New Era, 1987), and Subbarayalu, *South India under the Cholas*. See also Davis, *Lives of Indian Images*, (Princeton UP, 1999), pp. 51–87 for a suggestive interpretation of the semiotics of one particular class of plundered objects, temple icons.

36. On the much-discussed overseas conquests, the account in Cœdès' *Les Etats* remains an impressive achievement, however historiographically dated; see also Spencer *Politics of Expansion* and now the essays collected in Kulke et al., *Nagapattinam to Suwarnadwipa*, especially the refreshingly even-keeled account by Sen ("Military Campaigns of Rājendra Chola and the Chola-Srivijaya-China Triangle").
37. On the *senāpati* titleholders (more than a quarter of those charted in the *Concordance* are Brahmans; none are *mūventaveḷaṉ*), see Veluthat, *Political Structure*, pp. 90–91, Subbarayalu, "Chola State," p. 226.
38. See Subbarayalu, *Political Geography*, pp. 56–69, who adduces convincing evidence that the *vaḷanāṭu* scheme was premised on a survey conducted around 1002.
39. See the discussions in *Concordance* I, pp. xlvii–li; Veluthat, *Political Structure*, pp. 80–86; and Subbarayalu, "The Chola State" (in *South India under the Choḷas*), pp. 221–224.
40. See Subbarayalu, "The Chola State," p. 225, and Veluthat, *Political Structure*, pp. 89–90.
41. Shanmugam, *Revenue System*, is dedicated to the details of the Coḻa system of revenue assessment and collection; the nature of the *tiṇaikkaḷam* and its work of quantification are explored in the central chapters of Subbarayalu, *South India under the Cholas*. See Veluthat, *Political Structure*, p. 92 on the office of *tiṇai* under "chiefly rule."
42. A note on orthography: "*rājarājīśvara*" is the form found in the temple's own records (see SII 2:1 with reproduction, *et passim*); I have nevertheless corrected this to *rājarājeśvara*, "the Śiva[-liṅga] of Rājarāja"; on this usage, see the references assembled by Sanderson, "The Śaiva Religion among the Khmers (Part 1)," BEFEO 90–91, p. 415 n. 250.
43. Heitzman's intelligent analysis of the imperial temple network (*Gifts of Power*, pp. 121–142) forms the major statement on the social and economic history of the Tanjavur complex.
44. The expressly imperial land tenurial arrangements are detailed in three of the temple's major records: SII 2: 4, 5, and 92; altogether sixteen "extra-areal" villages were inducted into the revenue network. Heitzman's methods deliberately restricted his consideration to those sites he could securely locate on modern maps, and downplay the imperialist amplitude of the network: he only includes data for two of these sixteen sites, those in the Deccan (*Gifts*, pp. 127–8, 134).
45. The quote is from Heitzman (*Gifts*, p. 138, diacritics and italics added).
46. Veluthat, whose scholarship (*Political Structure, Early Medieval*) combines empirical exhaustiveness and conceptual vigor to produce the most satisfying political anatomy of medieval South India, nevertheless inadequately emphasizes the distinctiveness of the Coḻa polity in this regard. While the comparison with the data furnished by the Pāṇḍya, Cera, and Hoysaḷa

polities is certainly productive, the difference of scale (in terms of inputs and outcomes both) between these and the Co<u>l</u>a case is qualitative rather than simply quantitative.

47. See Chapter 2, "Adhirājendra's Tondaimandalam Mobilizations," especially the references contained in n. 44 there.
48. There is almost nothing written about these sub-imperial appanages; a good survey of the problem (and a presentation of the only extant evidence for a Sri Lankan incumbent) can be found in Indrapala, "Coḷalaṅkeśvara." The only detailed treatment for the Co<u>l</u>apāṇḍyas, the best-documented of these sub-imperial lines, is Sethuraman, *Mathematics*, pp. 49–69.
49. Subbarayalu, *South India under the Cholas*, p. 225.
50. On the temple at Gaṅgaikŏṇṭacoḷapuram, now in ruins, refer to Pichard, *Vingt ans après Tanjavur*, and to Ali, "Epigraphical Legacy." On the royal orders transferring the village revenue to Rājendra's foundation, see the discussion of Vīrarājendra's royal order (SII 4: 529), pp. 66ff.
51. Earlier political–historical scholarship drew on the *mĕykkīrtti* extensively in order to draw up a sequential record of a king's military victories and major public benefactions; it is the *mĕykkīrtti*s that provide, for instance, the major part of K. A. Nilakanta Sastri's connected account of the Co<u>l</u>a kings' reigns. Nilakanta Sastri in fact devoted some important critical attention to his reliance on this genre of a historical source: as much as they may have been prone to rhetorical inflations (leading him to waggishly refer to them as *pŏykkīrtti*s, "false fame"), he sharply distinguished their referential value from that of the other major set of sources, the Sanskrit *praśasti*s found largely in Co<u>l</u>a copperplate records, or the later testimony of court poetry.

    There has, however, until very recently been practically no attention to the poetics of the *mĕykkīrtti*, to its structure, its intertextual links with other literary genres, and the whole range of features that distinguish it as a form of verbal art. Nor until very recently has there been any critical thinking on its reception, the question of whom (if anyone) the eulogies were meant for and what (if any) extratextual effect they created. Davis' brief essay ("Cola Meykkīrttis as literary texts") and several contributions by Stein ("Circulation and Historical Geography in the Tamil Country"; *Peasant State*, pp. 352–358) are significant exceptions to the rule. Of crucial importance to any discussion of the form is Cuppiramaṇiyam, *Mĕykkīrttikaḷ*, which assembles eclectically edited, synoptic texts of the Co<u>l</u>a period, along with earlier and later eulogies to which Cuppiramaṇiyam assigns – wrongly, in my view – the name *mĕykkīrtti*. The appearance of Francis and Schmid's study of the *mĕykkīrtti*s found in the Pondicherry epigraphical corpus (*Pondicherry Inscriptions*, vol. 2, pp. v–xlvii) provides a useful corrective to much of this neglect. This suggestive essay represents the first real step forward in the form's interpretation in several decades.
52. See Schmid and Francis, *Pondicherry Inscriptions*, vol. 2, pp. xiii–xvi.
53. Pollock, *Language of the Gods*, pp. 115–161, is a magisterial account of the long history of the Sanskrit *praśasti* in South and Southeast Asia; as Schmid and Francis have pointed out (*Pondicherry Inscriptions*, vol. 2., pp. xvi–xviii),

Pollock mischaracterizes the *mĕykkīrtti* as genealogical in content (which it never is) and as a generic transposition of South Indian Sanskrit *praśasti* prototypes into Tamil (p. 323). While it would be specious to totally separate the two forms – both are, after all, epigraphical preambles meant to praise, an enormous overlap in their pragmatic purposes – the Coḻa texts were premised on a deliberately maintained particularity, set out from the cosmopolitan standard.

54. *Cf.* Francis and Schmid, pp. viii–xviii. Cuppiramaṇiyam includes the early Pāṇḍya copperplate texts within his collection (*Mĕykkīrttikaḷ*, pp. 169–217). Those eulogies of the renascent Pāṇḍya dynasty from Śrīvallabha onward (*ca.* 1120–1146) were composed in obvious imitation of the Coḻa prototype, and so could properly be called examples of the "*mĕykkīrtti* form"; the Vijayanagara examples that Cuppiramaṇiyam includes are simply lists of *biruda*s. On the *Paṉṉiruppāṭṭiyal*, see the excellent discussion in Clare, *Canons*, pp. 59–83.
55. On the *āciriyappā* of the *mĕykkīrtti*, see Francis and Schmid, *Pondicherry Inscriptions*, vol. 2 pp. xiii, esp. n. 47 (registering a difference of interpretation between Wilden and the present author). The question of the changing climate of literary style and taste in the period, traceable especially in the *Yāpparuṅkala Virutti*, is innovatively explored in Clare, *Canons*, pp. 26–31.
56. The scholarly discussion of this list is practically a subdiscipline in its own right, from its beginnings in Hultzsch and Venkayya's pioneering effort (scattered throughout SII vols. 2 and 3); Cœdès, "Le Royaume de Çrīvijaya," *BEFEO* 18 (1918); and Nilakanta Sastri, *The Cōḷas*, pp. 211–218, through Spencer, *Politics of Expansion: The Chola Conquest of Sri Lanka and Sri Vijaya* (Madras: New Era, 1983), to such recent accounts in Sakhuja and Sakhuja, "A nautical perspective," in *Nagapattinam and Suvarnadwipa* (Singapore: ISEAS, 2009). With the passage of time, the literary character of the *mĕykkīrtti* has tended to be subordinated to its denotative potential: where Cœdès once rightly saw the play of *figurae etymologicae* in the eulogy's jingling epithets, the work of toponymic assignment (pursued tenaciously, of course, by Cœdès himself) now holds the entire interest of the field.
57. Yāmunācārya, *Saṃvitsiddhi*, ll. 38–44: *yathā colanṛpaḥ samrāḍ advitīyo 'dya bhūtale | iti tattulyanṛpatinivāraṇaparaṃ vacaḥ | na tu tatputratadbhṛtyakalatrādinivāraṇam | tathā surāsuranarabrahmāṇḍaśatakoṭayaḥ | kleśakarmavipākādyair aspṛṣṭasyākhileśituḥ | jñānādiṣāḍguṇyanidher acintyavibhavasya tāḥ | viṣṇor vibhūtimahimasamudradrapsavipruṣaḥ |* "The statement 'the Coḷa king is now the emperor, one without a second throughout the earth' is meant to deny that there are any kings who are his equals; it does not deny that he has sons, courtiers, and wives. In the same way, all of the gods and anti-gods and the billions of universes are just drops in the ocean of the awesome power of Viṣṇu, the inconceivably powerful Lord of the Universe, untouched by the misfortunes of defilement and the effects of prior actions, who is the treasury of the six faculties beginning with [absolute] awareness." In calling the Coḻa king "the emperor, without a second," Yāmuna plays upon the famous *mahāvākya* of the *Chāndogya Upaniṣad* (6.2.1), *ekam evādvitīyaṃ tad brahma.*

58. The characterization of both of these (ultimately intercommunicating) views – respectively, the Hobbesian "great beast" and the Marxian "great fraud" interpretations of the state – is taken from Geertz, *Negara: The Theatre State in Nineteenth-Century Bali* (New York: Princeton UP, 1980), p. 122.
59. See for instance, Veluthat *Political Structure*, p. 21, with the significant caveat that Veluthat's awareness of the "royalist" character of this discourse leads him to emphasize that royal panegyric is only one among several other potential ideological systems.
60. See especially the critique found in Pollock, *Language of the Gods*, pp. 511–524, to which I can add little of substance; see especially his peroration (p. 524):

    There is in principle no contradiction between finding domination and the discourses of domination in the domain of everyday social relations or preserving for culture a role in the constitution of political life, and challenging the view that power deployed culture for mystifying or effacing the contingency of the political sphere, or harnessed culture to governance and control[.]

    For a view skeptical of the possibility of the ideological suasion of peasant peoples by central governments, see James Scott, *Domination and the Arts of Resistance: Hidden Transcripts* (New Haven: Yale UP, 1990).
61. Davis, "Chola *Meykkīrtti*s as literary texts," p. 1. In a way that deliberately gestures toward Ramanujan's exploration of the *akam–puṟam* dyad in classical Tamil, Davis understands the internal dynamic of the *mĕykkīrtti*s to be grounded in an opposition between the "landscape of battle" and the "landscape under the king's parasol," the former dominated by heat, violence, and the public display of martial virtue; and the second by coolness, whiteness, and the equally public virtue of generosity. While this is an attractive reading, it hardly manages to exhaust the repertoire seen in the Coḻa *mĕykkīrtti*s, or it does so in a way that flattens out much of their interest.
62. *Cf.* Nagaswami, "Cankam Traditions under the Colas" on the continuity of a nonprofessional cult of literary quality attributed to Caṅkam literariness in the Coḻa period.
63. The argument laid out here departs from Stein's suggestive interpretation of the long-term patterns of circulation and region-making in the Tamil country ("Historical Geography," esp. pp. 15, 17). Here Stein is especially attentive to the pragmatic dimensions of epigraphy in a way that sets him out from the many of his more empirically sound critics (*cf. Peasant State*, pp. 353–361). It is perhaps inadvertent that Stein – who resolutely denied there to be a successful project of state-making attested in the record – provides some of the best conceptual tools for thinking about the statist project, due to his sensitivity to the structuring limitations of real political control and his sharpened attention to the dissemination of these physical tokens of Coḻa rule.
64. In *Pondicherry Inscriptions*, II, pp. v–xlvii, esp. pp. xxiff.
65. Francis and Schmid, Pondicherry Inscriptions, II, especially pp. xxvii–xli (data on the important "*meykkīrtti*-sites" of Pākūr and Tirupuvaṉai), xlvi–xlvii (conclusions). As they note, their sense of the independence of the inscribing elites

derives from Orr's preface to the first volume of the same corpus ("Preface," esp. pp. XIX–XX), with the significant caveat that Francis and Schmid see this as a feature especially from 1050 or so onward, an advance on Orr's broader characterization.

66. I base my remarks here on the text given in Cuppiramaṇiyam, *Mĕykkīrttikaḷ*, no. 15, pp. 76–81, and on the readings found in SII 3:20, 3:30, 5:97 and EI 21:38. Vīrarājendra's records present a test-case for the limitation of Cuppiramaṇiyam's policy of eclectic editing: the text he has produced is a hotchpotch of readings that corresponds to no surviving exemplar. Very much to the point is Hultzsch's still-exemplary running discussion in SII 3 (pp. 31–33, 64–65, and 190–197) on the shifting versions of Vīrarājendra's two major eulogies. The wider logic of recension that can be seen throughout his reign – if this can even be recovered from the abundant surviving data – lies beyond the limits of the present discussion.
67. I adopt Sethuraman's estimate of Vīrarājendra's accession between March 24 and May 28, 1063 (*Mathematics*, p. 12).
68. SII 5:976, ll. 4–7, *cf.* *Mĕykkīrttikaḷ*, no, 15, ln. 6–13.
69. SII 3:30, ll. 21–22, *Mĕykkīrttikaḷ*, no. 15, ll. 93–95, 99–101.
70. The text of SII 3:30, l. 27, and Hultzsch's translation thereof must be supplemented by the additional reading given in EI 21:38l, ln. 5; Hultzsch's rendering of *piraṭṭaṉ* here and elsewhere as the "the liar" is an overtranslation, influenced by the colloquialism *piraṭṭu* (thus Fabricius' *Dictionary*, *s.v.*). The word, a *tadbhava* of Sanskrit *bhraṣṭa*, is wider in its sense, i.e. "ruined, defeated, cast off, fled": this is more contextually appropriate. Nilakanta Sastri (*The Cōḻas*, p. 282, n. 150) identified the correct etymon, but his own rendering ("outcaste") is, if anything, even more reaching an overinterpretation. Hultzsch's attempt to understand the *piraṭṭaṉ* here as the future Vikramāditya VI was questioned by Sastri, on the authority of Venkatarama Ayyar (*Caḷukki Vikkiramātittaṉ Carittiram*, pp. 23ff.), who falsifies on philological grounds Hultzsch's interpretation of the passage, especially the key word *meṉāḷ* ("previously").
71. See Monius, *Imagining a Place for Buddhism* (New York: Oxford UP, 2001), pp. 116–155, for an exhaustive synthesis on this text, though *cf.* pp. 120–22, where she underplays the significance of the text's location in Vīrarājendra's court. See more generally, Pollock, *Language of the Gods*, pp. 162–184, on the royal patronage of grammar.
72. See again Brocquet, "Epopée epigraphique."
73. EI 25:25, ll. 56–58, vs. 26; here and in the following verses, I refer to the version found in the Cārāla plates, which transmits a generally better text than the Kanyakumari pillars.
74. My interpretation of these verses owes much to Shulman's translation and discussion of them (*The King and the Clown in South Indian Myth and Poetry* (Princeton: Princeton University Press, 1980), pp. 25–28); see also Pollock, "*Rāmāyaṇa* and the Political Imagination," p. 271.
75. The expression *prakṛtidakṣiṇaḥ*, the inclusion of which is evidently motivated by the wordplay with the phrase *haritaṃ* … *dakṣiṇām*, is ambiguous; it may equally mean "gracious to his subjects" (thus Shulman, *King and*

Clown, p. 25). On the semantics of *dakṣiṇa/dākṣiṇya cf.* Ali, *Courtly Culture*, pp. 135–137.

76. EI 25: 25, ll. 61–71, vv. 28–34.
77. EI 25: 25, ll. 151–153, vs. 79.
78. Hultzsch (SII 3, p. 194) notes the change in record but not in rhetoric.
79. SII 5: 468, compared against *Mĕykkīrttikaḷ*, no. 14.
80. *A History of South India from the Earliest Times until the Fall of Vijayanagar* (Oxford University Press, 1966), p. 188: "a total revolution in the diplomatic relations among the states and a virtual partition of the Chālukyan kingdom").
81. See EI 7, Sk. 136 for this date; this is discussed further in Chapter 3, "Bilhaṇa's Double Game."
82. Compare SII 7: 877 (cited earlier) and SII 3: 82.
83. The evidence for Vijayāditya VII's triangulations between the Kalyāṇa Cālukyas, Gaṅgas, and Coḻas is reviewed in "Epic and Cognomen," earlier.
84. SII 4: 529 (=ARE 82 of 1892); for help in the interpretation of this very long and difficult text, whose garbled nature was already noted by Hultzsch (SII 3, p. 195), I rely on the accounts of Nagaswamy (*Gangaikondacholapuram*, Tamil Nadu State Department of Archaeology, 1970) and Ali ("Epigraphic Enigmas"). See also Karashima, *South Indian History and Society*, pp. 40–55.
85. Nagaswamy's tabulation of these figures (*Gangaikondacholapuram*, pp. 49–54, registering sixty-four figures) needs to be supplemented by the *Concordance* (nos. 2065–2118, registering fifty-three) and checked against the published record. While Nagaswamy adheres more closely to the serial order of the record, the *Concordance* includes some names that he doesn't register; for instance, the figure recorded in the Concordance as no. 2065, *madurāntakabrahmādi*[*rāyaṉ*] is unmentioned by Nagaswamy, who supplies a number of blank or partial entries to account for gaps in the record. Following Nagaswamy, I read two officials responsible for setting down the initial order (the phrase *oppīṭṭu pukunta keḷvi* in ln. 26 is a fragmentary description of this action, to be filled in with *variyil iṭṭu kŏḷka ĕṉṟu paṭi* or something similar [Cf. ARE 74 of 1932, discussed later]), followed by the fifty figures responsible for the order's acclamation (up to Nagaswamy's no.51/*Concordance* no. 2108; ll. 27–44; there may be an intervening step after Nagaswamy's no. 4(/2069) lost here due to damage, if the SII editor's restoration of *paṭiye* in ln. 27 is correct), then the thirteen accountants and recording scribes (ll. 44–47).
86. At the beginning of the list of courtiers, we find Antaiyārveḷāṉāṉa Rājendravairākaracoḻaṉ (Nagaswamy 3/*Concordance* 2068), Arayaṉ Rājarājaṉ (4/2069), and Koṉārkoṉ Aḻakiyapāṇṭiyaṉāṉa Rājarājakkumaṇarājaṉ (6/2071); their names possibly suggest magnate status, but they are more likely gentry. More distinctive, and associated by his title with the formerly magnate polity of Tirumuṉaipāṭi, is Kāmaṉ Veṅkātaṉārāṉa Vīrarājendramuṉaiyatariyar (16/2082); significantly, he is one of three named figures from Tondaimandalam.
87. These are, respectively, EI 22: 38, ll. 12–16 and ARE 74 of 1932 (transcribing and partly translated in the *Report* for 1931–32, pp. 51–55). The degree to which these three records overlap in their personnel will have to await study elsewhere.

Chapter 2

1. Significant contributions to this interpretation include Hultzsch in SII 1 (pp. 97–99) and 3 (esp. pp. 125–131, the essential overview, subsequently revised but never replaced; and his translation pp. 133–134); Hira Lal (EI 9:23 ["Rajapura Plates of Madhurantakadeva"] p. 179); Fleet 'Eastern Cālukya Chronology,' *IA* 20 (1891) and *Dynasties of the Kanarese Districts* (Bombay: Government Central Press, 1882, p. 66n); the crowning synthesis of this belongs to Nilakanta Sastri (*The Cōḷas*, pp. 290–294, 301–304). I reproduce the lineation given by Cuppiramaṇiyam (*Mĕykkīrttikaḷ*, no. 18, pp. 95), and follow his explication in places (*ibid.*, pp. 104–105): this text, being considerably more stable than other Coḻa *mĕykkīrtti*s, allows his synoptic editorial method to be used to particularly good effect.
2. On the metaphysics and mechanics of the opening sound or sounds of a poetic text, see inter alia, Shulman, "Notes on *Camatkāra*"; Clare, *Canons, Conventions*, pp. 72–80.
3. As per the MTL, s.v., citing *Īṭu ad Tiruvāymŏḻi* 5.5.7.
4. Notably, the word *tuṇai* only occurs in Vīrarājendra's short eulogy prior to Rājendracoḷa's first records.
5. The identification was first proposed by Hira Lal ("Rajapura Plates of Madhurantakadeva"), relying on a reference to Dhārāvarṣa in a record of his grandson's time, dated Śaka 1033 (1111 CE). It was later adopted by Nilakanta Sastri (*The Cōḷas*, pp. 298, fn. 25).
6. See for instance, *cakkarakoṭṭatt' appuṟatt'aḷavum evarun tāṉait tāvaṭi cĕlutti* (SII 3:30, ll. 29–30; *Mĕykkīrttikaḷ*, no. 15, ln. 138–139). The reference to Vikramāditya follows the account in *Vikramāṅkadevacarita*, 4.30.
7. Hultzsch (SII 3, p. 132) was correct in his understanding of this meaning, though he does not find a pun here; Nilakanta Sastri (*The Cōḷas*, pp. 298–299, n. 26) unaccountably sees this as "mere poetry" that "contains no geography."
8. Reference to *pukaḻ* is omnipresent throughout the Coḻa *mĕykkīrtti*s; by contrast, *dharma* (whether given as *tarumam* in Tamil orthography, or in its pure Dravidian cognate *aṟam*) is surprisingly almost unattested in earlier eulogies, with only a single mention in a short and poorly represented *mĕykkīrtti* of Rājamahendra, who never ruled independently (Rājamahendra 1, ln. 3: *tarumanĕṟi niṟpa maṉunĕṟi naṭāttiya*; this and subsequent references to the text of pre-Rājendracoḷa *mĕykkīrtti* are drawn from Cuppiramaṇiyam, *Mĕykkīrttikaḷ*).
9. Compare, for example, *Puṟanāṉūṟu* 2.16–19: *pāal puḷippiṉum, pakal iruḷiṉum / nāal vetanĕṟi tiriyiṉum / tiriyāc cuṟṟamŏṭu muḻutuceṉ vilaṅki* "Even if milk becomes something sour, or the sun goes dark, / or the Four Vedas swerve from the truth, / may you shine on, with no loss, on and on with your unswerving ministers!" (trans. Hart and Heifitz, *The Four Hundred Songs of War and Wisdom* (New York: Columbia University Press, 1999), p. 4), *Cilappatikāram* 2.88, *urimaic cuṟṟamoṭ' ŏrutaṉi puṇarkka*, "[Kovalaṉ's mother] gave [a house and retinue to Kaṇṇaki] to be her's alone, like her rightful companions"; and the late-eighth century Pāṇḍyan Veḷvikkūṭi plates (EI 17: 16, ln. 57).

10. *Urimai* occurs at the opening of Rājarāja's inauguration of the *mĕykkīrtti* form (ll. 1–2: *tirumakaḷ polap pĕrunilaccelviyum / ta<u>n</u>akke urimai pūṇṭamai ma<u>n</u>akkŏḷa*, "as the goddess of the great earth, just like Śrī, accepted the rightful husbandry of him alone"), and in Rājendra's account of the justice of his campaign across the sea (ln. 51, *urimaiyil pi<u>r</u>akkiya pĕrunitip pi<u>r</u>akkamum*, "[Rājendra seized], according to his right, the wondrous great treasures stored up [at Kaṭāram]," *pace* Hultzsch). The word also finds a place in Rājādhirāja's shorter eulogy but, perhaps significantly, not in its expanded versions (no. 1, ll. 13–14: *ta<u>n</u>kulatt' ava<u>n</u>ipar na<u>n</u>kutaru takaimaiyil / araciyalurimai mu<u>r</u>aimaiyil etti*, "given the fitness that lends virtue to the earth-lords of his family, [the king] honors the right to rule that comes to him in unbroken succession [*mu<u>r</u>aimai*, see further];" see Sastri, *The Cōḷas*, p. 247 on his different eulogies), as well as in the expanded conclusion to Vīrarājendra's long text (no. 2, ln. 155–156, . . . *porttŏ<u>l</u>il / urimaiyil ĕytiy aracu vi<u>r</u>r'iruntu*, "he took up the task of war-making, as was his right, and sits in state in kingship").
11. *Kula*: Rājendra, ll. 13, 34 (both references to the *kulata<u>n</u>am* or ancestral wealth of the king's enemies; for the first of these, see further); Rājādhirāja, first eulogy, ln. 1–2 *aṅkatirkaṭavuḷ / tŏlkulam vilaṅka* ("so to make flourish the ancient family of the bright-rayed god," a highly marked opening move, later adopted by Adhirājendra's eulogists, see further) and ln. 13 (see note 10; Rājendradeva, fourth eulogy, ll. 23–25, investing one member of his family with the grandiloquent title *ti<u>n</u>akarakkulattuc ci<u>r</u>app'amar co<u>l</u>a janakarājan*, "Co<u>l</u>a Janakarāja<u>n</u>, in whom the virtue of the family of the Sun is fixed"). *Mu<u>r</u>aimai*: Rājendra, ll. 12–13, *ĕ<u>r</u>ipaṭai keraḷar mu<u>r</u>aimaiyil cūṭum / kulata<u>n</u>am ākiya palarpuka<u>l</u> muṭiyum* ("[he seized] the abundant fame and the crown, which were the ancestral wealth, worn by right by the spear-fighter lord of Keraḷa"); Rājādhirāja, first eulogy, ln. 14 . . . *mu<u>r</u>aimaiyil etti* (translated earlier, n. 10); Vīrarājendra, second eulogy, ln. 6, *mu<u>r</u>aimaiyil* (Cuppiramaṇiyam reads this as a variant).
12. *The Cōḷas*, p. 296, quoting Bühler without attribution; see further Chapter 3, "Bilhaṇa's Double Game,", page 129, n. 20.
13. This is the unpublished record ARE 823 of 1945–1946 from Siddhamalli, dating itself to day 329 of Adhirājendra's third regnal year, and containing astronomical data yielding the corresponding civil date of May 3, 1071: see the discussion in Sethuraman, *Mathematics*, pp. 11–12.
14. Though I once again rely on Cuppiramaṇiyam, the text of Adhirājendra's *mĕykkīrtti* is considerably less certain than that of Rājendracoḷa. I include here a small *apparatus criticus* of the readings I accept in the body text:

sigla

PC: Pu. Cuppiramaṇiyam's *Mĕykkīrttikaḷ*; PCv: Cuppiramaṇiyam's variants
TI SII 3.57 (Tiruvallam)
P1: SII 4:1388 (Polonnaruwa)
P2: SII 4: 1392 (Polonnaruwa)
K: SII 7: 442 (Kalavai)
VE: SII 8:4 (Veppankulam, Kanci district)
VI: SII 8: 754 (Villupuram, Villupuram district, fragmentary)

variants
4.*cĕlla*] P1 P2 Ve; *cĕlva* PC
5.*valannoḻi nīvaṟkku*] Ti PCv; *valaner*[*pu*]*ṉivaṟku* Ve; *valicer puvaṉikkum* PC P1 P2; K lacunose
8.*kīrttiyaṅ*] K; *kīrttiyum* PC Ti P1 P2 Ve; Vi fragmentary
10.*ākki*] K; *āka* PC *marapiṉil*] PC; *viravi naṟ-* K
9.*tuṟantu*] PC; *t[ī]rntu* K
11.*cūṭṭi*] Ti, K, Vi; *cūṭi* PC

after line 13, PC includes: *vīrasiṃhāsanattu ulaka / muḻutuṭaiyāḷŏṭum vīṟṟ'irunt'aruḷi* (Ve,Vi, K all omit).

15. The reading adopted here by Cupiramaṇiyam *vali cer puvaṉikkum* is metrically sound and gives a plausible meaning "[his matchless wheel goes forth] to the whole world, touched by the power of the sun." This reading, however, is only attested (as far as I am aware) in two records found in the same site in Polonnuruwa in Sri Lanka. This may have been a local variation upon the *mĕykkīrtti* text, but there is no warrant to believe that it was known to the Coḻa subjects on the mainland.

    Nevertheless, the translation here is uncertain: *ŏḻi* (from the verb *ŏḻital*, "to cease, to decline, to die") does not generally form its noun directly from the root (the commonly occurring form is *ŏḻipu*, which in any case has the meaning "exclusion, elimination"). *nīvaṟku*, while more easy of interpretation, is itself somewhat uncertain: I take it as the dative-case inflection of the verbal noun *nīval*, an allegro syncopation of the more usual *nīvutal*. Given these several difficulties, this translation can only be considered tentative. Hultzsch, adopting the same reading in SII 3.57, translates (pp. 116–117) "in order to remove and wipe away the force [?] of the sun," understanding *ŏḻi* evidently as a serial adverbial participle (for which the expected form would be *ŏḻintu*).
16. Again, this is problematic: *matuvai* is unattested, but cf. *matukai* and *mataṅya* in this meaning.
17. After this point, the text in Cuppiramaṇiyam may be translated as "sitting in state atop a throne of heroes with the mistress of the entire earth," a royal style that would go on to become standard in post-Kulottuṅga *mĕykkīrtti*s, but that was first employed in the final redaction of Vīrarājendra's short eulogy. While this may just be a copyist's or engraver's error, it is possible that the presence of this formula may allow for an internal chronology of those records of Adhirājendra's that lack a day in the third regnal year, presuming that the king was married at some point during the intervening time.
18. To give just a few examples of the incessant repetitions met with in the Coḻa *mĕykkīrtti*s in the period from Rājarāja to Vīrarājendra: there are the realia such as [*cuṭar-*, *maṇi-*,]*muṭi*, *ceṅkol*, and *kuṭai*; personal names and toponyms like *āhavamallaṉ*, *iraṭṭapāṭi eḻarai ilakkam*, *kārkaṭal ilaṅkai*; and such stock phrases as *muṭi cūṭṭi*/*muṭi kŏṇṭu*, *eṇṭicai nikaḻa*, and *maṉu nĕṟi*, the repetition of all of which is so frequent that a tabulation would impose on the reader's patience.

19. The case has been made eloquently in the domain of European political thought by Quentin Skinner (*Visions of Politics* (Cambridge: Cambridge University Press, 2001), vol. 1, esp. pp. 114–118). I have discussed elsewhere the applicability of this model in the context of the study of medieval South Indian works on poetics ("Source Criticism to Intellectual History," pp. 148–154).
20. 7:985 in Tirunamanallur locates itself in Muṉaipāṭi in the Rājendracoḻavaḷanāṭu, as does Rājendracoḷa's record 193 of 1906. Adhirājendra's record from Tirukkovalūr (7:884), part of the old Milāṭu lordship, expressly locates itself in Kuṟukkaikuṟṟam in Jananāthavaḷanāṭu, as do the cluster of Rājendracoḷa records in the same locale (SII 7:875, 876 [where it is expressly identified with Milāṭu, ll. 15–16], and 877). It is unclear whether any other kings used the name Jananāthavaḷanāṭu for this territory; it does not occur among those discussed by Subbarayalu (*Political Geography*, pp. 58–69 and map 12).
21. Not every one of Rājendracoḷa's records includes the *mĕykkīrtti* beginning *tirumaṉṉi viḷaṅkum*. A number (*e.g.* SII 7: 498, 541, 748, 749, 875, 877, 979; ARE 193 of 1906, 172 of 1920) have the following truncated and banal opening (cf. Cuppiramaṇiyam, *Mĕykkīrttikaḷ*, no. 22):

pūmiyum tiruvum tāme puṇara
vikkiramattāl cakkiram naṭātti
vijayāpiṣekattup paṇṇi
vīrasimhāsanattup puvaṉa-
muḻutuṭaiyāḷŏṭu vīṟṟ'irunt'aruḷiṉa
kovirājakesarivaṉmarāṉa uṭaiyār śrīrājendracoḻadevaṟku

As the goddesses of earth and sovereignty join with him alone; having set the wheel of rule in motion through his martial valor, and performed the consecration of victory; sitting in state on the heroic lion's throne along with his queen, lady of the entire earth, Rājakesarivarman Uṭaiyār Rājendracoḷadeva ...

This *mĕykkīrtti* notably lacks the rhetorical and intertextual flair of Rājendracoḷa's other eulogy. Many of the Coḻas possessed a similarly brief and subdued eulogy, among them Rājādhirāja and Rājendradeva; Vīrarājendra's short *mĕykkīrtti* may have grown out of a similarly unambitious opening. The logic of the distribution and variation of such texts would repay further study: the cluster of occurrences in SII 7 suggests that the use of this second early *mĕykkīrtti* was concentrated on the southern borders of the Tondaimandalam area (with the exception of 7:541, from within the city limits of modern Chennai).

There are also a number of Adhirājendra inscriptions that bear a similarly underwhelming alternate *mĕykkīrtti* (*e.g.* SII 7:884, SITI 821 [fragmentary], ARE 219 of 1912, 113 of 1929/30):

tirumaṭantaiyum jayamaṭantaiyum
tiruppuyaṅkaḷil iṉit'iruppa
irunilan taṉ ŏrukuṭainiḻal

aṉaitt'ūḻiyum maṉṉi
vāḻa meruviṟ puliy irutti
vīrasiṃhāsaṉattu vīṟṟ'irunt'aruḷi
māppukaḻ maṉuvuṭaṉ vaḷartta kopparakesarivarmarāṉa uṭaiyār śrī adhirājendradevaṟku

As the goddesses of sovereignty and victory rest gently in his two arms; as the entire world, its wide lands fixed beneath his matchless parasol, abides; the one who set the tiger [-emblem] on Mount Meru, who sits in state atop the hero's lion-throne, who has made flourish Manu of great fame, Parakesarivarman Uṭaiyār Adhirājendradeva.

Though one can detect some resonances here with Rājendracoḷa's 'main' *mĕykkīrtti*, the text is basically a pastiche derived from Vīrarājendra's long text: compare, again with reservations, the text edited by Cuppiramaṇiyam (*Mĕykkīrttikaḷ*, no. 15), ll. 1–5.

22. The score assigned to each record was arrived at by tabulating the inclusion of the following features:
    1. *mĕykkīrtti*
        1.a long (2 points).
        1.b short (regarding which see n. 21)
    2. officials
    3. magnates
    4. royal order (5 points)
    5. cash transaction
    6. named local elites
    7. queen (3 points)
    8. reference to transregional collective group (*cittirameḻi/nagaram/valaṅkai*)

    Given the rarity of royal orders in this corpus, and their obvious significance as a gauge of courtly investment, they have been weighted especially strongly, as have the records where a queen is the agent, for identical reasons. Similarly, the inclusion of the *mĕykkīrtti* texts discussed earlier in the chapter has been weighted more than a text with a shorter eulogy.

    Adhirājendra's records are scored as follows:

	Long mĕy. (2 pt)	Short mĕy.	Officials	Magnates	R. order (5 pt)	Cash	Named locals	Queen (3 pt)	Collective	Score
A	X		X	X		X	X			6
B	X		X			X				4
C	X					X				3
D	X					X	X			4
E				X					X	2
F		X		X			X			3

	Long měy. (2 pt)	Short měy.	Officials	Magnates	R. order (5 pt)	Cash	Named locals	Queen (3 pt)	Collective	Score
G										1
H	X		X	X					X	5
I				X						1
J	X						X			3
K	X					X				3
L		X								1
M	X									2
N	X									2
O	X					X				3
P		X								1
Q	X						X			3
R				X			X			2
S		X	X	X	X					9

Rājendracoḷa's records, in turn, are scored as follows:

No.	Long měy. (2 pt)	Short měy.	Officials	Magnates	R. order (5 pt)	Cash	Named locals	Queen (3 pt)	Collectives	Score
1	X		X	X		X				5
2	X		X		X					8
3	X		X			X	X			5
4	X									2
5	X		X							3
6		X								1
7		X					X			2
8	X						X			3
9		X		X			X			3
10		X		X			X			3
11		X		X			X			3
12		X								1
13	X						X			3
14							X			1
15	X		X						X	4
16		X					X	X	X	6
17		X						X		4
18	X		X						X	4
19	X		X		X		X			10
20	X		X	X			X			5
21	X					X	X			4
22		X					X			2
23	X						X			3

No.	Long mĕy. (2 pt)	Short mĕy.	Officials	Magnates	R. order (5 pt)	Cash	Named locals	Queen (3 pt)	Collectives	Score
24	X			X				X	X	8
25	X		X	X	X					10
26	X									2
27	X							X		5
28										1
29	X									2
30										1
31	X									2
32	X						X		X	4
33	X									2
34						X				1
35		X								1

It needs to be emphasized that the importance assigned to these records is an artifact of the present analysis, and that their significance is relative. I do not mean to imply that the actions of kings, their courts, and the upper reaches of the gentry are somehow more *intrinsically* important than those of others.

23. SII 3, p. 132.
24. Of those instanced by Sastri (*The Cōḷas*, pp. 296 and 300nn.) ARE 358 of 1917, 497 of 1920, 279 of 1929, 185 of 1919, and 101 of 1928 have all been included here. ARE 425 of 1912, issued in the second year of Tribhuvanacakravartin Rājendracoladeva, though lacking a cognomen, is correctly assigned in the ARE report to the final king of the dynasty, Parakesarivarman Rājendra ("Rājendra III"), r. 1246–1279: though its date is difficult to calculate, it borrows the "*mĕykkīrtti*" (properly so-called) of Māṟavarman Sundarapāṇḍya (r. 1215–1239), and so must postdate that king's reign. ARE 55 of 1911, as its ASI transcript indicates, belongs to the reign of Kulottuṅga III (r. 1178–1218); the epigraphists' office tentatively assigns 156 of 1923 to Kulottuṅga II (r. 1133–1150; the *mĕykkīrtti* is a garbled bricolage based on Vīrarājendra's short eulogy, referring to the king [ln. 2] as *kov[ī]raśekharadeva*, a name otherwise unparalleled). ARE 468 of 1913, the final record cited by Sastri, presents a fascinating anomaly, returned to later (see n. 98).
25. The suggestion is Sethuraman's (*Mathematics*, pp. 63–64); the two inscriptions issued in this king's name are SII 14:194 and 195, both dated in the third regnal year (although 14:194 is oddly dated to year 3, day 380; this record is notable in that it reproduces a truncated version of Vīrarājendra's short *mĕykkīrtti* [ll. 11–14] and in its scrupulous adherence to Coḻa chancellery norms). This presumption accounts of the extreme southern end of Adhirājendra's inscriptions in Tirunelveli and Polonnaruwa. *Ex hypothesi*, his political network in the far south and Sri Lanka continued to pay honor to

Adhirājendra after his translation into Coḻa kingship. This hypothesis, and indeed Sethuraman's conjectural identification, finds support in the problematic testimony in the Tirunelveli record (SITI 821, discussed n. 54).

26. On the institution of the *nagaram*, see Hall, *Trade and Statecraft in the Age of the Cōḻas* (Delhi: Abhinav Publications, 1980) and Champakalakshmi, *Trade Ideology and Urbanization* (Delhi: Oxford University Press, 1996), esp. pp. 203–310 and 371–423; for the Five Hundred Masters, see Abraham, *Two Medieval Merchant Guilds of South India* (New Delhi: Manohar Publications, 1988).
27. Subbarayalu, *Political Geography*, p. 15, citing ARE 22 of 1922, dated to 1009 as the first attestation of the name Jayaṅkŏṇṭacoḻamaṇḍalam.
28. A list of the traditional *koṭṭam*s can be found in Mahalingam, *Kāñcīpuram in Early South Indian History* (London: Asia Publishing House, 1969), p. 3n (based on accounts in the Mackenzie collectanea); Subbarayalu, *Political Geography*, p. 30 discounts the evidentiary value of such late accounts, while conceding that "the number of Kōṭṭams comes to about twenty-four" in this period.
29. The understanding of the Tondaimandalam *taṉiyūr* system described here derives from Champakalakshmi's admirable study ("The City and the Hinterland" in *Trade, Ideology and Urbanization*). The *taṉiyūr* did exist outside of Tondaimandalam, but only in a vestigial way and significantly only in adjacent territories: see the list and description in Subbarayalu, *Political Geography*, pp. 92–94. On Cidambaram's status as the only major temple center classed as a *taṉiyūr*, see pp. 180ff.
30. Champakalakshmi, "The City and the Hinterland", p. 381; on Kāñci, pp. 389–398. The study of Pallava royal ideology has been recently revived and raised to a new level of both empirical and conceptual sophistication by the work of Emmanuel Francis: see *Le Discours Royal, passim*, and especially his "Praising the King," on the halo effect of Pallava royalist self-presentation in lesser lordly lineages.
31. On the *pallavaraiyaṉ* title (and the closely associated *viḻupparaiyaṉ*), see Karashima et al., *Concordance of Names*, vol. 1, pp. lii–lv; and Subbarayalu, "The Chola State," in *South India under the Cholas*, pp. 222–225.
32. The most significant early account of these records is that of Subrahmanya Aiyer, "Largest Provincial Organisations," *QJMS* 45–46 (1954–56); Stein (*Peasant State*, pp. 217–225) characteristically rejects Aiyer's overdrawn centralized-bureaucratic interpretation, while – again, characteristically – relying heavily on his presentation of the evidence, for which the most significant records are those found in Tirukkoyilur (SII 7: 129) and the cluster found in Mannargudi (SII 6: 48, 50, 58), all datable to the thirteenth century.
33. The Tāmaraippākkam inscriptions were first noted in ARE 179, 183 and 188 of 1974, and were subsequently published as *Tāmaraippākkam Kalvĕṭṭukaḷ* (hereafter TK) nos. 1, 26 and 29). There is an early notice of these records by Nagaswamy (*Studies in Ancient Tamil Law and Society* (Madras: Institute of Epigraphy, 1978), pp. 75–78, limited to TK 29); Krishnan's important study was the first to really exploit their evidence ("Chittiramelip-Periyanadu – an

agricultural guild of medieval Tamil Nadu." *Journal of the Madras University* 56, 1 (1982)). The Tāmaraippākkam records have been recently discussed in Karashima (*Ancient to Medieval*, pp. 115–135, records summarized on pp. 119–120) and Subbarayalu (*South India under the Cholas*, pp. 132–135).

34. The three records uniformly report themselves to be work of a scribe bearing the title Cittirameḻinā ṭṭup paṭṭaṉ, i.e. "brahman of the Cittirameḻi country (or assembly)." It is unclear whether this is the same individual or a title held by a series of professional literates. Neither TK 1 nor TK 26 explicitly names itself a record of the *cittirameḻi* assembly (*pace* the editor Kŭ. Tāmotaran's summary for the first of these, pp. 1–2); the group in TK 1 refers to itself as the *rājentiracoḻanil pĕriyaṉāṭu* ("the great assembly in the Rājendracoḻa hall"); the nature of the collective decision in TK 26 (see further) clearly links it to the later "translocal" assemblies. The Tamil prose style of all three records, especially of the court case in TK 29, is unusual, as are several instances of the records' lexis, which will be noted later.

35. The opening Sanskrit *śloka* reads (in corrected orthography, but retaining its faulty meter): *śrīma[d]bhūdevīputrā[n]āṃ cāturva[r]ṇṇya[j]anodbhava[m]* | *sarvalokhitārthāya citrameḷasya śāsanam* | |. This is a close parallel to a pair of verses later found in Tirukovalur (SII 7:129). The record's opening "*mĕykkīrtti*'" also resembles that found in the later records, though here the relationship is more attenuated. On the wider history of collective groups issuing decisions with the force of *dharma*, see Davis, "Intermediate Realms of Law," *JESHO* 49, 1 (2005).

36. TK 1; as Tāmotaraṉ notes, the abbreviated eulogy given here describes Rājendra as *pūrvatecamum kaṅkaiyum kiṭāramum kŏṇṭa*, when the king's conquests in Southeast Asia are never claimed before his fourteenth year in his genuine records. Tāmotaraṉ is perhaps too ready to gloss over this inconsistency when he assigns the record to Rājendradeva's time, as if this was simply a scribal error: this may represent a concerted effort to backdate an arrangement to the earlier reign of the totemic Coḻa empire-builder, paralleling what we see in the *valaṅkai mahāsenai* records in Kolar (see pp. 103ff.)

37. The title *piṭārar* and the role *piṭārañ cĕykiṟa* are unclear in their signification: the TKC, *s.v.*, cites only this instance. The word tends to have medical or ethnic connotations (MTL, *s.v.*); the latter sense – "man of the *kuṟava* caste" – is perhaps likely to be the etymon here; in its non-honorific form *piṭāraṉ*, it occurs relatively frequently as a proper name (there are twenty occurrences in the *Concordance*, largely as a personal name or a patronym). It is perhaps suggestive of a lordly figure with strictly local loyalities, who – though possessed of a title redolent of Coḻa courtly grandeur – nevertheless aligned himself with the decision of the corporate group. The conclusion to the record is eloquent (ll. 11–12): *...tirutāmaraippākkattu tiruvaṅkīśvaramuṭaiyār koyiliṟ silālekai rājapiṭārar taṭutta taṭaiye pĕriyanāṭṭomum tiruvāṇai ĕṉṟu taṭuttom*, "Following the opposition registered by Rāja[rāja]piṭārar in a stone inscription in the Tiruvagnīśvara temple in Tāmaraippākkam, we of the *pĕriyanāṭu* have also opposed the command of the king."

38. The crucial phrase here is ll. 4–5: *ĕṅkaḷil icaintu nāṭṭāṇmai cĕyya iṭṭa kaiccavolaippaṭi kalvĕṭṭum paricāvatu*: "Having agreed amongst ourselves and so arranged the government of the country, we inscribe the following ordinance, in accord with the documented agreement that we have set down." Subbarayalu (*South India under the Cholas*, pp. 101, 133), with characteristic interpretative caution, wishes to only understand *nāṭṭāṇmai* to mean "major land tax," rather than referring to the larger politico-juridical *authority* to regiment such a tax. I choose to understand the term more expansively following the MTL, *s.v.*, "Office of village headman; sovereignty, over-lordship of a country." Tāmotaraṉ rightly draws attention to the term *kaiccavolai*, which he glosses as *tīrmāṉam* ("decision"). I would link the first element in this compound *kaicca*[*m*] with *kaccam* ("agreement," MTL *s.v.*, *cf.* skt. *kārya* via pkt. *kajja*), though whether this represents a regional pronunciation or simply a misrendering is unclear. On the similar, Kerala-specific use of *kaccam* (especially as in the frequently cited "Mūḻikkaḷam *kaccam*"), see Veluthat, "Literacy and Communication" (in *The Early Medieval in South India*. New Delhi: Oxford University Press, 2010), pp. 174–175 and references cited there. The whole agreement is described in the record's conclusion as a *tiruvāṇai* (ln. 7), ordinarily the term for a royal order. On the list of *nāṭu*s mentioned here, see Subbarayalu, "*Ūrār, Nāṭṭār*" (in *South India under the Chōḷas*), especially his map 10.2 on p. 134.
39. See Subbarayalu, *Political Geography*, pp. 83–86; on Tirukkovalūr (/Tirukkoyilur) Heitzman, *Gifts*, pp. 28–30, 90–99 (as already noted, this was a significant location for the inscriptions of both Adhirājendra and Rājendracoḷa, as well as the site of one of the most important later *cittirameḻi* charters).
40. So, for instance, ARE 123 of 1926 (Tiruvilakkudi, Tanjavur dist. Adhirājendra, year two) or 165 of 1911 (Tirukkāṉūr, same district, Adhirājendra year 3=SITI 1178A). Notably, neither of these records includes a *mĕykkīrtti*.
41. This is SII 17: 227. The hypernym is erratic in that Centaṉ is itself the Tamil transformation of Skt. Jayanta. It is unclear whether this was a deliberate decision or a misunderstanding by the author of the Sanskrit verse, which is an underwhelming and not quite metrical effort.
42. SII 7: 854: the parcel is described ll. 4–7; the Cĕṅkaṇicāttaṉ mentioned here is an ancestor of the Cāmpuvarāyar families who figure so prominently in the epigraphy of the final decades of Coḷa rule: see Govindasamy, *The Role of Feudatories in Later Chōḷa History* (Annamalainagar: Annamalai University, 1979), pp. 188ff.
43. *Ibid.*, ll. 7–8: *ivvūrt tirukkauriśvaramuṭaiyār mahādevar koyilil nān eḻuntaruḷuvitta* [*sic*] *āṭiyaruḷuvār cittirameḻiviṭaṅkarkku santi oṉṟu.*
44. On the *paḷḷi* warrior groups, refer to the evolving ideas of Karashima and Subbarayalu: beginning with the former's *South Indian History and Society*, pp. 27–28, where the introduction of movable wealth acquired through war into the agrarian order of Tiruchirappalli and Tanjavur districts was first suggested as a causative agent in the emergence of large-scale non-Brahman landholding. This was later refined to suggest that "the old warlike

communities such as Surutiman, Palli [N.B.] and Nattaman" were responsible for the major acquisition of land (*Ancient to Medieval*, p. 72). These groups would go on to claim the authority to exercise so-called *pāṭikāval* rights ("territorial protection," the extortionist nuance of this comes over intact into modern English) in late Coḻa times: *ibid.*, pp. 143ff. Parenthetically, one of these *pāṭikāval* groups, the so-called Sambuvaraya chiefs who emerge in the twelfth century, are likely the direct descendants of one of our two *nāṭāḻvaṉ*s, especially the epigraphically well-attested Ammaiyappaṉ Pāṇṭiyaṉ Naralokavīrapperaiyaṉ, a self-professed *kuṭipaḷḷi* from Ceṅkeṇi (on this figure, refer to the *Concordance*, 3, s.v. *ceṅkeṇi*).

Subbarayalu emphasizes the place of the militarization of society in the rise of private landholding (see *South India under the Cholas*, pp. 170ff.). The origins of private property within the confines of the *brahmadeya* were first proposed by Karashima (*History and Society*, pp. 5–12); the wider social-theoretical consequences of this remain underresearched.

45. On *nāṭāḻvaṉ*, see *Concordance*, I, Appendix 3, pp. lv–lvi (= Karashima, *History and Society*, pp. 63–64) and again Subbarayalu, *South India under the Cholas*, pp. 171–172, noting the coincidence of this title with members of the *paḷḷi* caste.
46. The formulary was adopted from Vīrarājendra's chancellery: SII 5.976 from Tiruveṅkāṭu, dated to the 233rd day of that king's second year (sometime between November 1065 and January 1066), includes an identical schedule of revenue terms, and employs the same formula for dating the application of fiscal arrangements (ll. 48–49 *yāṇṭiraṇṭāvatiṉ ĕtirām āṇṭu mutal iṟaiyiliyāka*, see note 47).
47. The records are SII 3:57 (with Hultzsch's translation) and 8:4. "From the year": *cakravartikaḷ śrīvirarājendratevaṟku yāṇṭu ēḻāmvatiṉ ĕtirāmāṇṭu mutal* (ll. 11–12; ln. 2): this may be meant to suggest that Vīrarājendra's eighth year was current (which it was), and – significantly – that the king was still himself ruling (though *cf.* the convoluted reasoning in Sethuraman, *Mathematics*, p. 12, who sees in this record acknowledgment that Vīrarājendra had died between the promulgation of his revenue order and his son's agents' execution of it). On the type of cash levies recorded here (all of which are generically classed as *antarāyam*, and assessed at a rate of 25 *kācu* per thousand *kalam* of paddy), see Shanmugam, *Revenue System*, pp. 27–28; Subbarayalu, "Revenue System" (in *South India under the Cholas*, pp. 97–98); and, more generally, Karashima, "Revenue Terms" (in *History and Society*, pp. 69–84).
48. As attested in SII 4: 529 (*Concordance*, no. 2077); see Chapter 1, "Vīrarājendra: Crisis and Revolution."
49. Tiraimūrnāṭu is the area around Tiruvidaimarudur; on the *Veḷ* lords, originally from Kodumbalur, see Govindaswamy, *Feudatories*, pp. 6–25; Veluthat, *Political Structure*, p. 122; and references *ad loc.*
50. The one exception (ll. 22–23: *rājentiracoḻavaḷanāṭṭup poykaipākkattuk kuḷamuḻāṉ eṟaṉ īcaraṅkiricekaraṉāṉa cayatuṅkamūventaveḷaṉ*) is himself significant: Rājendracoḻavaḷanāṭu was the Coḻa name for the magnate territory of Pāṇakoppāṭi, which was centered on Tiruvallam as its ancient capital (thus Hultzsch, SII 3, p. 89). This man's *mūventaveḷaṉ* title, however, suggests a

member of the gentry rather than a lordly figure. His other title, *kuḷamuḻā<u>n</u>*, is obscure: Hultzsch (SII 3, p. 118n.) suggests a connection with the equally unclear *komuḻā<u>n</u>* found in SII 3:10; another occurrence of the title (in the honorific form *kuḷamuḻār*) seems to be this man's brother (as they share a patronymic and a native place) who, as *atikārikaḷ* for Kulottuṅga, conducted an investigation at Tiruvo<u>rr</u>iyūr in 1076 (SII 5:1356, ll. 3–4 *Concordance*, no. 8854).

51. The logic similar to this is outlined by Heitzman (*Gifts*, p. 221): referring specifically to temple land transfers, he explains how

    [a]lienation of tax revenues for a temple did not necessarily result in economic loss in the long run, and may have resulted in economic and political gain for a powerful donor. When taxes went to the neighbouring temple rather than to the state, there was an immediate exclusion of state scrutiny of the annual produce of donated fields and villages, and an annual transfer of the upper share to a local temple's storerooms. There its allocation and redistribution were potentially under the influence of the donors. The appointment of ritual officiants and the gift or sale of sanctified offerings were lucrative perquisites.

52. Adhirājendra's inscriptional traces in Sri Lanka are amenable to similar explanation: the existence of these records likely depended less on shoring up support in the Coḻa-ruled north of the island as it did on the king's efforts to secure the loyalty of Tŏṇṭaiyar lords. Both records (SII 4: 1388 and 1392) detail donations made to support permanent lamps; only one (1388, ll. 10–12) contains fragmentary details of the donors, one of whom evidently comes from Tondaimandalam (the edition reads *coḻamaṇṭalattu tak..koṭṭattu vi<u>r</u>peṭṭunāṭṭu*), and another of whom bears the title [*jayaṅ*?]*kŏṇṭacoḻapallavaraiyan*. The donations appear to be cash, rather than in land: given the limitations of our knowledge about the Coḻa economic history other than land use and ownership, it is not possible to say what significance we can give to the repeated obtrusion of money-payments in these records. Was monetization on the rise in this period, outside of the elite circumstances of royal and imperial donation? Was the increased pervasion of the money-form in any way influential on the kinds of social transformations evident in the early appearances of the *cittirameḻi* assemblies, in Tāmaraippākkam and elsewhere? Studies of Coḻa monetary history are few: I know of nothing beyond the positivist numismatics of Biddulph, *Coins of the Cholas* (Varanasi: Numismatic Society of India, 1968) and Chattopadhyaya's insightful *Coins and Currency Systems in South India, c. A.D. 225–1300* (New Delhi: Munshiram Manoharlal Publishers, 1977), esp. pp. 51–62, 136–148.

53. As we saw earlier (see note 47), Vīrarājendra's royal orders extend to at least his eighth year, but there is scant evidence that lived on to the middle of 1071, which would have marked his ninth regnal year. SII 1:42, from the Shore Temple in Mamallapuram, is a short donation dated in the ninth year of (a) Vīrarājendracoḻa, but lacks a *varman* title, a *mĕykkīrtti*, or any other details associated with that king. See further (n. 54) on ARE 128 of 1912 from Tiruvo<u>rr</u>iyūr, detailing donations by his queen.

54. See Sethuraman, *Mathematics*, pp. 11–12, based on Adhirājendra's Siddhamalli inscription (the only one to furnish reliable chronological details: see n. 13) dated May 3, 1071. Sethuraman oddly presumes that Adhirājendra died nearly immediately after this record's issue (p. 92). All of the three records recording observances for the sake of the king's *tirumeṉi* (his "auspicious body") are in their several ways problematic. SITI 821 – from Mannargudi in Tirunelveli district, the sole Adhirājendra record from the Pāṇḍya country – was recorded by Mackenzie's pandits in an almost unintelligibly corrupt eye-copy; I quote Mahalingam's conjectural version (with my own further suggestion preceded by an asterisk): *ulakamuḻututaiyāloṭum vīṟṟirunaruḷiya māmutalmatikkulam viḷakkiya koccaṭaiyavaṉmarāṉa... maṉuvuṭaṉ vaḷartta śrī adhirājentirateva̱rku avar tirumeṉikku naṉṟāka *veṇṭum ... āṇṭu 3-vatu* "sitting in state with his queen, the mistress of the entire earth, bringing luster to the family whose august ancestor is the moon, the king, Caṭaiyavarman ... he who has made flourish Manu of great fame, Adhirājendra ... that what his auspicious body needs in order to be well again ... in his third year of rule ..." (N.B. that, as restored by Mahalingam, this is the sole piece of direct evidence – unnoticed by Sethuraman but supporting his conclusions – that identifies the Coḻa prince with Jaṭāvarman Coḻapāṇḍyadeva). An undated and now only partly visible inscription (128 of 1912) from Tiruvoṟṟiyūr records a donation by a queen of Vīrarājendra's. In his report (1913, pt 2, §32), Krishna Sastri described how from this record "we learn that 60 *veli*s of waste land in Siṃhaviṣṇu-chaturvedimaṅgalam were brought under cultivation and designated Vīrarājendraviḷāgam; while its income in paddy, gold and *kāśu* was allotted under various items of expense 'for the health of *Chakravartin* Vīrarājendradeva, for the increase of his race, for the prosperity of the marriage badge (*tirumaṅgalyam*) of the queen and for the glorious health of her children.'" This is indeed a close explanation of the record's text, which reads (ln. 3) *cakkiravartti śrīvirarājentratevar tirumeṉi kalliyāṉa tirumeṉiyākavum tirukkulam vattikkavum nampirāṭṭimār tirumaṅkalliyam perukavum piḷḷaikaḷ ti[ru]meṉi kalliyāṇatirumeṉiyākavum.* Sethuraman (*Mathematics*, p. 86) misunderstands the record when he writes

the queen of Vira Rajendra donated lands to the temple and prayed God, "for the safeguard of her 'Thirumangalyam' (marriage badge); for the recovery of her husband from disease; for the recovery of her son from some disease and for male issue for her son."

For the other record, the fragmentary 280 of 1917, I have at my disposal only its mention in the ARE report: from Kukūr near Kumbhakonam and dated to Adhirājendra year three, it "registers a gift of land by a certain individual who had daily to recite the Tiruppadiyam twice before Māmbaḷamuḍaiya-Mahādeva for (the recovery of the health of?) the king" (*Cf.* Heitzman, *Gifts*, pp. 145–46). The view that Adhirājendra was simply the victim of epidemiological bad luck is championed by

Sadasivapandarathar (*History of the Later Cholas*, vol. 1, pp. 269–272), on the basis of the record from Kukūr.

55. *Divyasūricarita* 18.86 describes the Coḷa king's post-*abhicāra* condition (*taddhatipradalitakaṇṭhanālarandhrāt niḥsīmoṣadhimanubhedadurnivārāt* | *uttasthau krimipaṭalaṃ yatas tadāsīt tasyāptaṃ krimigalanāma pāpalakṣma*; the verse concludes "as this was the case, his name 'Worm-throat', the mark of his evil, was apt"); the Tiruvārūr Śiva's declaration is found in 18.84 (*tyāgeśaḥ purajid upendrabhaktamukhyaḥ coleśānvayavasudhādhipatyamudrāṃ* | *adyādām iti* **kamalālaye* [em. Svamin; *kamaṭhālaye* Ed.] * *'śarīrāṃ* [em.; *'śarīraṃ* Svamin and IA] *vāgbherīṃ mukharayati sma gopurāgre* | |). The suggestion to link the Kṛmikaṇṭha narrative to Adhirājendra's brief reign was first made over a century ago by Bhattanatha Svamin in the pages of the *Indian Antiquary* ("The Cholas and the Chalukyas in the XIth Century," *IA* 41 (1912)). Judiciously discussed by Nilakanta Sastri (*The Coḷas*, pp. 295–297), this identification has continued to find defenders in popular para-scholarly forums (as a Google search will readily attest). Svamin's larger historical narrative is similar to the one argued for here: before the discovery of the index record for Adhirājendra's regnal dates, he conjectured the precariousness of Rājendracoḷa's early position, and suggests that Adhirājendra likely died (in a rebellion, he argues) sometime in 1074. Though not acknowledging Svamin, and favoring the view that Adhirājendra died of disease, Sadasivapandarathar reviews the Adhirājendra-as-Kṛmikaṇṭha account and finds it unsatisfying (*Later Cholas*, vol. 1, pp. 269–270). The Vaiṣṇava persecution narreme, though unconnected to either of the Coḻa kings ruling in 1070–72, itself possesses a historical referent in the removal of the "galling nuisance" of a Viṣṇu image from Cidambaram, a deed claimed explicitly by Kulottuṅga II (r. 1133–1150; on the account of this in the *Kulottuṅkacoḻavulā*, see Wentworth, *Yearning*, pp. 197ff.).

56. See his "New Approach," but cf. the critique found in Subrahmanyam, "Whispers and Shouts."

57. SII 8:701. For any study of the prosopography of Coḻa inscriptions, the absolutely indispensable resource is of course Karashima, Subbarayalu, and Matsui's *Concordance*. This research tool – produced at the dawn of academic computing, through enormous painstaking effort – certainly deserves to be reckoned one of the greatest scholarly monuments of Coḻa studies. It is limited, however, to a considerable sample of published records, and lacks toponymic identifiers that are a part of premodern Tamil name conventions. I am deeply grateful to Professor Subbarayalu for kindly sharing with me a provisional electronic version of the name database, greatly expediting my work of cross-checking.

58. In this group we may include 497 of 1920–21 (year three, from Papanasam, within the Kāveri delta), SII 7:498 (year three, from Kovilāṭi, again in the delta; beginning with the short *tiruvum pūmiyum mĕykkīrtti*), SII 3:67 (also year three, from Comaṅkalam, firmly in Tondaimandalam) and 193 of 1906 (year four, from Tirukovalūr also including the *tiruvum pūmiyum* introduction, characteristic of that region: see n. 60).

59. The *veḷḷāṭṭi* record was first published as SII 7:807 (refer, however, to the superior text given in PI 28); it is dated to Rājendracoḷa's year four. The rendering "maid-servant" follows the MTL and Vijayavenugopal's translation of the inscription (*Pondicherry Inscriptions* vol. 2, p. 15); the term might possibly instead mean "female Veḷḷāḷa" (see SII 17:518, 528 and Ali, "Service Retinues of the Chola Court: A Study of the Term *Veḷam* in Tamil Inscriptions," *BSOAS* 70, 3 (2007): p. 507n). The Tirupuvaṉai records mentioning the magnate-official are PI 113 and 114, both year three. The first of these fills out some of the details of his retinue with the mention of one Villavarājar and a V[ī]rarā[jendraco]ḻamūventaveḷār, equally generic titles. The actions of the *atikārikaḷ* here may be compared to the similar figure, *atikārikaḷ* Coḻamūventaveḷār, seen in a record from Kavantamangalam (SII 3:77, dated Thursday, November 7, 1073), where the official is responsible for oversight in a strictly local decision.
60. The Rājendracoḷa records, all beginning with *tiruvum pūmiyum*, are SII 7:877 (year two), 7:875 and 7:876 (both year four); compare these to the six earlier records from nearby Tirunamanallur (the ancient Nāvalūr) edited by Hultzsch in EI 7: 19. SII 7:884 records a similar transaction dated in Adhirājendra's third year; none of these records bear an exact day, so it is not possible to more precisely specify the chronological gap separating this record from 7:877. Every one of the named figures here, donors and beneficiaries alike, bear lordly titles; none, however, claim any official role.
61. SII 7:748: the date here is not given in the body text of the published inscription, though in a footnote the editor suggests that the date "may be read as *5-āvatu.*" This seems unlikely, given that the inscription gives the *tiruvum pūmiyum mĕykkīrtti* and is in Rājendracoḷa's name, though it wrongly gives his cognomen as Parakesarivarman.
62. SII 3:65.
63. SII 3:64.
64. ARE 138 of 1923, ln. 4; the mention of this record in the *Report* for 1923 (part 2, para. 33, p. 104) decrees in the absence of any evidence this titleholder to be "probably [Umainaṅkai's] husband." More information about the identity of either of these royal women is not forthcoming; while it is entirely likely that Rājendracoḷa had already wed his Coḻa cousin Ammaṅgai by this point, there is no way of knowing whether this records her action.
65. ARE 138 of 1923, ln. 8; the donor's full recorded name is Nakkan Cāṇanāna Cittirameḻikkon. While the name of the first donor is lost, both are characterized as *maṉṟāṭi cuṟṟi caṅka . . .*, *maṉṟāṭi* possibly referring to Śiva as Naṭarāja or to an ethonym of sheep-tending pastoralists. The grammar of the truncated phrase suggests the former ('the assembly [?] around Naṭarāja'), while the location of the grant in a Vaiṣṇava temple (called Vīraviṇṇakarāḻvār in the record) perhaps argues in favor of the latter. *Koṉ* is notoriously ambiguous: taken in the sense of a "member of the Iṭaiyār community" (MTL, s.v. *koṉāṉ*), this might lend supporting evidence to the interpretation of *maṉṟāṭi* as an ethnonym.
66. The text of the record is given in SITI no. 743; the record has no ARE number and is unnoticed in Mahalingam's *Topographical List*. In the SITI

version of the record, which was made from the manuscript eye-copies of Mackenzie's pandits, the issuers' names are given as Teṉkarai Rājātirājaṉ Rājaparamecuvara maṉṉaṉ, Pitiṉāṭṭu Iḷaṅkuḷattūr Matirāntaka uṭaiyār, and Kumāraṉ Pilipāṇa uṭaiyār; given the philological limitations of the SITI texts, these renderings should not be considered secure.

67. SII 24: 53, ll. 10ff.; *cf.* the editor Narasimhaswamy's comments, p. vii, who attributes this affray to the "political feud" between Rājendracoḷa and Adhirājendra; see also Sastri, *The Cōḻas*, p. 551; and Stein, *Peasant State*, p. 174. This record may be the earliest reference to conflicts between the two caste-blocs, which would later prove endemic down to colonial times (cf. Appadurai, "Right and Left Hand Castes" (*IESHR* 11 (1974)) and Stein *Peasant State*., p. 173ff.).
68. See Sastri, *The Cōḻas*, pp. 333–334, and see pp. 281ff. and 307ff.
69. For reviews of the testimony of *Vikkiramacoḻavulā*, vv. 68–90, refer to Sastri, *op. cit.*, pp. 347–348 and now to the definitive translation and study in Wentworth, *Yearning*, pp. 364–366, upon which I draw here. Of the fourteen named individuals, at least six hailed from Jayaṅkōṇṭacoḻamaṇḍalam, especially from the former magnate polities that it contained: Karuṇākaraṉ and Naralokavīraṉ (both mentioned already in connection with Kulottuṅga); Coḻakoṉ, "Lord of the Muṉaiyar" (thus from Tirumuṉaippāṭi, near Milāṭu); Vāṇaṉ (Sastri suggests this may be the Cuttamallaṉ Muṭikōṇṭāṉāṉa Vāṇakovaraiyar mentioned in ARE 229 of 1929; in any case, this is likely a man from Vāṇakoppāṭi, again near Milāṭu; this may be an underlord of Karuṇākaraṉ's mentioned in the *Kaliṅkattupparaṇi*); "the Kāṭava, lord of Ceñci" (Kāṭava[r] is a traditional synonym for the Pallavas; this is likely, as Sastri notes, the earliest reference to Gingee); and "the royal lord of Ceti" (if, as Sastri suggests (n. 40), this refers to a Cetirāyar, this is one of the Malaiyamans of Tirukkovalūr). A seventh figure, "the generous Nuḷampaṉ, who took Kollam and Koṭṭāṟu," is particularly interesting. Noḷambavāḍi is the part of southern Kannada country incorporated into the Coḻa territories as Nikarilicoḻamaṇḍalam (regarding which see further in this chapter); the conquests in which this figure participated link him with the martial career of Naralokavīra. Govindasamy (*Feudatories*, p. 286) suggests that this may be the same figure as one Rājendracoḻa Gaṅga Nuḷambaṉ Mulvāymaṇḍalikaṉ Nuḷambadevar, mentioned in a Chittoor record of Kulottuṅga's time (568 of 1906). This is possible (the Chittoor record actually concerns the man's son), but his connection with the campaigns to the southwest make it equally likely this is the *maṇṭalamutalikaḷ* Nuḷampātarāyar who authorized a royal order far to the south (in modern Tirumayyam taluk, Pudukottai, IPS no. 124, dated in Kulottuṅga's year 46, 1116).

As for the other figures in this remarkable poetic attestation of the state of play in Vikrama's court society, while a few figures seem to be from the delta, such as Kaṇṇaṉ, "the holy brahman from walled Kañcai," which Wentworth identifies with Kañcāṟu, near Mayiladuturai, or the Anantapālaṉ that Sastri would identify with the figure of the same epithet mentioned in ARE 71 of 1926, the remainder are either unlocatable or are situated by the poet in an increasingly implausible radiatory spatial network. Thus the king of Venāṭu (modern Travancore) gives way to "the lord of Vatsa" (*vattavaṉ*) and "the Trigarta" (*tikkataṉ*), through to such figments of Kūttaṉ's classical literary education as the lords of Kosala, Mālava, and Māgadha. However, all of these would later supply the names of post-Coḻa magnate polities, and Kūttaṉ may be adopting them before their appearance in the epigraphical record.

70. The Vīrarājendra record is EC 10, Cintāmaṇi taluq no 161, dated to his sixth year or 1069; instead of a *mĕykkīrtti* it is prefaced by a characteristically Deccani *birudāvali* (including a reference to the Coḻa king as *poḷakulatilaka*, "pinnacle of the Hoysaḷa family"). Prior to that time, the most recent Coḻa record was that of Rājendradeva (Mb 107, 1057), one of only two inscriptions of that king in the region.
71. I draw here on Gururaja Rao, "The Kolāramma Temple and the Cōḷas" (*Tamil Civilization* 3, 2–3 (1985): pp. 101–106) and the political-geographic discussion in Adiga, *Making of Southern Karnataka* (Chennai: Orient Longman, 2006), pp. 7–10; Adiga classes Kolar within the residual hills of "the southern Maidan", pp. 75ff., 100–115. Greater detail can be gleaned from the district's *Gazetteer* (Bangalore: Government Press, 1968), esp. pp. 9–26 (physical landscape and natural history), 42–47 (medieval history) and 82ff. and 541ff. (description of the Kolāramma temple and modern Kolar town).
72. In certain cases, as in some of the Rājendracoḷa's records referred to here, this alternates with Vijayarājendracoḻamaṇḍalam.
73. On the limited applicability of the Tamil country's system of *nāṭu*s in southern Karnataka, see Adiga *Making*, pp. 10–21.
74. EC 10 Mulbagal taluk no. 49(a), from the Bharateśvara temple, Avani, and *ibid.* no. 119, on a rock "in the field of Maḍivāḷa." The discussions of these records include Sastri, *The Coḷas*, pp. 538–539; Stein, *Peasant State*, pp. 125–131, 192–196; Karashima, *Ancient to Medieval*, pp. 121, 133; and Subbarayalu, *South India under the Cholas*, pp. 132–133. All of these interpretations rely on the unsatisfactory texts printed by Rice and on the frequently obtuse translations provided by R. Narasimhachar. The transliteration scheme employed for this (as for other Tamil records that Rice collected) is idiosyncratic and "Kannada-izing"; even worse is the back-transcription into the Tamil script, which is essentially worthless. Of the earlier interpreters of these records, only Subbarayalu (p. 137, n. 34) makes any reference to the limitations of the EC editions; G. Vijayavenugopal is currently re-editing the Avani record along with the other Tamil-language inscriptions of modern Karnataka (the text of Uttanur record is no longer accessible); until the appearance of this new edition, all readings from this significant corpus should be considered provisional.
75. *tecam ĕllām tirumeḻi kūṭi*; better sense might he had from the emendation *tirumeḻi[k]kuṭi* "the families of the sacred plow"; this seems to be tacitly adopted by Karashima (*Ancient to Medieval*, p. 121: "All the agriculturalists (*mēḻi kudi*) of the country").
76. *kāṇi* does not yield any sense in its usual meaning ("possession, property"); the emendation *kāṭṭa* ("having been imposed") gives meaning, but is awkward in its syntax: read as an absolute phrase, it is oddly interposed between

the subject and predicate *aḻakiyacoḻa°...ēṉṟum*. G. Vijayavenugopal (in a personal communication dated March 19, 2013) plausibly suggests that this might be a case of metathesis, for **kāṇi iṟai* ("property tax"), thus perhaps giving the truncated meaning, "this property text [being] spurious ..."

77. The text is tentative reconstruction, based on EC 10 Mu 49(a) [=A] and Mu 119 [=U], with some emendations and restoration to Tamil orthography: *śrīrājentiracoḻatevar tiruvaruḷiṉāl* [U; A *tiruvaruḷi...*] *tecam ēllām tirumeḻi kūṭi vantu nir[*a]nta* [AU *nirnta*] *coḻamaṇṭalam eḻupatteṭṭu nāṭum jayaṅkŏṇṭacoḻamaṇṭalam nāṟpatteṉṉāyiram pūmiyum pĕrumpaṭai valaṅkai* [A; U omits *passim*] *mahācĕṉaiyum* [corr; A *mahāce...*; U *mahā...*] *...tarkku nir [a]nta śrīrājentiracoḻappatiṉeṉpūmi-pĕriyaviṣayamum pĕrumpaṭai mahācĕṉaiyum* [U; A *-pĕriyaviṣayaṅ*] *kaṇṭa matam* [.]

    coḻakala tirukulan toṉṟiṟṟu mutal pacuvukkum ĕrumaivukkum iṟaiy illai [A; U lacunose] *ippatiṉeṉpūmiyil illātav iṟai kaṭṭattu* [...AU both lacunose here] *atikārikaḷ aḻakiyacoḻamūventaveḷār* [U; A *...kiyacoḻa-*] *pacuvukkum ĕrumaivukkum illātav iṟai kāṇi* [A *sic leg;* U omits] *ivviṟai iṟukka vĕṇṭām ĕṉṟum*

78. *ippaṭikkup patiṉeṉpūmi pĕriyaviṣaiyamum pĕrumpaṭai* [U; A *patiṉeṭṭu viṣaiyamum pĕrumpaṭai*] *valaṅkai mahācĕṉaiyum* [emend; A *valaṅkai mahā...ṉaiyum;* U *mahā...ṉaiyum*] *kaṇṭa matam* [U; A *pataṅ kaṇṭum*] [.] *akappaṭu* [A; U omits] *kalvĕṭṭi cācaṉañ cĕytom. pattiṉeṉpūmippĕriyaviṣaiyamum* [U; A *-pĕriya...perukki ūrum*] *pĕrumpaṭai mahācĕṉaiyum evviṟai [*a]ḻittu ... iṟai... iṟuppāṉum gaṅgaikaraiyil* [A; U lacunose] *gobrāhmaṇaraiyum niraiyum* [U; A *naraiyām*] *kurāluṅ govāraṇavāciyum aḻittavantu mahāpātakar āvar* [U; A *aḻittāṉ brahmavattiyum paṭuvatākavum*] *pĕriyaviṣaiyattukkum pĕrumpaṭai* [A ends] *mahācĕṉaikkum [a?]varkup pakaivarāvar ākavum inta cilālekaip pa... niṟuttiṉār śāśvan me...ntumatapalam pĕṟuvar ākavum* [.] *ippaṭi cilālekai cĕytom patiṉeṉpūmiviṣaiya... pĕrumpaṭaimahācĕṉaiyum*

79. The phrases are Stein's, *Peasant State*, pp. 125, 127, which I cautiously adopt here.

80. Alongside the anomaly of the label *valaṅkai* being present in only one of the two copies of this order, the name of this warrior group appears to have been defaced in both of the records: only the closing sentence of the Uttanur text seems to record it undamaged. *Cf.* Stein, who argues rather too neatly that "shortly after the A.D. 1072 inscription [from Avani] was engraved, it was defaced" (*Peasant State*, p. 194, citing the opinion of Rice in his footnote to the translation of no. 119, which Stein seems to have misunderstood).

81. On the differing historical semantics of *nāḍu* and *viṣayam* in medieval Kannada sources, see again Adiga, *Making*, pp. 10–21. The long-term interrelationship between the *[cittirameḻi-] pĕriyanāṭu* and the Ayyāvoḷe organization is discussed in Krishnan, "Agricultural Guild," pp. 101–103 and Abraham, *Two Medieval Merchant Guilds*, pp. 82–86; on p. 77 she notes "In many inscriptions of merchants in Kannada and in Tamil areas, the number eighteen is frequently attached to the terminology used to describe merchant groups. The *padineṉ-bhūmi* so frequently referred to could have been the name of a merchant group or a semi-mythical eighteen districts on either side

of the Kaveri." On this latter set of eighteen (which is, of course, an auspiciously round number throughout South Asia), *cf.* Stein, *Peasant State*, pp. 285–286.

82. The common text to be eked out between these two exempla is ambiguous in its construction: I construe *śrīrājentiracoḻatevar tiruvaruḷiṉāl* grammatically with the immediately following *tecam ĕllām tirumeḻi kūṭi vantu niranta*, and take that this refers to Parakesarivarman Rājendra. Rice and Narasimhachar's translation here is cautious: "by the grace of śrī-Rājendra-Śoḻa-devar, the ? farmers of the whole country came and settled." The minatory presence of the question mark in this translation has not stopped others from tacitly adopting it: Stein (*Peasant State*, p. 125), though eliding this troubling passage from his quotation, nevertheless unhesitatingly takes this as historical evidence of "the conquest during Rajendra's time" of the region.
83. Sastri, *The Cōḷas*, p. 539, taken up and discussed in Stein, *Peasant State*, pp. 193ff. Stein presumes that the *mūventaveḷar* was himself "most likely . . . a leader of the conquering Tondaimandalam *valangai* forces claiming to exercise the superior prerogatives of a chief." This is exceedingly unlikely, given the disconnect between the gentry *mūventaveḷar* figures and the martial leadership of the *senāpati*s and *daṇḍanāyaka*s. Caution about this line of interpretation has already been expressed by Subbarayalu, *South India under the Choḷas*, pp. 133, 137.
84. Given the evident connections between these records and those from Tāmaraippākkam, the official's role here can be compared to that of the Rājarājapiṭārar mentioned in TK 1 (see note 37). The likelihood of Aḻakiyacoḻaṉ being a valued member of Rājendracoḷa's court society is increased if he is the same man as the Paṭaiyamuḻāṉ Perumān Kuppai āṉa Aḻakiyacoḻan Vecālippāṭi Mūventaveḷān involved in a lamp donation in Kulottuṅga, year forty-four, 1114 (SII 17:149), part of a cluster of similar donations involving titled officials in the Naṭanapādeśvara temple in Cuddalore taluk.
85. All references to the Kolaramma records are drawn from EC 10, Kolar taluk (hereafter Kl): Kl 111 details the land transfers in year sixteen (1027); Kl 112a includes transfers from year eleven (1022) seemingly back-dated to year seven (1018). Both of these are royal orders with the complex lists of officials typical of such documents. The reconstructions described in Kl 109a were overseen by the *seṉāpati* Mārayan Arumoḻi, alias Uttamacoḻabrahmamārayaṉ, a member of the Narākkaṉ line of Brahman officials from Amaṇkuṭi (now Ammangudi, Tanjavur district; the same man's brother is also one of the officials mentioned in Kl 111: on this family, see Subbarayalu, *South India under the Cholas*, pp. 53–57, 232). The record is rounded off by the donations of perpetual lamps by two Brahmans, one from Tondaimandalam, the other from the coastal delta, near Nagappattinam.
86. Kl. 25 and 26, both fragmentary; Kl. 24 (not reproduced by Rice) is a Kannada transcription of Kl. 25. Kl 26 bears the date *varmanāna uṭaiyār śrīrājendracoḻatevarkku yāṇṭu āṟāvatu*, and Rice accordingly dates this to 1017. This could, however, possibly be attributed to Rājendracoḷa (in 1076–1077, though in Kl 91, regnal year seven, he is called Kulottuṅga) or

indeed to Rājendradeva (which would be in 1058–1059), though the latter's limited epigraphic profile in Kolar makes this unlikely. Kl 25 refers to an individual as *iṟai taṇṭukiṟa koyiṟṟamaṉ*, "he of the king's house, collecting taxes" and, seemingly, by another name given in the irremediably corrupt transcription **alginaṟal yiṟṟaman*; this person is tasked with collecting fines from individuals and from *kāmuṇṭaṉ*s (Ka. *gāvuṇḍa*) of the *ūr* and the *nāṭu* in the event of the livestock's nondelivery. The *soi-disant Kaivvāranāṭṭunāṭṭom* ("we, the assembly of Kaivāra *nāṭu*") institutes the weekly animal offering in Kl 26, again charging the local leader (*nāṭṭukkāmuṇṭucĕyvāṉ*) with its observance: see Adiga, *The Making of Southern Karnataka*, p. 19. Rice and Narasimhachar render *innāṭṭuk kuṟaṭṭiyar* as "the guardian deity of this *nāṭu*," though on what authority I am uncertain. Correcting the reading to *kuṟatti*- would seem warranted: while in Tamil, this is strictly an ethnonym (thus the MTL: "woman of the hilly tract, woman of the *kuṟava* tribe"); Malayalam preserves the meaning "a mask representing Bhadrakāḷi" (*Malayalam Lexicon*, vol. 4, p. 310); I am grateful to Rich Freeman for bringing this to my attention. Notably, judging from its name, the village inhabited by this nonvegetarian goddess is a *brahmadeya*.

87. The single record is spread over two entries in EC vol. 10: Kl 108 (containing the *tirumaṉṉi mĕykkīrtti*) and 106d. The paired phrases *māṭāpattiyañ cĕykiṉṟa* and *patipātamūlappaṭṭuṭai*, respectively, characterizing the *paṇḍitar* and the *pañcācāriyattevakaṉmikaḷ* ("the temple priests affiliated with the five teachers") were not translated by Rice and Narasimhachar: these are, respectively, 'head of a *maṭha*' (thus TKC, from Skt. *māṭhādhipatya*?) and "those possessed of a place at the base of the Lord's feet" (*cf.* TKC, s.v. *patipātamūlattār*). The phrase *patipātamūlappaṭṭuṭai pañcācāriyattevakaṉmikaḷ* reoccurs in a later inscription (Mu. 54) from the Rāmeśvara temple in Āvani, dated to Kulottuṅga's thirty-third year or 1103–1104; some of its occurrences in records from the Tamil country proper are collected by Hultzsch in SII 3, p. 138 n. 12 and *ibid.*, p. 158.

88. Sanderson noticed the relationship between temple and *tantra* in passing in an article ("Atharvavedins in Tantric Territory," pp. 277–278 with nn.); his longer demonstration of this relationship is as yet unpublished. As he notes, the "southern" *Brahmayāmala* is attested in two manuscripts, which in fact transmit completely different texts: one is held in the Trivandrum University Library (no. 1982) and the other is in the collection of the IFP, Pondicherry (T.522; cited as "P" in further occurrences, both by page number in the ms. and by *paṭala* and verse); I only have access to the latter, much longer and more detailed text. On the "northern" *Brahmayāmala*, refer to Hatley's admirable doctoral dissertation ("*Brahmayāmalatantra* and the Early Cult of Śaiva *yoginī*s"). While the text transmitted in P does not contain a detailed description of its *mantra*-system, it does evince familiarity with the northern *Brahmayāmala*: it includes repeated reference to the *navākṣara* formula that is the latter's principal *mantra* (P, pp. 8 [4.6a, 7b], 15 [6.13d], 28 [7.106b], 65 [17.11d, 12a] etc., etc.), and even employs the latter's technical term *smaraṇam* to describe its seed-syllable HŪM (P, pp. 21 [7.38b], 27 [7.103b, 110a], 47 [12.28a, where it is correctly identified, correcting ms.'s unmetrical

hūṃ iti smaran śrutvā to *hūṃ iti smaraṇaṃ kṛtvā*]). On the *smaraṇam* in the northern text, see Hatley, pp. 255ff.; and Sanderson, "History through Textual Criticism," pp. 44ff.

89. *Cf.* the following passages from P (p. 2; *cf.* Sanderson "Atharvavedins," p. 278, n. 143): *bhadrakālī tu cāmuṇḍī sadā vijayavarddhinī* || (1.16cd) ... *tasyās sarvaprayatnena* **caturmūrtiṃ* [em. Sanderson; *caturmūrtiḥ* ms.] *prapūjayet* | **deśaśāntikaraṃś* (em. Sanderson; *daśa-* ms.) *caiva nṛpāṇāṃ vijayaṃ bhavet* || *sarvapāpaharaṃ śāntaṃ sadā vijayasaṃbhavam* | (1.18–19ab), "Bhadrakālī [that is,] Cāmuṇḍī always guarantees victory...One should make every effort to worship her four forms [black, white, red, and yellow, according to 1.14–16ab], and it will bring peace to the country, and victory to kings" (p. 75); *mātṛśāntividhiṃ vakṣye sarvaśāntikaraṃ śubham* | *sarvavyādhiharaṃ śubhraṃ sadā vijayavardhanam* || *akālamṛtyuśamanaṃ putrapautrādivardhanam* | *mahāvighnapraśamanaṃ mahāśāntikaraṃ param* || (18.1–2), "I shall now teach the ordinance for the pacification of the Mothers, a pure [rite] which puts all things at peace, which removes disease, guarantees constant victory, puts to rest untimely death, gives increase to one's sons and grandsons, ends great obstacles, and puts all things at peace to the utmost." Among the several passages on this theme in the Trivandrum text adduced by Sanderson (*op cit., ibid.*, with his emendations), see for instance 3.172: *yaś caināṃ saṃpratiṣṭhāpya* **kārayen* (em; *kārayan* ms.) *nityam arcanam* | *sa nṛpaḥ sarvabhaumatvaṃ prāpnuyād iti* **niścayaḥ* (corr.; *niścayam* ms.) ||, "There is no doubt that king who establishes her and arranges for her worship in perpetuity shall attain universal imperium."

90. The *Brahmayāmala*'s *Kujavārabalipaṭala* ("chapter on the Tuesday worship") begins with a encomiastic description of its benefits (p. 100, 22.1–4): *athātas sampravakṣyāmi kujavārabaliṃ śṛṇu* | *sarvapāpaharaṃ rājñe sarvasampatpravardhanam* || *brāhmaṇānām hitañ caiva mahāmārīvināsanam* |**rājarāṣṭrajayañ* (corr.; *rājārāṣṭra-* ms.) *caiva putrapautravivardhanam* || *mṛtajvaravināśañ ca* **bhūtadṛṣṭivināśanam (em.* [*cf.* P p. 64, 17.3d]; *bhūtaduṣṭa-* ms.) | *mahāśāntikarañ caiva mahāvṛṣṭivivardhanam* || *rājasenāsukhārthañ ca hastyaśvanaravardhanam* | **taskarānnābhayaṃ (em.; taskarānnabhayañ* ms.) *caiva mātṝṇāṃ prītivardhanam* ||, "Listen: I will now teach the Tuesday offering, which removes all sins from the king, and increases all of his accomplishments, which benefits Brahmans and destroys pestilence, which brings victory to the king and to country and which gives increase to one's sons and grandsons, destroys death and fever, destroys the evil eye, puts all things at peace, and guarantees abundant rain. It puts the king's army at ease, giving increase to its elephants, horses, and men; gives security from brigands and [shortages of] food, and it makes the Mothers happy." The chapter then describes the apportionment of responsibilities for the goat-offering, with an officiant (*deśikaḥ, deśikottamaḥ*) responsible for invoking the goddess in her solitary form in a decorated pot with the principal nine-syllable *mantra* of the *Brahmayāmala* system (p. 100 [=22.8] *ekavīrīṃ nyaset kumbhe mūlamantreṇa deśikaḥ*), who then displays Śaiva emblems to a low-caste priest and has him dispatch the animal with a razor (p. 101 [=22. 17–18]: *śūlaṃ dhvajañ ca paraśuṃ* †*cānnaliṅgaṃ kriyākaram*† | *kapālaṃ ḍamaruñ caiva*

ratna†vyāgh†ādikan tathā | *etāṃś ca tān samuddhṛtya dīkṣite paraśaivake* | *kṣurikāhastasaṃyuktaṃ baliñ caiva hi kārayet* | "The trident, the flag, the axe, † and the *liṅga* made of cooked rice, the reservoir of all actions [?] † the skull-bowl, rattle-drum, the jewel . . . and others: he should show all of these before an initiate *paraśaiva* and then have him, razor in hand, perform the offering"). On the *paraśaiva* – a pious transformation of the caste-title *paraśava* – see Sanderson, "Atharvavedins," p. 277, n. 142.

91. These figures are drawn from Kl 108, where they are also broken down on a per diem basis. In addition to the office of *māṭāpattiyam* ascribed to the *kannāṭapaṇḍitar* – which is reminiscent of Kālamukha institutional figures from elsewhere in the Kannada world – the suffix *-paṇḍita*, while hardly decisive, is suggestive of connections with the order. *Cf.* for instance the very similar *kāśmīrapaṇḍita* (SII 15: 32 [1147]: see Lorenzen, *Kāpālikas and Kālāmukhas: Two Lost Śaiva Sects* (Delhi: Motilal Banarsidass, 1991), pp. 108, 140–141), the famous Caturānanapaṇḍita who gave his title to a line of Śaiva abbots in Tiruvoṟṟiyūr (EI 27: 47 with Raghavan's valuable introduction, pp. 292–301), or the list of figures officiating at the Tripurāntaka temple in Balligave: Vareśvarapaṇḍita, Caturānanapaṇḍita [a different man from the above], Kriyāśaktipaṇḍita, and Jñānaśaktipaṇḍita (see Lorenzen, pp. 138–140, citing EC 7 Sk. 99, 106, 118, 119, 123, and 292).

Māraciṅkabhaṭṭaṉ is likely the same person as the Āḷan Māraciṅganāna Rājaparākramabrahmamārayan mentioned in a donation made to the same temple eighteen years earlier (Kl 107, 1054). Rice, without apparent reason, claims that this latter man was of the Kauśika *gotra*, as was the man listed before him in the record, Śaṅkaran Tiyampakan. The Māraciṅkaṉ in the present record is expressly said to belong to the Gautama *gotra*.

92. The *vyākaraṇamum yāmalamum vakkāṉippāṉ*, like the *karaṇaṉ* and the *taccaṉ* received thirty *kalam* of paddy and one *kācu* per annum. The P text of the *Brahmayāmalam*, amidst its generally stiff and not infrequently barbaric Sanskrit, contains some evidence that its author/compiler was a Tamil speaker, whose native language occasionally left accidental traces on his composition. Among the features, in addition to those that are possibly the result of transmission by Tamil-speaking scribes (e.g. epenthetic *ya-śruti*s [as in 6.25d: *tasmād yetāni varjayet*] or hypercorrections [e.g. 5.12cd *tadarthaṃ kaṇṭavistāraṃ tadarthaṃ bilam ucyate*, in both cases for correct *tadardhaṃ*]) see e.g. 6.5ab *āgneyayamayor madhye pitarasthānam uttamam*, "the best shrine to the **ancestors** is located in the south-southeast" [thematization of Skt. *pitṛ* to *pitara*, *cf.* MTL *pitarar*] 6.27a, *nallamallasamākīrṇaṃ*, "[the village for picked for a temple-site should be] filled with **good** wrestlers" [*nalla-*, *cf.* Tamil *naṉmai*, adj. stem *nalla-*, "fine, good"] and 7:23cd: *śikhāyān tu śikhāṃ nyasya kavacaṃ tanamastake*, "placing the crest [*-mantra*] on the [goddess'] crest, [place] the armor [*-mantra*] on **her** head," understanding *tana-* to be a thematization influenced by the Tamil reflexive pronominal base *taṉ*; the correct form and *sandhi* (**tanmastakam*) would break the meter.

93. There is another, more tangible benefit to Rājendracoḷa's interest in Kolar. Though its industrial exploitation dates to the nineteenth century, the region's reserves of gold were known in premodern times. It is thus likely

not a coincidence that Kulottuṅga was the last Coḻa dynast to issue gold coinage, though the coins struck in his name are only extant with high regnal years, closely reproduced the fabric of Veṅgī Cālukya coins rather than earlier Coḻa types, and were possibly meant only to circulate in the Cālukya territories to the northeast (see Balakrishnan Nayar, *Dowlaishweram Hoard* (Chennai: The Commissioner of Museums, 2002) and the illuminating discussion in Chattopadhyaya, *Coins and Currency Systems*, pp. 57–60). Note that the Kolaramma inscriptions are atypically centered on the conversion of land revenue into gold *māṭai*s, perhaps indicative of a higher degree of monetization in the region; the use of gold as a transactional medium seems generally to have been more advanced in the Deccan than in the Tamil country.

94. The record is EI 9: 23, edited with an introduction by Hira Lal ("Rajapura Copper Plates of Madhurāntakadeva," introduction, pp. 174–179). Despite the record's barbarous Sanskrit, its elaborate dating formula was confirmed by Kielhorn (p. 176), save for a mistake in the record's name for the Jovian year. While some of Lal's argumentation seems questionable, his connection between the *meḍipota* who are the donees of the grant and the so-called meriah (variant spellings include *melliah, maliah*) cult suppressed by the colonial state in the 1850s seems sound. Note also the strikingly Coḻa regnal name borne by the local king who, along with members of his family and other notables, was responsible for the donation.

95. The *tantra*'s seventh *paṭala*, detailing the initial installation (*pratiṣṭhā*) of the goddess, supplies a prototype for the nine-pot liturgy (P, pp. 18–19, 7.13–18): *kalaśān vinyaset tatra sarvagandhāni tāni tu* | *caturdikṣu nyaset kumbhān pūrvādikramayogataḥ* || [x x x] *vā śāli yavās tilān koṇeṣu vinyaset* | *pañcaratnena* **saṃyuktān* (em; *saṃyuktā* ms.) *navākṣareṇa mantravit* || *madhye tu vinyaset* **kumbhe vīreśīṃ* (em.; *kumbhaṃ vīreśī-* ms.) †**tantra* (em. *tantram* ms.) *ucyate*† | *raktākṣī[ṃ] vinyaset* **pūrve* (em; *pūrvaṃ* P) *karālīṃ dakṣiṇe nyaset* || *caṇḍākṣī[ṃ] paścime nyasya mahocchiṣṭhottare nyaset* | *ambikā caṇḍikā caiva ghorā ghoreśvarī tathā* || *koṇeṣu* **kalaśān* (em.; *kalaśā* ms.) *nyasya śāstradṛṣṭena karmaṇā* | *svasvenaiva tu bījena navākṣarayutena ca* || *kalaśaṃ vinyased vidvān śūlamudrāṃ pradarśayet* | *gandhapuṣpādibhiś caiva vastrayugmena veṣṭayet* ||

The officiant should arrange the [nine] pots and [should place] all sorts of fragrant substances [with]in [them]. He should place pots in the cardinal directions, beginning with the east and proceeding from there. He should place . . . or rice or millet seeds in the [pots in the] intermediate directions. All of these the mantra-knower should [have?] filled with the Five Jewels, accompanied by the Nine-syllable formula. Now, in the central pot he should install Vīreśī, the heroic Goddess † as is taught in the tantra [?] † He should install Raktākṣī in the east, Karālī in the south, Caṇḍākṣī in the west and Mahocchiṣṭhā in the north. Establishing with actions taught in the śāstra Ambikā, Caṇḍikā, Ghorā, and Ghoreśvarī in the pots in the intermediate directions, the learned one should establish each pot through the seed-syllable particular to it, as joined to the Nine-syllable formula; he should display the Trident hand-signal. Along with perfumes and flowers, he should wrap [the central pot] with a pair of cloths.

The *pañcaratna* or Five Jewels is likely a reference to the set of transgressive substances (urine, feces, semen, menstrual blood, and phlegm) used sacramentally in certain Tantric circles (see Sanderson, "Opening Verses," n. 63, pp. 110–112 for references). The *navākṣara* or Nine Syllable formula is the core mantra of the original *Brahmayāmala*: HŪM CAṆḌAKAPĀLINI SVĀHĀ refer to Hatley's discussion, "*Brahmayāmalatantra*," pp. 251–258. While I have retained some of the peculiarities of the text's language (presuming them to be authorial, rather than transmissional, errors), the cruxed **tantra ucyate* (for P's *tantram ucyate*) calls for comment: it may be a telegraphed expression (I have translated it as if it were something similar to the clichéd *yathāśāstram*, *cf.* *śāstradṛṣṭena karmaṇā* in 17b) or it may conceal a deeper corruption. The passage continues to detail the mantric construction of a sculpted image (*pratimā*) of the goddess in her solitary form (*ekavīrī*) through the instantiation of the other six Mothers along with Vināyaka and Vīrabhadra (pp. 19–20, 7.21–31), before turning to a description of the qualified officiant (pp. 21–22, 7.42–51) who should oversee the *homa*-fire sacrifice to the installed goddess. Ectypic variations of this basic ritual can be seen in e.g., P, pp. 67–68 (17.31cd-35, "*Dundhubhipraharaṇapaṭala*") and 101 (22.6-9, "*Kujavārabalipaṭala*," cf. n. 90).

96. In arguing for the political agency exercised by the goddess, I take my inspiration from Dipesh Chakrabarty's ambition to "pluraliz[e] the history of power" in the postcolonial study of the Indian past (*Provincializing Europe*, p. 14). Chakrabarty is eloquent in his critique of the "assumption running through modern European political thought and the social sciences ... that humans are ontologically singular, that gods and spirits are in the end 'social facts,' that the social somehow exists prior to them." He goes on to throw down the methodological gauntlet:

> I take gods and spirits to be existentially coeval with the human, and think from the assumption that the question of being human involves the question of being with gods and spirits. (*Ibid.*, p. 16; *cf.* also pp. 104–106)

This jibes with the position of another Indianist, Ronald Inden. It is in the course of his systematic account, extending Collingwood, of complex agency that Inden argues there to be

> some agents, to wit, the gods Vishnu and Siva ... whom some might wish to dismiss as agents. I am going to assume, however, that such agents, whose very existence may be contested, may in a sense be real. The persons and institutions of a community may indeed attribute a great deal of or even a determining power to a god or gods, ancestors, ghosts, to the state, to reason, to law, to the market, to society, to the party, to the crown, to the people. We may take such agents to be real to the extent *that complexes of discursive and nondiscursive practices constitute and perpetuate them*, even if some would deny their reality. (*Imagining India*, p. 27, my emphasis; *cf.* also pp. 235–239)

Perhaps the most powerful, if idiosyncratic, effort in this direction comes from outside South Asian studies, in the "symmetrical anthropology" practiced by Bruno Latour in *On the Modern Cult of Factish Gods* (Durham: Duke

University Press, 2010), esp. pp. 1–66. Similar in its intent to Latour, but directly concerned with the political agency of the nonhuman and the inanimate, is Jane Bennett's *Vibrant Matter: A Political Ecology of Things* (Durham: Duke University Press, 2010).

97. The record is the unpublished 68 of 1921, dated to the 329th day of the king's fourth regnal year, or approximately May 8, 1074.
98. The Tirukaccālai transcript reads *kamalāmakaḷ*; subsequent versions (and so the text published by Cuppiramaṇiyam, *Mĕykkīrttikaḷ*, no. 21) read the synonymous *malarmakaḷ*. There is perhaps one earlier occurrence of this *mĕykkīrtti*, in a record now built into the floor of the Brahmapurīśvara temple at Kokkarayanpet in Salem district. This record (468 of 1913) is cited by Sastri (*The Cōḷas*, p. 334, n. 6) as an attestation of the eulogy in the fourth year; it records the donations to support food offering made by one Kaṅkaikoṇṭāṉ Ammaiyappaṉ, alias Mādhavarāja, for the bodily health (*tirumeṉi*) of Kulottuṅga, whom it styles as "emperor" (*cakkiravartti*, N.B. not *tiripuvaṉacakkiravarttikaḷ*); its draft of the *mĕykkīrtti* contains extra lines not found in 68 of 1921, but attested in later examples. This incomplete record lacks an exact date and is found in an upland locale otherwise isolated from the machinery of Coḻa power (it is the *only* medieval inscription in this temple, according to Mahalingam, *Topographical List*, vol. 6, p. 442). Given all of these oddities, it seems best to bracket this record as a fascinating anomaly.
99. In the second invocatory verse to the *Kaliṅkattupparaṇi: nilamakaḷai*. . .*urimaiyiṉiṟ kaipiṭittav upayakulottamaṉ aṉapayaṉ vāḻkav ĕṉṟe*, "We say 'hail!' to Anapayaṉ, supreme in both his families, who took the earth-goddess by the hand, as was his right."
100. A possible exception here, though only an inchoate one, is the invocation in the third and latest of the Tāmaraippākkam inscriptions of its authorizing assembly's right to *nāṭṭāṇmai*, the "governance" of their territory (see n. 38). This single instance, however, is an insufficient warrant to inferring a wider language of politics at work outside the epigraphical record.
101. See Cox, "Law, Literature and the Problem of Politics," esp. pp. 172–74.

Chapter 3

1. Fleet, "The Eastern Cālukya Chronology," pp. 277, 281, was the first to argue that Kulottuṅga "acquired the Chôḷa crown by hostile invasion and conquest" and to link this with the evidence already introduced by Bühler in the introduction to his edition of the *Vikramāṅkadevacarita* (see further, n. 28).
2. The first place all of these works were brought together was Fleet's 1891 account of Veṅgī Cālukya dynastic history in the pages of the *Indian Antiquary* ("Eastern Cālukya Chronology," *IA* 20 (1891), esp. pp. 276–285); he did not have access to the full Tamil text of the *Kaliṅkattupparaṇi* and instead relied on Pillai's extracts from it, earlier published in the same journal (see n. 101). Bühler's introduction to his *editio princeps* of Bilhaṇa's poem (published 1875) is the earliest attempt to colligate the literary evidence with the testimony of epigraphy; this was in turn synthesized in Hultzsch's

introduction to Kulottuṅga's inscriptions in the third volume of *South Indian Inscriptions* (pp. 125–131).

3. On the "worldly," see Said, *The World, The Text and the Critic* (Cambridge: Harvard University Press, 1983), pp. 35ff., and especially p. 39: "texts [are] objects whose interpretation – by virtue of the exactness of their situation in the world – *has already commenced* and are objects already constrained by, and constraining their interpretation" (emphasis Said's).

4. Since Georg Bühler's pioneering edition of 1875, furnished with a lengthy introduction, the poem has been the subject of repeated, if unresolved, debates. For Bühler, Bilhaṇa's work was peculiarly valuable as one of the few survivals of what he correctly identified as a once-flourishing genre of biographical and eulogistic writing, the transmission of which suffered owing to its supposedly limited interest to a far-flung Sanskrit readership. While Bilhaṇa's poem was certainly read, studied, and imitated for centuries after its initial dissemination, its remarkably shallow transmission goes some way to support this hypothesis: only a single complete manuscript of the poem seems to survive, despite the fact that it was once evidently read from Kashmir to Kanyakumari.

   Bühler was clear as to its limited value as a source for history: "the importance of Charitas like ... the Vikramāṅkacarita lies chiefly in that, however much a vitiated taste and a false conception of the duties of a historiographer Royal may lead their authors astray, the main facts which they relate, may be accepted as historical" (Introduction, p. 3). This limited value arose, again according to Bühler, from the poet's adherence to the genre conventions of the *mahākāvya* and its restricted and stylized narrative register: Bilhaṇa "never makes exact statements" as to the length of time passing between the episodes he narrates, while his "heroes are painted all white and the enemies all black. Āhavamalla and Vikrama have no more individuality than Rāma, Dushyanta, or Purūravas. They are simply perfection and their enemies are entirely contemptible and wicked" (p. 4).

   There is much here that is unarguable: Bilhaṇa's reckoning of time is highly conventionalized, and his adherence to the descriptive set pieces laid down for the *mahākāvya* leads him to include a great many extended passages of apparently nonnarrative poetic description. The only real limitation to the editor's interpretation is his readiness to take Bilhaṇa's eulogistic depiction of his patron at face value: this is not an adequate understanding of the mordant, cynical vision of kings and kingship that the poet subtly but definitively puts forward in the poem. Bilhaṇa's skeptical, even anarchic, view of royal power provides the shared point of departure for the articles by Bronner ("Poetics of Ambivalence"), Cox ("Sharing a Single Seat"), and McCrea ("Poetry beyond Good and Evil"), all of which appeared together in a special issue of the *Journal of Indian Philosophy* (vol. 38, no. 5, 2010). I would like to record my gratitude to Yigal Bronner and Lawrence McCrea, with whom I have jointly developed much of the details of this dissident reading of the *Carita*: their ideas, expressed in these articles and in several years' worth of conversation, have been of great influence on my thinking about Bilhaṇa.

   These recent studies excepted, subsequent scholarship has not gone beyond the terms set out by Bühler. V. S. Pathak's was perhaps the best attempt, but even his sprightly account (*Ancient Historians of India* (Bombay: Asia Publishing House, 1966), esp. pp. 56–83) is committed to an understanding of Bilhaṇa as an apologist, an unscrupulous "defense counsel" wishing to clear his patron's name in the court of public opinion. Warder's *Introduction to Indian Historiography* (Bombay: Popular Prakashan, 1972, pp. 45–50) simply parrots Pathak, while Mishra (*Studies on Bilhaṇa*, New Delhi: K.B. Publications, 1976), offers no comments on the value or valence of Bilhaṇa's historical narrative. Nagar, though deserving of great credit as the *Carita*'s best editor, is far too hagiographical about the poet and too damning of other scholars' efforts – venomously so in the case of Mishra's work – to make a positive contribution (*Bilhaṇa's Vikramāṅkadevacarita and Its Neo-Expounders*, International Library Center, 1991). Nilakanta Sastri makes extensive use of the poem for his reconstruction of Kulottuṅga's accession, but in his hands, it is subject to an oft-revised situational logic: sometimes treated as a sort of fun-house mirror of real events (*The Cōḷas*, pp. 292–294, 306ff.), while also considered as a reliable source for the chronology of Adhirājendra's reign.

5. EC 7, Sk. 136 contains the precise date of his death, the eighth day of the waning fortnight of Caitra, *Śaka* 990 or March 29, 1068, and the accession of Someśvara II two weeks later, the plausibility of which is confirmed by Fleet (*Dynasties of the Kanarese Districts*, Bombay: Government Press, 1882, p. 438).
6. Despite the abundant epigraphical and literary remains of the Kalyāṇa Cālukyas in Sanskrit and Kannada, the difference in methodological and interpretative sophistication between their modern study and that of the Coḷas is stark. Along with much of the rest of early-medieval west Deccani history, the Cālukyas' basic political-dynastic details were worked out by the indefatigable J. F. Fleet, in a long series of publications in the IA and EI, synthesized in his still valuable *Dynasties of the Kanarese Districts*, pp. 426–467: I adopt Fleet's account particularly as touching chronology (see especially pp. 442–448). As far as more recent scholarship, one can only agree with Veluthat's assessment that "in spite of the greater success of conceptual exercises in other parts of India, historiography in Karnataka has remained at the same conventional level" (*Early Medieval*, p. 325).
7. On the numerical reckonings attached to the western Deccan territories, see Fleet, "Ancient Territorial Divisions" (IA 20 (1891)); Stein, *Peasant State*, pp. 128–130; Inden, *Imagining India*, p. 224 (approvingly citing Stein); and most recently Adiga, *Making of Southern Karnataka*, pp. 10–21, esp. 14–18. As early as 1055, Vikrama was described as the ruler of the Banavāsi 12,000 and the Gaṅgavāḍi 96,000 territories: see EI 13:14, where the language of the record suggests that the future king (who must have been a pre-adolescent at this time) was acting as a ceremonial overlord to the *mahāmaṇḍaleśvara* Harikesarideva, the actual executor of the order; similarly, Vikramāditya is in association with Someśvara in an inscription from Hangal (mod. Dharwad district, EI 16:10b) dated to 1074.
8. Pollock, *Language of the Gods*, p. 159, n. 90.
9. Among Bilhaṇa's models here, the most eminent is the opening to Bāṇa's *Harṣacarita* (esp. vv. 4–6).

10. See 1.16: and 1.29cd; *cf.* Bronner, "Poetics of Ambivalence," p. 463.
11. 1.19 and 1.24, and *cf.* 1.3, 1.30, and 1.54.
12. 1.9: Bilhaṇa's major inspiration here is Padmagupta's *Navasāhasāṅkacarita*; on the adoption of this artfully simple style as an integral part of the patron-centered epic culminating in Bilhaṇa, see McCrea, "Poetry beyond Good and Evil," pp. 504–505.
13. 18.70–108; these verses have been well translated in Bühler's introduction to his edition (pp. 10–16) and again in Miller, *Phantasies of the Love-Thief* (New York: Columbia, 1971), pp. 188–191. See also Cox, "Scribe and Script," pp. 15–17.
14. 18.92cd.
15. Compare 1.26–27 with 18.106–107. The theme is an older one, with a classical precedent to be seen, e.g. in *Kāvyādarśa* 1.5. On Bilhaṇa's subversive remounting of this theme, especially the paradigm case of Vālmīki's creation of the *Rāmāyaṇa*, see the essays by Bronner (esp. pp. 463–464) and McCrea (pp. 506, 512ff.), both emphasizing the radical relativism that underlies the poet's thinking here. As McCrea puts it (p. 514), in the *Carita* "we are reminded again and again of the mirroring of Rāma and Rāvaṇa and the implication that, but for their poetically generated reputations, they are more or less interchangeable."
16. As argued by Bühler in the introduction to his edition, pp. 20–22.
17. 4.1–20; vs. 18 *tena keralabhūpālakīlālakaluṣīkṛtaḥ . . . payodhiḥ.*
18. 4.105, *cf.* McCrea, "Poetry beyond Good and Evil," pp. 516–517, drawing attention to a parallel in 3.47.
19. Here Bilhaṇa explores one of the central but largely unremarked-upon themes of Sanskrit literature: see Cox, "Sharing a Single Seat"; on the "displacement" of power in the poem, see my "Law, Literature, and the Problem of Politics," pp. 172ff.
20. These two verses have elicited comment since the poem's publication, yet their understanding has, I think, eluded its modern readers. Bühler, in the introduction to his edition, sees the first verse as describing how the Coḻa prince had "lost his life in a fresh rebellion," commenting in a footnote that "I conclude this from the expression *prakṛtivirodhahatasya*, which I translate by 'of the Cola prince, who had been slain in consequence of a disagreement with his subjects,'" before going on to acknowledge that "[it] might be taken to mean 'of the Chola prince, who had been killed (by Rājiga) in consequence of an invenerate emnity'" (p. 35). Bühler offers no suggestions on the meaning of the second verse. Mishra has, I think, offered the correct interpretation for the second of these two twinned attributes: grounded in parallels elsewhere in the text, he suggests that *prakṛtivirodhin* should be understood as "'who is in conflict with nature,' i.e. 'unnatural' " (*Studies*, p. 12), but goes on to argue quite wrongly that this suggests the need to emend the previous verse in line with this interpretation. Banerji and Gupta (*Bilhaṇa's Vikramāṅkadeva caritam*, p. 98) translate the first compound phrase as "who was distressed [*sic*!] by the revolt of his subjects" and the second as "who was naturally hostile to him [i.e. Vikramāditya]." Mishra's unnecessary emendation occasioned a

jeremiad by Nagar (*Neo-Expounders*, pp. 109–113); in the commentary to his own edition, Nagar only provides a Sanskrit translation of Buhler's earlier remark.

21. The relevant part of the *Arthaśāstra* is found in its sixth *adhikaraṇa* or topic (called *maṇḍalayoniḥ*, "the basis [of policy] that is the circle [of elements]): see especially 6.1.17: *tataḥ sa duṣṭaprakṛtiś cāturanto 'py anātmavān | hanyate vā prakṛtibhir yāti vā dviṣatām vaśam* | |, "Thus, a king whose *prakṛti* is ruined, even if he rules to the ends of the earth, has no control over himself. He is either slain by his *prakṛti*-s, or is dominated by his enemies." Kangle (*Kauṭilīya Arthaśāstra*, vol. 2, p. 317n) argues that in *duṣṭaprakṛti*, the ambiguous term must mean "constituent element," but that "in *prakṛtibhiḥ* in the second half subjects are clearly to be thought of." Thus Bilhaṇa's equivocation is potentially a deliberate reaction to the wavering technical language found in his source. See also, further in the same *adhikaraṇa*, 6.2.19: *bhūmyanantaraḥ prakṛtyamitras tulyābhijanaḥ sahajo viruddho virodhayitā vā kṛtrimaḥ*, "A king's natural [*prakṛti*-] enemy possesses contiguous territory, an innate enemy is equal to him in nobility, the enemy by circumstance has either been opposed by the king [*viruddhaḥ*] or opposes him [*virodhayitā*]." On the wider occurrence of the ideologeme of the "natural enemy," see for instance, Fleet, *Dynasties*, p. 316n (describing the Pallavas in Cālukya epigraphy): *prakṛtyamitra* (IA 8:26), *svakulavaira* (*ibid.*); (describing the Rāṣṭrakūṭas from the Cālukya perspective): *prakṛtisapatna* (IA 20: 266 and n. 1). See also Pollock, *Language of the Gods*, p. 151, on the Bādāmi Cālukyas as the *prakṛtyā śatravaḥ* of the Pallavas. Further echoes in Deccani epigraphy of the language of Kauṭalya can be seen in Cox, "Scribe and Script," p. 10n; on the status of "natural enmity" within the *Pañcatantra* literature, compare Taylor, *Fall of the Indigo Jackal* (Albany: SUNY Press, 2007), pp. 75–97. On *paścātkopa*, see *Arthaśāstra*, 9.3.

22. I can find no attestation of the two members in juxtaposition; the closely related *prakṛtiviruddha* does occur in *Suśrutasaṃhitā*, 35.39 (a reference I owe to Dominik Wujastyk).

23. See Chapter 2, n. 54, on the kingdom-wide recognition of Adhirājendra's illness within the Coḻa domains.

24. The ramifications of his carefully chosen words are redoubled by the verses' structure: in each case, the aggressors ("Rājiga" and Someśvara) swarm around the Cālukya and his brother-in-law (*colasunoḥ ... rājigābhidhānaḥ prakṛtivirodhahatasya veṅgināthaḥ* and *praguṇam akṛta ... prakṛtivirodhinam asya somadevam*) in a way that verbally enacts the crisis faced by Vikrama: he is hemmed in on all sides, just as it appears that his forces will be crushed between the armies of the Coḻa and his brother.

25. Some of the other verses in this segment have been translated and discussed in Cox, "Scribe and Script," pp. 15–16; see also Bronner, "Poetics of Ambivalence," pp. 474–476.

26. Uneven meters, since Kālidāsa's time at least, are also associated with lamentation (as in the Aja- and Rati-*vilāpa* cantos of the *Raghuvaṃśa* and the *Kumārasaṃbhava*, respectively, though in these classic cases the carrying meter is the ten-eleven syllable *viyoginī*). Perhaps evincing a metapoetic self-

awareness here, Bilhaṇa refers to Vikrama's lament for his father-in-law early in the *sarga* (6.8cd: *himakarakarakāṇḍapāṇḍugaṇḍasthalagaladaśrujalaś ciraṃ lalāpa*)

27. Compare Bronner, "Poetics of Ambivalence," p. 476, who finds a possibly anti-Buddhist satirical undertone in *sakalam api vidanti hanta śūnyaṃ*.
28. On staining and marking, see Bronner, pp. 465ff.; the ambiguity of the noun *vārākī* ("miserable harlot") suggests both pity and censure.
29. This is one of the few verses where the fragmentary second source for the *Vikramāṅkadevacarita* contains a substantively different and credible reading. The manuscript discovered by R. G. Bhandarkar in 1883 in Ahmedabad reads *anucitam idam āḥ* at the beginning of the first half-verse and *unnatacetaso yad asya* at its end (as reported by Bhandarkar, *Report* Appendix 3, and in the apparatus to this verse in Nagar's edition, who further notes that the particle *āḥ* bears a superscribed note *khedaḥ* ["distress"; this is likely wrong writing for *khede*, "in the sense of distress"]). Should we adopt these readings, the first half of verse construes slightly differently: "Why, oh why, was there this wrongful resolution on the elder brother's part? Because of this, he joined with their family's enemy, Rājiga the Cola, in the hope of doing harm to that noble-minded man."
30. In the *sarga*'s final verse, after Jayasiṃha's defeat on the battlefield, Bilhaṇa playfully returns to patently Kauṭalyan language to account for his betrayal: "[Vikrama,] the earth's ornament, made his camp there on the bank of the [Krishna] river, and set himself to the task of statecraft, to righting him [i.e Jayasiṃha] through conciliation. But his heart was twisted [*kuṭilahṛdayaḥ*, N. B.], so he did not accept the peace-offer: once one's fortunes have collapsed, the mind becomes totally ungovernable."
31. This is a theme that has been trenchantly explored by David Shulman (*The King and the Clown in Tamil Myth and Poetry*, Princeton: Princeton University Press, 1985; "From Author to Non-Author in Tamil Literary Legend," in *The Wisdom of Poets*, Delhi: Oxford 2001).
32. On the verse *sarvasvaṃ gṛhavarti kuntalapatiḥ, etc.* (cited in Śrīdharadāsa's *Saduktikarṇāmṛta*), see Bronner, "Poetics of Ambivalence," pp. 480–481. My larger argument on the so-called *Bilhaṇacarita* tradition and the ascription to him of the *Caurapañcāśikā* will have to await publication elsewhere.
33. See Cox, "Scribe and Script," esp. p. 14, n. 23, and compare Pollock, *Language of the Gods*, pp. 157ff.
34. Sir Walter Elliot was the first modern scholar to draw attention to one of these plates in two nearly simultaneous publications, his *Coins of Southern India*, first published in 1886 and in a brief communication in the *Indian Antiquary* in 1885 (referring to the other publication). It is from this record, the so-called Chellur plates, that Hultzsch produced an edition as the last of the "Eastern Chalukya Grants" in the first volume of the *South Indian Inscriptions*, which appeared in 1890 (SII 1:39, pp. 49–62). Shortly thereafter, Fleet attempted to exploit the evidence of this record for his systematic review of Veṅgī Cālukya chronology (IA 20, pp. 276–285, calling them the "Chellûrî" plates). Fleet reproduced there the incorrect conclusions that Hultzsch had earlier drawn. Almost a decade passed before the introduction into evidence

of the other two plates, in the editions of Krishna Sastri and Hultzsch, both of which appeared in *Epigraphia Indica* (respectively, EI 5:10, pp. 70–100 and EI 6:35, pp. 334–347). In his subsequent publication, Hultzsch corrected his earlier chronological and dynastic-historical conclusions. Throughout this discussion, I refer to these charters by the names given them by their editors, after the modern names of their initial findsites (in order of issue) Teki, Chellur, and Pithapuram; in the notes, I refer to these by the sigla T, C, and P.

35. On the general format of copperplate charters in classical and medieval India, see the still-useful discussion in Chhabra, "Diplomatic of Sanskrit Copper-Plate Grants," *The Indian Archives*, vol. 5, no. 1, 1955. This may be supplemented by Salomon, *Indian Epigraphy*, pp. 113–118 and Ali, "Royal Eulogy as World History" (in *Querying the Medieval*, Oxford: Oxford University Press, 2000), esp. pp. 169–175.
36. The Teki charter styles itself as an address to the king's leading subjects from the river Manneṟu to Mount Mahendra (T ll. 83–84: *manneṭimahemdramadhyavarttino rāṣṭrakūṭapramukhān kuṭumbinas sarvvān*), describing an area from the vicinity of Nellore in modern Tamilnadu to Odisha's Ganjam District (see Hultzsch's introduction to the plates, EI 6, pp. 335–336).
37. See Chapter 1, "Epic and Cognomen."
38. He is called Coḍagaṅga only in vs. 25; Rājarāja is given as a sort of *abhiṣeka* name in vs. 26, while he is again called Rājarāja in reference to the date of his coronation (Śaka 1006, 1084 CE) and finally both names occur in the art prose description at the outset of his order.
39. See Krishnan, *Karandai Tamil Sangam Plates of Rajendrachola I*. Memoirs of the Archaeological Survey of India, New Delhi: ASI, 1976, pp. 1–5; and cf. Ali, "Royal Eulogy," p. 170.
40. See Venkataramanayya, *Eastern Chalukyas*, pp. 1–4, 16–40.
41. As Pollock has demonstrated, a Veṅgī record seems to have been consulted by the author of the eulogy of the western king Vikramāditya V's innovative Kauṭhem plates, issued *ca.* 1008–1009 (Pollock, *Language of the Gods*, p. 157).
42. The format is repeated in the grants of Śaktivarman's brother Vimalāditya and in the inscriptions of the latter's sons Rājarājanarendra (Kulottuṅga's father, see e.g. his Korumelli plates in IA 12) and Vijayāditya VII (see his Pāmulavāka and Ryāli plates JAHRS 2:3–4 and 9:2). In all of the revised eastern Cālukya charters (including the three considered here), the transition between the newer, "mythical" preamble and the king-list beginning with Pulakeśin and Kubja Viṣṇuvardhana is awkwardly affected by a formulaic prose bridge, similar to but not identical with that of the Kalyāṇa Cālukya records (*cf.* T: 16–17; C: 27–33 [reading the longer prose formula with the earlier grants]; P: 19–21), seemingly borrowed from those or another source without any effort at integrating the older material.
43. *Cf.* Pollock, *Language of the Gods*, p. 155; and Venkataramanayya, *Eastern Chalukyas*, pp. 6–8; as both of these note, the earliest attestation of the

Ayodhyā connection appears to be Ranna's Kannada *Sāhasabhīmavijaya* (composed 982).

44. The reference to the conjoint heritage (*mānavyasagotrahārītiputradvipakṣagotrakramocitāni karmāṇi*) is a part of the earlier shared Cālukya prototype, adopted from yet earlier Deccani dynasties, the Kadambas and the Cuṭus (*cf.* Pollock, *Language of the Gods*, p. 150); the interpretation of this as indicative of a kṣatriya–Brahman dynastic fusion is peculiar to the Veṅgī line.
45. Contrastively, the Cālukyas of Kalyāṇa seem to have increasingly cast themselves as members of the solar dynasty, picking up the thread of their putative origin in Ayodhyā. Bilhaṇa directly contributed to this reimagining: see here especially *Carita* 1.63 and 2.53, and cf. Bronner, "Poetics of Ambiguity". On the *Mahābhārata*'s own vagaries in the assignment of its characters to the two great dynasties, see Brodbeck's suggestive essay ("Solar and Lunar Lines," *Religions of South Asia*, vol. 5 (2011)).
46. See Vimalāditya's Ranastipundi grant EI 6: 347ff. and Rājarāja Narendra's Nandamapundi grant (EI 4, no. 43). The balance of the opening matter was given in prose, following the family's earlier records.
47. On the title *kāvyakartṛ*, compare the colophon to Kulottuṅga's father Rājarājanarendra's Korumelli plates (IA 12: ln. 114): *karttā cetanabhajaḥ* (read *-bhaṭṭaḥ*?, thus Fleet) *kāvyānām* and his Nandamapundi plates (EI 4: 309, ln. 92) *kāvyānāṃ karttā nanniyabhaṭṭo*; in *ibid.*, p. 303, fn. 3, Hultzsch suggests that this might in fact be Nannayabhaṭṭa, the author of the *Āndhramahābhāratamu;* for more on this connection, see further.
48. They are sometimes in secondary scholarship referred to as "viceroys" or "governors," but these terms have no basis in any Sanskrit, Tamil, or Telugu titles. While they continued to date their records in Kulottuṅga's regnal years (see Hultzsch's introduction to the edition of Teki [EI 6, p. 335, retracting his earlier argument in SII 1, p. 50]), they are otherwise operating within the prerogatives of an independent king.
49. The two names are essentially synonymous, Mummuḍi (Ta. *mummuṭi*, "[he who possesses] the three crowns") being a common *biruda* of RKV Rājarāja I. According to the testimony of Teki (see n. 51), Coḍagaṅga is awarded the title Rājarāja as a regnal name upon his commission to rule over Veṅgī, presumably necessitating the retroactive alteration of his brother's name.
50. TCP vs. 17ab: *śrīpādasevāsukhato gurūṇām na jātu rājyaṃ sukham ity avekṣya.*
51. CP vs. 25 *yo ... cakravartinā | āhūto yauvanoddāmadehalakṣmīdidṛkṣayā* versus the version seen in T vs. 20 *gurubhrātṛsamāgamaikamanorathaṃ ... samānayan mānavadevadevaḥ.*
52. For the chronological details here, refer to the second of Hultzsch's two discussions (EI 6, pp. 334–335, substantially revising his own early remarks in SII 1, pp. 51–52).
53. Refer again to Pollock (*Language of the Gods*, pp. 159–161), who gives a lucid sketch of Veṅgī's role in the endemic warfare of the late tenth and eleventh centuries.
54. In keeping with its anomalous status relative to the other two texts elsewhere (see further), the opening of Chellur differs from the other two. It begins with a different invocatory verse, shared with the first verse of the Ryāli plates of

Vijayāditya VII, covering the same mythical genealogical material – the sequence Viṣṇu–Brahmā–Atri-Moon – but in a different meter and with different wording than T or P; Chellur then follows this with an *anuṣṭubh*, unparalleled in the other versions, introducing Purūravas. In the C version, the moon is called *vaṃśakāra* ("the lineage founder," vs. 1, ll. 2–3); not surprising in itself, this title and its variants (e.g. *vaṃśakara, vaṃśakartṛ*) occurs attached to different figures in the lineage narrative. So in T (ln. 6) and P (ln. 8) Arjuna is the *vaṃśakara*, while elsewhere in C it is Yayāti. Contrariwise, Arjuna is distinguished in the C version by another lyric verse (again shared with Ryāli, with which C's variants are only trivial). The king-list shared by C and the Ryāli plates is further enlivened by several expansions; C also contains an expanded list of royal regalia (ll. 24–25), as opposed to the comparatively brief *śvetatapatraikaśaṅkhapañcamahāśabdādīni*, seen in TP (resp. ll. 13, 16).

55. T, vs. 6 (ll. 28ff.) C: vs. 7 (ll. 50ff.); P vs. 6 (ll. 35ff.). (Hereafter in citations of the conjoint text of the charters, I only give the verse, rather than the line number, for each charter): *rājāsāv anurūparūpavibhavām* (TP; *tasyāsīd apakalmaṣā sucaritair* C) *ammaṃganāmnā bhuvi prakhyātām* (T; *prakhyātā* C; *prakhātām* P [*sic*]) *upagacchati sma vidhivad devīṃ jagatpāvinīṃ* (T; *upayacchata* ... P [*sic* for *upayacchate*]; *śubhalakṣaṇaikavasatir devī jagatpāvanī* C) | *yā jahnor iva jāhnavī himavato gaurīva lakṣmīr iva kṣīrodād divaseśavaṃśatilakād rājendracoḍād abhūt* | |
56. Though Rājarājanarendra's own records mention his own maternal connection to the Coḻas – his mother Kundavvā (Ta. Kuntavai) was Rājarāja I's daughter (Korumelli, ll. 63–65, and Nandamapundi, vs. 14), this is unmentioned in all of Viddaya's eulogies.
57. It is possible that the revision was made to remove a potential impropriety in the other versions, which might connote sexual congress instead of matrimony. Pāṇini 1.5.36 (*upād yamaḥ svakaraṇe*) specifies that the form *upayacchate* is limited to a matrimonial sense: this might – its incorrect reading notwithstanding – be evidence of a tertiary correction in P, which otherwise simply reverts to the readings of T without remedying the problems identified by C.
58. TP, vs. 7; C, vs. 8: *putras tayor abhavad apratighātaśakti*-(PC; *śaktiṃ* T) *niśśeṣitārinivaho mahanīyakīrttiḥ* | *gaṃgādharādrisutayor iva kārttikeyo rājendracoḍa iti rājakulapradīpaḥ* | |
59. TP, vs. 8; C, vs. 9: *bhāsām unnatihetuṃ prathamaṃ* (corr.; *pradhamaṃ* TPC) *veṃgīśvaratvam adhyāsya* | *yas tejasā digantān ākramata sahasrabhānur udayam iva* (TP [in P, the editor unhappily emends to *ākramati*]; *ākramad udayaṃ sahasraraśmir iva* C) | |
60. According to Pāṇini 7.3.76, the radical vowel of the verb √*kram* should be lengthened in its *parasmaipada* inflections, a problem that the TP version avoids. Perhaps the change – whether introduced by Viddaya, Penna, or someone else – was motivated by the attractive assonance of *sahasraraśmi*-, though this would by itself fail to explain the need to rearrange the line, or to introduce the errant form.
61. Compare especially the discussion of verse 3.1.141 of Nannaya's *Mahābhāratamu* (*jaladhivilolavīcivilasat, etc.*), as translated and discussed

by Narayana Rao and Shulman (*Classical Telugu Poetry*, p. 12). If, as Hultzsch suggested (see n. 47), Nannaya was the composer of some of the (Sanskrit) *praśasti* verses of Rājarājanarendra's time, this idea of interlinguistic poetic modeling becomes even more feasible.

62. In the T and P versions, the first *pāda* lacks a necessary heavy fourteenth syllable.
63. T, vv. 11–13 (orthography as in the plates): *prakhyātabhūbhṛtkulajanmabhājas sadābhimukhyas sarasāḥ prasannāḥ | tasyābhavan pā[r]tthivapuṃggavasya devyaś śubhā nadya ivāmburāśeḥ || ātmānurūpair atha tāsu labdhai[r] devīṣu devapratimaḥ kumāraiḥ | sa naṃdyamāno naradevavaṃdyair nnūnaṃ hasaty [e] kakumāram īśaṃ || ātmeve[n]driyavargaṃ sutavargaṃ teṣu teṣu viṣayeṣu | kramaśas sa niyuṃjāno mummuḍicoḍaṃ kumāram ity avadat ||*
64. C, vs. 12; P, vs. 11: ... *sūryavaṃśatilakād rājendradevārṇavāt* [||] *saṃbhūtāṃ madhurāntakīti viditāṃ nāmnāpareṇa ... lakṣmīṃ.*
65. This is stated indirectly in T, vs. 19 (where Mummuḍi[/Rājarāja] "was eager to bow to the lotus-feet of the eldest of his brothers," *bhrātṛṣu pūrvajasya caraṇāṃbhojapraṇāmārtthinā*) and directly in vs. 21.
66. Here once again, C stands on its own in reading *mayā veṃgīmahīrājyaṃ coḍarājyābhilāṣiṇā* instead of the practically synonymous *vatsa veṃgīmahīrājyaṃ mayā digvijayeṣiṇā* in vs. 14 (due to differences in the intervening text, the verse numeration is now shared in all three versions), though P sides with it against T in vs. 15, in the grammatically indifferent variant *abdān/abdāni.*
67. CP, vs. 18: *tadanujam atha dhīraṃ vīracoḍaṃ kumāraṃ guṇam iva tanubaddhaṃ vikramaṃ cakravarttī | udayam iva ravis tvaṃ prāpya veṅgīśvaratvaṃ vitanu śirasi pādaṃ bhūbhṛtām ity avocat ||*
68. *guṇam iva tanubaddhaṃ vikramaṃ* is obscure; this translation follows Hultzsch's in SII 1 (he eschews translating this passage in his edition of Teki). It would perhaps make better sense if *vikrama* here could be understood as both a noun and a proper name ("he addressed the prince Vīracoḍa [also known as] Vikrama, who was indeed like the quality [of *vikrama*, valor] embodied"). There is, however, no other reference to Vīracoḍa bearing this name, and his step-brother who would ultimately succeed Kulottuṅga on the Coḻa throne ruled under the name Vikramacoḻa. Still, given the fact that two of his sons deputed by Kulottuṅga to Veṅgī shared the title Rājarāja, it is perhaps not too great a stretch.
69. This is the case in verses found in Pithapuram only, again showing the affinity between it and Teki: P, vs. 22 resembles T, vs. 26 (*abhivāṃchitavastudānair ... samastabhuvanāśraya nāma sārthaṃ dhatte* versus *rājarājābhidhānena sārthenāhvaya sādaraṃ*), P, vs. 23=T, vs. 26, and P, vs. 24, recycles some of the material seen in T, vs. 31 (the verses are in the same meter, the first *pāda*s of which read (P:) *tyaktvā bhūbhārakhedaṃ p[h]aṇipatir acalaṃ pāti pātālalokaṃ* and (T:) *pātālaṃ pāti yāvat* [*t*]*vam iva phaṇipatir nnāgayūthaikanā[th]o.*
70. T, ll. 76–77; C, ll. 78–79; P, ll. 68–69 ... *sarvalokāśrayaśrīviṣṇuvardhanamahārājādhirājo rājaparameśvaraḥ paramamāheśvaraḥ paramabhaṭṭārakaḥ paramabrāhmaṇyaḥ ...*

71. On the invention of the Telugu *campū* attributed to Nannaya and its literary and performative ramifications, see Narayana Rao, "Multiple Literary Cultures in Telugu" (in *Literary Cultures in History: Reconstructions from South Asia*. Berkeley: California University Press, 2003), pp. 391–395.
72. C, vs. 25, *guṇādhiko guṇajñena rājarājādhipena yaḥ | rājarājabrahmamahārāja-nāmnā stuto mudā | |*
73. This was a common Co̱la official title, in its Tamil orthography *rājarājabrahmamārāyaṉ*[*/-mārāyar*]. There are also a *rājarājabrahmamahārāja* mentioned among the honorees of the Pithapuram plates (ln. 176). This last, unnamed figure – who receives more shares in the *brahmadeya* than any of the more than 500 Brahmans named there – is also a *senāpati* and of the Mudgala *gotra* and is thus likely Meḍama himself.

   Hultzsch did not notice the Co̱la valence of the title in his edition of the inscription (which was published in 1890, at the dawn of Co̱la epigraphical studies), though he did register that something was unusual about it, in that he found it "somewhat lengthy" (SII 1, p. 53). He was of the opinion (*ibid.*, n. 3) that the Rājarāja referred to here could only be Kulottuṅga's father Rājarāja Narendra. This is certainly possible: the same king's Kalidiṇḍi grant (published in the Telugu-language journal *Bhāratī* (vol. 20), which is unavailable to me; see Venkataramanayya *Eastern Cālukyas*, pp. 38–39, 241–242), details the memorial temples erected in honor of Co̱la generals who served under him, one of whom bears this exact title (the other two were, in Tamil orthography, Uttamaco̱la Co̱lakoṉ and Uttamaco̱la Milāṭuṭaiyāṉ). It is however also possible that, despite the short time-frame involved, this title may have been granted by either Rājarāja Mummuḍicoḍa or Rājarāja Coḍagaṅga. As the former was very likely Vīracoḍa's uterine brother, he is the most likely candidate, despite the brevity of his reign in Veṅgī.
74. The most notable of the verses celebrating Meḍama describes his household in this way (vs. 32, ll. 95–96):

   In his courtyards, each and every day there are floods of water, dripping from the feet of countless Brahmans – those gods on earth – as they are bathed there. Forever filling thousands of paths, wondrous to say, they best the floods of the Ganges, which drip from merely one of the gods, and which exhaust themselves with only three paths [of heaven, earth, and the underworld].
75. On the donees' onomasty, see Krishna Shastri's brief but thorough discussion in the introduction to his edition (EI 5, pp. 72–73), and his tabulation of their proper names and *gotra*s (pp. 96–100); many of the names are only orthographic transcriptions of pure Tamil epithets, and many are directly tied to the Vaiṣṇava sacred landscape of Co̱lamaṇḍalam.
76. Vv. 28–29.
77. Vs. 30: *yeṣāṃ prabhāve*[*ṇ*]*a sahasradhāmā rakṣāṃsi saṃdhyādvitay*[*e*] *vidhūya | vibhāti nirvvighnaviyatpracāro jagaṃti rakṣa*[*ñ*] *jagadekacakṣuḥ | |*. C's account of Mudgala also contains a slight echo of the luni-solar theme: see its vv. 22–23 (ll. 81–83: Mudgala emerges from the race of Brahmans as the moon from the milk-ocean, and once arrested the sun with his Brahmanical

walking-stick); the honoree Meḍama is himself sunlike in vs. 28 (ll. 87–89, an admittedly stock punned comparison).

78. Both, along with Rājarāja-Mummuḍi, subsequently disappear from the epigraphic record, at least under those names. There is speculation that either of the two brothers bearing the title Rājarāja (that is, Mummuḍi or Coḍagaṅga) might have patronized a work of Sanskrit lexicography, Keśavasvāmin's *Nānārthārṇavasaṃkṣepa* or *Rājarājīya* (see Vogel, *Indian Lexicography*, Wiesbaden: Harrassowitz 1979, p. 346). There is an unclear contemporary reference to Vīracoḍa in a poorly preserved inscription of the Nāgavaṃśi lord Someśvaradeva (EI 10: 4), dating perhaps to the turn of the century, who is described as *vīracoḍanṛpa*[*sa*]*ṃvarakāmaḥ* (vs. 4, ln. 15), "eager for the wealth [?] of King Vīracoḍa." Very implausibly, B. Venkatakrishna Rao takes this to imply the Coḻa prince's death on the battlefield (*Eastern Chalukyas of Vengi*, p. 435).

79. Hultzsch's characteristically clear-sighted review of the evidence is worth quoting in detail (SII 3, pp. 177–78, retaining his scheme of transliteration):

> [We see] that the official title of the chief queen is often mentioned twice – first in connection with her proper name, and a second time immediately before the name of the king himself, with whom she is stated to be seated on the throne. [So] we find that, in an inscription of his 26th year [= SII 3:72], there are mentioned (1) Dīnachintāmaṇi with the title Bhuvanamuḻuduḍaiyāḷ, (2) Eḻiśai-Vallabhī with the title Eḻulagamuḍaiyāḷ, (3) Tyāgavallī with the title Ulaguḍaiyāḷ, and (4) once more Bhuvanamuḻuduḍaiyāḷ (*i.e.* Dīnachintāmaṇi) as seated on the throne with the king. In two inscriptions of the 30th and the 42nd year [SII 3:73 and SII 3:75], the order is (1) Tyāgavallī Avanimuḻuduḍaiyāḷ, (2) Eḻiśai-Vallabhī Eḻulaguḍiayāl or Eḻulagamuḍaiyāḷ, and (3) again Avanimuḻuduḍaiyāḷ (*i.e.* Tyāgavallī). In two inscriptions of the 45th and 47th years [ARE 44 of 1891 and SII 3: 76], we have (1) Tyāgavallī Ulaguḍaiyāḷ and (2) Eḻiśai-Vallabhī Eḻulaguḍaiyāl and [the latter] adds Ulaguḍaiyāḷ (*i.e.* Tyāgavallī) a second time. It follows from these references that in A.D. 1095–96 Dīnachintmaṇi occupied the place of chief queen, while Eḻiśai-Vallabhī and Tyāgavallī were the second and third queens. In A.D. 1099–1100, Dīnachintāmaṇi had died, Tyāgavallī had been made chief queen and Eḻśai-Vallabhī remained second queen. This arrangement was still in force in A.D. 1116–1117 [SII 3:76] . . . Dīnachintāmaṇi is perhaps identicial with the Madhurāntakī of the Chellur and Pithapuram plates.

See also Sastri, *The Cōḻas*, p. 332 and n. 157.

80. According to Kielhorn's calculations (EI 7, p. 5).

81. This has gone unnoticed in earlier scholarship; the closest I can find is Hultzsch's observation, "As the two copper-plate grants which mention Madhurāntakī do not contain the name Vikrama-Choḍa, it remains doubtful whether his mother was Madhurāntakī or another of the queens of Kulottuṅga I" (SII 3, p. 179).

82. Among the records referring to Vikrama by the title *tyāgasamudra* (a functional synonym of the Dānārṇava, the eastern Cālukya who ruled *ca.* 970–973) are the first verse of his own Cevvilimedu *praśasti* (EI 6:21, ln. 1),

where he is in fact referred to by the synonymous *tyāgavārākara*, and the Pithapuram pillar inscription of Mallapa (EI 4:33, vs. 24 *tasmiṃs tyāgasamudrāparanāmani coḍamaṃḍalaṃ trātum | gatavati veṃggībhūmir nnāyakarahitā tadaṃttare jātā* | |). Both of these epigraphs are in Sanskrit; the epithet also occurs in Oṭṭakkūttar's *Vikkiramacolanulā* (vs. 331 *eṉaik kaliṅkaṅkaḷ eḻiṉaiyum poykkŏṇṭa* [||] *tāṉait tiyākacamuttirame māṉappor*: see Wentworth, *Yearning*, p. 385). The name was to insinuate itself into lordly onomasty after Vikrama's reign: a Tiyākasamuttirap pallavarāyan is mentioned in a record of 1124 (SITI 99), while multiple occurrences of the Brahman name Tiyākasamuttirapaṭṭaṉ can be found from the final decades of the twelfth century (*e.g.* SII 7:1026, *ca.* 1174).

On Tyāgapātakā, see SII 3, pp. 181–2; and *Coḷas*, p. 346: The chief queen of Vikrama's own son and successor Kulottuṅga II (r. 1133–1150) was also called Tyāgavallī (*The Coḷas*, p. 349); given the widely seen habit of adopting names from two generations earlier, this has the value of corroborative evidence.

The relevant passage from the *mĕykkīrtti* (Mĕykkīrttikaḷ, no. 24) reads: *kaliṅkam eḻum kaṉalĕri parappi/aimpaṭaip paruvattuv ĕmpaṭai tāṅki*: "Spreading fire through all of the seven Kaliṅgas, wielding a fierce weapon in the age [when he should be wearing] a child's five-piece amulet." *Cf.* Nilakanta Sastri, *Cōḷas*, p. 338, n. 91. This claim is itself grounded in an intertextual reference to Kulottuṅga's later *mĕykkīrtti*s, which places his own Veṅgī campaigns *iḷaṅkoparuvattil* ("when he was a prince"), as well as possibly to Cayaṅkŏṇṭār's poem (cf. *Kaliṅkattupparaṇi*, vs. 240, also noted by Nilakanta Sastri).

83. From the time of its publication, the problem of history has been a prominent concern of the modern scholarship that has taken notice of the *Paraṇi*. Beginning with the earliest essay on the text written in a European language – V. Kanakasabha Pillai's "Tamil Historical Texts no. 2, The Kalingattu Parani" of 1890 (*IA*, vol. 19) – scholars have repeatedly engaged with the question of what sort of historical data can be gleaned from the text, and what sort of source it can be understood to be. Pillai was concerned with the status of the *Paraṇi* as a source of genealogical data about the Coḻas as well as of the events of Kulottuṅga's accession; here the avowedly "most important portion of the poem" is that containing the royal genealogy (pp. 338–339), as it provided corroboration of epigraphical accounts already published.

Beside its utility as a source of Tamil dynastic history, early scholarship concentrated on the constitution of the text of this at-times obscure poem. There have been six published editions of the poem, of predictably variable quality (see the review in Aravāṇaṉ, *Kaliṅkattupparaṇi: ŏru matippīṭu* (Ceṉṉai: Jaiṉa Iḷaiñar Maṉṟam, 1976), pp. 36–39, for details). The greatest testament to the poem's philological and historical problems can be seen in the researches of the great Mu. Irākavaiyaṅkār. Initially confining himself to the textual criticism of the edition of A. Kopālaiyar in the pages of the journal *Centamiḻ*, Irākavaiyaṅkār subsequently published a brief monograph (*Kaliṅkattupparaṇiy ārāycci*, Maturai: Tamiḻccaṅkamuttiracālai, 1925, hereafter *Ka. ār.*), as well as including these materials in his collected papers (*Ārāyccit tŏkuti*, Chennai: Pari nilayam, second edition, 1938, pp. 406–445, hereafter *Ār. tŏ.*). Though the latter is more readily available (it was reprinted in 1964), the interested reader would do well to seek out the earlier study: it contains more than twice as many disputations on particular readings, and includes in its final section ("*caṅkot-taram*," pp. 57–71) both Kopālaiyar's responses to Irākavaiyaṅkār's criticisms and his own further defenses of them.

Among the *Paraṇi*'s recent interpreters, the works of Shulman (*King and Clown*, esp. pp. 276–292) and Ali ("Violence, Gastronomy, and the Meaning of War," *Medieval History Journal*, vol. 3, 2000) especially call for comment. Placing the work in the context of the mythopoetics of Co<u>l</u>a-era kingship, Shulman focuses attention on the *Paraṇi*'s comic, anti-structural features, linking its oneirically erotic early section, its comico-horrific descriptions of the denizens of Kāḷi's court, and the cataclysmic violence of the Kaliṅga battlefield within a single logic of deliberate, controlled transgression. Shulman takes the poem to be an "explosive fantasy that seeks to open up a dimension of experience normally contained or denied" (pp. 284–285), depending on the depiction of a wild "anti-space" projected beyond the confines of the ordered world of dharmic kingship, only to have that same space suddenly yawn open in the midst of the settled selves of the kingdom. Expressly interested in a synchronic *histoire des mentalités* for all of medieval South India, Shulman would likely resist my desire to see this as an outcome of the poet's reflexive gloss of this *particular* court society.

Ali's reading of the *Paraṇi* broadly agrees with Shulman's totalizing vision of the poem: like Shulman, he draws attention to the interbraided worlds of war and the demonic onto which the settled world of the court projects its dystopic underside. Extending from this, he focuses on the poem's consistent linkage of comedy, horror and violence with the consumption of flesh (especially human flesh, the essential element in the Paraṇi's zombie apocalypse aesthetic), severed from the reciprocity marking the concerns with feasting and hospitality that had characterized the classical Vedic sacrificial order. In all of this, Ali urges an understanding of a transformed, distinctly medieval sense of the politics of expansion and of "the wider social 'meaning' of war" in this period (p. 263). Suggestively, Ali also urges that we might see real historical actors transfigured into the guise of Kāḷi's ghoul-courtiers, speculating that in them we might see the various tricksters and conjuremen who adopted the lifeways of the *kāpālika* and other extreme mortuary Śaiva orders.

84. The references to the **Kŏppattupparaṇi* and the **Kūṭalcaṅkamattupparaṇi* derive from references contained in Ŏṭṭakūttar's *Irācarācaco<u>l</u>avulā* (vv. 24, 25; see Wentworth, *Yearning*, p. 401; in vs. 27 it goes on to mention the *Kaliṅkattupparaṇi*); one of the *mĕykkīrtti*s of Rājādhirāja mentions the performance of a 'Tami<u>l</u> *paraṇi*' on the battlefield itself (Cuppiramaṇiyam *Mĕykkīrttikaḷ*, no. 6, ln. 14 *ta<u>nn</u>āṭiyi<u>r</u> <u>r</u>ami<u>l</u>pparaṇi kŏṇṭu*; this revises the account of the other version of this *mĕykkīrtti*, which only mentions his "victory" at this same place, *ta<u>nn</u>āṭiyi<u>r</u> cayaṅ kŏṇṭu*). *Cf.* Venkataramanayya, *Eastern Cālukyas*, pp. 233 and 235n, who identifies this location as the fortress of Dannaḍa, the modern Amaravati in Andhra Pradesh's Guntur district. Does this imply that this *tami<u>l</u>pparaṇi* was an impromptu entertainment for the

troops? On these early, supposedly "lost" examples of the genre, see Aravāṇan, *Ŏru matippīṭu*, pp. 26ff. On the *Paṉṉiruppaṭṭiyal*, see Clare, *Canons, Conventions*, pp. 59–83 and Wentworth, *Yearning*, pp. 157–159.

85. See the discussion in Mu. Aruṇācalam, *Tamiḻ ilakkiya varalāṟu*, vol. 5, pp. 1–6. Both Aruṇācalam and Irākavaiyaṅkār quote the verse ascribed to Cayaṅkŏṇṭār from *Tamiḻ nāvalar caritai* (no. 115):

   kāvalar īkai karutuṅkāṟ kāvalarkkup
   pāvalar naṟkum paric'ŏvvā pūviṉilai
   yākāp pŏruḷaiy anapayaṉ aḷittāṉ pukaḻām
   ekāp pŏruḷ aḷitteṉ yāṉ

   When you think about the gifts of kings,
   the presents poets give to kings are incomparably better:
   Anapayaṉ offers wealth that will not remain on the earth,
   But the wealth *I* offer – fame – won't ever fade away.

86. The passage is drawn from Nacciṉārkkiṉiyar's commentary on the *Tŏlkāppiyam*'s *Cĕyyuḷiyal: paraṇiyāvatu: kāṭukĕḻucĕlvikkup paraṇināṭ kūḻum tuṇaṅkaiyum kŏṭuttu vaḻipaṭuvat' or vaḻukkuppĕṟṟiyatu. atu pāṭṭuṭaittalaivaṉaip pĕytu kūṟaliṟ puṟattiṇai palavum virāyiṟṟu.* I follow Irākavaiyaṅkār (*Ka. ār.*, pp. 62–63, *Ār. tŏ*, pp. 409–10) in his emphasis on the passages gendered valence; drawing on a range of classical and post-classical texts, he argues that the *tuṇaṅkai* was a dance performed by female performers (*ibid.*). This categorical judgment can be further nuanced by the conclusions advanced by Sivathamby in his study of the dramatic repertoire in classical literature (*Drama in Ancient Tamil Society*, Madras: New Century Book House, 1981, pp. 185–187, 341–343), who suggests an earlier association between the dance-form, the *pey*s that haunt the battlefield, and the gory martial cult.

87. See Shulman's reading of this part of the poem (*King and the Clown*, pp. 281–284); see p. 280 for his review of the several theories as to the identity of the speaker (critically extending the workmanlike review in Aravāṇaṉ, *Ŏru matippīṭu*, pp. 43–49). Once again, I follow Irākavaiyaṅkār's interpretation.

88. The phrase is Shulman's (*King and the Clown*, p. 278).

89. The surviving Sanskrit genealogical accounts are found largely in the relatively small corpus of copperplates issued by the Coḻa kings; recall that the early *mĕykkīrtti*s of the Coḻas never contain a genealogical section. For discussions of the Coḻa genealogy, see Wentworth, *Yearning.*, pp. 131–142; and Broquet, "Une epopée epigraphique."

90. It is in this context that I must demur from Shulman's interpretation of the *paraṇi*. When he writes "[Cayaṅkŏṇṭār's] text is not a farce; not a satire; not a parodic or carnivalesque extravaganza; not a comic semiotic commentary of the serious life of the court – it is wholly remote from those genres. Moreover, several of its chapters are quite 'straight' or serious, in the conventional meaning of the word (for example, those dealing with the royal genealogy and with Kulottuṅga's birth and childhood" (*King and Clown*, p. 279), he is, I

suppose, trying to avoid the premature reduction of the poem to a framework introduced from outside the world in which the KP was created, especially in analogizing the poem to something like the grotesquerie of European Romanticism (*ibid.*, responding critically to Zvelebil, *Smile of Murugan*, Leiden: Brill, 1973, p. 207). There is much in the sections of the *Paraṇi* relating to the Co̱la *vaṃśa* and to Kulottuṅga's place in it that is most definitely skewed rather than "straight"; and much of its peculiar power derives, I think, precisely from this oblique angle from which it depicts Kulottuṅga's court society.

91. In his learned edition of the poem, Kaṉṉaiya Nāyuṭu notices both of these parallels in his comments to vv. 178 and 180; the *Cilappatikāram*'s medieval commentator Aṭiyārkkunallār in turn cites vs. 178 on 5.90–98.
92. This multiple-emboxed narration concludes twenty-seven stanzas later, in vs. 209, with a closing benediction written out by Karikālaṉ ("may my descendants forebear any and all errors by those who will read out what I have written," *ĕḻuti maṟṟ' uraicĕytavar avarkaḷ cĕypiḻāy ĕlām ĕmar pŏṟukka*), a closely observed variation on a scribe's or engraver's colophon.
93. I do not follow Kaṉṉaiya Nāyuṭu here, who understands this verse very differently. He finds no ambiguity of referent in the verse's first words, taking them to speak only of the *Mahābhārata* narrative ("*ataṉ mutal kaṇ – antap pāratak kataiyiṉ mutalil*"), and he understands *patam* and *pātam* (my "word" and "line of verse") as, respectively, "world(s)" and "species of creature" (*ulakaṅkaḷ* and *piṟappiṉ pirivukaḷ*). I cannot see what motivated this interpretation, which takes these words out of their straightforward, attested senses and fails to articulate with what immediately follows in vs. 183.
94. Vs. 179 is built around a similar, epicyclic variation of this, based on the verb *pukaṟṟal* ("to declare"), swirling around Nārada: *pukalāp pukalvatu* ... *pukalvāṉ*, stringing together in rapid succession a verbal participle ("saying"), a future participle ("something to say") and an imperfective participial noun ("he says").
95. There is a single classical occurrence of *varalāṟu* in one of the songs of the *Paripāṭal* (6.42, *āṟu varalāṟu*, where it seems to mean "set of circumstances"); a generation or more after Cayaṅkŏṇṭār, it occurs in the *Kamparāmāyaṇam*, *kulamuṟai* vs. 29, in something closer to the sense of "sequential narrative" (I am grateful to Blake Wentworth for first pointing out this occurrence to me; it is also the citation in MTL *s.v.*).
96. Kanakasabha Pillai's translation and analysis of this section ("Tamil Historical texts part 2") can still be read with profit.
97. Cayaṅkŏṇṭār interlaces references to this luni-solar theme elsewhere in the poem. It can be seen first of all in the poem's opening invocation, where Kulottuṅga is identified as *upayakulottamaṉ apayaṉ*, "Apayaṉ, supreme in both his families." More substantively, there is the following example from the head-to-toe description of Kāḷi (vs. 123):

    King Apayaṉ in lineage as rare as the Veda,
    and in virtue joining grace with wisdom,
    took birth into two fine families:

first of all, that of the lovely moon and that of the Sun, the Day-bringer.
Suited to these both, on her radiant face, [Kāḷi] had a beautiful *tilaka*.

As Kaṉṉaiya Nayuṭu suggests *ad loc.*, Kāḷi's face is likened to the moon (whiteness, coolness, etc) and the *sindur* mark to the sun (roundness, redness). Note also the use of the adjectival participle *utitta* (translated here "took birth"); this is derived from the same loan-root as vs. 232's *utittāṉ*.

98. See the early interpretations referred to in Sastri, *The Cōḻas*, p. 293, n. 33; Sastri himself does not follow these.
99. vs. 240, *paṇṭu vacutevaṉ makaṉāki nilamātiṉ paṭarkaḷaiyu' māyaṉ ivaṉ ĕṉṟuteḷiv ĕyta* ... *tiruvaimpaṭai taritte*; vs. 242, *tirumārpiṉ malarmaṭantai tirukkaḻuttiṉ maṅkalanāṇ ĕṉṉa*. On the genre of *piḷḷaittamiḻ*, codified in later theoretical treatises, refer to Richman, *Extraordinary Child* (Honolulu: University of Hawai'i Press, 1997); on the set of five Vaiṣṇava emblemata as markers of childhood, see the parallel description of Vikramacoḻa (cited earlier in this chapter, n. 82).
100. Compare the translation by Sastri, *The Cōḻas*, p. 305.
101. See Thapar, *Time as a Metaphor for History* (Delhi: Oxford University Press, 1996), for a brief but suggestive characterization of this temporal-historical model.
102. See above, Chapter 2, "Forging Rājendracoḷa's Political Network, 1071–1073."
103. This is especially the case in vv. 265–272, written in metrical counterpoint to vv. 258–264.
104. Irākavaiyaṅkār first proposed this identification, based on his own emendation for the masculine *uriyāṉ* given in Kopālaiyar's text (Kaṉṉaiya Nāyuṭu accepts this proposed reading, while reporting the variant *–ulakiṉ eḻicaikaḷ cūḻa varuvār*): see *Ka. ār.*, pp. 16–17; *Ār. tŏ.*, pp. 418–419.
105. Vv. 315 and 328; in the latter, Irākavaiyaṅkār correctly identified and elucidated the poet's *tirumantiravolaiyāṇ* as a Coḻa chancellery title (*Ka. ār.*, p. 18, *Ār. tŏ.*, pp. 419–420).
106. The record is SII IV:862 (ARE 43 of 1893); the credit for its identification belongs once more to Irākavaiyaṅkār (*Ka. ār.*, pp. 35–36; *Ār. tŏ.*, pp. 427–428). Nilakanta Sastri repeats much of this information (*The Cōḻas*, pp. 334 and nn.) without credit. I propose Karuṇākaraṉ's social profile to be similar, though not identical, to that of the *kuṭippaḷḷi* figures attested in Adhirājendra's epigraphy (see Chapter 2, "Adhirājendra's Tondaimandalam Mobilizations, 1071–1071"). Karuṇākaraṉ was in all likelihood at least a generation younger than these figures, as he was still active in Vikramacoḻa's court some years after the completion of the *Paraṇi*. If this presumption of his *arriviste* status in Colamandalam is correct, we must abandon Irākavaiyaṅkār's suggestion that the early tenth-century *mūventaveḷāṉ* Cāttaṉ Ulakaṉ, a possessor of the same village, be considered Karuṇākaraṉ's ancestor (SII 17: 482, *ca.* 925).
107. The last of these is unaccountably not included in Kaṉṉaiya Nāyuṭu's edition, though it is found in both Kopālaiyar's and the text published by

Kaḻakam; in vs. 363 Kopālaiyar proposed the conjecture *coḻaṉicakkaramām* "the Coḻa's own hand"; this was rejected by Irākavaiyaṅkār, whom Nāyuṭu follows.

108. Here I depart from Irākavaiyaṅkār (*Ka. ār.*, pp. 18–24, 38–40; *Ār. tŏ.*, pp. 429–431). He would have these three verses refer to *four* separate individuals: Karuṇākaraṉ, his elder brother Pallavarayar, Vāṇakovaraiyaṉ and Muṭikŏṇṭacoḻaṉ; the latter three he refers to, without any support in the text, as the army's *upaceṉāpatikaḷ* ("lieutenant generals"). In his convoluted understanding of vs. 364 Pallavarayar (the title is taken as a proper name) is described as "generous" (*curapi*, a "wish-giving cow") who precedes Karuṇākaraṉ (*tŏṇṭaiyaṛkk' aracin muṉvarum*, "coming before the lord of the Tŏṇṭaiyar"), while less senior to him in the army's chain of command. He is followed once again by Nilakanta Sastri (*The Coḷas*, p. 334), who cites as corroboration the existence of a *senāpati pallavaraiyar* in ARE 46 of 1914; it is difficult to credit this as decisive evidence given the impersonal nature of the title. I understand the entire phrase *muṉvaruñ curavi tuṅkavĕḷviṭai* to refer to the Tŏṇṭai standard (Kaṉṉaiya Nāyuṭu reports the variants *veḷviṭai* ["lovely bull"] and *vĕḷkŏṭi* ["white banner"]; both are unobjectionable in sense and in meter, though the second sounds like a banalization. Absent a clearer sense of the distribution of these readings, I am unable to weigh their value).
109. There is, admittedly, no direct echo of the Kolar cult in the *Kaliṅkattupparaṇi*, but in his *Takkayākapparaṇi* of about a generation later, Ŏṭṭakkūttar, a very close student of Cayaṅkŏṇṭār's poem, makes direct references to *yāmaḷam* in the context of the Kāḷi-cult: see vv. 113 (*paravuvaṉa yāmaḷamo*), 136 (Kāḷi is *yokayāmaḷattiṉāḷ* [v.l. *yāmaḷākamattiṉāḷ*]). The learned author of the poem's surviving early commentary peppers his scholium with references to the *yāmala*-based temple cult (see the remarks to the above-cited verses, as well as his comments on vv. 67, 91, 112, 117 [referring, *inter alia*, to *pāracava* temple-officiants], 534. The specificity of the connection between the cult inaugurated at Kolar and the imaginal world centered upon Kāḷi remained strong in the Tamil country; *cf.* Nagaswamy, *Tantric Cult of South India*, Delhi: Agam Kala Prakashan, 1982, pp. 22–34, who projects much of this cultic specificity back onto Cayaṅkŏṇṭār's text, not always convincingly.
110. The notion of the transference of "social energy" ("how collective beliefs and experiences were shaped, moved, from one medium to another, concentrated in manageable aesthetic forms, offered for consumption") is indebted to Greenblatt, *Shakespearean Negotiations* (Berkeley: University of California Press, 1988), p. 5 and, more generally, pp. 1–20.

Chapter 4

1. *The Cōḷas*, p. 330.
2. Among the large bibliography of works on the temple, several can be singed out as exemplary. Younger, *The Home of Dancing Śivaṉ* (New York: Oxford University Press, 1995) provides an overview of the site's history of religions. Kulke, *Cidambaramāhātmya; eine Untersuchung der religionsgeschichtlichen und*

historischen Hintergründe für die Entstehung der Tradition eines südindischen Tempelstadt (Wiesbaden: Harrassowitz, 1970), while concentrating on a single text, seeks to offer a larger integrative picture of the site's history; this is discussed at length later in the chapter. Smith, *The Dance of Śiva* (Delhi: Oxford University Press, 1996), presents a wide-ranging interpretation of a single Sanskrit hymn; his book also contains a great deal that is of interest to the generalist. Much of the scholarship on this most famous of temples has, unsuprisingly, been art-historical: important works include Harle, *Temple Gateways of South India* (New Delhi: Munshiram Manoharlal Publishers, 1995); Balasubrahmanyam, *Middle Chola Temples* (Faridabad : Thomson Press, 1975); and Michell, *Chidambaram: Home of Nataraja* (Mumbai: Marg Publications, 2004). The leading example of revisionist scholarship is B. G. L. Swamy, *Cidambaram and Naṭarāja: Problems and Rationalization* (Mysore: Geetha Book House, 1979). A fine survey of the problems of writing the history of South Indian Śaivism from the available Tamil sources can be found in Goodall, *Parākhyatantra* (Pondicherry: EFEO/IFP, 2004), pp. xxix–xxxiv. Of the studies focusing on epigraphy, the pioneering work of Subrahmanyam, "The Oldest Chidambaram Inscriptions" (*Journal of Annamalai University*, vol. 13, 1944), merits special mention; Hall's "Merchants, Rulers, and Priests: Cidambaram in the Age of the Cōḻas" (in *Structure and Society in Early South India*, Delhi: Oxford University Press, 2001) attempts to produce an economic history with slender evidence. More successful is Orr, "Temple Life at Chidambaram in the Chola Period" (in *Sri Puspanjali*, Delhi: Bharatiya Kala Prakashan, 2004). The bilingual eulogy to Naralokavīra presents a special case, with its own scholarship: see further, n. 15, for references. The complaining epigraphist – cited without name in *The Cōḻas*, p. 16, n. 18 – was H. Krishna Sastri in his *Annual Report* of 1902 (p. 8); he repeated the sentiment in the preface to SII 4.

3. Quoted in Balasubrahmanyam, "Oldest Chidambaram Inscriptions", p. 56.
4. The record, which I have not been able to consult, is ARE 330 of 1958/1959, a fragmentary inscription dated to the third year of a Parakesarivarman, in what the epigraphist took to be a tenth-century character: it seems to be this record, as yet without an ARE number, that Balasubrahmanyam briefly mentions at the close of his article ("Earliest Inscriptions (part 2)" pp. 90 and 91, no. 1); he also notes a fragment in what he assesses to be the same script (*ibid.*, p. 91, no. 5). It records a gift of gold, but to the temple of Anantīśvaram rather than the Little Shrine. For Appar's poems, see for instance the second *patikam* of the fifth book of the *Tirumuṟai*, the Tamil Śaiva canon: vs. 2, *cĕmpŏṉampalatt' uḷ niṉṟa tāṇuvai … maṟantu*, "forgetting Sthāṇu, who stands within the hall of fine gold" and vs. 8, *tūya cempoṉṉiṉāl ĕḻuti meynta ciṟṟampala kūttaṉai … maṟantu*, "forgetting the Dancer of the Little Hall covered in finely worked pure, bright gold." Citations taken from Subrahmanya Aiyar, Chevillard, and Sarma, *Digital Tēvāram* (Pondicherry: IFP/EFEO, 2006). For Appar's date, see Zvelebil, *Lexicon of Tamil Literature* (Leiden: Brill, 1994), pp. 51ff.
5. For Rājarāja's title *śivapādaśekhara*, see e.g. SII II:1, ln. 55; as was already noted by Subrahmanyam ("Earliest Inscriptions (part 2)," p. 61n), this has no probative value whatsoever for the king's devotion to the Cidambaram

Śiva. On the iconographic program of the Tanjavur temple, see Champakalakshmi, *Trade, Ideology, and Urbanization* (Delhi: Oxford University Press, 1996), pp. 429–430. Kulottuṅga II's Cidambaram coronation is discussed in *The Cōḻas*, p. 348; even this depends on the interpretation of an ambiguous phrase in the king's *mĕykkīrtti*.

6. See Orr, "Temple Life," p. 231: "of the 288 inscriptions, only 6 date from the tenth century and 7 from the eleventh."
7. The characterization belongs to Hall, whose study ("Cidambaram in the Age of the Cōḻas") is largely based on the evidence of this one record; as Hall himself concedes (p. 103), however, references to Cidambaram's Coḻa-period *nagaram* marketing center are otherwise sparse, with one passing reference in a Kulottuṅga-era record (317 of 1958–1959) and another from a century later (SII 12: 154; this record, though ascribed by Hall to Kulottuṅga III's reign, is dated to year eight of the post-Coḻa warlord Koppĕruñciṅkaṉ).
8. On the *taṉiyūr*, refer especially to Champakalakshmi, "*Brahmadeya* and Its Ramifications" (in *Structure and Society in Early South India*, Delhi: Oxford University Press, 2001), drawing on the earlier discussions in *Political Geography*, pp. 92–94 (concentrating especially on Cidambaram) and *Peasant State*, p. 152 (focusing especially on Uttaramerūr).
9. For the conjoint *brahmadeya* Udaiyargudi-Kattumanarkoyil, alias Vīranārāyaṇacaturvedimaṅgalam, see Champakalakshmi, "*Brahmadeya,*" pp. 77–79, and *Political Geography*, Appendix 4 ("Kār-nāḍu") and Map 10.
10. These are Parākramacoḻanallūr (which contained the merchant center Guṇamenākai nagaram), Tillai Aḻakunallūr, Rājarājanallūr, Kuntavainallūr, and Aruṇmoḻinallūr (4: 223, ll. 18–19). These names, all of which are derived from personal names or titles of Coḻa royalty, indicate by their *-nallūr* segment that they were Brahman habitations. Most *taṉiyūr*s seem to have had a dozen such satellites; Cidambaram would eventually have twenty-two: see Champakalakshmi, "*Brahmadeya,*" and Thirumoorthy, "Settlement Patterns" (in *Kāveri*, Chennai: Panpattu Veliyiittakam, 2001). Also noteworthy at this early date is that these are related to named *periḷaimaināṭu*s; these, unlike the customary *nāṭu*s of the region, appear to be *ex nihilo* creations of the Coḻa land tenure system, as can be seen from their own highly royalist nomenclature (the two mentioned here are Kiṭāraṅkŏṇṭacoḻa-*p* and Maturāntaka-*p*). These seem to have been invented as representative bodies (or possibly units of revenue account?) for the gentry-cultivator communities in the vicinity (*Political Geography*, pp. 45–46); they are exclusively associated with the *taṉiyūr*s of Cidambaram, Udaiyargudi, and Mannargudi, and most of the references to them date from the early thirteenth century. The name of this unusual unit or assembly has eluded interpretation: Subbarayalu suggests (*ibid.*) that "it can be asserted with good authority that *Pēriḷamaiyar* were the same as the *Veḷḷāḷas*" of the region, while Champakalakshmi suggests that the semantics of *iḷamai* ("youth") suggest a connection with "younger/subordinate lineage groups" ("*Brahmadeya,*" p. 72n). Given its artificial, state-sponsored status, I would suggest that—along the lines of *vaḷanāṭu*, "prosperous *nāṭu*" – the name might be understood as a piece of

propagandistic salesmanship on the part of the agents of the Co<u>l</u>a state, and that it be understood as something like "great new-model *nāṭu,*" a more-or-less transparent attempt to turn its institutional novelty to its advantage.

11. Younger, *Dancing Śivaṉ*, pp. 92–104. He sensibly suggests (p. 97) that an earlier boundary wall was likely demolished in the course of the early twelfth-century renovations. This likely would have had nothing in common with the *gopuram*-dominated gigantism of the present day. Younger suggests that stones from this wall may have been used for the nearby Tiruvanantīśvaram temple (citing ARE 331 and 337 of 1958–1959).
12. Kuntavaiyāḻvār's record (ARE 119 of 1888, EI 5: 13c) is dated Kulottuṅga, year forty-four; in corrected Tamil orthography, the donation of the king of Kambhoja (Sūryavarman II?) reads (ll. 10–11): *śrīrājendracoḻadevaṟku kāmbocarājaṉ kāṭciyākak kāṭṭiṉa kallu*. Maturāntiki's record (ARE 117 of 1888, SII IV: 222, lines 7ff.) is tentatively dated to year forty-six (1116). The problem with the record's date, and its genuineness more generally, centers on its anomalous *mĕykkīrtti*. As published, it is a fusion of the opening of Śrīvallabha Pāṇḍya's eulogy (who did not begin to reign until 1120! See Cuppiramaṇiyam, *Mĕykkīrttikaḷ*, p. 219) and individual lines from Kulottuṅga's own late *mĕykkīrtti, pukaḻ cūḻnta*, etc. (I thank K. Vijayavenugopal for bringing this anomaly to my attention). Vācciyaṉ Iravi is mentioned in ln. 10; for the significance of his *gotra* name, see further.
13. This record has been edited and translated by Hultzsch: EI 5,13a (pp. 103–104).
14. The name Naralokavīra was Nilakanta Sastri's suggestion for a single title of reference for this Tondaimandalam lord, in his classic short study devoted to him ("Naralokavīra: A Cōḷa Feudatory" in *Studies in Chōḷa History and Administration*, Madras: University of Madras, 1932), from which much of my account derives. Besides variations on his Tamil *iyaṟpĕyar* (*kūttaṉ*[*ār*], *velkūttaṉ*, [*sabhā*]*nartaka*), other titles associated with him include *aruḷākara* and *mānāvatāra*. The epithet *naralokavīra* occurs frequently in the Sanskrit verses of this inscription (Skt vv. 8, 12, 21, 24, 30), but only once in the Tamil (vs. 7 [=1065], *cf.* Tiruvatikai, 1114; see note 15 for these references). The epithet likely derives from a metrical cliché in the resolution to a Sanskrit *upajāti* or *vasantatilaka* verse (the meter of all but one of these instances; *cf.* *Bhagavadgītā* 11.28).
15. The earliest published reference to the inscription was Hultzsch's notice of it as ARE 120 of 1888, while the first attempt at publication as SII IV: 225 resulted in a poor edition. The Sanskrit text had been copied down by one of the pandits working under Colin Mackenzie and was subsequently published (with some different readings and a Tamil paraphrase) as SITI nos. 1271–1273. A somewhat different Sanskrit text was published by B. G. L. Swamy as an appendix to his revisionist tract on Cidambaram (*Chidambaram and Naṭarāja*, pp. 121–134); this is accompanied by a very unreliable translation, based presumably on the SITI gloss. Another, more careful attempt at translation of the Sanskrit verses can be found in Balasubrahmanyam, *Later Chola Temples*,

pp. 23–26. Irākavaiyaṅkār's reconstruction appeared in his *Pĕruntŏkai* (Maturai: Tamiḻccaṅkamuttiracālai, 1936), as nos. 1059–1094; this is immediately followed by an edition of Naralokavīra's Tiruvatikai record (nos. 1095–1119): these verses so closely accord in metric, style, and points of phrasing that they were certainly written by the same poet at the Cidambaram *veṇpā*s. Irākavaiyaṅkār's repairs to the text of the Tamil eulogy are a remarkable work of scholarship, and I closely follow him for the text of these verses; where I disagree with his conjectures, I indicate it in the notes. Nilakanta Sastri's "Naralokavīra" contains careful discussion of several of the Tamil verses from Cidambaram as well as Tiruvatikai, and a summary of the Sanskrit *praśasti*.

One feature of the inscription's presentation of the Sanskrit verses evidently puzzled Krishna Sastri, the SII editor: in a footnote appended to the text in *South Indian Inscriptions*, he notes,

> The numbering of the verses in the original is not clear. While the first six are marked 11, 60, 68, and 60 (thrice) respectively, the succeeding 25 verses are marked with double figures. The first of these is the serial number of the verses (7 to 31) and the second is irregularly 56, 76, 44, 60, 64, 77 or 22. Could the verses be quotations from a recognized work? (SII IV: 225, p. 31).

Leaving aside the anomalous 11 for the first verse, in every case this number correctly corresponds to the number of syllables in each Sanskrit verse, a few errors notwithstanding (thus vs. 25 [*anuṣṭubh*] should read 32 instead of 22, and vs. 27 [*śārdūlavikrīḍita*] should read 76 instead of 77). I presume this to be an artifact of the fair copy given to the engraver in order to calculate the necessary space on the stone, something that the more regular Tamil *veṇpā*s would not have required. That these numbers were inadvertently included in the final version suggests that the inscription may have been made inattentively, in haste, or under adverse circumstances; this might suggest an explanation for the inferior quality of the Sanskrit and Tamil texts.

I presented a working version of the text and translation of this record to a workshop in Pondicherry as long ago as 2007, and much of my understanding I owe to the participants, especially Dominic Goodall and G. Vijayavenugopal. Subsequently, in a brief article ("Purāṇic Transformations in Coḻa Cidambaram"), I announced my intention to publish a critical edition and philological translation of the *praśasti*. Should I (or someone else) eventually gain access to the original text in situ – the ASI can no longer locate the record's estampage or any transcript made from it – this might prove worthwhile, but this is not possible given the materials that are presently available to me.

16. See Pollock, *Language of the Gods*, p. 50, for a characterization of the "linguistic division of labor" that came to be standard throughout the Sanskrit cosmopolis.
17. In all quotations from Naralokavīra's Cidambaram *praśasti*, the siglum A refers to the edition of the text in SII volume IV, B to the text of the Sanskrit given in SITI, referred to by their serial numbering there; C

refers to Irākavaiyaṅkār's edition of the Tamil verses, with two sets of numbering, one serial and the other the number assigned to them in *Pĕruntŏkai*. In the accompanying apparatus, an asterisk in the established text precedes each lemma; "conj." refers to my own conjectures. Skt vs. 1: *cakre tena sabhāpates tribhuvanakṣemāya nṛttam paraṃ kurvāṇasya tadekatānamanasā mānāvatāreṇa yat* | *tan mattaś śṛṇu sāvadhānam adhunā yatstotra* **pātrāśrayair* (conj.; *pātraśśatair* AB) *vvaktrair dehabhṛtaś caranti sarasan* **dyāvāpṛthivyor dvayoḥ* (B; *dyāvāpṛthivyonvayoḥ* A) | |

18. Vs. 1 [1059]: **ĕllai kaṭavāv ikalventaraik kavarnta* (C; *ellai kaṭalāl ikal* [*lenta*]*ṇakka vanta* A) *celvam elān tillaiccirrampalattut tŏllait tirukkŏṭuṅkai* **pŏṉmeyntāṉ* (A; *pŏṉveyntāṉ* C) *ṟiṇmaik kaliyiṉ tarukk'ŏṭuṅka velkūttaṉ ṟāṉ*; Vs. 2 [1060]: *tillaiyiṟ poṉṉampalattaic cempoṉāl* **meyntu* (A; *veyntu* C *passim*) *vāṉ ĕllaiyaip pŏṉṉākkiṉāṉ ĕṉparāl ŏllai vaṭaventar cĕlvam ĕlām vāṅka vel vāṅkuṅ* **kuṭaiventar* (A; *kuṭaiventaṉ* C) *tŏṇṭaiyār* **kŏl* (A; *ko* C)
19. The word supplies the verse's *taṉicŏl* or "independent word" occurring at the end of its second metrical line (*aṭi*, "foot") and sharing the pattern of front-rhyme (*ĕtukai*) with the opening two lines (on these terms, and the description of the *vĕṇpā* more generally, see U. Niklas, "Introduction to Tamil Prosody," BEFEO vol. 77, 1991, esp. pp. 177–178 [*ĕtukai*], 180 [§ 7.6, *taṉicŏl*], and 180–181 [§8.1, *vĕṇpā*].
20. This interpretation depends on undoing one of Irākavaiyaṅkār's emendations: he reads *ko* ("king") instead of the dubitative marker *kŏl*. While the expression *tŏṇṭaiyar ko(ṉ)* occurs regularly here and in Tiruvatikai, this reading would eliminate the contrast that is central to the verse.
21. Vs. 16 [/1074]: ... *tollainīr* [/] **maṇmakaḷait taṅkoṉ* (C; *maṇmakaḷaik* [*ka*] *ṅkoṉ* A) *matikkuṭaikkīḻ vīṟṟirutiv* [/] **uṇmakiḻun* (C; *urai makuḻum* A) *tŏṇṭaiyarkoṉ*; vs. 22 [/1080]: *pĕrolinīr motāv* [/] *alaikiṉṟav ĕllaiy apayaṉkke yāka* [/] *malaikiṉṟa tŏṇṭaiyār maṉ*.
22. Compare Nilakanta Sastri, "Naralokavīra," p. 185–186: the absence of a Coḻa regnal year "may raise a doubt that at some time he might have set up independent rule, throwing off his allegiance to his Cōḷa overlord." Against this, the great historian suggests that the statements of subordination to Apayaṉ/Kulottuṅga were "sufficiently precise."
23. Ta. vs. 30 [/1086]: *tillait tiyākavali* †*viṇciṟ pañcaviṇi*† [/] ĕllai nilaṅkŏṇṭ' iṟaiyiḻiccit tillai [/] *maṟaimuṭippārvītimaṭañ* **camaittāṉ* (A; *caṟaittāṉ* [?] C) *maṇṇor* [/] *kuṟai muṭippāṉ tŏṇṭaiyar ko*. Along with Irākavaiyaṅkār, I am unable to make sense of the crux in the first line; it is only a guess that *pañcaviṇi* might represent Skt. *pañcaviṃśat* (the form is not attested, to my knowledge).
24. This is most obvious in vs. 12 [/ 1070]: *cāla mutu pey taṭikkat* **tāraṭṭikait* [conj.; *tāraṭikkattaṅ*[*ku*] A; *tāraṭikkat* (?) C] *tŏṇṭaiyarkoṉ* / *pālamutu cĕyvittāṉ* **purintu* [conj.; *parintu* A *pārttu* C], "... so that the old ghoul[s?] grew hugely fat, the lord of the Tŏṇṭaiyar, with his garland and necklace, carefully arranged offerings of milk."

The occurrence of the *mutupey* here is a clear homage to the poem; on the verb *taṭittal* "to grow fat," *cf.* KP vs. 228 (*taṭittaṉam eṉat talai taṭittaṉam eṉa*, "[the ghouls said] 'We have grown fat, our heads have grown fat'"). The sole reference to Kulottuṅga as *apayaṉ* (see n. 21) also connects the eulogy with the court poem. The poet pursues a similar theme in the Tiruvatikai inscription, vs. 1104 *māṟupaṭuttār uṭalam vaṉpey pakirnt' uṇṇa*, "so the savage ghouls, bickering, divided up the corpse between them and ate it up." Beside these intertextual connections, there is also the real world resonance of the major sites of Naralokavīra's activity with the court's represented movement within the poem: Cayaṅkŏṇṭār depicts a royal progress from Cidambaram to Tiruvatikai to Kāñcī (vv. 299–300, see above, Chapter 3, "Time-Warp and Incarnation"), precisely the three places where Naralokavīra left his most conspicuous donations.

25. Skt. vs. 29cd: *cakāra* **yo* [conj.; *yad* AB] *vairivilāsinīnāṃ vanāgnidhūmāmbaratām karoti*. On this misogynist topos of the exile and destitution of the women of a *praśasti*'s subject's foes, see Ingalls, *Anthology of Sanskrit Court Poetry*, Cambridge: Harvard University Press, 1965, pp. 372–373, § 4.
26. Vs. 5: *śucikusumasamudragrastadigvyomasīma drumavanam anurūpan tatra* **bhaktyā vyadhatta* (B (conj.?); *pa*[*tyābhya*]*dhatta* A) [|] *viśama-nayana-lāsyālokanāyāgatānāṃ vibudhaparibṛḍhānāṃ vy*[*ā*]*hṛtair vyāptapārśvam* [||]
27. Vs. 30: *kiñcāyam atraiva cakāra sālam bāhyam śilābhir naralokavīraḥ* [|] *yacchṛṅgameghastanitaiś śivāyāḥ krīḍāmayūrā racayanti lāsyam* [||]
28. *nāmnā tan naralokavīram akarot sālam mahāntam prabhor* **tasminn* (B; *tasi*[*n*] A) *eṣa sabhānaṭaḥ parapurapradhvaṃsadīkṣāguruḥ* [|] *yacchṛṅgāgranibaddhaketanapaṭā nedīyasā* **bhāsvatā* (B; *bhāsvatās* A) **taptāḥ takṣaka-* (conj.; *taptāntaḥkṣiti-* B; *taptāntakṣiti-* A)*val* **lihanti* (B; *labhanti* A) *śiśiraṃ vyomāpagāyāḥ payaḥ* [||], The phrase "like Takṣaka" in the translation is based upon my own tentative conjecture: compared to the two published readings, this yields better grammar (*taptāḥ* agreeing with *ketanapaṭā*[*ḥ*]), and provides an appropriate standard of comparison for the conceit of the flags "licking" the waters. Against this, I know of no poet's convention especially connecting Takṣaka with the Gaṅgā.
29. The synonymous *sabhānartaka* is found in Sanskrit prose inscription recording Naralokavīra's constructions in Siddhalingamadam (ARE 267 of 1909, SII 26: 388).
30. Swamy, *Chidambaram and Naṭarāja* (p. 125) anticipates some of the interpretation given here. His rendering of the verse, however, is absolutely unreliable: for instance, he is unaware of the referential doubling between man and god in the name *sabhānaṭa*.
31. Cuppiramaṇiyam, *Mĕykkīrttikaḷ* no. 24, ll. 30–38 p. 113 (*cf.* SII 5: 458, dated to year eleven) *pattāṇṭu varumuṟai* [/] *muṉṉe maṉṉavar cumant'* / **uḷḷ'iṟai* [SII] *niraittuc cŏrinta cĕmpoṟkuvaiyāṟ* [/] *taṉkulanāyakaṉ tāṇṭavam puriyuñ* [/] *cĕmpŏṉampalañ cūḻtirumāḷikaiyuṅ* [/] *kopuravāyiṟkūṭa cāḷāmum* [/] *ulakavalaṅkŏṇṭav ŏḷiviḷaṅku nemik* [/] *kulavaraiy utayakkuṉṟamŏṭu niṉṟ' ĕṉap* [/] *pacumpŏṉ mĕyntu* ...

32. *Cf.* Nilakanta Sastri, *The Cōḻas*, pp. 344–345, who, however, downplays the novelty of this claim.
33. Cuppiramaṇiyam, *Mĕykkīrttikaḷ* pp. 113–114, ll. 52–56 *pattām āṇṭir̲ cittiraittiṅkaḷ / attam pĕr̲r̲a ātittavārattut / tiruvaḷarmatiyiṉ trayodaśipakkattu / iṉṉaṉa palavum iṉitu camaitt'aruḷit /taṉ ŏrukuṭainiḻar̲ talamuḻutun taḻaippa.*
34. The calculations are Franz Kielhorn's, in EI VII: 1 (p. 5); this is broadly confirmed by that fact that in a fragmentary record from the south face of the second *prākāra* (ARE 314 of 1958/1959), an inscription of Vikrama's tenth year announced two royal visits and tax remissions to the temple's benefit. These are dateable to October 22, 1128 (day 115) and May 8, 1129 (day 313), neatly bookending the *mĕykkīrtti*'s date. *Cf.* Orr, "Temple Life at Cidambaram," p. 237, who notes this unpublished record.
35. *Vikkramacoḻaṉulā*, vv. 78–79 (trans. Wentworth, *Yearning for a Dreamed Real*, p. 364): the conquests detailed in the first of these match those of both the Cidambaram and the Tiruvatikai eulogies; while *kāliṅkarkoṉ* does not occur in the Cidambaram verses (the synonymous *kāliṅkar er̲u* and *kāliṅkar* each occur once) it is found *passim* in Tiruvatikai.
36. See Orr, "Temple Life at Chidambaram," p. 233, from whom I draw my figures.
37. See again Orr, "Temple Life," pp. 233ff., and especially n. 7. Vācciyaṉ perhaps suggests a role in ritual or other public performance (*cf.* Skt. *vācaka*, "reciter" or *vādya*, "musical instrument"; *cf.* TKC, *s.v. vācciyaṅkaḷ*). The name *uḻaiccaraṇaṉ*, which is found almost exclusively in Cidambaram, remains opaque even in its orthography: Orr, for instance, reads "*uḻaiccāṇaṉ*" (I follow the transcription in Orr's prepublication manuscript, as the names given in the published version are incorrect). I choose to give the name that seems to yield some sense ("deer foot"); the two renderings are graphically indistinguishable in inscriptional Tamil. The *Concordance of Names* only lists eight figures bearing the name-segment Uḻaiccaraṇaṉ or its variants (*uḻaiccāṇan, uḻaiccāḷaṉ*); six of these (75 percent) are found in Cidambaram (the majority of Orr's references to *uḻaiccaraṇaṉ* figures are found in unpublished inscriptions not taken into account in the *Concordance*); of the thirty-seven figures in the concordance with name-segment Vācciyaṉ, seven (19 percent) are from Cidambaram. While the distribution of ninety-eight figures bearing the name Kavuciyaṉ or one of its variants (*kavucikaṉ/kavuṇiyan/kaviṇiyaṉ, etc.*) shows no clear regional focus, it is notable that among these figures there is a high incidence of personal names connecting their bearers to the Cidambaram temple (e.g. *tillaināyakabhaṭṭan*, no. 5146; *mūvāyirapaṭṭaṉ* no. 4659, *āṭaviṭaṅkapaṭṭaṉ*, no. 4669; *aḻakaviṭaṅkapaṭṭaṉ*, no. 4692; *tiruccir̲r̲ampalamuṭaiyāṉ*, no. 1239; *tillaippirāṉ*, the father of the single man recorded under nos. 1818 and 1836).
38. The best evidence of the acculturation to Brahmanical norms by the Pāñcarātrikas can be found in the *Āgamaprāmāṇyam* of Yāmunācārya, who wrote in the first half of the eleventh century. In the course of his defense of the validity of the Pañcarātra scriptures, Yāmuna refutes a presumed

objection that the practitioners of their ritual precepts, whom he called *bhāgavatas* or *sāttvatas*, were not in fact a part of the Brahman *varṇa*, but members of a ritually impure caste of temple servants. See *Āgamprāmāṇyam*, pp. 11–17 (*pūrvapakṣa*), 105ff. (*siddhānta*). Yāmuna's natal village of Kāṭṭumaṉṉārkuṭi is less than sixteen miles to the southwest of Cidambaram.

39. Kulke, *Cidambaramāhātmya, Eine Untersuchung*, pp. 159–213 and "Functional Interpretation of a South Indian Māhātmya" (in *Kings and Cults*, Delhi: Manohar, 1993). I am very pleased to acknowledge the interest and warm encouragement that I have received from Professor Kulke ever since I first began this research, including the access he has allowed me to the two MSS he used in his 1967 dissertation (see n. 43).
40. Kulke, "Functional Interpretation," pp. 199–202; *Cidambaramāhātmya*, pp. 200–206.
41. "Functional Interpretation," p. 203; for this conjecture's afterlife as fact see Witzel, "Toward a History of the Brahmans," p. 267.
42. "Functional Interpretation," pp. 192–194, 206–207, on Berg; Kulke is quick to acknowledge the difficulty in simply imposing the cultural logics of pre-Islamic Java onto southern India.
43. All citations from the text here are based on three sources: the edition published by Somasundara Dikshitar (=Ed.), and the paper transcripts of two MSS held in the Government Oriental Manuscripts Library, Chennai: D. No. 19347 (designated with the siglum A, this is Kulke's CM1) and R.7632 (siglum B, Kulke's CM2). I am very grateful to Kulke for sharing these with me, as I am to David Smith and David Shulman, who jointly provided me with Dikshitar's very rare edition. This workmanlike effort makes no reference to its sources, and records no variants; I presume it to be based on a single good manuscript of the CM. Given the edition's inaccessibility, and the degree of variation between the three sources, it seemed prudent to constitute the text in all passages cited here. For short passages, I have indicated the rejected variants in brackets; for longer ones I have provided a critical apparatus. In the apparatus, letters enclosed in hash marks (# ... #) indicate syllables that are unclear in the source; "ac" and "pc" stand, respectively, for *ante correctionem* and *post correctionem* ("before" and "after correction"); "conj." indicates my conjectural emendations. I have not been able to assess the value, whether attestational or as an independent literary work, of the Tamil transcreation attributed to Umāpatiśiva, the *Koyiṟpurāṇam*.
44. Kulke, *Cidambaramāhātmya*, p. 156:"... in Stil der purāṇas die Schöpfungsgeschichte."
45. Ed, pp. 101–102; A p. 108; B p. 88:

tasmin mahati saṃhārasamaye parameśvaraḥ |
rudrarūpadharas sākṣād akaroc caṇḍatāṇḍavam || 6
punas svatantro bhagavān icchāśaktipracoditaḥ |
saṃhārasyāntasamaye sargaṃ sthāpya svaśaktiṣu || 7
prakāśya ca mahāmāyāṃ tasyām adbhutasaṃsadi |
nādādipañcatattvāni sasarja jagatāṃ prabhuḥ || 8
śuddhamārgaṃ tataś caivaṃ sṛṣṭvā vācaṃ caturvidhām |
mātṛkāyās turīyāyā varṇān utpādya śaṃkaraḥ || 9

sasarja teṣāṃ prathamaṃ mātrātritayalakṣaṇam |
sargādikṛtyasahitaṃ praṇavaṃ svaprakāśakaṃ || 10
tataś ca vyāhṛtīs tābhyo gāyatrīṃ vedamātaram |
tasyās sasarja bhagavān sarvān vedān atandritaḥ || 11
tebhyas sasarja bhagavān saptakoṭi mahāmanūn |
upamantrāṃs tatas tebhyas tatsaṃkhyātas sasarja ha || 12
tad anyasyāś ca māyāyās tattvajātaṃ sasarja saḥ |
kālādyavaniparyantaṃ carācarasamanvitam || 13

6a *tasmin mahati AB; tasminn ahani Ed.*
6b *samaye EdApcB; samaveśa Aac [sic],*
7d *sargaṃ EdA; svargaṃ B*
8a *prakāśya EdB; pradarśya A*
8b *tasyām EdB; tasminn A (sic)*
8d *jagatāṃ B; jagataḥ EdA*
9a *śuddhamārgaṃ EdB; śuddhamārgāṃ A*
9b *vācaṃ caturvidhām EdA; vācaś caturvidhāḥ B*
10c *sahitaṃ EdA; tritayaṃ sahitaṃ B [sic]*
10d *svaprakāśakaṃ EdB; suprakāśakaṃ A*
11b *veda- B; loka- EdA*
11c *sasarja EdB; santuṣṭa- A*
12d *tatsaṃkhyātas Ed; tatkhātāṃś ca A tatsaṃkhyātāṃs B; ha AB; saḥ Ed*
13b *saḥ EdB; ha A*
13c *kālādya- EdB; javādya- A.*

46. While this passage is resonant with a spectrum of Śaiva texts, I have been unsuccessful in locating any of the author's direct sources: invaluable here is the information contained in the *Tāntrikābhidhānakośa* (Wien: Verlag der Österreichischen Akademie der Wissenschaften, 2000–): see ss.vv. *icchā* [*śakti*], *tattva*, *nāda*, and [*mahā*]*māyā*. On the phrase *nādādipañcatattvāni* in 8c, with its correlation between the reality-levels of the Śaiva "Pure Universe" or *śuddhādhvan* and the production of articulate sound, refer to the discussion in Goodall, *Bhaṭṭarāmakaṇṭhaviracitā Kiraṇavṛttiḥ* (Pondicherry: IFP/ EFEO, 1998), pp. 290–293 (f.n. 392), citing a range of primary sources.
47. Vs. 9bcd's reference to the fourth and hindmost part of language giving rise to articulate sound pointedly recalls the phrase *turīyam vācaḥ manuṣyāḥ vadanti* ("men speak the fourth part of language") quoted and discussed by Patañjali in the *Paspaśādhikaraṇa* of the *Mahābhāṣya* (p. 3). On the wider history of the synthesis between Veda-congruent Brahmanism and tantric Śaivism, refer to Sanderson's magisterial *Śaivism and Brahmanism in the Early Medieval Period.*
48. Ed pp. 102–3; A pp. 110–111 B p. 89:

mahānto vaidikā mantrās sarve yāgāya matkṛtāḥ || 16
teṣām adhyayanārthāya sṛṣṭāś caiva dvijātayaḥ |
yāgasyāpi ca siddhyarthaṃ gāvas sasṛjire mayā || 17
havirbhis tadbhavair eva taiś ca mantrair dvijātayaḥ |
matprīṇanāya manmūrtāv agnau juhvati ye narāḥ || 18
duṣprāpam anyais te svargaṃ labhante nātra saṃśayaḥ |

madāgameṣu ye saktāś caryāyogakriyāparāḥ | | 19
sārūpyāvadhikā muktis teṣāṃ sidhyen na saṃśayaḥ |
ye vaidikāḥ punar yāgān niṣkāmāḥ kurvate dvijāḥ | | 20
trividhām api vindanti muktiṃ te nātra saṃśayaḥ |
vedāntaniṣṭhitā ye tu jñānino vītakalmaṣaḥ | | 21
madāgamaparā ye ca jñānapāde vyavasthitāḥ |
ubhaye 'pi ca vindanti sāyujyam atidurbalam | | 22

16d *yāgāya* Ed; *yāgāś ca* AB
17b *dvijātayaḥ* Ed; *dvijādayaḥ* AB
17d *gāvas* EdB; *yāgās* A
18a *tadbhavair* EdB; *tadbhayair* Aac; *tanmayair* Apc
18b *dvijātayaḥ* Ed; *dvijādayaḥ* AB
18c *manmūrtāv agnau* EdBpc; *manmūrtavahnau* A
18b *juhvati* Ed; *jihūs ta* Aac (*sic*); *juhuvus te* Apc (*sic*); *juhvanti* B (*sic*)
19a *te* EdB; *tat* A
19c *saktāś* EdB; *kartāś* Aac (*sic*; canceled)
20a *sārūpyāvadhikā* A; *sārūpyād adhikā* Ed; *sārūpyadadhikā* B (*sic*)
20b *sidhyen* A *siddhā* Ed; *siddher* B
20c *yāgān* EdA; *yāgās* B
20d *niṣkāmāḥ* EdB; *niṣkrāntāḥ* A
21a *vindanti* EdB; *kurvanti* A
21c *niṣṭhitā* AB; -*niratāḥ* Ed
22d *ati*- EdA; *api* B

While it is also explicable as the characteristic voicing of Sanskrit consonant when pronounced by a Tamil speaker, AB's *dvijādayaḥ* ("twice-borns and other men") might represent a shared secondary attempt to remove the logical absurdity of the passage only accounting for the creation of Brahmans.

49. Ed. pp. 103–4; A pp. 111–112; B pp. 89–90.

ubhayeṣu ca mārgeṣu karmabrahmapareṣu ca |
vedāgamaprasiddheṣu ye na tiṣṭhanti pāpinaḥ | | 23
caturvidhaiś ca te daṇḍyāḥ daṇḍaiś śāstrapracoditaiḥ |
asmād grāhayituṃ śaktāṃś śāstrārthān adhikāriṇaḥ | | 24
pravartayitum etāṃś ca dharmān sthāpayituṃ tataḥ |
nivartayitum evāsmad asato 'nadhikāriṇaḥ | | 25
pravṛttān apy anuncite mārge śāsayituṃ tathā |
atra rājā hi śaknoti prajāpālanadīkṣitaḥ | | 26
rājā durātmanaś śāsti rājā kālasya kāraṇam |
eṇāṅkamaulir bhagavān iti niścitya cetasā | | 27
sarvalokādhirājyasya śaktaṃ kaṃcin nirūpya ca |
tatas tv āhūya dharmajñau savitus tanayāv ubhau | | 28
nigrahānugrahābhyāṃ ca dharmasthāpanatatparau |
tayor ekasya bhagavān daṇḍaṃ datvā jagatprabhuḥ | | 29
dakṣiṇāśāpatiṃ cakre trailokyasamavartinam |
rājñāṃ kakudam anyaṃ ca kṛtvā makuṭadhāriṇam | | 30

23a *ca* EdB; *tu* A
24a *te* EdB; *tair* A
24b *daṇḍaiś* AB; *daṇḍyaiś* Ed
24c *asmād* EdB; *tasmād* A
24d *śaktāṃṣ* conj.; *śaktāḥ* B; *muktāś* EdA
25a *evāsmad* Ed; *etasmā* A; *asm#ān#* B
25d *asato* EdA; *#da tha to#* B; *'nadhikāriṇaḥ* EdB; *nādhikāriṇaḥ* A
26a *pravṛttān apy anuncite mārge* EdB; *pravṛttānumate mārge tāṃś ca* A
26c *rājā hi śaknoti* EdB; *rājātiśakto hi* A
27a *śāsti* EdB; *śāstā* A
27c *eṇāṅkamaulir* AB; *śaśāṇkamaulir* Ed
27d *niścitya* AB; *niścita-* Ed
28a *adhirājyasya* EdB; *adhikārājyasya* A (canceled)
28b *śaktaṃ* AB; *śaktiṃ* Ed *kaṃcin* conj.; *kiṃcin* EdAB
28c *dharmajñau* B; *dharmajño* EdA 30a *dakṣiṇāśāpatiṃ* EdB; *dakṣiṇāśāpatiś* A.

50. The list for four modes of punishment (reprimand, censure, fines, and execution) is found in *Manusmṛti* 8.129; the phrase *rājā kālasya kāraṇam* is a commonplace in the *Mahābhārata* (e.g. 5.13.15d and 12.7.6d).
51. On the textual interrelationship between the *Cidambaramāhātmya* and the *Sūtasaṃhitā*, see Cox, "Purāṇic Transformations." In a forthcoming study, I document the latter's complex process of textual synthesis as a leading example of the anonymous Tantric and purāṇic philology of its period.
52. 20.35ab: *āsīd bhāgirathīpūraparipanthiyaśoṃkuraḥ* | (*panthiyaśo-* EdB; *-panthī yaśo-* A). *cf.* Kulke, *Cidambaramāhātmya*, pp. 203–204.
53. 25:16 *vyāghradhvajaṃ dadāv* **asmai* (EdA; *asair* B) *varaṃ rājñāṃ sudurlabham* | *avalambya kareṇainaṃ praviśyāśu cidambaram* || *pādas* CD are missing in A.
54. The phrase is van Buitenen's: see his general "Introduction," in *The Book of the Beginning*, Chicago: University of Chicago Press, 1973, pp. xvi–xix.
55. 20:40–50; 22:5–14.
56. 22.1: *prathamo gauḍanāthasya* **rājñas sūnur* (EdB; *rajasūnur* A) *ahaṃ mune.* Kulke unconvincingly attempted to link the name Gauḍa with the name of the Godāvari river (*Cidambaramāhātmya*, p. 200). The young Simhavarman's itinerary (20: 51–56) is equally problematic: though it seems to link the prince with the Bhimavaram temple in Andhra where both Kulottuṅga and his sons were prominent donors, it places the temple in Orissa (or in central India), which seems to be located near Java (20:52–53 *anyedyuḥ prāviśad rājyaṃ tasmād yāvakanāmakaṃ* | *tad atītya punas so 'yam* **oḍra*(Ed; *oḍya-* A; *madhya-* B)*deśaṃ suvistṛtam* || 52 *praviśya tan* **namaskṛtya* (EdA; *namas kṛtvā* B) *bhīmanāthaṃ tadantare* | *sthānāny api tadanyāni* **tatra natvā* (EdB; *tan natvā* A, canceled) *mahāyaśāḥ* || 53).
57. All three sources diverge on the sole mention of what might be the figure's name: 20.34cd reads in Dikshitar's edition *śrīmān rājā lekhendrasaṃjñakaḥ* in A (p. 112) *rājā lokeśavikramaḥ* (either a proper name or an epithet), and in B *rajo* [*sic*; read *rājā*] *lekhendravikramaḥ.* The reading shared by Ed and B, *lekhendra-*, is unconvincing as a proper name. Kulke adopts A's reading

throughout (*Cidambaramāhātmya,* pp. 19ff., 203ff.); the presence of the epithet *vikramaḥ* in one of Rājendra's copperplate inscriptions suggests to him that this is yet another linkage with the apex ancestor of the imperial Coḻas ("Legend of Hiraṇyavarman," p. 199). While both Siṃhavarman and Hiraṇyavarman are attested names of Pallava kings (see Francis, *La discours royal dans l'Inde du Sud ancienne*, "Généalogie, no. 6," p. 255), there is no real historical sense in the CM's invocation of them. The actual Pallava kings bearing these regnal titles were separated by (at least) five generations, and Hiraṇyavarman is barely represented in the available genealogical sources for the dynasty, the sole attestation being the testimony of the Kasakudi plates (see Francis, *La discours,* pp. 296–297, and Hultzsch's introduction to his edition of the plates SII 2: 73, p. 344). To think that the authors of the CM might have preserved some memory of this dynastic situation half a millennium later seems impossible; I presume that these were simply names to them, perhaps resonant of the ancient past of Tondaimandalam.

58. Cf. Orr, "Temple Life at Chidambaram," p. 233: "There are no indications in the inscriptions of Chidambaram of the 'importation' or immigration of Brāhmaṇs from North India. We do not even find at Chidambaram evidence that we see at other temples of Brāhmaṇa families whose names indicate origins in villages in Andhra Pradesh."
59. Kulke, *Cidambaramāhātmya*, pp. 168–170; *Ibid.*, "Functional Interpretation," p. 204.
60. The final Tamil verse of the Naralokavīra inscription (37/1094) mentions that a drainage sluice was constructed "so to increase the prosperity of the Three-Thousand of Tillai." The only published inscription in the region that uses the label is of the thirteenth century: SII 8:43, dated in the thirty-sixth regnal year of the warlord Koppĕruñciṅkaṉ (*ca.* 1279?). Occurrences of the name-segment [*tillai*]*mūvāyira-* found in Karashima *et al.*'s *Concordance* are all dateable to the late twelfth century at the earliest.
61. 25.32cd-33: *cidambaram idam divyaṃ navīkartum *ihotsahe* (Ed; *ihotsave* AB) | *eteṣām ca samastānāṃ munīnāṃ divyatejasām* | *āśramāṇi viśālāni cikīrṣāmi samantataḥ* |
62. I find that Kenneth Hall, in his economic-historical review of the temple city, comes to similar conclusions about the text, via a very different route: "Cidambaram in the Age of the Cōḻas," pp. 111–112.
63. "Dikshitars' Right to Manage Natarajar Temple Cannot Be Taken Away" *The Hindu*, January 7, 2014 (accessed online on April 28, 2015). It is unclear when the group began to identify itself as Dikshitars (*dīkṣitāḥ, tīṭcitar*). The name is unknown to the CM, though the summary verses in the *śārdūlavikrīḍita* meter appended to the beginning of each chapter of the published edition (possibly the work of its modern editor?) use the title *passim* as a synonym for the 3,000 Brahmans. Studies of the community and its unusual status can be found in John Loud, *The Dikshitars of Chidambaram* (PhD. thesis, University of Wisconsin-Madison, 1990), and Younger, *Home of the Dancing Śivaṉ*, pp. 13–39.
64. I refer to two records, both from the Kuntīmādhava temple in Pithapuram and both published by Hultzsch in volume 4 of *Epigraphia*

Indica: no. 4, issued by the Veḷanāḍi king Pṛthivīśvara in *śaka* 1108 (*ca.* 1186) and no. 55, issued in *śaka* 1124 (1202) by the supposed Cālukya Mallapadeva. I hope to discuss these two interesting records in a later publication.

65. For Virūpākṣa's *campū*, see Raghavan's introduction to his edition of the text. What I know of *Navacoḷacaritramu*, I owe to my student Jamal Jones of the University of Chicago.

Conclusions

1. The theory underlies the several studies comprising Sahlins's *Islands of History* (Chicago: University of Chicago Press, 1985), and is expressly discussed in its final chapter, "Structure and History" (pp. 136–156). Sahlins expanded on this in a subsequent article, "The Return of the Event, Again," cited as it appears in Marshall Sahlins, *Culture in Practice: Selected Essays* (New York: Zone Books, 2000), pp. 293–351.
2. See William Sewell, "A Theory of the Event: Marshall Sahlins' 'Possible Theory of History,'" in *Logics of History: Social Theory and Social Transformation* (Chicago: University of Chicago Press, 2005), pp. 197–224, and the practical exercise in its application in the same volume's "Historical Events as Transformation of Structures: Inventing Revolution at the Bastille" (pp. 225–270). My reference to Banks derives from a section of his novel *Excession* (London: Orbit, 1996); Sahlins's quotation is from p. 138 of *Islands of History*; Sewell's discussion of it can be found in *Logics of History*, pp. 200ff.
3. *Islands, ibid.*; I cite the text as emended by Sewell (*Logics, ibid.*, et passim); Sahlins's earlier published version reads "in actions *or* in the world" (italics added).
4. *Islands*, p. 145; *Logics*, pp. 205–213, esp. 206, 209.
5. *Islands*, pp. 149–50; cf. *Logics*, p. 203.
6. *Logics*, p. 199 and pp. 221–223 and "The Return of the Event, Again," pp. 341–344.
7. *Logics*, p. 224.
8. Richard Rorty, "On Ethnocentrism: A Reply to Clifford Geertz," in *Objectivity, Relativism and Truth: Philosophical Papers* (Cambridge: Cambridge University Press, 1991), pp. 203–210.

Bibliography

Abbreviations

ARE	Annual Report on Epigraphy (later Annual Report on Indian Epigraphy)
ASI	Archeological Survey of India
BEFEO	*Bulletin de l'École française d'Extrême-Orient*
BEI	*Bulletin d'Études Indiennes*
BSOAS	*Bulletin of the School of Oriental and African Studies*
CIS	*Contributions to Indian Sociology*
CSSH	*Comparative Studies in Society and History*
EC	*Epigraphia Carnatica*
EFEO	École française d'Extrême-Orient
EI	*Epigraphia Indica*
IA	*Indian Antiquary*
IESHR	*The Indian Economic and Social History Review*
IFP	Institut Français de Pondichéry
IPS	*Inscriptions (texts) of Pudukottai State*
JAHRS	*Journal of the Andhra Historical Research Society*
JAOS	*Journal of the American Oriental Society*
JAS	*Journal of Asian Studies*
JESHO	*Journal of the Economic and Social History of the Orient*
JIP	*Journal of Indian Philosophy*
JRAS	*Journal of the Royal Asiatic Society*
JSAS	*Journal of South Asian Studies*
MTL	University of Madras *Tamil Lexicon*
PI	*Pondicherry Inscriptions*
QJMS	*Quarterly Journal of the Mythic Society* (Bangalore)
SII	*South Indian Inscriptions*
SITI	*South Indian Temple Inscriptions*
TKC	*Tamiḻk kalvĕṭṭuc cŏllakarāti*

Primary Sources in Sanskrit and Tamil

Āgamaprāmāṇyam
Āgamaprāmāṇyam of Yāmunācārya. Edited by N. Narasimhachari. Baroda: Gaekwad's Oriental Series, 1976.

Arthaśāstra
The Kauṭilīya Arthaśāstra. Edited by R. P. Kangle. Bombay: University of Bombay, 1969.

Brahmayāmalatantra
IFP T.522 (*'mātṛtantra'*), paper, Devanāgarī script; cover page reads "copied from a ms. belonging to Candraśekharagurukkal, Tirukkalukkunram."

Chāndogya Upaniṣad
Olivelle, *The Early Upaniṣads*.

Cidambaramāhātmya
Edited by Somasundara Dikshitar. Kadavasal: Sri Meenakshi Press, 1968.
Also GOML ms. D. No. 19347 (=A) and ms. R.7632 (=B), both paper, Devanāgarī script.

Cilappatikāram
Iḷaṅko Aṭikaḷ, *Cilappaṭikāram*. Edited by U. Vē. Cāminātaiyar. Ceṉṉai: Makāmakōpāttiyāya Ṭakṭar U. Vē. Cāminātaiyar Nūl Nilaiyam, 2011 (reprint).

Coḷacampū
Virupaksakavi, *Cola campū*. Edited with critical introduction and notes by V. Raghavan. Tanjore: Administrative Committee, T.M.S.S.M. Library, 1951.

Divyasūricaritam
Garuḍavāhana Paṇḍita, *Śrīdivyasūricaritam*. Edited by Ko. Ka. A. Veṅkaṭācārya. Bambaī: Anantācārya Risarca insṭīṭyūṭa, 1978.

Irācarācacōḻaṉulā
Kaviccakkaravartti Oṭṭakkūttar iyaṟṟiya mūvarulā: paḻaiya urai, kuṟippuraikaḷuṭaṉ. Edited by U. Ve Cāminātaiyar. Ceṉṉai: Makāmakōpāttiyāya Ṭākṭar U. Ve. Cāminātaiyar Nūl Nilaiyam, 1992.

Kaliṅkattupparaṇi
Kaviccakaravartti Cayaṅkoṇṭār pāṭiya Kaliṅkattupparaṇi mūlamum arumporuḷviḷakamutaliyaṉavum. Edited by A. Kōpālaiyar. Ceṉṉai: Nārāyaṇaiyaṅkār, 1923.
Kaliṅkattupparaṇi. Edited by A. V. Kaṉṉaiya Nāyuṭu. Ceṉṉai: P. N. Accukkuṭam, 1944.
Kaliṅkattupparaṇi, tĕlipŏruḷ viḷakkak kuṟipuraiuṭaṉ. No editor given, annotated by Pĕ. Paḻaṉivel Piḷḷai. Tirunĕlveli: South India Saiva Siddhanta Works Publishing Society (=Kaḻakam), 1968 (reprint).

Kāvyādarśa
Kāvyalakṣaṇam of Daṇḍin. Edited by Anantalal Thakur and Upendra Jha. Darbhanga: Mithila Institute of Post-Graduate Studies and Research in Sanskrit Learning, 1957.

Kulottuṅkacolavulā
Kaviccakkaravartti Oṭṭakkūttar iyaṟṟiya mūvarulā: paḻaiya urai, kuṟippuraikaḷuṭaṉ. Ceṉṉai: Makāmakōpāttiyāya Ṭākṭar U. Vē. Cāminātaiyar Nūl Nilaiyam, 1992. See also Wentworth, *Yearning for a Dreamed Real.*

Harṣacarita
Harṣacarita of Bāṇabhaṭṭa. Edited and translated by P. V. Kane. Delhi: Motilal Barnasidass, 1986 (reprint).

Mahābhāṣya
The Vyākaraṇa-Mahābhāṣya of Patañjali. Edited by Franz Kielhorn. Bombay: Government Central Book Depot, 1885–1909.

Manusmṛti
Olivelle, *Manu's Code of Laws.*

Navasāhasāṅkacarita
The Navasâhasâṅka charita of Padmagupta alias Parimala, part I, containing the preface, the text with various readings, and an index to the ślôkas. Edited by Vâmana Śâstrî Islâmpurkar. Bombay: Government Central Book Depot, 1895.

Nītivākyāmṛta
Śrīmatsomadevasūriviracitam Nītivākyāmṛtam. Edited by Pannalal Soni. Bombay: Māṇikyacandra Digambara Jaina Granthamālā, 1922–1933.

Paripāṭal
Eṭṭuttokaiyuḷ aintāvatākiya Paripāṭal mūlamum Parimēlaḻakaruraiyum. Edited by U. Vē. Cāminātaiyar. Ceṉṉai: Makāmakōpāttiyāya Ṭakṭar U. Ve. Cāminātaiyar Nūl Nilaiyam, 1980 (reprint).

Puṟanāṉūṟu
Puṟanāṉūṟu: mūlamum paḻaiya uraiyam. Edited by U. Vē. Cāminātaiyar. Ceṉṉai: Makāmakōpāttiyāya Ṭakṭar U. Ve. Cāminātaiyar Nūl Nilaiyam, 1971 (reprint).

Rājataraṇgiṇī
Kalhaṇa's Rājataraṅgiṇī: A Chronicle of the Kings of Kaśmīr, 3 vols. Edited and translated by Sir Aurel Stein. Westminster: A. Constable, 1900.

Tēvāram
Subramanya Aiyar, V. M., Jean-Luc Chevillard, and S. A. S. Sarma. *Digital Tēvāram. Kaṇiṉit Tēvāram* [CD-ROM]. Pondicherry: IFP/EFEO, 2007.

Saṃvitsiddhi
Yāmunācāryas Saṃvitsiddhi: Kritische Edition, Übersetzung und Anmerkungen mit einem Rekonstruktionsversuch der verlorenen Abschnitte. Edited by Roque Mesquita. Wien: Verlag der Österreichischen Akademie der Wissenschaften, 1988.

Takkayākapparaṇi
Kaviccakkaravarttiyākiya Oṭṭakkūttar iyaṟṟiya Takkayākapparaṇi: mūlamum uraiyum. Edited by U. Ve. Cāminātaiyar. Ceṉṉai: Makāmakōpāttiyāya Ṭākṭar U. Ve. Cāminātaiyar Nūlnilaiyam, 1992.

Vikramāṅkadevacarita

Vikramāṅkadevacaritaṃ Mahākāvyaṃ. Edited by Murari Lal Nagar. Benares: Government Sanskrit College, 1945.

Vikramāṅkadevacarita. Edited by Georg Bühler. Bombay: Government Central Book Depot, 1875.

Epigraphy: Texts and Reports

Annual Report on (South Indian) Epigraphy. Madras: Archeological Survey of India, 1887–1955. Followed by *Annual Report on Indian Epigraphy*. New Delhi: Government Publications, 1952–present.

Epigraphia Carnatica. Edited by B. Lewis Rice and R. Narasimhacarya. Bangalore: Mysore Government Central Press, 1886–1919.

Epigraphia Indica. Vols. 1–42. Delhi: Archaeological Survey of India, 1892–1978.

Indian Antiquary. Vols. 1–62. Bombay: Education Society's Press, 1872–1933.

Inscriptions (texts) of the Pudukottai State, Arranged According to Dynasties. Chennai: Government Museum, 2002.

Journal of the Andhra Historical Research Society. Rajahmundry: Andhra Historical Research Society, 1925–.

Karandai Tamil Sangam Plates of Rajendrachola I. Memoirs of the Archaeological Survey of India. New Delhi: ASI, 1976.

Mĕykkīrttikaḷ. Edited by Pū. Cuppiramaṇiyam. Ceṉṉai: Ulakat Tamiḻārāycci Niṟuvaṉam, 1983.

Putuccēri Māṉilakkalveṭṭukkaḷ. Pondicherry Inscriptions. Edited by S. Bahour Kuppusamy and G. Vijayavenugopal. 2 vols. Pondicherry, IFP/EFEO, 2006.

South Indian Inscriptions. Vols. 1–24. Madras: Archeological Survey of India, 1890–1982.

South Indian Temple Inscriptions. Edited by T. Subrahmaniam. Madras: Government Oriental Manuscripts Library, 1953.

Tāmaraippākkam kalveṭṭukaḷ. Edited by Ku. Tāmōtaram. Ceṉṉai: Tamiḻnāṭu Aracu Tŏlpŏruḷ Āyvuttuṟai, 1999.

Secondary Literature

Abraham, Meera. *Two Medieval Merchant Guilds of South India*. New Delhi: Manohar Publications, 1988.

Adiga, Malini. *The Making of Southern Karnataka: Society, Polity and Culture in the Early Medieval Period*. Chennai: Orient Longman, 2006.

Ali, Daud. *Courtly Culture and Political Life in Early Medieval India*. Cambridge and New York: Cambridge University Press, 2004.

Ali, Daud. "The Epigraphical Legacy at Gangaikondacholapuram: Problems and Possibilities." In *New Dimensions in Tamil Epigraphy: Select Papers from the Symposia held at EPHE-SHP, Paris in 2005, 2006 and a Few Invited Papers*, edited by Appasamy Murugaiyan, 3–34. Chennai: Cre-A Publishers, 2012.

Ali, Daud. "Royal Eulogy as World History: Rethinking Copper-Plate Inscriptions in Cola India." In *Querying the Medieval: The History of Practice in South Asia*, edited by Daud Ali, Ronald Inden, and Jonathan S. Walters, 165–229. Oxford: Oxford University Press, 2000.

Ali, Daud. "Service Retinues of the Chola Court: A Study of the Term *Veḷam* in Tamil Inscriptions." *BSOAS* 70, 3 (2007): 487–509.

Ali, Daud. "Violence, Gastronomy and the Meaning of War in Medieval South India." *Medieval History Journal* 3 (2000): 261–289.

Appadurai, Arjun. "Right and Left Hand Castes in South India." *IESHR* 11 (1974): 216–259.

Aravāṇaṉ, Ka. Pa. *Kaliṅkattup paraṇi: oru matippīṭu*. Ceṉṉai: Jaiṉa Iḷaiñar Maṉṟam, 1976.

Aruṇācalam, Mu. *Tamiḻ ilakkiya varalāṟu*, 14 vols. Ceṉṉai: Ti Pārkkar, 2005.

Arunachalam, B. *Chola Navigation Package*. Mumbai: Maritime History Society, 2004.

Balakrishnan Nayar, T. *The Dowlaishweram Hoard of Eastern Chāḷukyan and Chōla Coins*. Chennai: The Commissioner of Museums, 2002.

Balasubrahmanyam, S. R. *Later Chola Temples: Kulottunga I to Rājendra III (AD 1070–1280)*. Madras: Mudgala Trust, 1979.

Balasubrahmanyam, S. R. *Middle Chola Temples: Rajaraja I to Kulottunga I, A.D. 985–1070*. Faridabad: Thomson Press, 1975.

Banerji, Sures Chandra and Amal Kumar Gupta, trans. *Bilhaṇa's Vikramāṅkadeva Caritam; Glimpses of the History of the Cālukyas of Kalyāṇa*. Calcutta: Sambodhi Publications, 1965.

Banks, Iain. *Excession*. London: Orbit, 1996.

Bayly, Susan. *Saints, Goddesses, and Kings: Muslims and Christians in South Indian Society, 1700–1900*. New York: Cambridge University Press, 1989.

Becker, Alton. *Beyond Translation: Essays Towards a Modern Philology*. Ann Arbor: University of Michigan Press, 1995.

Bennet, Jane. *Vibrant Matter: A Political Ecology of Things*. Durham and London: Duke University Press, 2010.

Bhandarkar, R. G. *Report on the Search for Sanskrit Manuscripts in the Bombay Presidency in the Year 1882–1883*. Bombay: Government Central Book Depot, 1884.

Bhattanatha Svamin. "The Cholas and the Chalukyas in the XIth Century." *IA* 41 (1912): 217–227.

Biddulph, Charles Hubert. *Coins of the Cholas*. Varanasi: Numismatic Society of India, 1968.

Bourdieu, Pierre. *Outline of a Theory of Practice*. Cambridge and New York: Cambridge University Press, 1977.

Brocquet, Sylvain. "Une Épopée epigraphique." *BEI* 22 (2007): 73–103.

Brodbeck, Simon. "Solar and Lunar Lines in the Mahābhārata." *Religions of South Asia* 5 (2011): 127–152.

Bronner, Yigal. "The Poetics of Ambivalence: Imagining and Unimagining the Political in Bilhaṇa's *Vikramāṇkadevacarita*." *JIP* 38, 5 (2010): 457–483.

van Buitenen, J. A. B, trans. *The Mahābharata: I. The Beginning*. Chicago: University of Chicago Press, 1973.

Chakrabarty, Dipesh. *Provincializing Europe: Postcolonial Thought and Historical Difference*. Princeton: Princeton University Press, 2000.

Champakalakshmi, R. "Reappraisal of a Brahminic Institution: The Brahmadeya and Its Ramifications in Early Medieval South India." In *Structure and Society in Early South India: Essays in Honor of Noboru Karashima*, edited by Kenneth R. Hall, 59–84. New Delhi: Oxford University Press, 2001.

Champakalakshmi, R. *Trade, Ideology and Urbanization: South India 300 BC to AD 1300*. Delhi: Oxford University Press, 1996.

Chattopadhaya, Brajadulal. *Coins and Currency Systems in South India, c. A.D. 225–1300*. New Delhi: Munshiram Manoharlal Publishers, 1977.

Chattopadhaya, Brajadulal. *The Making of Early Medieval India*. Delhi: Oxford University Press, 1994.

Chhabra, Bahadur Chand. "Diplomatic of Sanskrit Copper-Plate Grants." *The Indian Archives* 5, 1 (1955): 1–20.

Clare, Jennifer Steel. *Canons, Conventions and Creativity: Defining Literary Conventions in Premodern Tamil South India*. PhD dissertation, University of California at Berkeley. Berkeley: ProQuest/UMI, 2011.

Cœdès, George. "Le royaume de Çrīvijaya." *BEFEO 18*, 1 (1918): 1–36.

Cœdès, George. *Les états hindouisés d'Indochine et d'Indonésie*. Paris: Éditions de Boccard, 1948 (translated as *the Indianized States of South-East Asia*. Trans. by Susan Cowling. Honolulu: East-West Center Press, 1968).

Cohn, Bernard. "Indian Histories and African Models." In *An Anthropologist among the Historians and Other Essays* by Bernard Cohn. Delhi: Oxford University Press, 1990.

Collingwood, Robin George. *The New Leviathan, or Man, Society, Civilization and Barbarism*. Oxford: The Clarendon Press, 1942.

Cox, Whitney. "From Source-Criticism to Intellectual History in the Poetics of the Medieval Tamil Country." In *Bilingual Discourse and Cross-Cultural Fertilisation: Sanskrit and Tamil in Medieval India*, edited by Whitney Cox and Vincenzo Vergiani, 115–160. Pondicherry: IFP/EFEO, 2013.

Cox, Whitney. "Law, Literature, and the Problem of Politics in Medieval India." In *Law and Hinduism: An Introduction*, edited by Donald Davis, Timothy Lubin, and Jayanth Krishnan, 167–182. New York: Cambridge University Press, 2010.

Cox, Whitney. "Scribe and Script in the Cālukya West Deccan." *IESHR* 47, 1 (2010): 1–28.

Cox, Whitney. "Sharing a Single Seat: The Poetics and Politics of Male Intimacy in Bilhaṇa's *Vikramāṅkakāvya*." *JIP* 38, 5 (2010): 485–501.

Davis, Donald. "Intermediate Realms of Law: Corporate Groups and Rulers in Medieval India." *JESHO* 49, 1 (2005): 92–117.

Davis, Richard H. "Chola *Meykkīrttis* as Literary Texts." *Tamil Civilization* 3, 2–3 (1985): 1–5.

Davis, Richard H. *Lives of Indian Images*. Princeton: Princeton University Press, 1997.

Derrett, J. and M. Duncan. *The Hoysalas: A Medieval Indian Dynasty*. Madras: Oxford University Press, 1957.

Dumont, Louis. "The Concept of Kingship in Ancient India." *CIS* 6 (1962): 48–77.
Dumont, Louis. *Homo Hierarchicus: The Caste System and Its Implications*. Translated by Mark Sainsbury, Louis Dumont, and Basia Gulati. Chicago: University of Chicago Press, 1980.
Dumont, Louis. *Religion, Politics, and History: Collected Papers in Indian Sociology*. Paris and The Hague: Mouton Publishers, 1970.
Elliot, Walter Sir. *Coins of Southern India*. Varanasi: Prithivi Prakashan, 1970 (reprint).
Fleet, John Faithful. "Ancient Territorial Divisions of India." *Journal of the Royal Asiatic Society of Great Britain and Ireland* (1912): 707–710.
Fleet, John Faithful. "Eastern Chalukya Chronology." *IA* 20 (1891): 1–15, 93–104, 266–285.
Fleet, John Faithful. *The Dynasties of the Kanarese Districts of the Bombay Presidency, from the Earliest Historical Times to the Musalman Conquest of A.D. 1318*. Bombay: Government Central Press, 1882.
Francis, Emmanuel. *Le discours royal dans l'Inde du Sud ancienne. Inscriptions et monuments pallava (IVème – IXème siècles). Tome I. Introduction et sources*. Louvain: Peeters, 2013.
Francis, Emmanuel. "Praising the King in Tamil during the Pallava Period." In *Bilingual Discourse and Cross-Cultural Fertilisation: Sanskrit and Tamil in Medieval India*, edited by Whitney Cox and Vincenzo Vergiani, 359–410. Pondicherry: IFP/EFEO, 2013.
Francis, Emmanuel and Charlotte Schmid. *Preface to Putuccēri Māṉilakkalveṭṭukkaḷ. Pondicherry Inscriptions*, vol. 2.
Geertz, Clifford. *Negara: The Theatre State in Nineteenth-Century Bali*. Princeton: Princeton University Press, 1980.
Gonda, Jan. *Ancient Indian Kingship from the Religious Point of View*. Leiden: Brill, 1966.
Goodall, Dominic, ed. and trans. *Bhaṭṭarāmakaṇṭhaviracitā Kiraṇavṛtti*. Pondicherry: IFP/EFEO, 1998.
Goodall, Dominic, ed. and trans. *Parākhyatantram: The Parākhyatantra, a Scripture of the Śaiva Siddhānta*. Pondicherry: IFP/EFEO, 2004.
Govindasamy, M. S. *The Role of Feudatories in Later Chōḻa History*. Annamalai Nagar: Annamalai University, 1979.
Greenblatt, Stephen. *Shakespearean Negotiations: The Circulation of Social Energy in Renaissance England*. Berkeley: University of California Press, 1988.
Gros, François and R. Nagaswamy. *Uttaramerūr: Légende, Histoire, Monuments; avec Le Pañcavaradakṣetra māhātmya édité par K. Srinivasacharya*. Pondichéry: IFP, 1970.
Gururaja Rao, B. K. "The Kolāramma Temple and the Cōḷas." *Tamil Civilization* 3, 2–3 (1985): 101–106.
Hall, Kenneth R. "Merchants, Rulers and Priests in an Early South Indian Sacred Center: Chidambaram in the Age of the Colas." In *Structure and Society in Early South India: Essays in Honor of Noboru Karashima*, edited by Kenneth R. Hall, 59–116. New Delhi: Oxford University Press, 2001.
Hall, Kenneth R. *Trade and Statecraft in the Age of the Cōḻas*. Delhi: Abhinav Publications, 1980.

Harle, James C. *Temple Gateways in South India: The Architecture and Iconography of the Cidambaram Gopuras*. New Delhi: Munshiram Manoharlal Publishers, 1995.
Hart, George and Hank Heifetz, trans. *The Forest Book of the Rāmāyaṇa of Kampaṉ*. Berkeley: University of California Press, 1989.
Hatley, Shaman. *The Brahmayamalatantra and Early Saiva Cult of Yoginis*. PhD Dissertation, University of Pennsylvania. Philadelphia: ProQuest/UMI, 2007.
Heitzman, James. *Gifts of Power: Lordship in an Early Indian State*. New Delhi: Oxford University Press, 1997.
Henige, David P. "Some Phantom Dynasties of Early and Medieval India: Epigraphic Evidence and the Abhorrence of a Vacuum." *BSOAS* 38, 3 (1975): 525–549.
Inden, Ronald. *Imagining India*. Oxford: Basil Blackwell, 1990.
Indrapala, Karthigesu. "An Inscription of the Tenth Year of Cōḷa Laṅkeśvara Deva from Kantalai, Sri Lanka." In *Senarat Paranavitana Commemoration Volume*, edited by L. Prematilleke, K. Indrapala, and J. E. van Lohuizen-deLeeuw. Leiden: Bill, 1978.
Ingalls, Daniel H. H., trans. *An Anthology of Sanskrit Court Poetry*, Cambridge: Harvard University Press, 1965.
Irākavaiyaṅkār, Mu. *Arāyccit tokuti*. Ceṉṉai: Pāri Nilaiyam, 1938.
Irākavaiyaṅkār, Mu. *Kaliṅkattupparaṇiyārāycci*. Maturai: Tamiḻccaṅkamuttiracālai, 1925.
Irākavaiyaṅkār, Mu. *Pĕruntŏkai*. Maturai: Tamiḻccaṅkamuttiracālai, 1936.
Kanakasabhai Pillai, V. "Tamil Historical Texts: No. 2 – The Kalingattu Parani." *IA* 19 (1890): 329–345.
Karashima, Noboru. *Ancient to Medieval: South Indian Society in Transition*. New Delhi: Oxford University Press, 2009.
Karashima, Noboru. *South Indian History and Society: Studies from Inscriptions, A.D. 850–1800*. Delhi: Oxford University Press, 1984.
Karashima, Noboru. "South Indian Temple Inscriptions: A New Approach to Their Study." *JSAS* 19, 1 (1996): 1–12.
Karashima, Noboru, Y. Subbarayalu and Toru Matsui, eds. *A Concordance of the Names in Cōḻa Inscriptions*. Madurai: Sarvodaya Ilakkiya Pannai, 1978.
Karashima, Noboru, Y. Subbarayalu and P. Shanmugam. *Land Control and Social Change in the Lower Kaveri Valley from the 12th to 17th Centuries*. Tokyo: Institute for the Study of Languages and Cultures of Asia and Africa, 1980.
Krishnan, K. J. "Chittiramelip-Periyanadu – An Agricultural Guild of Medieval Tamil Nadu." *Journal of the Madras University* 56, 1 (1982): 89–106.
Kulke, Hermann. *Cidambaramāhātmya; eine Untersuchung der religionsgeschichtlichen und historischen Hintergründe für die Entstehung der Tradition eines südindischen Tempelstadt*. Wiesbaden: O. Harrassowitz, 1970.
Kulke, Hermann. "Funktionale Erklärung eines südindischen Māhātmyas: die Legende Hiranyavarmans und das Leben des Cōḷa-Königs Kulottunga I." *Saeculum* 20 (1969): 412–422.
Kulke, Hermann. *Kings and Cults: State Formation and Legitimation in India and Southeast Asia*. Delhi: Manohar Publishers, 1993.

Kulke, Hermann, K. Kesavapany and Vijay Sakhuja. *Nagapattinam to Suvarnadwipa. Reflections on the Chola Naval Expeditions to Southeast Asia.* Singapore: Institute of Southeast Asian Studies, 2009.

Latour, Bruno. *On the Modern Cult of the Factish Gods.* Durham: Duke University Press, 2010.

Latour, Bruno. *We Have Never Been Modern.* Cambridge: Harvard University Press, 1993.

Lorenzen, David N. *The Kāpālikas and Kālāmukhas: Two Lost Śaivite Sects.* Delhi: Motilal Barnasidass, 1991.

Loud, John. *The Dikshitars of Chidambaram.* Unpublished PhD thesis, University of Wisconsin-Madison, 1990.

Ludden, David. *An Agrarian History of South Asia.* Cambridge: Cambridge University Press, 1999.

Mahadevan, T. P. "On the Southern Recension of the *Mahābhārata*, Brahman Migration and Brāhmī Paleography." *Electronic Journal of Vedic Studies* 15, 2 (2008): 1–143.

Mahalingam, T. V. *Kāñcīpuram in Early South Indian History.* London: Asia Publishing House, 1969.

Mahalingam, T. V. *Topographical List of the Inscriptions in the Tamil Nadu and Kerala States.* 9 vols. Delhi: Indian Council of Historical Research, 1985–1995.

Malayalam Lexicon. 5 vols. Trivandrum: Kēraḷa Sarvakalāśālā Prasiddīkaraṇam, 1965–.

McCrea, Lawrence. "Poetry beyond Good and Evil: Bilhaṇa and the Tradition of Patron-Centered Court Epic." *JIP* 38, 5 (2010): 503–518.

McCrea, Lawrence. "*Śāntarasa* in the *Rājataraṅgiṇī*: History, Epic, and Moral Decay." *IESHR* 50, 2 (2013): 179–200.

McGann, Jerome. "Philology in a New Key." *Critical Inquiry* 39, 2 (2013): 327–346.

Michell, George and Vivek Nanda, eds. *Chidambaram: Home of Nataraja.* Mumbai: Marg Publications on behalf of the National Centre for the Performing Arts, 2004.

Miller, Barbara Stoler, trans. *Phantasies of a Love-Thief: The Caurapañcāśikā Attributed to Bilhaṇa; A Critical Edition and Translation of Two Recensions.* New York: Columbia University Press, 1971.

Mishra, B. N. *Studies on Bilhaṇa and His Vikramāṅkadevacarita.* New Delhi: K.B. Publications, 1976.

Monius, Anne E. *Imagining a Place for Buddhism: Literary Culture and Religious Community in Tamil-Speaking South India.* New York: Oxford University Press, 2001.

Mysore State Gazetteer, Kolar District. Bangalore: Director of Printing, Stationery and Publications at the Government Press, 1968.

Nāgar, Murari Lal. *Bilhaṇa's Vikramāṅkadevacarita and Its Neo-Expounders.* n.p: International Library Center, 1991.

Nagaswamy, R. [=Irā. Nākacāmi]. *Cōlmālai.* Chennai: Tamil Arts Academy, 2000.

Nagaswamy, R. *Gangaikondacholapuram.* Madras: State Department of Archaeology, Government of Tamil Nadu, 1970.

Nagaswamy, R. "Sangam Poetic Traditions under the Imperial Cōḻas." In *South Indian Horizons: Felicitation Volume for François Gros on the Occasion of his 70th Birthday*, edited by J.-L. Chevillard and Eva Wilden, 487–494. Pondicherry: IFP/EFEO, 2004.

Nagaswamy, R. *Studies in Ancient Tamil Law and Society*. Madras: Institute of Epigraphy, 1978.

Nagaswamy, R. *Tantric Cult of South India*. Delhi: Agam Kala Prakashan, 1982.

Narayana Rao, Velcheru. "Multiple Literary Cultures in Telugu: Court, Temple and Public." In *Literary Cultures in History. Reconstructions from South Asia*, edited by Sheldon Pollock, 383–436. Berkeley and Los Angeles: University of California Press, 2003.

Narayana Rao, Velcheru and David Shulman, eds. *Classical Telugu Poetry: An Anthology*. Berkeley and Los Angeles: University of California Press, 2002.

Narayana Rao, Velcheru, David Shulman and Sanjay Subrahmanyam. *Symbols of Substance. Court and State in Nāyaka Period Tamil Nadu*. Delhi and New York: Oxford University Press, 1992.

Narayana Rao, Velcheru, David Shulman and Sanjay Subrahmanyam. *Textures of Time: Writing History in South India 1600–1800*. Delhi: Permanent Black, 2002.

Niklas, Ulrike, "Introduction to Tamil Prosody." *BEFEO* 77 (1991): 165–227.

Nilakanta Sastri, K. A. *The Cōḻas*. Madras: University of Madras, 1935.

Nilakanta Sastri, K. A. *A History of South India from Prehistoric Times to the Fall of Vijayanagar*. Madras: Oxford University Press, 1955.

Nilakanta Sastri, K. A. *Studies in Chola History and Administration*. Madras: University of Madras, 1932.

Olivelle, Patrick, ed. and trans. *The Early Upaniṣads*. New York: Oxford University Press, 1998.

Olivelle, Patrick. *King, Governance, and Law in Ancient India: Kauṭilya's Arthaśāstra*. New York: Oxford University Press, 2013.

Olivelle, Patrick and Suman Olivelle, eds. *Manu's Code of Law: A Critical Edition and Translation of the Mānava-Dharmaśāstra*. New York: Oxford University Press, 2005.

Orr, Leslie. "Preface" to *Putuccēri Māṉilakkalveṭṭukkaḷ. Pondicherry Inscriptions*, vol. 1. Pondicherry: IFP/EFEO, 2006.

Orr, Leslie. "Temple Life at Chidambaram in the Chola Period: An Epigraphical Study." In *Sri Puspanjali (Recent Researches in Prehistory, Protohistory, Art, Architecture, Numismatics, Iconography and Epigraphy): Dr. C.R. Srinivasan Commemoration Volume*, edited by K. V. Ramesh et al., 227–241. Delhi: Bharatiya Kala Prakashan, 2004.

Orr, Leslie. "Words for Worship: Tamil and Sanskrit in Medieval Temple Inscriptions." In *Bilingual Discourse and Cross-Cultural Fertilisation: Sanskrit and Tamil in Mediaeval India*, edited by Whitney Cox and Vincenzo Vergiani, 325–357. Pondichéry: IFP/EFEO, 2013.

Pathak, Vishvambhar Sharan. *Ancient Historians of India: A Study in Historical Biographies*. Bombay: Asia Publishing House, 1966.

Pichard, Pierre. *Vingt ans après Tanjavur, Gangaikondacholapuram*. Paris: EFEO, 1994.

Pocock, J. G. A. *The Machiavellian Moment: Florentine Political Thought and the Atlantic Republican Tradition.* Second edition, New York: Princeton University Press, 2003.

Pocock, J. G. A. *Political Thought and History: Essays on Theory and Method.* Cambridge: Cambridge University Press, 2009.

Pollock, Sheldon. "Crisis in the Classics." *Social Research* 78, 1 (2011): 22–48.

Pollock, Sheldon. "Future Philology? The Fate of a Soft Science in a Hard World." *Critical Inquiry* 35, 4 (2009): 931–961.

Pollock, Sheldon. "Indian Philology and India's Philology." *Journal Asiatique* 299, 1 (2011): 423–442.

Pollock, Sheldon. *Language of the Gods in the World of Man: Sanskrit, Culture and Power in Premodern India.* Los Angeles: University of California Press, 2006.

Pollock, Sheldon. "Mīmāṃsā and the Problem of History in Traditional India." *JAOS* 109, 4 (1989): 603–610.

Pollock, Sheldon. "Rāmāyaṇa and the Political Imagination in India." *JAS* 52, 2 (1993): 261–279.

Raman, Bhavani. *Document Raj: Writing and Scribes in Early Colonial South India.* Chicago: University of Chicago Press, 2012.

Richman, Paula. *Extraordinary Child: Poems from a South Indian Devotional Genre.* Honolulu: University of Hawai'i Press, 1997.

Rorty, Richard. *Objectivity, Relativism and Truth: Philosophical Papers.* New York: Cambridge University Press, 1991.

Sadasivapandarathar, T. V. *History of the Later Cholas* [=*Piṟkālacoḻar carittiram*], 3 vols. Annamalainagar: Annamalai University, 1957–1958.

Sahlins, Marshall. *Islands of History.* Chicago: Chicago University Press, 1985.

Sahlins, Marshall. *Culture in Practice: Selected Essays.* New York: Zone Books, 2000.

Said, Edward K. *The World, the Text and the Critic.* Cambridge: Harvard University Press, 1983.

Sakhuja, Vijay and Sangeeta Sakhuja. "Rajendra Chola's Naval Expedition to Southeast Asia: A Nautical Perspective." In *Nagapattinam to Suvarnadwipa: Reflections on the Chola Naval Expeditions to Southeast Asia*, edited by Hermann Kulke, K. Kesavapany and Vijay Sakhuja, 168–177. Singapore: Institute of Southeast Asian Studies, 2009.

Salomon, Richard. *Indian Epigraphy: A Guide to the Study of Inscriptions in Sanskrit, Pāli and Other Indo-Aryan Languages.* New York: Oxford University Press, 1998.

Salomon, Richard. "The Men Who would be King: Reading between the Lines of Dynastic Genealogies in India and Beyond." *Religions of South Asia* 5, 1 (2011): 267–291.

Sanderson, Alexis. "Atharvavedins in Tantric Territory: The Āngirasakalpa Texts of the Oriya Paippalādins and Their Connection with the Trika and the Kālīkula, with Critical Editions of the *Parājapavidhi*, the *Parāmantravidhi*, and the **Bhadrakālī-mantravidhiprakarana*." In *The Atharvaveda and Its Paippalāda Śākhā: Historical and Philological Papers on a Vedic Tradition*, edited by Arlo Griffiths and Annette Schmiedchen, 195–311. Aachen: Shaker Verlag, 2007.

Sanderson, Alexis. "A Commentary on the Opening Verses of the *Tantrasāra* of Abhinavagupta." In *Sāmarasya: Studies in Indian Arts, Philosophy, and Interreligious Dialogue in Honour of Bettina Bäumer*, edited by Sadananda Das and Ernst Fürlinger, 89–148. New Delhi: D. K. Printworld, 2005.
Sanderson, Alexis. "History through Textual Criticism in the Study of Śaivism, the Pañcarātra and the Buddhist Yoginītantras." In *Les Sources et le temps. Sources and Time: A Colloquium, Pondicherry, 11–13 January 1997*, edited by François Grimal, 1–47. Pondicherry: IFP/EFEO, 2001.
Sanderson, Alexis. "The Śaiva Age: The Rise and Dominance of Śaivism during the Early Medieval Period." In *Genesis and Development of Tantrism*, edited by Shingo Einoo, 41–349. Tokyo: Institute of Oriental Culture, 2009.
Sanderson, Alexis. "The Śaiva Religion among the Khmers, Part I." *BEFEO* 90–91 (2003–2004): 349–463.
Sanderson, Alexis. *Śaivism and Brahmanism in the Early Medieval Period.* Forthcoming.
Sathianathaier, R. *Studies in the Early History of Tondamandalam.* Madras: Rochouse, 1944.
Scharfe, Hartmut. *Investigations in Kauṭalya's Manual of Political Science.* Wiesbaden: Harrassowitz Verlag, 1993.
Scott, James C. *Domination and the Arts of Resistance: Hidden Transcripts.* New Haven: Yale University Press, 1990.
Sethuraman, N. *The Cholas: Mathematics Reconstructs the Chronology.* Kumbakonam: Sethuraman, 1977.
Sewell, William. *Logics of History: Social Theory and Social Transformation.* Chicago: Chicago University Press, 2005.
Shanmugam, Palani. *The Revenue System of the Cholas, 850–1279.* Madras: New Era Publications, 1987.
Shulman, David. *The King and the Clown in South Indian Myth and Poetry.* Princeton: Princeton University Press, 1985.
Shulman, David. "Notes on *Camatkāra*." In *Language, Ritual and Poetry in Ancient India and Iran: Studies in Honor of Shoul Migron*, edited by David Shulman, 257–284. Leiden: Brill, 2010.
Singh, Upinder, "Violence, Politics, and War in Kāmandaka's *Nītisāra*." *IESHR* 47 (2010): 29–62.
Sivathamby, Karthigesu. *Drama in Ancient Tamil Society.* Madras: New Century Book House, 1981.
Skinner, Quentin. *Machiavelli.* New York: Hill and Wang, 1981.
Skinner, Quentin. *Visions of Politics. 3 volumes.* Cambridge and New York: Cambridge University Press, 2002.
Smith, David. *The Dance of Śiva: Religion, Art and Poetry in South India.* Delhi: Oxford University Press, 1996.
Spencer, George W. *The Politics of Expansion: The Chola Conquest of Sri Lanka and Sri Vijaya.* Madras: New Era Publications, 1983.
Spencer, George W. "The Politics of Plunder: The Cholas in Eleventh-Century Ceylon." *JAS* 35, 3 (1976): 405–419.
Spencer, George W. "Temple Money-Lending and Livestock Redistribution in Early Tanjore." *IESHR* 5 (1968): 277–293.

Stein, Burton. "Circulation and the Historical Geography of Tamil Country." *JAS* 37 (1977): 7–26.
Stein, Burton. *Peasant State and Society in Medieval South India*. New Delhi: Oxford University Press, 1980.
Subbarayalu, Y. *Political Geography of the Chōḷa Country*. Madras: State Department of Archeology, 1973.
Subbarayalu, Y. *South India Under the Cholas*. Delhi: Oxford University Press, 2012.
Subrahmanya Aiyar, K. V. *Historical Sketches of Ancient Deccan*. Madras: Modern Imprint, 1917.
Subrahmanya Aiyer, K. V. "Largest Provincial Organizations in Southern India." *Quarterly Journal of the Mythic Society* 45–46 (1954–56): 29–47, 70–98, 270–286 and 8–22.
Subrahmanyam, S. R. "The Oldest Chidambaram Inscriptions. Chapters I and II." *Journal of Annamalai University* 13 (1944): 53–91.
Subrahmanyam, Sanjay. "Whispers and Shouts: Some Recent Writings on Medieval South India." *IESHR* 38 (2001): 453–465.
Swamy, B. G. L. *Chidambaram and Naṭarāja: Problems and Rationalization*. Mysore: Geetha Book House, 1979.
Talbot, Cynthia. *Precolonial India in Practice: Society, Region, and Identity in Medieval Andhra*. Oxford and New York: Oxford University Press, 2001.
Tamil Lexicon. 7 vols. Madras: University of Madras, 1924–1936.
Tamiḻk kalvĕṭṭuc cŏllakarāti (Glossary of Tamil Inscriptions). 2 vols. Chennai: Santi Sadhana Trust, 2002.
Tāntrikābhidhānakośa. Edited by Hélène Brunner, Gerhard Oberhammer, Andre Padoux et al. 3 vols. Wien: Verlag der Österreichischen Akademie der Wissenschaften, 2000–.
Taylor, McComas. *The Fall of the Indigo Jackal. The Discourse of Division and Pūrṇabhadra's Pañcatantra*. Albany: State University of New York Press, 2007.
Thapar, Romila. *Time as a Metaphor of History: Early India*. Delhi: Oxford University Press, 1996.
Thirumoorthy, G. "Settlement Patterns in Medieval Cidambaram." In *Kāveri – Studies in Epigraphy, Archaeology, and History: Professor Y. Subbarayalu Felicitation Volume*, edited by S. Rajagopal, 438–444. Chennai: Panpattu Veliyiittakam, 2001.
Tieken, Herman. *Kāvya in South India: Old Tamil Caṅkam Poetry*. Groningen: Egbert Forsten, 2001.
Trautmann, Thomas. *Dravidian Kinship*. Cambridge and New York: Cambridge University Press, 1981.
Veluthat, Kesavan. *The Early Medieval in South India*. New Delhi: Oxford University Press, 2010.
Veluthat, Kesavan. *The Political Structure of Early Medieval South India*. New Delhi: Orient Longman, 1973.
Venkatakrishna Rao, Bhavaraju. *History of the Eastern Chalukyas of Vengi (610–1210 A.D.)*. Hyderabad: Andhra Pradesh Sahitya Akademi, 1973.
Venkatarama Ayyar, A. V. *The Life and Time of Chalukya Vikramaditya VI [=Caḷukki Vikkiramātittaṉ carittiram]*. Madras: K. Abhiirama Ayyar, 1922.

Venkataramanayya, N. *The Eastern Cāḷukyas of Vēṅgi*. Madras: Vedam Venkataraya Sastry, 1950.
Vogel, Claus. *Indian Lexicography*. Wiesbaden: Harrassowitz Verlag, 1979.
Wagoner, Phillip. "Precolonial Intellectuals and the Production of Colonial Knowledge." *CSSH* 45, 4 (2003): 783–814.
Warder, Anthony K. *Introduction to Indian Historiography*. Bombay: Popular Prakashan, 1972.
Weber, Max. "Politics as a Vocation." In *From Max Weber: Essays in Sociology*, edited and trans by H. H. Gerth and C. Wright Mills, 77–128. New York: Oxford UP, 1946.
Wentworth, Blake. *Yearning for a Dreamed Real: The Procession of the Lord in the Tamil Ulās*. Unpublished PhD dissertation, University of Chicago, 2011.
White, David Gordon. *The Alchemical Body: Siddha Traditions in Medieval India*. Chicago: Chicago University Press, 1996.
Wickham, Chris. *Framing the Early Middle Ages: Europe and the Mediterranean 400–800*. Oxford and New York: Oxford University Press, 2005.
Willis, Michael. "Later Gupta History: Inscriptions, Coins and Historical Ideology." *JRAS* 15, 2 (2005): 131–150.
Witzel, Michael. "Toward a History of the Brahmans." *JAOS* 113, 2 (1993): 264–268.
Younger, Paul. *The Home of Dancing Śivaṉ: The Traditions of the Hindu Temple in Citamparam*. New York: Oxford University Press, 1995.
Zvelebil, Kamil. *Lexicon of Tamil Literature*. Leiden and New York: Brill, 1994.
Zvelebil, Kamil. *The Smile of Murugan on Tamil Literature of South India*. Leiden: Brill, 1973.

Index

Abhimanyu, 37
Adhirājendra (r. 1069–1072), 27, 40, 78–81, 85–86, 90–95, 97–98, 99–100, 101, 114, 116, 201, 243n67
  accession of, 71, 78
  death of, 30, 113, 116, 119, 128, 131, 202, 240n54, 241n55
  Jaṭāvarman Uṭaiyār Co̱lapāṇḍyadeva, 86
  Kaliṅkattupparaṇi does not mention, 164
  as Kopparakesarivarma, 79
  records or epigraphs of, 79, 81, 90, 93, 210, 229n13, 230n17, 231n20, 231n21, 232n22, 234n25, 237n39, 239n52, 240n54, 268n106
  Vikramāditya VI and, 128
Africa, 12, 14, 214n12
Aghoraśiva, 178, 192
*agrahāra*s, 13, 21, 136
agriculture, 8, 43, 50, 86, 102
Āhavamalla Someśvara (r. 1044–1068), 36, 61, 64, 65, 124
  sons of, 64, 122, 123
  suicide of, 64, 65, 123, 127
A̱lakiyaco̱la̱n, 104
Āḷavantā̱n, 60
Ali, Daud, 265n83
Amma II, 36
Ammaṅgādevī, 36
Ammaṅgai, 242n64
Anantavarma Coḍagaṅga, 153
Andhra Pradesh, 21, 26, 36, 37, 38, 135, 142, 145, 153, 198, 203, 265n84
Āndhramahābhāratamu. *See Mahābhāratamu*
Apaya̱n. *See under* Kulottuṅga Co̱la I; Vīrarājendra Co̱la
appanage, 52, 123, 140
Appar, 179, 270n4
archaeology, 10
Arjuna, 37, 260n54
Arthaśāstra, 17–18, 129–130, 131, 256n21
aru̱l, 65, 74, 104, 115, 158
Arumuga Navalar, 178
assemblies
  brahmadeya. *See* brahmadeyas:assemblies governing
  cittirame̱li, 87–89, 92, 94, 103, 113, 236n34
  *sabhā*s, 52, 96–97, 99, 134, 212, 221n32
authority, 12, 13, 60, 85, 117, 190, 197, 212, 237n38
  Co̱la central, 97, 204
  Co̱la state, 6, 27, 34, 56, 115, 201, 210
  Dumont on, 19
  feminine, 164
  local, 88, 89, 96, 99, 108, 238n44
  royal, 5, 27, 33, 41, 55, 78, 90, 98, 100, 104, 121, 147
  textual, 106
Avani, 102–104
Ayodhyā, 136, 138, 148, 259n43, 259n45
Āys, 42
Ayurveda, 130

Balasubrahmaniyam, S. R., 270n4
Bāṇa, 125
Banavāsi region, 123
Bangalore, 85
Becker, Alton, 216n25
Berg, C. C., 190
Bhadrakālī, 109, *See also* Kāḷi
Bhagavadgītā, 17, 272n14
bhakti, 179, 220n31
Bhartṛhari, 172
Bhīma I (r. 892–922), 36
Bhuvanaikamalla Someśvara, 123
Bilhaṇa, 6, 18, 26, 65, 68, 78, 119, 121, 202, 210, 253n4
  as author, 124, 126, 140, 141
  as Cālukya propagandist, 122
  Cayaṅkōṇṭār compared to, 121, 153, 154, 155, 157, 165, 169, 172, 173, 174
  influences on, 254n9, 255n12
  Kashmirian, 122